*access to history*

# Russia 1894–1941

MICHAEL LYNCH

**SECOND EDITION**

***In memory of Philip James Lynch, 1934–2007***

The Publishers would like to thank Nicholas Fellows and John Short for their contribution to the Study Guide.

The Publishers would like to thank the following for permission to reproduce copyright material:

Routledge for The Routledge Atlas of Russian History by Martin Gilbert, published by Routledge 2007, pages 151 and 163.

**Photo credits: p6** David King; **p33** https://commons.wikimedia.org/wiki/File:Батька_Гапон.jpg; **p35** World History Archive/TopFoto; **p44** Library of Congress, LC-DIG-ggbain-07327; **p69** Punch Ltd; **p81** Library of Congress, LC-DIG-hec-04921; **p98** Hulton Archive/Getty Images; **p103** Library of Congress, LOC-3c01877; **p108*t*** The Granger Collection/TopFoto, ***b*** ITAR-TASS/TopFoto; **p116** Fine Art Images/Heritage Images/TopFoto; **p117** TopFoto; **p142** Hulton-Deutsch Collection/Corbis; **p149** Punch Ltd; **p156** Roger-Viollet/Topfoto; **p168** Topham/AP; **p192** Library of Congress LOC-35130; **p207** Bettmann/Corbis; **pp233, 237** David King; **p249** University of Kent Cartoon Archive/Solo Syndication.

**Acknowledgements:** are listed on page 276.



Orders: please contact Bookpoint Ltd, 130 Milton Park, Abingdon, Oxon OX14 4SB. Telephone: +44 (0)1235 827720.
Fax: +44 (0)1235 400454. Lines are open 9.00a.m.–5.00p.m., Monday to Saturday, with a 24-hour message answering service.
Visit our website at www.hoddereducation.co.uk



First published in 2008 by
Hodder Education
An Hachette UK Company
Carmelite House, 50 Victoria Embankment
London EC4Y 0DZ

Impression number 10 9 8 7 6 5
Year 2019 2018



Cover photo: Bolshevik, 1920 (oil on canvas), Kustodiev, Boris Mikhailovich (1878–1927)/
© Tretyakov Gallery, Moscow, Russia/Bridgeman Images
Produced, illustrated and typeset in Palatino LT Std by Gray Publishing, Tunbridge Wells
Printed and bound by CPI Group (UK) Ltd, Croydon CR0 4YY

A catalogue record for this title is available from the British Library

**ISBN 978 1471838316**

# Contents


| | | |
|---|---|---|
| **CHAPTER 1** | **Late Imperial Russia 1894–1905** | **1** |
| 1 | The land, the people and tsardom | 1 |
| 2 | The problem of reform in Imperial Russia | 9 |
| 3 | Economic reform under Witte 1893–1903 | 14 |
| 4 | The opponents of tsardom | 18 |
| 5 | The Russo-Japanese War 1904–5 | 28 |
| 6 | The 1905 Revolution | 31 |
| **CHAPTER 2** | **From revolution to war 1905–14** | **42** |
| 1 | Economic policy under Stolypin | 42 |
| 2 | The dumas 1906–14 | 47 |
| 3 | Growing tensions in Russia 1911–14 | 52 |
| 4 | Russia's foreign policy before 1914 | 55 |
| 5 | The tsar's position at the outbreak of war in 1914 | 60 |
| 6 | Key debate | 62 |
| **CHAPTER 3** | **From war to revolution 1914–17** | **67** |
| 1 | Russia's entry into the war in 1914 | 68 |
| 2 | The impact of war on Russia | 71 |
| 3 | The growth of opposition to tsardom | 80 |
| 4 | The February Revolution 1917 | 85 |
| 5 | Key debate | 92 |
| **CHAPTER 4** | **1917: From Provisional Government to October Revolution** | **96** |
| 1 | The Dual Authority | 97 |
| 2 | The return of the Bolsheviks | 100 |
| 3 | The Provisional Government and its problems | 104 |
| 4 | The October Revolution | 112 |
| 5 | Reasons for the Bolshevik success | 119 |
| 6 | Key debate | 123 |
| **CHAPTER 5** | **Lenin's government of Russia 1917–24** | **129** |
| 1 | The Bolsheviks in power | 130 |
| 2 | Dissolution of the Constituent Assembly | 134 |
| 3 | Treaty of Brest-Litovsk 1918 | 136 |
| 4 | Russian Civil War 1918–20 | 139 |
| 5 | Foreign interventions 1918–21 | 148 |
| 6 | Lenin's methods of imposing control 1917–21 | 153 |
| 7 | War Communism 1918–21 | 160 |
| 8 | Kronstadt Rising 1921 | 165 |
| 9 | New Economic Policy (NEP) | 169 |
| 10 | Lenin's legacy | 174 |
| 11 | Key debate | 178 |

**CHAPTER 6** **Stalin's rise to power 1924–9** **183**

1 Stalin's character and background 183
2 The power struggle within the Communist Party 188
3 'Permanent Revolution' versus 'Socialism in One Country' 195
4 Stalin's defeat of Trotsky and the Left 196
5 Stalin's defeat of the Right 198

**CHAPTER 7** **Stalin and the Soviet economy 1929–41** **203**

1 Stalin's economic aims after 1929 203
2 Collectivisation: the war against the peasantry 205
3 Industrialisation: the first three Five-Year Plans 213
4 Key debate 221

**CHAPTER 8** **Stalin's dictatorship 1929–41** **225**

1 The purges 225
2 Stalin's totalitarianism 239
3 Stalin and the cult of personality 242
4 Stalin's foreign policy 246
5 Stalin's record by 1941 251
6 Key debate 252

**Study guide** **257**

**Glossary of terms** **265**

**Further reading** **271**

**Index** **274**


## Dedication

**Keith Randell (1943–2002)**

The *Access to History* series was conceived and developed by Keith, who created a series to 'cater for students as they are, not as we might wish them to be'. He leaves a living legacy of a series that for over 20 years has provided a trusted, stimulating and well-loved accompaniment to post-16 study. Our aim with these new editions is to continue to offer students the best possible support for their studies.

CHAPTER 1

# Late Imperial Russia 1894–1905

The Russian Empire of which Nicholas II became tsar in 1894 was beset by many long-standing difficulties that had prevented its achieving modernity. This chapter describes the basic features of the Russian Empire at the beginning of Nicholas II's reign, and examines the opposition groups that had developed by 1905, the year which saw the greatest challenge tsardom had yet faced: the 1905 Revolution. The analysis falls under the following headings:

★ The land, the people and tsardom
★ The problem of reform in Imperial Russia
★ Economic reform under Witte 1893–1903
★ The opponents of tsardom
★ The Russo-Japanese War 1904–5
★ The 1905 Revolution

## Key dates

| | |
|---|---|
| **1894** | Start of Nicholas II's reign |
| **1894–1906** | Sergei Witte's economic reforms |
| **1897** | Jewish Bund formed |
| **1898** | Social Democratic Party formed |
| **1901** | Formation of the Social Revolutionary Party |
| **1903** | Social Democratic Party split into Bolsheviks and Mensheviks |
| **1904–5** | Russo-Japanese war |
| **1905** | Revolution |
| | All-Russian Union of Peasants set up |
| | October Manifesto created a *duma* (parliament) |
| | Formation of the Kadet and Octobrist parties |

## The land, the people and tsardom

▶ *Why had Imperial Russia not modernised its governmental, political and economic systems?*

The following sections describe the main characteristics of Imperial Russia.

### Russia's geography and peoples

In 1894 Imperial Russia covered over 8 million square miles (22 million square kilometres), an area equivalent to two and a half times the size of the

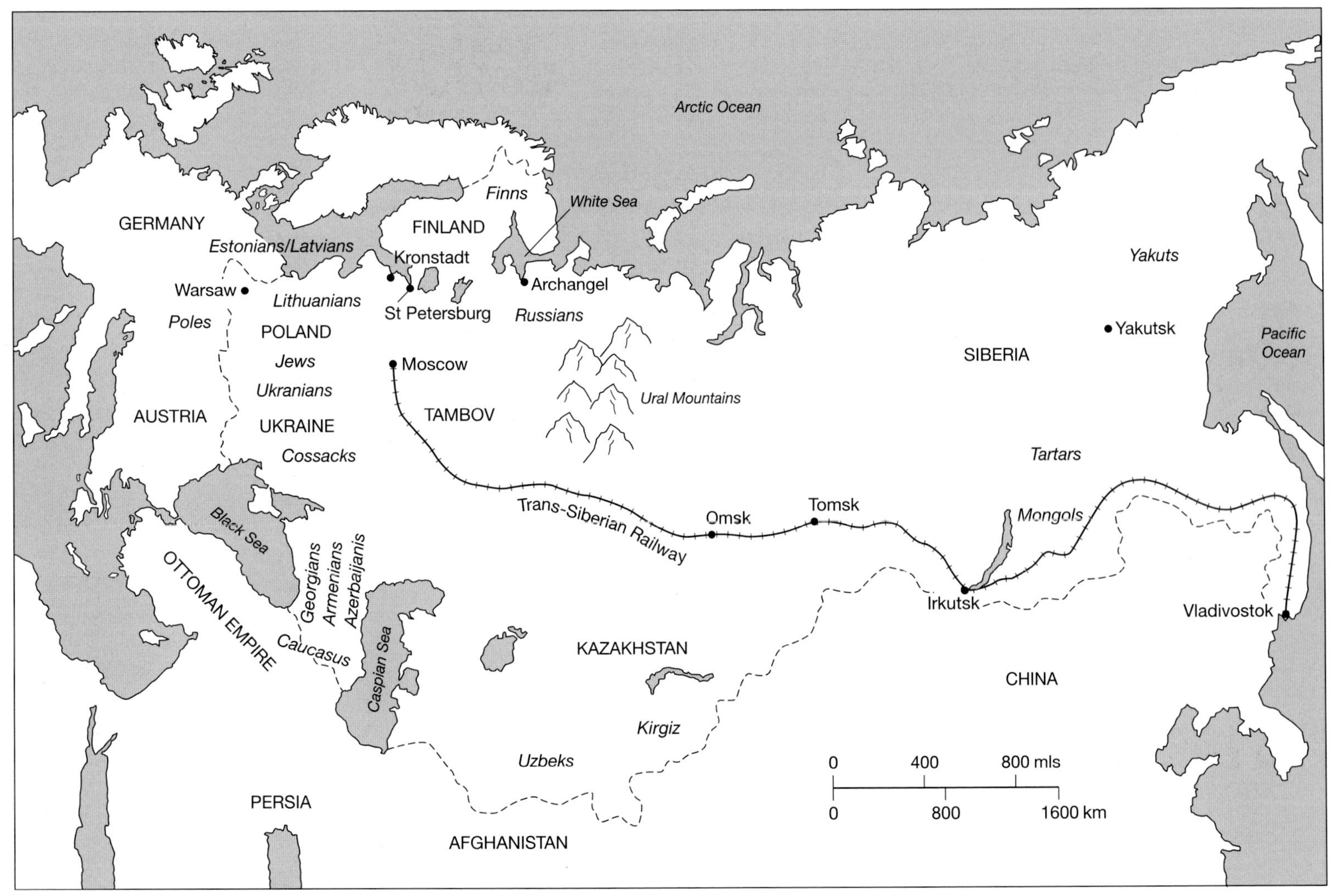


Figure 1.1 Imperial Russia.

USA today. At its widest, from west to east, it stretched for 5000 miles; at its longest, north to south, it measured 2000 miles. It covered a large part of two continents. European Russia extended eastward from the borders of Poland to the Urals mountain range. Asiatic Russia extended eastward from the Urals to the Pacific Ocean. The greater part of the population, which between 1815 and 1914 quadrupled from 40 million to 160 million, was concentrated in European Russia. It was in that part of the empire that the major historical developments had occurred and it was there that Russia's principal cities, Moscow and St Petersburg, the capital, were situated.

The sheer size of the Russian Empire tended to give an impression of great strength. This was misleading. The population contained a wide variety of peoples of different race, language, religion and culture. Controlling such a variety of peoples over such a vast territory had long been a major problem for Russian governments.

**Table 1.1** The major nationalities of the Russian Empire according to the census of 1897 (in millions, defined according to mother tongue)

| | | | | | |
|---|---|---|---|---|---|
| Great Russian | 55.6 | German | 1.8 | Mordvinian | 1.0 |
| Ukrainian | 22.4 | Azerbaijani | 1.7 | Georgian | 0.8 |
| Turkic/Tatar | 13.4 | Latvian | 1.4 | Tadzhik | 0.3 |
| Polish | 7.9 | Bashkir | 1.3 | Turkmenian | 0.3 |
| White Russian | 5.8 | Lithuanian | 1.2 | Greek | 0.2 |
| Yiddish (Jewish) | 5.0 | Armenian | 1.2 | Bulgarian | 0.2 |
| Kirgiz/Kaisats | 4.0 | Romanian/Moldavian | 1.1 | | |
| Finnic | 3.1 | Estonian | 1.0 | | |

## The tsar (emperor)

The peoples of the Russian Empire were governed by one person: the tsar (emperor). Since 1613 the Russian tsars had been members of the **Romanov dynasty**. By law and tradition, the tsar was the absolute ruler. Article I of the 'Fundamental Laws of the Empire', issued by Nicholas I in 1832, declared: 'The Emperor of all the Russias is an autocratic and unlimited monarch. God himself ordains that all must bow to his supreme power, not only out of fear but also out of conscience.'

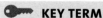

**KEY TERM**

**Romanov dynasty**
The royal house that ruled Russia between 1613 and 1917.

There were three official bodies through which the tsar exercised his authority:

- the Imperial Council, a group of honorary advisers directly responsible to the tsar
- the Cabinet of Ministers, which ran the various government departments
- the Senate, which supervised the operation of the law.

These bodies were much less powerful than their titles suggested. They were appointed, not elected, and they did not govern; their role was merely to give advice. They had no authority over the tsar, whose word was final in all governmental and legal matters.

## Russia's political backwardness

What the tsar's power showed was how little Russia had advanced politically when compared with other European nations. By the beginning of the twentieth century all the major Western European countries had some form of democratic or representative government. Not so Russia; although it had been frequently involved in European diplomatic and military affairs, it had remained outside the mainstream of European political thought.

There had been reforming tsars, such as Peter I (1682–1725), Catherine II (1762–96) and Alexander II (1855–81), who had taken steps to modernise the country, one example being the emancipation of the serfs in 1861 (see page 7). But their achievements had not included the extension of political rights. In Russia in 1894, it was still a criminal offence to oppose the tsar or his government. There was no parliament, and although political parties had been formed they had no legal right to exist. There had never been a free press in Imperial Russia. Government censorship was imposed on published books and journals.

**KEY TERMS**

**Liberal ideas** Notions that called for limitations on the power of rulers and greater freedom for the people.

***Okhrana*** The tsarist secret police, whose special task was to hunt down subversives who challenged the tsarist regime.

**Political activists** Those who believed that necessary change could be achieved only through direct action.

**Reactionary** Resistant to any form of progressive change.

Such restriction had not prevented **liberal ideas** from seeping into Russia, but it did mean that they could not be openly expressed. The result was that supporters of reform or change had to go underground. In the nineteenth century there had grown up a wide variety of secret societies dedicated to political reform or revolution. These groups were frequently infiltrated by agents of the ***Okhrana***. As a result, raids, arrests, imprisonment and general harassment were regular occurrences.

### Extremism

The denial of free speech tended to drive **political activists** towards extremism. The outstanding example of this occurred in 1881 when Tsar Alexander II was blown to bits by a bomb thrown by a terrorist group known as 'The People's Will' (see page 19). In a society in which state oppression was met with revolutionary terrorism, there was no moderate middle ground on which a tradition of ordered political debate could develop.

## The Russian Orthodox Church

The tsars were fully supported in their claims to absolute authority by one of the great pillars of the Russian system, the Orthodox Church. This was a branch of Christianity which, since the fifteenth century, had been entirely independent of any outside authority, such as the papacy. Its detachment from foreign influence had given it an essentially Russian character. The great beauty of its liturgy and music had long been an outstanding expression of Russian culture. However, by the late nineteenth century it had become a deeply conservative body, opposed to political change and determined to preserve the tsarist system in its **reactionary** form. How detached the Orthodox Church was from Russia's growing urban population was illustrated by the statistic that in 1900 a Moscow suburb with 40,000 people had only one church and one priest.

The Church did contain some priests who strongly sympathised with the political revolutionaries, but as an institution it used its spiritual authority to teach the Russian people that it was their duty to be totally obedient to the tsar as **God's anointed**. The **catechism** of the Church included the statement that 'God commands us to love and obey from the inmost recesses of our heart every authority, and particularly the tsar'.

**God's anointed** At their coronation tsars were anointed with holy oil to symbolise that they governed by divine will.

**Catechism** The manual used for instructing the people in the essential points of the faith.

**Capital** The essential financial resource which provides the means for investment and expansion.

## The social structure of tsarist Russia

The striking features of the social structure were the comparatively small commercial, professional and working classes and the great preponderance of peasants in the population. This is illustrated in Figure 1.2, which shows the class distribution of the population, as measured by Russia's 1897 census.

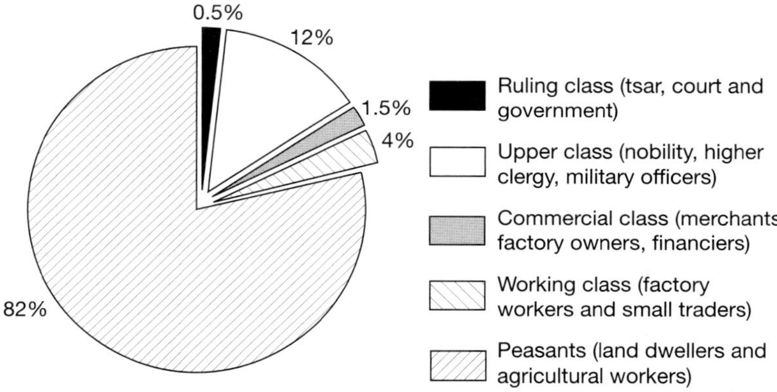


**Figure 1.2** The class distribution of the Russian population in 1897.

## The Russian economy

The remarkable difference in size between the urban professional and working classes and the rural peasants revealed a critical feature of Imperial Russia: its slow economic development. The low number of urban workers was a sign that Russia had not achieved the major industrial growth that had taken place in the nineteenth century in such countries as Germany, Britain and the USA.

This is not to say that Russia was entirely without industry. The Urals region produced considerable amounts of iron, and the chief western cities, Moscow and St Petersburg, had extensive textile factories. Most villages had a workshop for making iron tools, and most peasant homes engaged in some form of cottage industry, producing wooden, flaxen or woollen goods to supplement their income from farming. However, these activities were all relatively small scale. The sheer size of Russia and its undeveloped transport system had limited the chances for industrial expansion. A further restriction had been the absence of an effective banking system. Russia found it hard to raise **capital** on a large scale. It had not yet mastered the art of successful borrowing and investment, techniques which help to explain why expansion had been so rapid in Western countries. Russia's financial sluggishness had discouraged the rise of **entrepreneurialism**.

## Agriculture

Russia's unenterprising industrial system was matched by its inefficient pattern of agriculture. Even though four-fifths of the population were peasants, a thriving **agrarian economy** had failed to develop. Indeed, the land in Russia was a source of national weakness rather than strength. The empire's vast acres were not all good farming country. Much of Russia lay too far north to enjoy a climate or a soil suitable for crop-growing or cattle-rearing. Arable farming was restricted mainly to the Black Earth region, the area of European Russia stretching from Ukraine to Kazakhstan.

### KEY TERMS

**Entrepreneurialism**
The dynamic, expansionist attitude associated with Western commercial and industrial activity in this period.

**Agrarian economy**
A system in which food is produced on the land by arable and dairy farming and then traded.

### SOURCE A

? Study Source A. How effectively does it portray the relationship between the various social classes in tsarist Russia?

**A mocking socialist cartoon of 1900 showing the social pyramid in Imperial Russia. The Russian caption for each layer reads (in ascending order): 'We work for them while they ...' '... shoot at us' '... eat on our behalf' '... pray on our behalf' '... dispose of our money.'**

The great number of peasants in the population added to the problem. There was simply not enough fertile land to go round. Under the terms of the **Emancipation Decree of 1861**, the ex-serfs were entitled to buy land, but they invariably found the price too high. This was caused both by a shortage of suitable farming territory and by the government's taxation of land sales, imposed in order to raise the revenue needed to compensate the landowners for the losses caused by emancipation. The only way the peasants could raise the money to buy land was by borrowing from a special fund provided by the government. Consequently, those peasants who did manage to purchase property found themselves burdened with large mortgage repayments which would take them and their families generations to repay.

**KEY TERMS**

**Emancipation Decree of 1861** This reform had abolished serfdom – a Russian form of slavery in which the landowner had total control over the peasants who lived or worked on his land.

**'Dark masses'** Used contemptuously in the imperial court and government circles to describe the peasants, who made up four-fifths of the population.

**Conscription** The forcing of large numbers of peasants into the army or navy.

## The peasant problem

Among Russia's governing class, which was drawn from less than one per cent of the population, there was a deeply ingrained prejudice against granting rights to the mass of the people. Over 80 per cent of the population were peasants. They were predominantly illiterate and uneducated. Their sheer size as a social class and their coarse ways led to their being regarded with a mixture of fear and contempt by the governing elite, who believed that these dangerous **'dark masses'** could be held in check only by severe repression. This was what Nicholas II's wife, the Empress Alexandra, meant when she said that Russia needed always to be 'under the whip'.

The existence in the second half of the nineteenth century of an uneducated peasantry suspicious of change, and living with large debts and in great poverty, pointed to the social, political and economic backwardness of Imperial Russia. Various attempts to educate the peasants had been made in the past, but such efforts had been undermined by the fear among the ruling class that any improvement in the conditions of the 'dark masses' might threaten its own privileges. It was commonplace for officials in Russia to speak of the 'safe ignorance' of the population, implying that any attempt to raise the educational standards of the masses would prove highly dangerous, socially and politically.

## The Russian Army

One common method of keeping the peasants in check was to recruit them into the Russian armed services. The lower ranks of the army and navy were largely filled by enforced enlistment. **Conscription** was regularly used as a form of punishment for law-breakers. Ordinary Russians dreaded this sentence; they knew that life in the armed forces was a brutalising experience for the common soldier. The Russian Army was notorious in Europe for the severity of its discipline and the grimness of the conditions in which its soldiers lived. Special military camps had been set up in the remoter regions of the empire which operated as penal colonies rather than as training establishments. The rigours of service life had accounted for the deaths of over a million soldiers in peacetime during the reign of Nicholas I (1825–55).

It was a persistent belief in Russia that, as a large empire, it needed a large army. Throughout the nineteenth century the Imperial forces were kept at a strength of around one and a half million men. The cost of maintaining the army and the navy accounted on average for 45 per cent of the government's annual expenditure. This was by far the largest single item of state spending, and, when compared with the four per cent devoted to education, showed how unbalanced government priorities were.

### KEY TERMS

**Commissions** The holding of officer rank.

**Nepotism** A system in which positions are gained through family connections rather than on merit.

**Militia** Local citizens called together and granted arms to deal with a crisis requiring force.

The higher ranks of the army were the preserve of the aristocracy. **Commissions** were bought and sold, and there was little room for promotion on merit. This weakened it as a fighting force, but the truth of this tended to remain hidden because, with the exception of the Crimean War (1854–6), Russia was not engaged in a major conflict with a Western European power for a whole century after 1815. The army's active service was essentially a matter of putting down national risings or serious disturbances within the empire or on its frontiers. There were frequent border clashes with Turkey throughout the nineteenth century, and at various times Russian forces saw action in Poland, Armenia and Persia.

## The bureaucracy (civil service)

### KEY FIGURE

**Alexander Herzen (1812–70)**

A leading revolutionary thinker and critic of the Russian government.

Ironically, it was in the area where there had been the largest attempted reform that the greatest corruption had developed. At the beginning of the eighteenth century, Peter I had attempted to modernise Russia by establishing a full-scale civil service with the aim of maintaining central government control throughout the empire. However, by the middle of the nineteenth century, many Russian critics had begun to condemn this civil service as a corrupt bureaucracy whose **nepotism** and incompetence were the principal reasons for Russia's backwardness. Writing in 1868, **Alexander Herzen** claimed that the bureaucracy had become 'a kind of civilian priesthood', a money-grasping elite, which used its power to tax people and direct their behaviour for its own ends. Herzen accused the bureaucrats who ran Russia of 'sucking the blood of the people with thousands of greedy, unclean mouths'.

By the middle of the nineteenth century, Herzen asserted, tsarist Russia was run by a bureaucratic class which, for all its incompetence, still possessed the power to control the lives of the Russian masses. At local and national levels, the law, the government, the police and the **militia** were in the hands of a set of men whose first thought was their own convenience and advantage. Against this injustice the ordinary citizen had no redress, since any challenge to the system was lost in bureaucratic procedures.

Herzen's savage attack provided powerful ammunition for those in Russia who wished to ridicule and undermine the tsarist system itself. However, it is important to remember that Herzen was a revolutionary propagandist intent on painting the blackest picture he could of tsardom.

Efforts were made in the nineteenth century to reform the administration and limit its abuses. Nevertheless, the fact remained that the corruption and efficiency which Herzen described was still operating when Nicholas came to the throne in 1894.

**Summary diagram: The land, the people and tsardom**

| **The land** | **The people** |
|---|---|
| Russia's geography<br>Its great size | The social structure<br>Tiny dominant elite<br>The 'dark masses'<br>80 per cent peasant population |
| **The economy** | **The tsarist system** |
| Undeveloped industry<br>Backward agriculture | Autocratic government<br>Reactionary Church<br>Corrupt bureaucracy<br>Oppressive army |

# 2 The problem of reform in Imperial Russia

▶ *Why did Imperial Russia find it difficult to modernise?*

Many members of the ruling class accepted that major reforms were needed if Russia was to modernise its social and economic structure. However, there were barriers in the way.

## Obstacles to reform

One major barrier to reform was a basic disagreement within the government elite over Russia's true character as a nation. Since the days of Peter the Great there had been serious differences between **'Westerners'** and **'Slavophiles'**. Their dispute made it difficult to achieve reform in an ordered and acceptable way.

Another barrier to planned reform was the **autocratic** structure of Russia itself. Change could only come from the top. There were no representative institutions, such as a parliament, with the power to alter things. The only possible source of change was the tsar. From time to time, there were **progressive** tsars who accepted the need for reform. Yet it was hardly to be expected that any tsar, no matter how enlightened, would go so far as to introduce measures that might weaken his authority.

**KEY TERMS**

**'Westerners'** Those who believed that to remain a great nation Russia would have to adopt the best features of the advanced countries of Western Europe.

**'Slavophiles'** Those who regarded Western values as corrupting and urged that the nation should preserve itself as 'holy Russia', glorying in its Slav culture and traditions.

**Autocratic** The absolute rule of one person – in Russia this meant the tsar.

**Progressive** Promoting necessary change.

The result was that reform in Russia had been piecemeal, depending on the inclinations of the individual tsar, rather than a systematic programme of change. It is notable that the significant periods of reform in Russia were invariably a response to some form of national crisis or humiliation. This was certainly true of the reforms introduced in Alexander II's reign (1855–81). His accession coincided with the defeat of Russia at the hands of France and Britain in the Crimean War (1854–6). The shock of this reverse prompted the new tsar into adopting a reform programme.

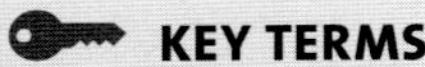

**KEY TERMS**

***Zemstva*** These local councils were elected bodies, but the voting regulations left them very much in the hands of the landowners.

***Mir*** The traditional village community.

**Intelligentsia** A cross-section of the educated and more enlightened members of Russian society who wanted to see their nation adopt progressive changes along Western lines.

## Local government reform

Alexander II's reforms began with the emancipation of the serfs in 1861, followed three years later by the setting up of a network of elected rural councils, known as ***zemstva***. Although these were not truly democratic, they did provide Russia with a form of representative government, no matter how limited, which offered some hope to those who longed for an extension of political rights. The authorities also emphasised the valuable role played in the countryside by the ***mir***, which they saw as a local organisation which would help to keep order and provide a cheap means of collecting taxes and mortgage repayments.

## Legal reforms

In addition, a number of legal reforms were introduced with the aim of simplifying the notoriously cumbersome court procedures whose delays had led to corruption and injustice. Of even greater importance was Alexander II's relaxation of the controls over the press and the universities. Greater freedom of expression encouraged the development of an **intelligentsia**.

## Limited nature of the reforms

Alexander II was not a supporter of reform simply for its own sake. He saw it as a way of lessening opposition to the tsarist system. He said that his intention was to introduce reform from above in order to prevent revolution from below. His hope was that his reforms would attract the support of the intelligentsia. In this he was largely successful. Emancipation, greater press and university freedoms, and the administrative and legal changes were greeted with enthusiasm by progressives.

No matter how progressive Alexander II himself may have appeared, he was still an autocrat. It was unthinkable that he would continue with a process that might compromise his power as tsar. Fearful that he had gone too far, he abandoned his reformist policies and returned to the tsarist tradition of oppression. His successor, Alexander III (1881–94), continued this, becoming notorious for the severity of his rule. During his reign a series of very restrictive measures known as 'the Reaction' had been imposed on the Russian people.

### Key measures of 'the Reaction'

*The Statute of State Security 1881*

- Special government-controlled courts were set up, which operated outside the existing legal system.
- Judges, magistrates and officials who were sympathetic towards liberal ideas were removed from office.
- The powers of the *Okhrana*, the tsarist secret police, were extended, and censorship of the press was tightened.

At its introduction in 1881, this Statute was described as a temporary measure brought in to deal with an emergency, but in essentials it remained in place until 1917.

*The University Statute 1887*

- Brought the universities under strict government control.

*The* Zemstva *Act 1890*

- Decreased the independence of the local councils and empowered government officials to interfere in their decision-making.

## Policies of Nicholas II

It was one of the ironies of Russian history that at a time when the nation most needed a tsar of strength and imagination, it was a man of weakness and limited outlook who reigned. The evidence suggests that Nicholas II was far from being as unintelligent as his detractors asserted. Nevertheless, his limited imagination was evident in the reactionary policies he followed. He seemed not to understand the real nature of the problems his nation and his dynasty faced.

The most pressing question was whether Imperial Russia could modernise itself sufficiently to be able to compete with the other European nations. Would the new tsar be a reformer or a reactionary? There was little doubt what the answer would be. Reform had a bad name by the time Nicholas became tsar. Furthermore, his upbringing and education made him suspicious of change. It was no surprise that he continued the repressive policies he had inherited. This further angered the intelligentsia and the critics of the tsarist regime; they began to prepare to challenge tsardom.

### The role of Pobedonostsev

As a young man, Nicholas had been tutored at court by **Konstantin Pobedonostsev**, a man of enormous influence in late Imperial Russia. Pobedonostsev was the chief minister in the Russian government from 1881 to 1905. His thin frame and pale skin stretched almost transparently across his bony features, giving him the appearance of a living corpse. In a macabre way this was wholly fitting since his fearful appearance was matched by the frightening nature of his ideas.

**KEY FIGURE**

**Konstantin Pobedonostsev (1827–1907)**

In addition to being chief minister, he was the Procurator (lay head) of the Synod, the governing body of the Russian Orthodox Church.

**KEY TERMS**

**Representative government** A form of rule in which ordinary people choose their government and have the power to replace it if it does not serve their interests.

**Pogroms** Fierce persecutions which often involved the wounding or killing of Jews and the destruction of their property.

**Ghettoes** Particular areas where Jews were concentrated and to which they were restricted.

Known as 'the Grand Inquisitor' because of his repressive attitudes, Pobedonostsev was an arch-conservative who had a deep distaste for all forms of liberalism and democracy. He dismissed the idea of **representative government** as 'the great lie of our time'. To his mind, autocracy was the only possible government for Imperial Russia. The Russians *en masse* were too uneducated, vulgar and uninformed to be able to govern themselves. They had to be controlled and directed. For the same reason, he rejected the notions of trial by jury and a free press. Such concessions would simply allow the ignorant and the troublemakers to cause disruption. Russia's rulers had a duty to govern with vigour and harshness, using the legal, religious and educational institutions to inculcate obedience in the people. Pobedonostsev was behind many of the **pogroms**, part of the organised attempt to enforce religious conformity in Russia. Nicholas took to heart the lessons he learned from Pobedonostsev.

## Russification

A policy of particular note that had begun under Alexander III and which Nicholas II carried on was Russification. This was a severely enforced method of restricting the influence of the non-Russian national minorities within the empire by emphasising the superiority of all things Russian. Russian was declared to be the official first language; this meant that all legal proceedings, such as trials, and all administration had to be conducted in Russian. Public office was closed to those not fluent in the language. The aim was to impose Russian ways and values on all the peoples within the nation.

Officials everywhere in the empire now had a vested interest in maintaining the dominance of Russian values at the expense of the other national cultures. Discrimination against non-Russians, which had previously been a hidden feature of Russian public life, became more open and vindictive in the 1890s. The nationalities that suffered most from this were the Baltic Germans, the Poles, the Finns, the Armenians and the Ukrainians. State interference in their education, religion and culture became widespread and systematic.

## Anti-Semitism

Undoubtedly, the greatest victims of Russification were the Jews. Over 600 new measures were introduced, imposing heavy social, political and economic restrictions on the Jewish population. The most onerous of these was the requirement that Jews live in discrete districts or **ghettoes**. This rendered them immediately identifiable and made it easy to characterise them as scapegoats who could be blamed for Russia's difficulties. Anti-Semitism was deeply ingrained in tsarist Russia. Pogroms had long disfigured Russian history. A group of ultra-conservative Russian nationalists, known as the 'Black Hundreds', were notorious for their attacks on Jews. During the reign of Nicholas II, the number of pogroms increased sharply. This was proof of the tsarist regime's active encouragement of the terrorising of the Jews. But what was disturbingly noticeable was the eagerness with which local communities followed the lead from above in organising the blood-lettings.

## The response to Nicholas II's policies

The tight controls that Nicholas II tried to impose did not lessen opposition to tsardom. The reverse happened; despite greater police interference, opposition became more organised. A number of political parties, ranging from moderate reformers to violent revolutionaries, came into being (see page 18). The government's policies of reaction and Russification produced a situation in which many political and national groups grew increasingly frustrated by the mixture of coercion and incompetence that characterised the tsarist system. As a policy, therefore, Russification proved remarkably ill-judged. At a critical stage in its development, when cohesion and unity were needed, Russia chose to treat half its population as inferiors or potential enemies. The persecution of the Jews was especially crass. It alienated the great mass of the 5 million Jews in the Russian population, large numbers of whom fled in desperation to Western Europe or North America, carrying with them an abiding hatred of tsardom. Those who could not escape stayed to form a large and disaffected community within the empire. It was no coincidence that the 1890s witnessed a large influx of Jews into the various anti-tsarist movements in Russia. In 1897, Jews formed their own revolutionary 'Bund' or union. Such developments suggested that troubles lay ahead for the tsarist government.

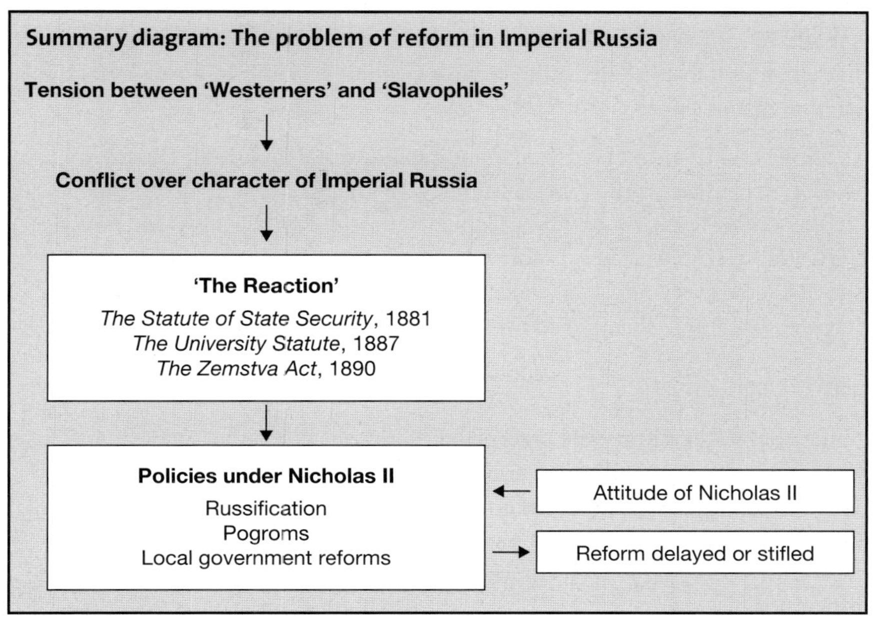

# Economic reform under Witte 1893–1903

 *What methods did Witte use to develop the Russian economy?*

 **KEY FIGURES**

**Sergei Witte (1849–1915)**
Minister of finance (equivalent to the British chancellor of the exchequer) 1893–1903 and chief minister 1903–6.

**Peter Stolypin (1862–1911)**
A political conservative but a progressive in agricultural matters, chief minister 1906–11.

 **KEY TERMS**

**'Great spurt'** The spread of industry and the increase in production that occurred in the 1890s.

**Private enterprise** Economic activity organised by individuals or companies, not the government.

**Capitalists** Russia's financiers and industrialists.

**State capitalism** The direction and control of the economy by the government, using its central power and authority.

For all the bitterness created by the government's repressive policies, the early years of Nicholas II's reign were a period of rapid economic expansion. For a time it seemed that Russia might become a modern industrial nation. This was largely due to the work of two outstanding ministers: **Sergei Witte**, who served during the early part of Nicholas II's reign, and **Peter Stolypin**, who held office during the middle years (see page 42). In the face of resistance from the very regime they were trying to serve, Witte and Stolypin sought to modernise Russia.

## The great spurt

In the 1890s, Russian industry grew so rapidly that the term the **'great spurt'** was used to describe the period. A major reason for the exceptional growth was the increase in the output of coal in Ukraine and of oil in the Caucasus. Economic historians are agreed that, although this sudden acceleration was the result of **private enterprise**, it was sustained by deliberate government policy.

The motives of the tsarist government were military rather than economic. It is true that the **capitalists** did well out of the spurt, but it was not the government's primary intention to help them. Economic expansion attracted the tsar and his ministers because it was a means of improving the strength of the Russian armed forces. A growing industry would produce more and better guns, equipment and ships.

As minister of finance and the outstanding individual involved in Russia's development at this time, Witte set himself the huge task of modernising the Russian economy to a level where it could compete with the advanced nations of the West. To help bring this about, he invited foreign experts and workers to Russia to advise on industrial planning. Engineers and managers from France, Belgium, Britain, Germany and Sweden played a vital role in the 'great spurt'.

## State capitalism

While not opposed to private enterprise, Witte considered that modernisation could be achieved only through **state capitalism**. He was impressed by the results of the industrial revolutions in Western Europe and the USA, and argued that Russia could successfully modernise by planning along the same lines. He admitted that, given the backwardness of Russia, this presented particular difficulties.

**SOURCE B**

**From Witte's memorandum to the tsar in 1899, quoted in T. Riha, editor, *Readings in Russian Civilization*, University of Chicago Press, 1964, volume 2, p. 431.**

*The economic relations of Russia to Western Europe are fully comparable to the relations of colonial countries with their metropolises [mother countries]. The latter consider their colonies as advantageous markets in which they can freely sell the products of their labour and of their industry, and from which they can draw with a powerful hand the raw materials necessary for them. Russia was, and to a certain extent still is, such a hospitable colony for all industrially developed states, generously providing them with the cheap products of her soil and buying dearly the products of their labour. But there is a radical difference between Russia and a colony: Russia is an independent and strong power. She has the right and the strength not to want to be the handmaiden of states which are more developed economically.*

According to Witte in Source B, what is the relationship between Russia and the advanced industrial nations?

Witte judged that, for Russia to avoid remaining the 'handmaiden' of the advanced industrial states, its greatest need was to acquire capital for investment in industry. To raise this, he negotiated large loans and investments from abroad, while imposing heavy taxes and high interest rates at home. At the same time as he encouraged the inflow of foreign capital, Witte limited the import of foreign goods. Protective **tariffs** were set up as a means of safeguarding Russia's young domestic industries, such as steel production. In 1897, the Russian currency was put on the **gold standard**. The hope was that this would create financial stability and so encourage international investment in Russia. The aim was largely successful but it penalised the consumers at home since they had to pay the higher prices that traders introduced to keep pace with the increased value of the rouble. Furthermore, prices tended to rise as a result of tariffs making goods scarcer.

**KEY TERMS**

**Tariffs** Duties imposed on foreign goods to keep their prices high and, therefore, discourage importers from bringing them into the country.

**Gold standard** The system in which a nation's basic unit of currency, in Russia's case the rouble, had a fixed gold content, thus giving it strength when exchanged against other currencies.

## The importance of the railways

Much of the foreign capital that Witte was successful in raising was directly invested in railways. He believed that the modernisation of the Russian economy ultimately depended on developing an effective railway system. His enthusiasm was an important factor in the extraordinary increase in lines and rolling stock that took place between 1881 and 1914. It would not be an exaggeration to describe this as a transport revolution.

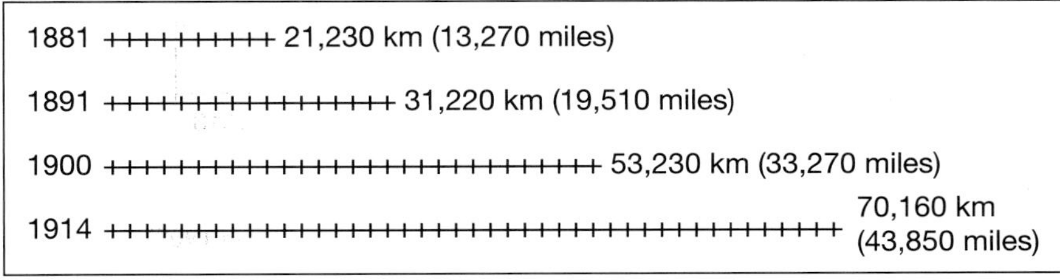


**Figure 1.3** The growth of Russian railways.

Witte's special prestige project was the Trans-Siberian Railway, which was constructed between 1891 and 1916. The line stretched for 5770 miles from Moscow to Vladivostok (see the map on page 2) and was intended to connect the remoter regions of the central and eastern empire with the industrial west, and so encourage the migration of workers to the areas where they were most needed. However, it promised more than it delivered. Sections of it were still incomplete in 1916 and it did not greatly improve east–west migration. The Trans-Siberian Railway proved more impressive as a symbol of Russian enterprise than as a project of real economic worth.

One of Witte's main hopes was that the major improvements in transport would boost exports and foreign trade. The trade figures suggest that his hopes were largely fulfilled. However, these figures of increased production are not so impressive when it is remembered that Russia was experiencing a massive growth in population. Production per head of population was lower than the aggregate figures suggested.

**Table 1.2** The Russian economy: annual production (in millions of tonnes)

| Year | Coal | Pig iron | Oil | Grain* |
|---|---|---|---|---|
| 1890 | 5.9 | 0.89 | 3.9 | 36 |
| 1900 | 16.1 | 2.66 | 10.2 | 56 |
| 1910 | 26.8 | 2.99 | 9.4 | 74 |
| 1913 | 35.4 | 4.10 | 9.1 | 90 |
| 1916 | 33.8 | 3.72 | 9.7 | 64 |

* European Russia only.

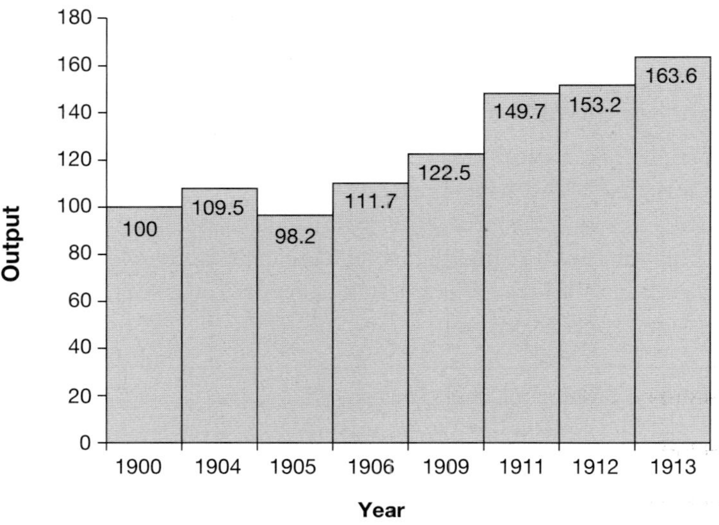


**Figure 1.4** Industrial output in the Russian Empire (base unit of 100 in 1900).

**Table 1.3** Population of Imperial Russia 1885–1913

| Region | 1885 | 1897 | 1913 |
|---|---|---|---|
| European Russia | 81,725,200 | 93,442,900 | 121,780,000 |
| Caucasus | 7,284,500 | 9,289,400 | 12,717,200 |
| Siberia | 4,313,700 | 5,758,800 | 9,894,500 |
| Steppes and Urals | 1,588,500 | 2,465,700 | 3,929,500 |
| Central Asia | 3,738,600 | 5,281,000 | 7,106,000 |
| Total | 98,650,500 | 116,237,800 | 155,427,200 |

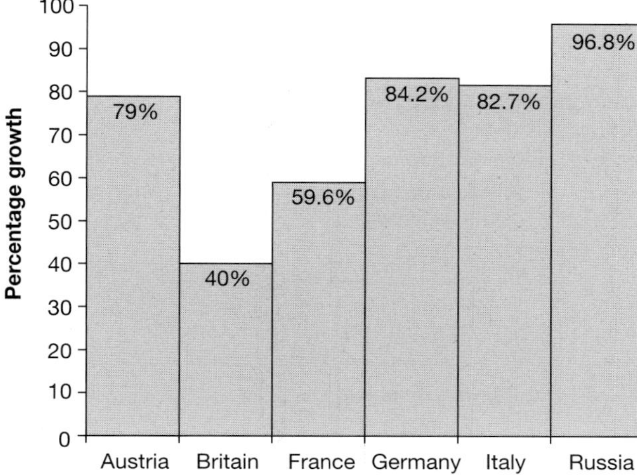


**Figure 1.5** Growth in national product 1898–1913.

Nevertheless, Russia was enjoying real economic growth. Figure 1.5 shows how favourably its industrial output compared with other European countries. Again, one has to be cautious in interpreting the data. Given its underdevelopment, Russia was starting from a much lower level of production. For example, although its 96.8% growth looks to be over twice that of Britain's, it was playing catch-up and had a long way to go.

## Witte's problems

There is no doubt that Witte's policies had a major impact on the expansion of the Russian economy. However, what can be questioned is whether the results were wholly beneficial. Critics have pointed to three drawbacks in his economic reforms:

- He made Russia too dependent on foreign loans and investments.
- In giving priority to heavy industry, he neglected vital areas such as light engineering.
- He paid no attention to Russia's agricultural needs.

Yet, any criticism of Witte should be balanced by reference to the problems he faced. The demands of the military commanders too often interfered with his plans for railway construction and the building of new industrial plant.

Moreover, his freedom of action was restricted by the resistance to change which he met from the court and the government. The main purpose of his economic policies was to make the nation strong and thus protect tsardom against the disruptive forces in Russian society, but he was disliked by the royal court and the government, which seldom gave him the support he needed.

Witte was not an easy man to get on with and he made enemies easily, but in ability he towered above all the other ministers and officials in the government. His tragedy was that despite his great talents, which, if properly recognised, might have led Russia towards peaceful modernisation, he was never fully trusted by the people of the tsarist system he was trying to save.

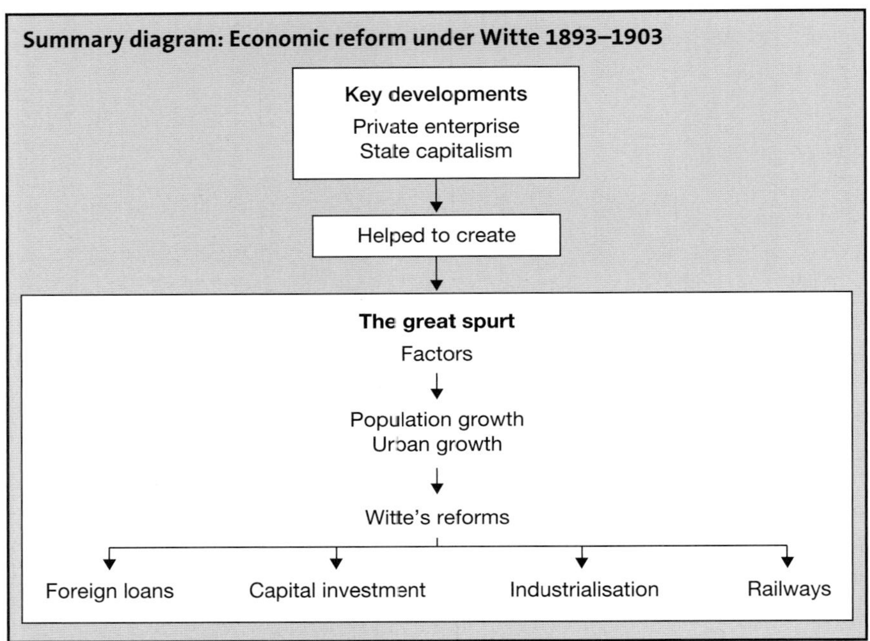

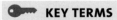

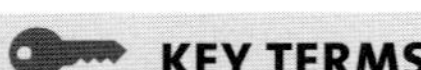
**KEY TERMS**

**Revolutionaries** Those who believed that Russia could not progress unless the tsarist system was destroyed.

**Reformers** Strong critics of the tsarist system who believed it could be changed for the better by pressure from without and reform from within.

**Populists** *Narodniks*, from the Russian word for 'the people'.

# 4 The opponents of tsardom

▶ *What forms did opposition to tsardom take?*

Two main groups opposed to tsardom can be identified in Nicholas II's reign: **revolutionaries** and **reformers** (liberals).

## Revolutionaries

The revolutionaries comprised three major forces:

- **Populists**.
- Social Revolutionaries (SRs).
- Social Democrats (SDs).

## The Populists (*Narodniks*)

This group regarded the future of Russia as being in the hands of the peasants who made up the overwhelming mass of the population. They argued that the peasants must take the lead in transforming Russia, beginning with the overthrow of the tsarist system itself.

Populism dated from the 1870s. As with all the significant political movements that came into being in this period, the Populist leaders were drawn, not from the peasants, but from the middle and upper classes. These leaders regarded it as their duty to educate the uninformed peasantry into an awareness of its revolutionary role. This involved 'going to the people', a policy by which the educated Populists went from the universities into the countryside to live for a period with the peasants in an attempt to turn them into revolutionaries.

The policy was seldom a success. The peasants tended to regard the students as airy-fairy thinkers and prattlers who had no knowledge of real life. In desperation, some Populists turned to terrorism, as the only way of achieving their aims. In 1879, a group calling itself 'The People's Will' was founded with the declared intention of murdering members of the ruling class. This group, which was reckoned to be no more than 400 strong, gained notoriety two years later when it successfully planned the assassination of Alexander II, who was blown to pieces by a bomb. However, this act weakened rather than strengthened the Populist movement. The murder of a tsar who had initiated many reforms seemed to discredit the idea of reform itself and so justified the repression imposed in the wake of the assassination.

The importance of populism lay in its methods rather than in its ideas. Its concept of a peasant-based revolution was unrealistic; the Russian peasantry were simply not interested in political revolution. What was lasting about populism was the part it played in establishing a violent anti-tsarist tradition. All the revolutionaries in Russia after 1870 were influenced, if not inspired, by the example of the Populist challenge to tsardom.

## The Social Revolutionaries (SRs)

The Social Revolutionary Party grew directly out of the Populist movement. The economic spurt of the 1890s had produced a quickening of interest in political and social issues. Seeing this as an opportunity to gain recruits from the rapidly growing urban workforce, the Populists began to agitate among the workers. The intention was to widen the concept of **the 'people'**, so that it encompassed not simply the peasants but all those in society who had reasons for wishing to see the end of tsardom.

**KEY TERM**

**The 'people'** The part of the population that the SRs believed truly represented the character and will of the Russian nation.

An important figure in the reshaping of Populist strategy was Victor Chernov, who played a key part in the formation of the Social Revolutionary Party in 1901 and became its leader. He was a member of the intelligentsia, and sought to provide a firmer base for populism than its previous passionate but vague ideas had produced. However, as with all the revolutionary groups in tsarist Russia, the SRs were weakened by disagreements among themselves. Leon Trotsky, who was later to play a major role as a revolutionary, pointed to this division when he described the SRs as being made up of two competing groups: 'Left Social Revolutionaries' and 'Right Social Revolutionaries'.

In distinguishing between the left and the right elements, Trotsky was referring to the division of the SR Party into anarchists and revolutionaries. The Left SRs were the faction who wanted to continue the policy of terrorism inherited from 'The People's Will'. The Right SRs were the more moderate element, who, while believing in revolution as their ultimate goal, were prepared to co-operate with other parties in working for an immediate improvement in the conditions of the workers and peasants. Between 1901 and 1905, it was the terrorist faction that dominated. During those years the SRs were responsible for over 2000 political assassinations, including Vyacheslav Plehve, the **interior minister**, and the tsar's uncle, the Grand Duke Sergei. These were spectacular successes but they did little to bring about the desired link with the urban workers.

**KEY TERMS**

**Interior minister** Equivalent to Britain's home secretary.

**Revolutionary socialism** The belief that change could be achieved only through the overthrow of the tsarist system.

**Social Democrats** The All-Russian Social Democratic Workers' Party.

**Class struggle** A continuing conflict at every stage of history between those who possess economic and political power and those who do not – in simple terms 'the haves' and 'the have-nots'.

**Dialectic** The violent struggle which takes place in nature and in human society between opposites.

The 1905 Revolution, which saw the first serious open challenge to tsardom in Nicholas II's reign, brought more gains to the liberals than to the revolutionaries (see page 36). One effect of this was that the more moderate Right SRs gained greater influence over party policy. This began to show dividends. From 1906, the SRs experienced growing support from the professional classes, from the trade unions and from the All-Russian Union of Peasants, which had been set up in 1905. At its first Congress in 1906, the SR Party committed itself to '**revolutionary socialism**' and gave a special pledge to the peasants that it would end 'private ownership by returning the land to those who worked it'.

It was their land policy that largely explains why the SRs remained the most popular party with the peasants. However, at the time, the Congress decisions brought disruption rather than unity. The left wing protested that the party's programme ignored the industrial workers, while the right asserted that Congress policy was unworkable in current Russian conditions. Chernov tried to hold the factions together, but from 1906 onwards the SRs were a collection of radical groups rather than a united party. Nevertheless, until they were outlawed by the Bolsheviks after the 1917 Revolution (see page 139), the SRs remained the party with the largest popular following in Russia.

## The Social Democrats (SDs)

The **Social Democrats** came into being in 1898; their aim was to achieve revolution in Russia by following the ideas of Karl Marx (1818–83), a German revolutionary, who had advanced the idea that human society operated according to scientific principles. Just as the physical universe was governed by the laws of chemistry and physics, so too, the behaviour of human beings was determined by social laws. These could be studied scientifically and implemented politically as communism. Marx claimed that the critical determinant of human behaviour was **class struggle**, a process that operated throughout history. He referred to this process as the **dialectic**.

For revolutionaries in the nineteenth century, the most exciting aspect of Marx's analysis was his conviction that the contemporary industrial era marked the final stage of the dialectical class struggle. Human history was about to reach its culmination in the revolutionary victory of the **proletariat** over the **bourgeoisie**, which would usher in 'the dictatorship of the proletariat'. This dictatorship would be the last but one stage of history in which the workers, having overthrown the bourgeoisie in revolution and taken power, would hunt down and destroy all the surviving reactionaries. It would be a violent and bloody affair but, once these final class enemies had been obliterated, all conflict would end and the perfect, harmonious society would emerge.

**KEY TERMS**

**Proletariat** The exploited industrial workers who would triumph in the last great class struggle.

**Bourgeoisie** The owners of capital, the boss class, who exploited the workers but who would be overthrown by them in the revolution to come.

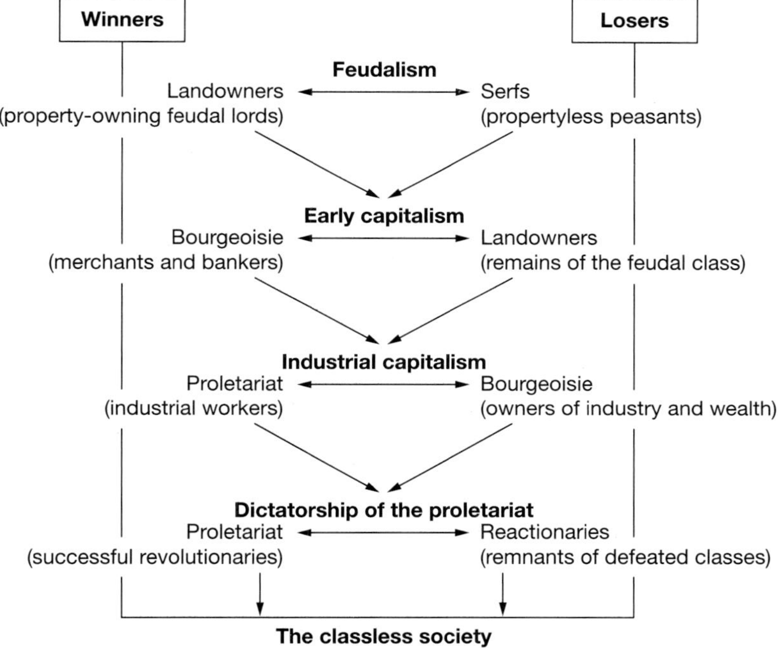


**Figure 1.6** A visual representation of the Marxist notion of the workings of the dialectic.

The attraction of Marx for Russian revolutionaries is easy to understand. His ideas had been known in Russia for some time, but what gave them particular relevance was the 'great spurt' of the 1890s. This promised to create the industrial conditions in Russia that would produce a politically conscious work force and thus make a successful revolution possible. The previously unfocused hopes for revolution could now be directed on the industrial working class.

The first Marxist revolutionary of note in Russia was **George Plekhanov**. He had translated Marx's writings into Russian and had worked to promote the idea of proletarian revolution. Despite his pioneering work, and his foundation of the SD party, a number of the members soon became impatient with Plekhanov's leadership. They found him too theoretical in his approach; they wanted a much more active revolutionary programme. The outstanding spokesman for this viewpoint was Vladimir Ulyanov, better known as Lenin (see profile on page 103).

**KEY FIGURE**

**George Plekhanov (1856–1918)**

Often referred to as 'the father of Russian Marxism'; it was under his leadership that the SD Party was formed in 1898.

## Lenin's impact on the SDs

When Lenin returned from exile to western Russia in 1900, he set about turning the SDs into his idea of what a truly revolutionary party must be. With a colleague, Julius Martov, he founded a party newspaper, *Iskra* (*The Spark*), which he used as the chief means of putting his case to the party members. Lenin criticised Plekhanov for being more interested in reform than revolution. He said that, under Plekhanov, the SDs, instead of transforming the workers into a revolutionary force for the overthrow of capitalism, were following a policy of '**economism**'. Lenin wanted living and working conditions to get worse, not better. In that way the bitterness of the workers would increase, and so drive the Russian proletariat to revolution.

**KEY TERM**

**Economism** Putting the improvement of the workers' conditions before the need for revolution.

In 1902, Lenin wrote his strongest attack yet on Plekhanov in a pamphlet called, *What Is To Be Done?* In it he berated him for continuing to seek allies among as broad a group of anti-tsarist elements as possible. Lenin insisted that this would lead nowhere. Revolution in Russia was possible only if it was organised and led by a party of dedicated, professional revolutionaries.

For Lenin, revolution was not a haphazard affair; it was a matter of applied science. He regarded the teachings of Karl Marx as having already provided the key to understanding how revolutions operated. It was the task of those select members of the SD party who understood scientific Marxism to lead the way in Russia. The workers could not be left to themselves; they did not know enough. They had to be directed. It was the historical role of the informed members of the SD party to provide that direction. Only they could rescue the Russian working class and convert it to true socialism.

## The Bolshevik–Menshevik split

The dispute between Lenin and Plekhanov came to a head during the second congress of the SD Party in 1903. Plekhanov tried to avoid confrontation, but Lenin deliberately made an issue of who had the right to belong to the Social Democratic Party. His aim was to force members to choose between Plekhanov's idea of a broad-based party, open to all revolutionaries, and his own concept of a small, tightly knit and exclusive party. The congress that met in a number of different places, including Brussels and London, was a heated affair, which frequently descended into a series of slanging matches over points of procedure. The London police, who had been asked by the Russian authorities to keep an eye on proceedings, tended to find the SDs a comical bunch. Their reports spoke of funny foreign gentlemen all speaking at the same time and trying to out-shout each other.

No matter how much the SDs may have amused the London bobbies, they took themselves very seriously. A deep divide developed between Lenin and one of his *Iskra* co-editors, Julius Martov, who shared Plekhanov's viewpoint about membership. Their quarrel was as much to do with personality as with politics. Martov believed that behind Lenin's tactics was a fierce determination to become dictator of the party. Martov's view was supported by Alexander

Potresov, another co-editor of *Iskra*, who wrote the following description of Lenin:

**SOURCE C**

**Adapted from the papers of Alexander Potresov, writing in 1903, quoted in David Shub, *Lenin*, Penguin, 1976, p. 76.**

*Lenin showed great cunning and a readiness to do anything to make his opinion prevail. Frequently my colleagues and I felt out of place in our own newspaper office. Lenin divided the world sharply between those who were with him and those who were against him. For him there existed no personal or social relationship outside of the two classes. When the political principle was enunciated that in the fight against the common enemy – the Tsarist government – it was desirable to present a common front by combining with other groups and parties, Lenin accepted it reluctantly and only in theory. In practice, it remained an idle phrase. He could not have acted on that principle even if he had wanted to, because he was incapable of co-operating with other people. It went against his grain.*

According to Source C, why was Lenin unwilling to join a common front against the tsarist government?

In a series of votes, the SD congress showed itself to be evenly divided between Lenin and Martov. However, after a particular set of divisions had gone in his favour, Lenin claimed that he and his supporters were the majority. This led to their being called **Bolsheviks** while Martov's group became known as **Mensheviks**. Initially, the main point dividing Bolsheviks and Mensheviks was simply one of procedure. However, following the split in 1903 the differences between them hardened into a set of opposed attitudes. These are shown in Figure 1.7.

**KEY TERMS**

**Bolsheviks** From *bolshinstvo*, Russian for majority.

**Mensheviks** From *menshinstvo*, Russian for minority.

| Menshevik view | Issue | Bolshevik view |
|---|---|---|
| Russia not yet ready for proletarian revolution – the bourgeois stage had to occur first | *Revolution* | The bourgeois and proletarian stages could be telescoped into one revolution |
| A mass organisation with membership open to all revolutionaries | *The party* | A tight-knit, exclusive organisation of professional revolutionaries |
| Open, democratic discussion within the party – decisions arrived at by votes of members | *Decision-making* | Authority to be exercised by the Central Committee of the party – this was described as 'democratic centralism'. |
| • Alliance with all other revolutionary and bourgeois liberal parties<br>• Support of trade unions in pursuing better wages and conditions for workers (economism) | *Strategy* | • No co-operation with other parties<br>• Economism dismissed as playing into the hands of the bourgeoisie<br>• The aim was to turn workers into revolutionaries |

**Figure 1.7** Main differences between the Mensheviks and the Bolsheviks.

### 'Democratic centralism'

This was Lenin's central notion that true democracy in the Bolshevik Party lay in the obedience of the members to the authority and instructions of the leaders. The justification for this was that while, as representatives of the workers, all Bolsheviks were genuine revolutionaries, only the leaders were sufficiently educated in the science of revolution to understand what needed to be done. In practice, democratic centralism meant that the Bolsheviks did what Lenin told them to do.

By 1912, Bolsheviks and Mensheviks had become two distinct, conflicting Marxist parties. Lenin deliberately emphasised the difference between himself and Martov by resigning from the editorial board of *Iskra* and starting his own journal, *Vyperod* (*Forward*), as an instrument for Bolshevik attacks on the Mensheviks. A Bolshevik daily paper, *Pravda* (*The Truth*), was first published in 1912.

## Lenin and the Bolsheviks before 1917

An important point to note is that the later success of Bolshevism in the October Revolution has tempted writers to overstate the importance of Lenin in the period before 1917. For example, Trotsky, who joined Lenin in 1917 after having been a Menshevik, argued in his later writings that the Bolsheviks had been systematically preparing the ground for revolution since 1903. But the fact was that during the years 1904–17 Lenin was largely absent from Russia. He lived variously in Finland, France, Switzerland and Austria, and his visits to Russia were rare and fleeting. Although he continued from exile to issue a constant stream of instructions to his followers, he and they played only a minor role in events in Russia before 1917.

## Bolshevik tactics

Lenin and his fellow exiles set up training schools for revolutionaries, who were then smuggled back into Russia to infiltrate worker organisations such as the trade unions. The Bolsheviks who remained in Russia spent their time trying to raise money for their party. This frequently involved direct terrorism and violence; post offices were favourite targets for Bolshevik attack. In one notorious episode in Tiflis in Georgia, a Bolshevik gang bomb-blasted their way into a post office, killed some twenty people before making off with a quarter of a million roubles. The money stolen in such raids was used to finance the printing of masses of handbills, leaflets and newspapers attacking the tsarist regime and calling for revolution.

Yet, the truth was that, despite such activities, Lenin's revolutionaries were regarded by the authorities during this period as merely a fringe group of extremists. Interestingly, the Bolsheviks were not listed by the police as a major challenge to the tsarist system. In the pre-1914 period, the numerical strength of the Bolsheviks varied between 5000 and 10,000; even in February 1917 it was no more than 25,000. Before 1917, the Mensheviks invariably outnumbered them. Numbers, of course, are not everything. Determination is arguably more important. Whatever the apparent lack of influence of Lenin's Bolsheviks before 1917, the fact is that when a revolutionary situation developed in 1917 it was they who proved the best prepared to seize the opportunity to take over government (see page 117). The Bolsheviks' readiness was one of Lenin's major political achievements.

## Reformers and Liberals

Apart from the revolutionaries, there were a number of reforming groups seeking non-violent change. These are usually referred to as liberals, although they never came together to form a common front.

Until the issuing of the October Manifesto in 1905 (see page 36) political parties had been illegal in Russia. This had not actually prevented their formation, but it had made it very difficult for them to develop as genuinely democratic bodies. There was no tradition of open debate. Since they were denied legal recognition, they often resorted to extreme methods in order to spread their ideas. As a result, during the brief period of their permitted existence from 1905 to 1921, before they were again outlawed, the Russian political parties proved to be suspicious and intolerant of each other. This made co-operation and collective action difficult to organise. Yet, although they were to have a short and inglorious life, the Russian liberal parties should not be ignored. In historical study, losers deserve as much attention as winners.

The economic boom of the 1890s saw the rapid development of a small but ambitious class of industrialists, lawyers and financiers. It was among such social groups that liberal ideas for the modernising of Russia began to take hold. There was also often a strong nationalist element in Russian liberalism. The national minorities viewed the liberal movement as a means of advancing their claim to be independent of Russian Imperial control. Three principal liberal parties came to prominence in the pre-1914 period: the Union of Liberation, the Octobrists and the Constitutional Democrats (Kadets).

### Union of Liberation

The first significant reforming movement to emerge was the Union (League) of Liberation. Its principal leaders were academics **Paul Milyukov** and **Peter Struve**. Formed in 1904, the Union drew up a programme which expressed its basic aim (Source D on the next page).

**KEY FIGURES**

**Paul Milyukov (1859–1943)**

The outstanding liberal critic of tsardom, he grew increasingly disillusioned with the tsar and doubted that the system he represented could be saved.

**Peter Struve (1870–1944)**

A radical thinker and writer who had first been attracted to Marxism and for a short time was an SD member.

? According to Source D, what is the basic aim of the Union of Liberation?

**SOURCE D**

**From the programme of the Union of Liberation, 1904, quoted in David Christian, *Imperial and Soviet Russia*, Macmillan, 1997, p. 135.**

*The first and foremost aim of the Union of Liberation is the liberation of Russia. Considering political liberty in even its most minimal form completely incompatible with the absolute character of the Russian monarchy, the union will seek before all else the abolition of autocracy and the establishment in Russia of a constitutional regime. In determining the concrete forms in which a constitutional regime can be realized in Russia, the Union of Liberation will make all efforts to have the political problems resolved in the spirit of extensive democracy. Above all, it recognises as fundamentally essential that the principle of universal equal, secret, and direct elections be made the basis of the political reform.*

The Union tried to bring the various liberal groups together by pointing out where there was common ground between them. Its influence helped to prepare the way for the 1905 Revolution and it continued to operate as a party until 1917. However, the Union was unable to create a single coherent reforming movement with a single purpose. The Union's deeper significance was in indicating the range of anti-tsarist feeling that existed and in advancing the arguments and ideas that the more progressive members of the government, such as Witte, took to heart.

**KEY TERM**

***Duma*** The Russian parliament, which existed from 1906 to 1917.

## The Octobrists

This group dated from the issuing of the tsar's manifesto of October 1905, which created the ***duma*** (see page 47). The Octobrists were moderates who were basically loyal to the tsar and his government. They believed in the maintenance of the Russian Empire and regarded the manifesto and the establishment of the *duma* as major constitutional advances.

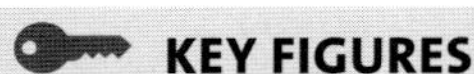

**KEY FIGURES**

**Alexander Guchkov (1862–1936)**

A major industrialist and factory owner.

**Mikhail Rodzianko (1859–1924)**

A large landowner.

The Octobrists were mainly drawn from the larger commercial, industrial and landowning interests. Their leading members were **Alexander Guchkov**, and **Mikhail Rodzianko**, both of whom were later to take a major part in the Provisional Government of 1917 (see page 88). How relatively restricted the Octobrists were in their aims can be gauged from their programme, issued in November 1905, which called for unity among all those who wanted the 'rule of law'. It appealed for the continuation of a 'strong and authoritative regime' to work with 'the representatives of the people' in bringing peace to the country.

The limited aims of the Octobrists led to their being dismissed by revolutionaries as bourgeois reactionaries who were unwilling to challenge the existing system. This was not wholly accurate. In the *dumas*, the Octobrists frequently voiced serious criticisms of the short-sightedness or incompetence of the tsarist government. They may not have wanted the overthrow of tsardom, but they were very willing to point out its failings.

## The Constitutional Democrats (Kadets)

The Constitutional Democrats also came into being as a party at the time of the 1905 Revolution. The Kadets, the largest of the liberal parties, wanted Russia to develop as a **constitutional monarchy** in which the powers of the tsar would be restricted by a democratically elected constituent (national) assembly. They believed that such a body, representative of the whole of Russia, would be able to settle the nation's outstanding social, political and economic problems. Lenin dismissed this as bourgeois political naïvety, but there is no doubt that the dream of a constituent assembly remained a source of inspiration to Russian reformers in the period before the 1917 Revolution.

**KEY TERM**

**Constitutional monarchy** A system of government in which the king or emperor rules but governs only through elected representatives whose decisions he cannot countermand.

The Kadet Party contained progressive landlords, the smaller industrial entrepreneurs and members of the professions. Academics were prominent in it, as typified by its leader, Paul Milyukov, who was a professor of history and had been a founder member of the Union of Liberation. In the *duma*, the Kadets proved to be the most outspoken critics of the tsarist system. They were to play a significant role in the events surrounding the February Revolution in 1917 (see page 86).

### The Kadet programme

- An All-Russian Constituent Assembly.
- Full equality and civil rights for all citizens.
- The ending of censorship.
- The abolition of the mortgage repayments on land.
- The recognition of trade unions and the right to strike.
- The introduction of universal, free education.

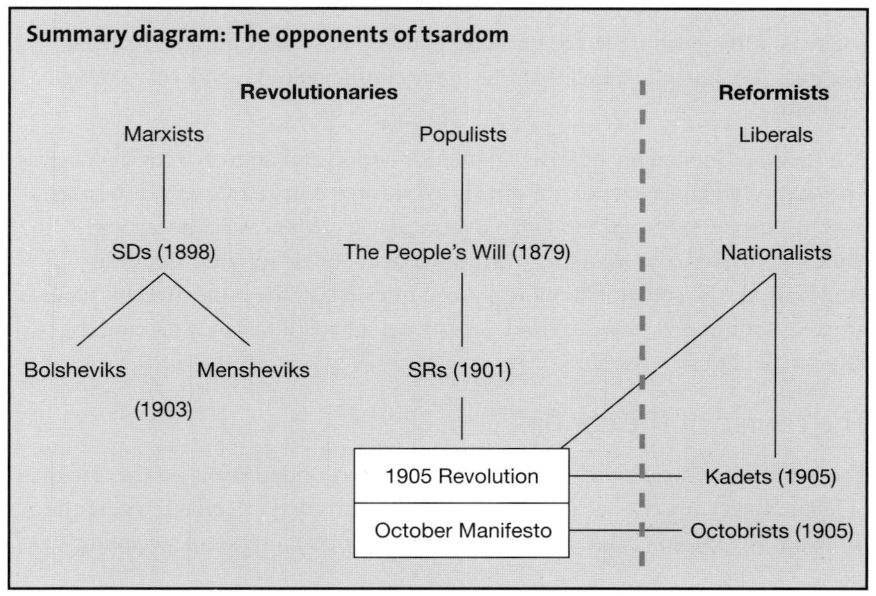

# The Russo-Japanese War 1904–5

► *Why did Russia go to war with Japan in 1904?*

In 1904, Nicholas II faced his first major test in foreign affairs when his country clashed with its far-eastern neighbour, Japan. It was a war largely of Russia's own making.

## The path to war

The foreign policy that Nicholas II inherited and continued was largely determined by the size of the Russian Empire. The protection of its many frontiers was a constant preoccupation. The Russian government had three main motives in going to war with Japan in 1904:

- to pursue an expansionist policy in the Far East, to make up for what it saw as its relative decline in Europe (see page 55)
- to obtain an ice-free port – all Russia's major ports on its northern coastline were frozen up for some part of the year
- to distract attention from Russia's domestic troubles by rallying the nation in a patriotic struggle.

In regard to the last point, it used to be thought that Vyacheslav Plehve, the interior minister, was the main force pushing for war. His words 'We need a small, victorious war to avert a revolution' were often quoted . However, recent research has shown that Plehve was deliberately misrepresented by his political opponent, Sergei Witte. We now know that Plehve was reluctant to go to war, whereas Witte, wishing to see Russia expand economically into the Far East (see page 16), knew full well that this made conflict with Japan a very strong possibility.

The Russians looked on Japan as an inferior nation and no match for themselves. They expected an easy victory. Pretexts for war were not hard to find. Territorial disputes between Russia and Japan over Korea and Manchuria were long-standing. In 1904, the Russian government deliberately rejected Japanese proposals for the settlement of the Korean question in the hope that this would provoke a military response. It did: Japan opened hostilities by attacking the Russian fleet in Port Arthur.

## The course of the conflict

The war itself soon showed that Russia had greatly underestimated the strength of Japan. It was not the backward state the Russians had imagined. Under the Emperor Meiji (1867–1912), Japan had embarked upon a series of sweeping

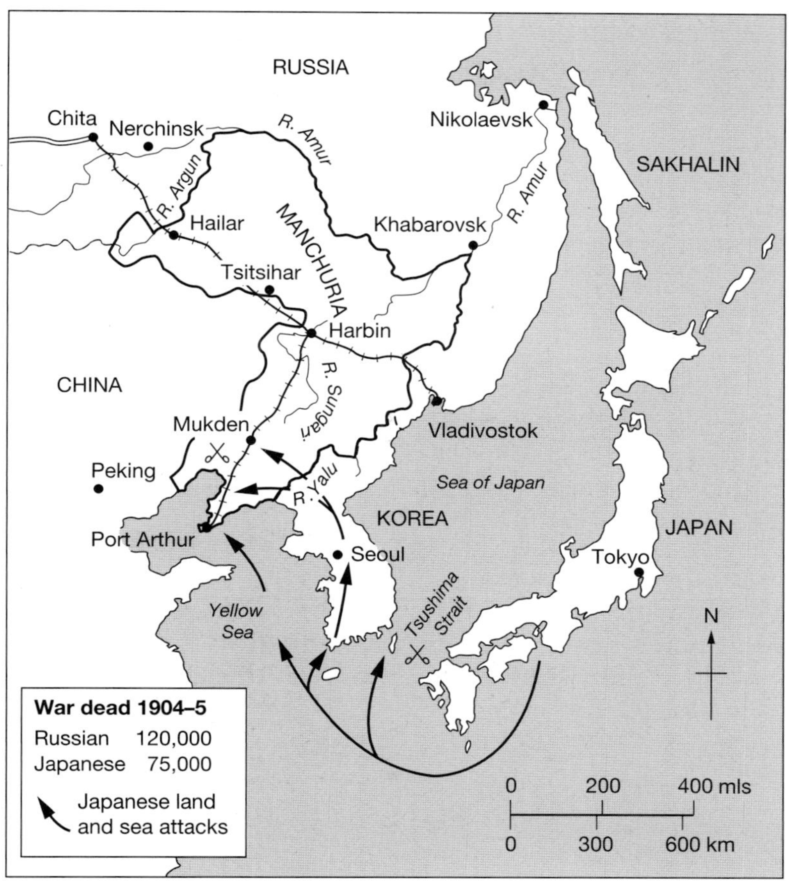


**Figure 1.8** The main areas of the Russo-Japanese War 1904–5.

reforms aimed at rapid modernisation along Western lines. The Japanese army and navy were far better prepared and equipped than the Russian forces and won a series of major victories. For Russia, the conflict was a tale of confusion and disaster. After a long siege, Port Arthur fell to Japan in January 1905. The following month, the Japanese exploited their advantage by seizing the key Manchurian town of Mukden.

The final humiliation for Russia came at sea. The Russian Baltic fleet, dispatched to the Far East in 1904, took eight months to reach its destination, only to be blown out of the water immediately on its arrival by the Japanese fleet at Tsushima in May 1905. Such defeats obliged the tsarist government to make peace. In the Treaty of Portsmouth (USA), Russia agreed to withdraw its remaining forces from Manchuria and accepted Japanese control of Korea and Port Arthur.

## Russia's defeat

The war was lost not because Russian troops fought badly, but because their military commanders had not prepared effectively. They understood neither the enemy they were fighting nor the territory in which the struggle took place. Their ignorance of the conditions allowed the Japanese to outmanoeuvre the Russian forces. The distance over which men and materials had to be transported from western Russia made it impossible to provide adequate reinforcements and supplies. The Trans-Siberian Railway, incomplete in a number of sections, proved of little value.

Russia's defeat at the hands of a small, supposedly inferior, Asian country was a national humiliation. Within Russia, the incompetence of the government, which the war glaringly revealed, excited the social unrest which it had been specifically designed to dampen. Russia's dismal performance contributed considerably to the build-up of tension which led to a direct challenge to tsardom: the 1905 Revolution.

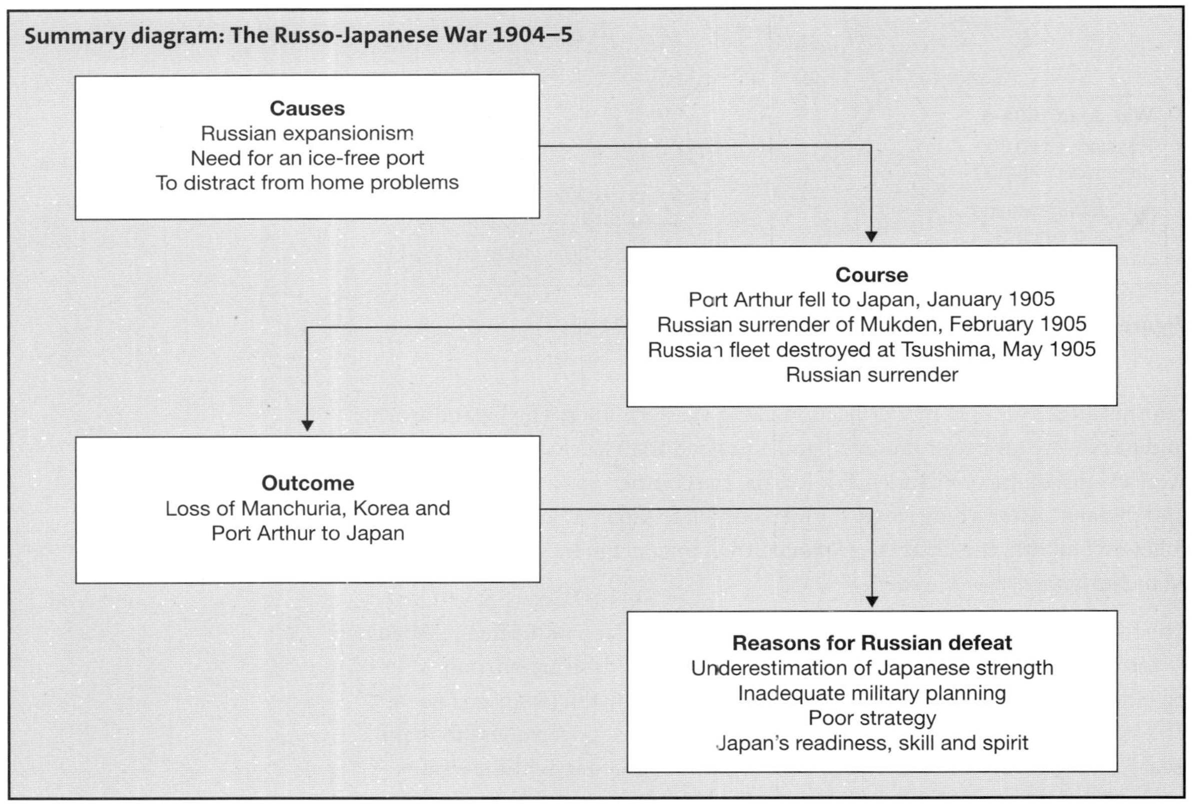

Summary diagram: The Russo-Japanese War 1904–5
Causes
Russian expansionism
Need for an ice-free port
To distract from home problems
Course
Port Arthur fell to Japan, January 1905
Russian surrender of Mukden, February 1905
Russian fleet destroyed at Tsushima, May 1905
Russian surrender
Outcome
Loss of Manchuria, Korea and
Port Arthur to Japan
Reasons for Russian defeat
Underestimation of Japanese strength
Inadequate military planning
Poor strategy
Japan's readiness, skill and spirit

# 6 The 1905 Revolution

*How far was the tsarist government responsible for the 1905 Revolution?*

In 1905, those angered by the government's policy of repression came together to present the tsarist system with the most serious challenge it had yet faced.

## The reasons for the 1905 Revolution

**KEY FIGURE**

**Leo Tolstoy (1828–1910)**

Internationally renowned Russian novelist and philosopher.

The situation which the tsar's government had created was graphically described by **Leo Tolstoy**. In 1902, in an 'Open address to Nicholas II', he detailed the persecution under which Russia groaned. Prisons were overflowing with convicts innocent of any real crime, the city streets were full of soldiers ready to shoot the people on a whim, and the censors' power stretched everywhere, denying freedom of religious and political expression. Things were no better in the countryside, where famine was a constant source of peasant misery. Presiding over this grim scene, Tolstoy asserted, was a government that squeezed money from the people through heavy taxation but was incapable of providing leadership. The result was 'the general dissatisfaction of all classes with the government and their open hostility against it'. Tolstoy's dispiriting conclusion was that it was 'impossible to maintain this form of government except by violence'.

The bleak picture Tolstoy painted did not necessarily mean that confrontation, still less revolution, was unavoidable. After all, if oppression is applied firmly enough, it prevents effective challenges to government. What weakened the tsarist regime in the period before 1917 was not its tyranny but its incompetence. It is certainly true that the crisis that occurred in Russia in 1905 was in large measure due to the mishandling of the situation by the tsar and his government. The year 1905 marked the first time the tsarist government had been confronted by a combination of the three main opposition classes in Russia:

- the industrial workers
- the peasantry
- the reformist middle class.

This was the broad-based revolt that most revolutionaries had been awaiting. Yet, when it came, it was accidental rather than planned. Despite the efforts of the various revolutionary parties to politicise events, the strikes and demonstrations in the pre-1905 period had been the result of economic rather than political factors. They had been a reaction to industrial recession and bad harvests. It was the tsarist regime's ill-judged policies that turned the disturbances of 1905 into a direct challenge to its own authority.

## The course of events

The 1905 Revolution was made up of a number of key developments.

### Bloody Sunday

The 1905 Revolution began with what became known as Bloody Sunday. On 22 January, Father Georgy Gapon, an Orthodox priest, attempted to lead a peaceful march of workers and their families to the Winter Palace in St Petersburg. The marchers' intention was to present a loyal petition to the tsar, begging him to use his royal authority to relieve their desperate conditions.

? What is the tone of the petition in Source E?

**SOURCE E**

**From a petition intended to be delivered by the marchers to Tsar Nicholas II on Sunday 22 January 1905, quoted in Lionel Kochan, *Russia in Revolution 1890–1918*, Granada, 1966, p. 99.**

*We working men and inhabitants of St. Petersburg, our wives and children, and our parents, helpless and aged men and women, have come to You, our ruler, in quest of justice and protection. We have no strength at all, O Sovereign. Our patience is at an end. We are approaching that terrible moment when death is better than continuance of intolerable sufferings.*

*Our first request was that our employers should discuss with us but this they refused to do. They regarded as illegal our other demands: reduction of the working day to eight hours, the fixing of wage rates in consultation with us, and investigation of our grievances against the factory managements. We have been in bondage [slavery] with the help and co-operation of Your officials. Anyone who dares to speak up in defence of the interests of the working class and ordinary people is jailed or exiled. Is this, O Sovereign, in accordance with the laws of God, by whose grace you reign?*

**KEY TERM**

**Little Father** A traditional term denoting the tsar's paternal care of his people.

The march induced panic in the police forces in the capital. The marchers were fired on and charged by cavalry. There are no precise casualty figures, but estimates suggest that up to 200 marchers may have been killed, with hundreds more being injured. The deaths were depicted by opponents of the tsarist regime as a deliberate massacre of unarmed petitioners. Although Nicholas II was in fact absent from St Petersburg when these events took place, they gravely damaged the traditional image of the tsar as the '**Little Father**', the guardian of the Russian people. In the midst of the death and confusion, Gapon had repeatedly cried out: 'There is no God any longer. There is no Tsar.'

### Disorder spreads

The immediate reaction to Bloody Sunday in Russia at large was a widespread outbreak of disorder, which increased as the year went on. Strikes occurred in all the major cities and towns. Terrorism against government officials and landlords, much of it organised by the SRs, spread to the countryside. The situation was made worse by Russia's humiliation in the war against Japan

## Father Georgy Gapon

| | |
|---|---|
| 1876 | Born in Ukraine |
| 1903 | Helped to found the Assembly of Russian Workers |
| 1904 | Involved in organising a mass strike |
| 1905 | Led workers' march to present a petition to the tsar |
| | Fled to Geneva after Bloody Sunday massacre |
| | Returned to St Petersburg |
| 1906 | Murdered |

Gapon remains an intriguing character about whom mystery still hangs. There were strong suspicions that he was an *Okhrana* **double-agent**. Sometimes he genuinely sympathised with the workers, as suggested by his efforts in organising the Assembly of Russian Factory and Plant Workers. He said he wanted to 'build a nest among the factory and mill workers where a truly Russian spirit would prevail'. Yet, on other occasions, he was willing to inform on those he led and to betray them to the authorities.

At the time of Bloody Sunday he appeared to be sincere in his wish to lead the workers in protest; indeed, he ignored a direct order from the authorities to call off the march. Having escaped serious injury or arrest during the suppression of the protest, he immediately fled from Russia to join a group of SDs in Geneva. It was there that he met Lenin. Krupskaya, Lenin's wife, recorded that her husband learned a great deal about Russian peasant problems from Gapon. For his part, Lenin tried to convert Gapon to Marxism.

Yet, by the end of 1905, Gapon had returned to St Petersburg, declaring that he no longer believed in revolution and that he wished to help the government to track down its enemies. This may have been a ruse. Perhaps he intended to infiltrate government circles as an SD spy. The only hard fact is that in March 1906 he was murdered, apparently by *Okhrana* agents, although even this is unclear.

Modern historians tend to agree that Gapon was naïve politically and became involved in events he never fully grasped. A contemporary was once asked whether Gapon was a supporter of constitutionalism. He replied, 'Support it? He can't even say it.' Whatever Gapon's real intentions may have been, his lack of understanding of political realities made him a fascinating but ultimately powerless participant in the 1905 Revolution.

(see page 30). The government was blamed for Russia's defeat, which led to further outrages, including the assassination of Plehve by SR terrorists. Public buildings in towns and large private estates in the country were attacked. Land and properties were seized by the peasants, who then squatted in the landlords' houses. An important factor motivating the peasants was the fear that the government was about to repossess the homes of those families who had failed to pay off the mortgages taken out in the post-emancipation years (see page 7).

The government's difficulties in containing the unrest encouraged the non-Russian minorities to assert themselves. Georgia declared itself an independent state, the Poles demanded **autonomy** and the Jews pressed for equal rights. In May, the Kadets, led by Paul Milyukov, persuaded the other liberal groups to join them in forming a 'Union of Unions', with the aim of organising a broad-based alliance that would include the peasants and the factory workers. A 'Union of Unions' declaration was issued, which referred to the government as 'a terrible menace' and called for a constituent assembly to replace 'the gang of robbers' now in power.

**KEY TERMS**

**Double-agent**
A government agent who pretends to be spying for the opposition against the authorities but who reports plans and secrets back to the authorities.

**Autonomy** National self-government.

## The *Potemkin* mutiny

The summer of 1905 brought disturbing news for the tsarist authorities of mutinies in the army and navy. The serving soldiers and sailors were conscripted peasants who were naturally reluctant to attack their own kind: workers on strike or rebellious peasants in the countryside. There were several instances of troops disobeying orders to shoot unarmed strikers or to use force to drive peasants from the properties they had occupied.

In June there were even worse tidings for the government. The crew of *Prince Potemkin*, a battleship of the Black Sea naval squadron, mutinied while at sea. The incident began as a protest by the sailors at having to eat putrid food and drink foul water; particular causes of complaint were *borsch*, a thin soup made from rotting beetroot, and scraps of meat crawling with maggots. The sailors elected a representative, Peter Vakulenchuk, to approach the captain with their complaints. The captain's immediate response was to have the man shot. In retaliation, the crew attacked the officers, killed several of them and then took over the ship. This was a desperate act and could have worked only if the other ships in the squadron had mutinied also. But they did not; despite the equally grim conditions in the other ships, the captains managed to maintain control. The crew of the *Potemkin* were on their own.

Hoping to arouse support on land, the mutineers sailed to the port of Odessa where a serious anti-government strike was taking place. The strikers welcomed the crew as heroes and formally honoured the body of Vakulenchuk by laying it on an elevated platform and surrounding it with flowers. It was a defiant gesture of solidarity but it enraged the authorities, who could not tolerate strikers and mutineers making common cause. Troops were ordered to disperse the crowds who had gathered in the harbour at the foot of a deep and wide flight of steps. With bayonets fixed, the soldiers marched resolutely down the steps trampling on those who fell in front of them and driving hundreds into the sea. The civilian death toll ran into thousands.

The massacre forced the *Potemkin* to leave Odessa. Since no other ships had sided with them, the crew decided to cut their losses. They sailed around the Black Sea looking for a safer area to land. Eventually they abandoned the ship in a Romanian port, hoping to find sanctuary for themselves in this remoter part of the Russian Empire.

Although the mutiny was restricted to one ship, there was no doubt the affair was deeply troubling to the Russian authorities. A government that cannot rely on the loyalty of its armed services, particularly in time of war, is in a very vulnerable position. The end of the Russo-Japanese War in August did little to ease the situation. Indeed, Witte feared that the returning troops would join the revolution. If this happened, he said, 'then everything would collapse'.

**SOURCE F**

**There are no photographs of the *Potemkin* mutiny. This shot is taken from the feature film *The Battleship Potemkin*, made in 1925 by Sergei Eisenstein, the pro-Bolshevik director. The still, from the film's opening section 'Men and Maggots', depicts the disgust of the crew at having to eat meat crawling with maggots, a disgust that turned to mutiny.**

## The tsar's response

Despite being the tsar's most able minister, Witte was not liked by the royal family or the court (see page 18). Nevertheless, it was to Witte that the tsar had turned in June 1905. Witte's first task was to negotiate peace terms with the Japanese. With this successfully completed, he then became chairman of the Council of Ministers, the effective head of the tsar's government. Yet, Witte remained frustrated by the inability of the tsar and his ministers to understand the crisis Russia was in. He referred to government policy as a 'mixture of cowardice, blindness and stupidity'. Nevertheless, he remained at

How might the photo in Source F support the view that Eisenstein's images are so powerful that they have conditioned the way we visualise the actual mutiny itself?

his post, driven by a sense of duty to do his best to steer the regime through its difficulties.

It was on Witte's advice that the tsar issued a Manifesto in August. This was an attempt to lessen the tensions by making concessions, the principal one being a promise to create a state assembly of elected representatives of the 51 provinces of the empire, to begin sitting in January 1906. However, the powers the assembly would have were not clearly defined. Moreover, since the tsar added the clause, 'We reserve to ourselves exclusively the care of perfecting the organisation of the Assembly', the clear implication was that he did not intend his royal authority to be restricted in any way. The limited concession the Manifesto represented did not work. In September, a series of strikes had begun in both St Petersburg and Moscow. Striking workers were joined by striking students, whose activities brought the universities to a standstill and added to the general disorder in the capital.

## Soviets formed

By October 1905, the industrial unrest had grown into a general strike. It was in this atmosphere that a development of particular moment occurred. In a number of cities, most notably in St Petersburg and Moscow, workers formed themselves into an elected **soviet**. The soviets began as organisations to represent the workers' demands for better conditions, but their potential as bases for political agitation was immediately recognised by revolutionaries. The Menshevik Leon Trotsky became chairman of the St Petersburg soviet and organiser of several strikes in the capital.

**KEY TERMS**

**Soviet** Russian word for a council made up of elected representatives.

**Legislative *duma*** A parliament with law-making powers.

## Government recovery

By October, the tsar was faced by the most united opposition in Romanov history. But, recognising the danger, the regime now began to show the sense of purpose that it had so far lacked. Concession was unavoidable, but, by giving ground, the government intended to divide the opposition forces ranged against it.

### The October Manifesto

The liberals were the first to be appeased. On Witte's advice, the tsar issued the October Manifesto in which, going further than he had in the August Manifesto, he made the following concessions:

- the creation of a **legislative *duma***
- freedom of speech, assembly and worship
- the right of political parties to exist
- the legalising of trade unions.

The liberals saw these as remarkable successes. Their appetite for reform was satisfied, at least temporarily.

### Pacifying the peasants

The peasants were the next to be quietened, by an announcement in November that the mortgage repayments which had so troubled them were to be progressively reduced and then abolished altogether. The response was an immediate drop in the number of land seizures by the peasants and a decline in the general lawlessness in the countryside.

### Crushing the workers

Having won over the liberals and peasants, the government was now seriously opposed by only one major group: the industrial workers. Here the policy was one not of concession but of suppression. The government felt strong enough to attempt to crush the soviets. Despite the mutinies earlier in the year, the troops who returned to Russia at the end of the war proved sufficiently loyal to be used against the strikers. After a five-day siege, the headquarters of the St Petersburg soviet were stormed and the ringleaders, including Trotsky, were arrested.

### Moscow uprising suppressed

The destruction of an uprising in Moscow proved even more violent. On 7 December, a group of Bolsheviks, Mensheviks and SRs came together in the recently formed Moscow soviet to organise a general strike. Encouraged by their success in this, they then seized a number of key installations, including post offices and railway stations, in an attempt to take over the whole city. However, tsarist regiments, some of whom had recently suppressed the St Petersburg soviet, were rushed to Moscow. There they used heavy artillery to force the insurgents into an increasingly confined area. To avoid being slaughtered, the soviet resisters surrendered on 18 December. Lenin, who had encouraged the uprising but had played no direct part in it, arrived in Moscow just in time to witness the flames of the gutted soviet buildings, set ablaze by government troops. The twelve-day uprising had led to the deaths of over 1000 people.

## The significance of the 1905 Revolution

A notable feature of the 1905 Revolution was how minor a part was played by the revolutionaries. With the exception of Trotsky, none of the SDs made an impact on the course of events. This throws doubt on the notion of 1905 as a revolution. There is the further fact that in a number of important respects tsardom emerged from the disturbances stronger rather than weaker. Despite its disastrous failure in the war against Japan, which produced protest throughout Russia and united the classes in opposition, the tsarist regime survived 1905 remarkably unscathed. The mutinies in the armed services did not spread and did not continue after the war. Loyal troops returned to destroy the soviets. The readiness of the liberals and the peasants to accept the government's political and economic bribes indicated that neither of those groups was genuinely ready for revolution.

It is true that the tsar appeared to grant significant concessions in the October Manifesto, but these were expedients rather than real reforms. The *duma* was not intended to be, nor did it become, a limitation on the tsar's autocratic powers. This was evident from the Fundamental Laws, which Nicholas II promulgated in April 1906: 'The Sovereign Emperor possesses the initiative in all legislative matters … The Sovereign Emperor ratifies the laws. No law can come into force without his approval.'

## The lesson of the 1905 Revolution

What 1905 showed was that as long as the tsarist government kept its nerve and the army remained loyal, the forces of protest would find it very difficult to mount a serious challenge. The events of 1905 also raised questions about the extent to which the liberals wanted change in Russia. Few of them enjoyed their experience of mixing with the workers during the revolution. They found proletarian coarseness unattractive and were frightened by the primitive forces they had helped to unleash. One middle-class proprietor, who had thrown his house open to the strikers, remarked on the difficulty of sustaining his belief in the goodness of people who abused his hospitality by molesting his daughters, urinating on his carpets and stealing everything they could carry. Peter Struve, who had been a founder member of the Union of Liberation before joining the Kadets in 1905, spoke for all frightened liberals when he said 'Thank God for the tsar, who has saved us from the people.'

Leon Trotsky reflected that 1905 had failed as a revolution because the protestors were disunited and inexperienced. Furthermore, the liberals had backed out of the revolution and betrayed the workers by leaving them to be crushed by government troops. He concluded that the tsarist system, 'although with a few broken ribs, had come out of the experience of 1905 alive and strong'.

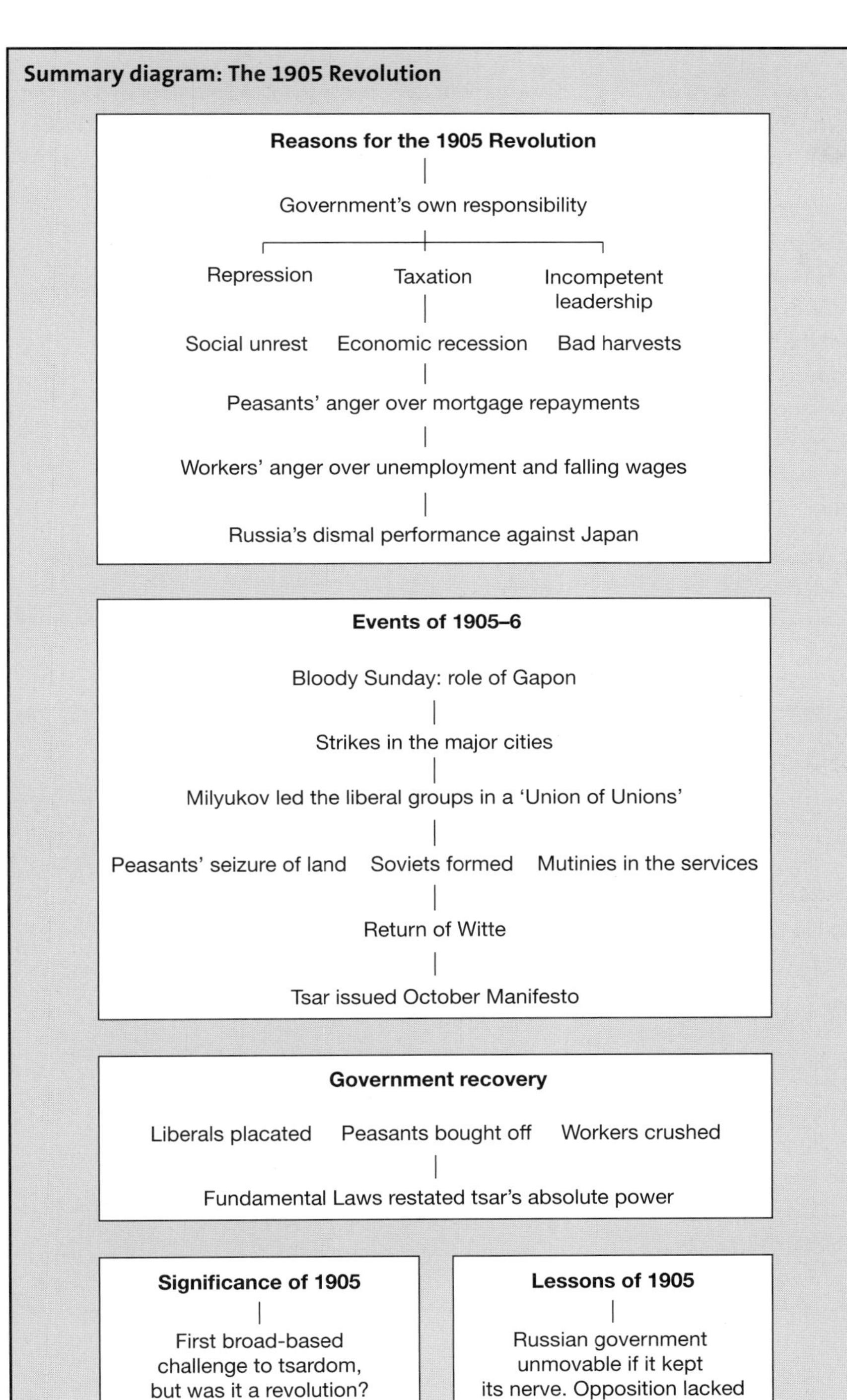
Summary diagram: The 1905 Revolution
Reasons for the 1905 Revolution
Government's own responsibility
Repression
Taxation
Incompetent leadership
Social unrest
Economic recession
Bad harvests
Peasants' anger over mortgage repayments
Workers' anger over unemployment and falling wages
Russia's dismal performance against Japan
Events of 1905–6
Bloody Sunday: role of Gapon
Strikes in the major cities
Milyukov led the liberal groups in a 'Union of Unions'
Peasants' seizure of land
Soviets formed
Mutinies in the services
Return of Witte
Tsar issued October Manifesto
Government recovery
Liberals placated
Peasants bought off
Workers crushed
Fundamental Laws restated tsar's absolute power
Significance of 1905
First broad-based challenge to tsardom, but was it a revolution?
Lessons of 1905
Russian government unmovable if it kept its nerve. Opposition lacked unity and direction

## Chapter summary

Led by a tsar and a government that were reluctant to engage in reform, Russia faced the problem of how to achieve modernity. The answer of tsardom's leading statesman, Witte, was to shape the economy in such a way that the nation could compete at parity with its European rivals. He encouraged industrial expansion and urged the state to take the lead in this by encouraging foreign investments. His efforts undoubtedly contributed to Russia's achieving the 'great spurt' of the 1890s.

Notwithstanding its economic growth, Russia's slowness in reforming politically led to the development of opposition from liberals and revolutionaries. While liberals believed that tsardom could be reformed into a constitutional monarchy, revolutionaries were convinced that only by the destruction of tsardom could Russia be modernised. Choosing to go to war with Japan in 1904, the government was shocked by Russia's defeat, which proved a major factor in the outbreak of the 1905 Revolution, when a loose alliance of peasants, industrial workers and liberals joined in resistance and protest. The government recovered its nerve and survived for the time being by satisfying the peasants with the cancellation of their mortgage repayments, placating the liberals by political concessions and physically suppressing the protesting workers.

## Refresher questions

Use these questions to remind yourself of the key material covered in this chapter.

**1** What powers did Nicholas II wield as tsar?

**2** Why was it so difficult for Russia to reform itself?

**3** What was Russification intended to achieve?

**4** What methods did Sergei Witte use to develop the Russian economy?

**5** How successful were Witte's policies?

**6** What were the main ideas of the Social Revolutionaries (SRs)?

**7** What was the impact of Marxism on the Social Democrats (SDs)?

**8** What led to the divide in the Social Democratic Party?

**9** How strong were the Bolsheviks before 1917?

**10** What had encouraged the growth of a liberal movement in tsarist Russia?

**11** How sweeping was the Kadet Programme for the reform of tsarist Russia?

**12** How critical of the tsarist system were the Octobrists?

**13** Why did Russia perform so badly in the Russo-Japanese war?

**14** What pattern did the 1905 Revolution follow?

**15** Why was the *Potemkin* mutiny such a serious threat to the tsarist regime?

**16** What steps did the government take to deal with the challenges facing it in 1905?

# Question practice

## ESSAY QUESTIONS

1. How far did Witte succeed in his plans to reform Russian industry in the years 1893–1903?
2. 'The only policy Nicholas II's government genuinely followed between 1894 and 1904 was one of repression.' How far do you agree with this statement?
3. To what extent was the defeat of tsarist Russia in its war against Japan, 1904–5, the result of its own mistakes?
4. Which of the following was the greater problem for the tsarist government in the 1905 Revolution? i) The liberals. ii) The workers. Explain your answer with reference to both i) and ii).
5. 'The tsar's government was stronger after the 1905 Revolution than before it.' How far do you agree?

# From revolution to war 1905–14

The period 1905–14 was a testing time for Imperial Russia. At issue was the question of whether it could become a modern state. The tsarist system had survived the 1905 Revolution by making concessions to its opponents. A parliament was granted and political parties were legalised. Whether such concessions weakened or strengthened tsardom is the underlying theme of this chapter, which sees Imperial Russia wrestling with its internal and external enemies. The key areas examined are:

- ★ Economic policy under Stolypin
- ★ The *dumas* 1906–14
- ★ Growing tensions in Russia 1911–14
- ★ Russia's foreign policy before 1914
- ★ The tsar's position at the outbreak of war in 1914

The key debate on *page 62* of this chapter asks the question: Was tsardom already doomed in 1914?

## Key dates

| | | | |
|---|---|---|---|
| **1905** | Revolution | **1907–12** | Third *duma* |
| **1906** | Fundamental Laws issued | **1911–14** | Serious internal unrest |
| | First *duma* | **1912** | Lena Goldfields episode |
| **1906–11** | Stolypin's years as chief minister | **1912–14** | Fourth *duma* |
| **1907** | Second *duma* | **1914** | Germany declared war on Russia |

## 1 Economic policy under Stolypin

► *What was Stolypin aiming to achieve in his dealings with the peasants?*

In the aftermath of the 1905 Revolution, the government entertained thoughts of limited reform. Peter Stolypin was appointed chairman of the Council of Ministers in July 1906. Like Witte before him, he was dedicated to strengthening tsardom in a time of crisis. He was a political conservative, whose attitude was clearly expressed in the coercive measures he introduced between 1906 and 1911. He declared his guiding principle to be 'suppression first and then, and only then, reform'. However, he also considered that, where possible, reform should be introduced as a way of reducing the social bitterness on which opposition fed. It was in this spirit that he approached the land problem in Russia.

## Land reform

Stolypin started from the conviction that industrial progress by itself could not solve Russia's most pressing need – how to feed the nation's rapidly growing population. The marked increase in population that occurred in the late nineteenth century had resulted in land shortage and overpopulation. This **rural crisis** was deepened by a series of bad harvests; the years 1891 and 1897 witnessed severe famines, which left millions starving. The government's land policies following the emancipation of the serfs in 1861 had not helped. The scheme under which state mortgages were advanced to the emancipated serfs to enable them to buy their properties had not created the system of stable land tenure that the government had expected. The high price of land, which led to heavy mortgage repayments being undertaken, had impoverished the peasantry. Their sense of insecurity both inhibited them from being efficient food-producers and made them a dangerous social force.

**KEY TERMS**

**Rural crisis** The problem of land shortage and overpopulation in the countryside produced by the huge increase in the number of people living in Russia by the late nineteenth century.

***Obschina*** Peasant communes set up within the localities.

### 'De-revolutionising' the peasantry

One of the reasons why the peasants had joined the Revolution in 1905 was their fear that the government was about to repossess the land of the mortgage-holders who had defaulted on their payments. When, under Stolypin's prompting, the government came to understand this fear, it bought off the peasants by announcing that the outstanding repayments would be cancelled. Stolypin referred to this tactic as 'de-revolutionising' the peasants.

### The 'wager on the strong'

Stolypin planned to build upon this successful treatment of the peasantry. In 1906–7, he introduced the following measures to restore the peasants' sense of security:

- Farmers were urged to abandon the inefficient strip system and replace it with fenced fields, based on the pattern that existed in Western Europe.
- The current trend of peasants grouping in ***obschina*** was discouraged and incentives were given to the peasants to return to individual farming.
- A special Land Bank was established to provide funds for the independent peasants to buy their land.
- Schemes for large-scale voluntary resettlement of the peasants were implemented, the aim being to populate the empire's remoter areas, such as Siberia, and turn them into food-growing areas.

## Peter Stolypin

| | |
|---|---|
| 1862 | Born into an aristocratic family |
| 1902 | Appointed as a regional governor |
| 1906 | Appointed interior minister and then prime minister |
| 1906–11 | Served as prime minister |
| 1906–7 | Introduced 'wager on the strong' |
| 1907 | Effective liaison with the second *duma* |
| 1911 | Assassinated |

Born into an aristocratic family, Stolypin studied agriculture at university and went on to hold minor government posts before rising to become governor of Kovno and then Saratov. His experience of the peasants led him to believe that in order to improve their conditions and make them more productive they needed both encouragement and stern political control.

Stolypin's aim was to break the peasants' dependence on collective and communal farming by giving them incentives to farm efficiently and profitably. This was not done out of pure altruism; if the peasants were left aggrieved, they would continue to be a dangerous source of social unrest. Stolypin's complementary policy of suppressing the 'dark masses' to prevent their becoming a disruptive force was evident in the harshness of the social policies he enforced, including anti-Jewish pograms. His political conservatism led him to attempt to manipulate the membership of the *duma* so that it became not a source of criticism of the tsarist system but a bulwark in its defence.

Stolypin was faced by the same problem that had confronted Witte; the leading members of the Russian establishment he was trying to save never gave him the support he needed. His attempt to convince them of the paradox that in order to conserve they had to be less conservative proved unavailing. They approved his repressive measures but never grasped that repression alone would not solve Russia's crises; it had to be coupled with economic modernisation.

Stolypin's uncompromising political stance, mixed with a strong sense of economic realism, offered a way out of the institutional crisis that threatened to destroy Imperial Russia. Tsardom's tragedy was that it never understood this. In 1911 Stolypin was assassinated by an SR member who was possibly in the pay of the secret police.

Stolypin defined his policy as a 'wager on the strong'. His intention was to create a layer of prosperous, productive peasants who would farm independently of the communes and whose new wealth would turn them into natural supporters of the tsarist system.

### Difficulties confronting Stolypin

The standard view of most scholars in this field has been that Stolypin had little real chance of reforming agriculture since the Russian peasantry was resistant to change and he had so little time to alter things. Others, however, have argued that, while it is true that the conservatism of most peasants prevented them from embracing progressive change, Stolypin was right, nonetheless, in thinking that he could 'wager on the strong' since there was, indeed, a layer of strong peasant farmers. This argument is based on evidence drawn from tsarist tax returns, which show that a significant minority of peasants were paying increasingly higher taxes in the decade before 1914, a sign that their farming was producing high profits.

However, even if one accepts that there was a progressive element among the peasants, there is no certainty that this would have been enough to modernise

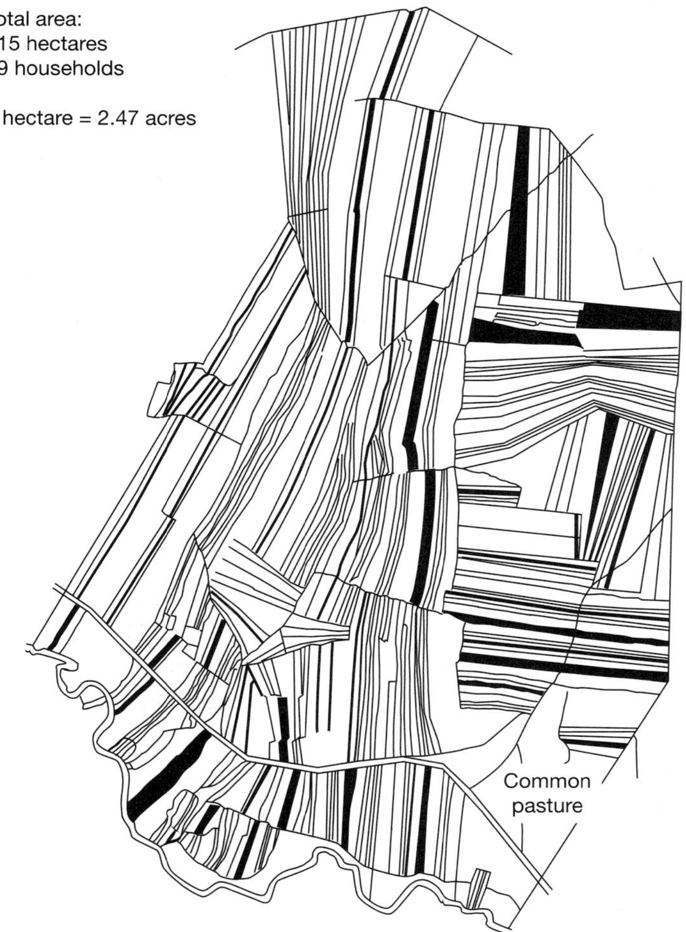


**Figure 2.1** Strip farming as practised in central Russia *c.*1900. Each scattered black strip represents the land farmed individually by one of the various nineteen households. The thicker the line, the larger the amount of land owned by a family.

Russian agriculture. Even in advanced economies, land reform takes time to work. Stolypin was well aware that, in a country as relatively backward as Russia, the changes would take even longer to become effective. He spoke of needing twenty years for his 'wager on the strong' to bring results. In the event, his assassination in 1911 allowed him personally only five years, and the coming of the war in 1914 allowed Russia only eight.

The doubt remains whether, even without the interruption of murder and war, his peasant policy would have succeeded. The deep conservatism of the mass of the Russian peasants made them slow to respond. In 1914, the strip system was still widespread. As Table 2.1 shows, only some 16 per cent of the land had been consolidated into farms. Most peasants were reluctant to leave the security of the commune for the uncertainty of individual farming. Furthermore, by 1913 the government's own Ministry of Agriculture had itself begun to lose confidence in the policy.

**Table 2.1** Number of peasant households that opted to set up independent farms (out of an estimated total of 12 million households)

|  |  |
|---|---|
| **1907** | 48,271 |
| **1908** | 508,344 |
| **1909** | 579,409 |
| **1910** | 342,245 |
| **1911** | 145,567 |
| **1912** | 122,314 |
| **1913** | 134,554 |
| **1914** | 97,877 |
| **Total** | 1,978,581 |

### Benefits of Stolypin's liaison with the *duma*

A notable feature of Stolypin's land policy was his effective working relations with the *duma*. The understanding which he developed with the Octobrists, the largest party in the third *duma* (see page 50), allowed him to pursue his reforms with little obstruction from the other deputies. His success here hinted at how much co-operation might have developed between government and progressive opinion had the tsarist regime been willing to trust its own ministers.

## The industrial front

Although Witte was no longer a minister after 1906, his earlier work still influenced Russian industrial development and it is arguable that had he remained in charge he might have been able to avoid or, at least, lessen the impact of the recurrent recessions that occurred. The period from 1908 to 1914 saw an overall increase in economic growth of 8.5 per cent (Table 2.2).

**Table 2.2** Economic growth in Russia 1908–14

| Assets | 1908 | 1914 |
|---|---|---|
| State revenues (in roubles) | 2 billion | 4 billion |
| Number of banks | 1,146 | 2,393 |
| Number of factories | 22,600 | 24,900 |
| Number of workers | 2,500,000 | 2,900,000 |

Nevertheless, against this bright picture has to be set the darker aspect. Few workers gained from the industrial and financial expansion. Weak trade unions and minimal legal protection left the workforce very much at the mercy of the employers. Little of the greater amount of money in circulation reached the pockets of the workers. Although the **inflation rate** rose by 40 per cent between 1908 and 1914, the average industrial wage rose from 245 to only 264 roubles per month (seven per cent) in the same period. Of course, a national average does not tell the whole story. Some workers did better than others; for example, wages were 30 per cent higher in St Petersburg than in Moscow. Nonetheless, the large number of strikes in the pre-1914 years, culminating with a **general strike** in 1914, shows the scale of the dissatisfaction with the conditions (see page 54).

**KEY TERMS**

**Inflation rate** A measure of the decline in the value of money over a period of time, more money being needed to buy the same quantity of goods.

**General strike** An organised stoppage by all or a majority of the workers.

### Stolypin and Witte

It is helpful to regard the work of Witte and Stolypin as complementary: Witte being mainly concerned with industry, Stolypin with agriculture. This is not to suggest that the two men fully co-operated in a common policy. Witte was deeply jealous of Stolypin. Nevertheless, they did share a basic objective – the preservation of the tsarist system. Had the tsarist government and bureaucracy been more willing to support Witte and Stolypin in their efforts to modernise the Russian economy, this might have prevented the build-up of social and political tensions.

The economic policies of Witte and Stolypin and the introduction of the *duma* were important advances but they were not enough to alter the essentially reactionary character of the tsarist system, which remained hostile towards reform. It was this that undermined the work of the few enlightened ministers, such as Witte and Stolypin, within the government.

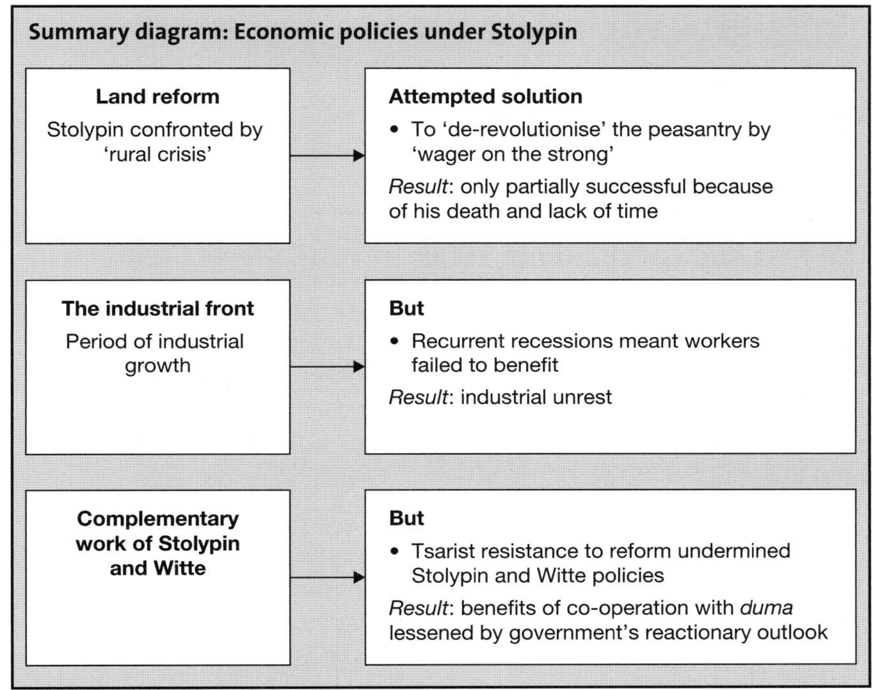

Summary diagram: Economic policies under Stolypin
Land reform
Stolypin confronted by 'rural crisis'
Attempted solution
• To 'de-revolutionise' the peasantry by 'wager on the strong'
Result: only partially successful because of his death and lack of time
The industrial front
Period of industrial growth
But
• Recurrent recessions meant workers failed to benefit
Result: industrial unrest
Complementary work of Stolypin and Witte
But
• Tsarist resistance to reform undermined Stolypin and Witte policies
Result: benefits of co-operation with duma lessened by government's reactionary outlook


# 2 The *dumas* 1906–14

▶ *How did the composition of the* dumas *change over the period 1906–14?*

The tsar's granting of a *duma* in the October Manifesto had been the most striking of the concessions made to the liberals. The new electoral laws laid down:

- All male citizens over 25 years had the right to vote.
- Women and military servicemen were debarred from voting.
- Votes were not equal since the constituencies differed in size.

It remained to be seen what role this new parliament, the first in Russian history, would play. There were four *dumas* in the years between the 1905 Revolution and the February Revolution of 1917 (see page 84). The four elections produced the results shown in Table 2.3.

**Table 2.3** *Duma* election results 1906–17

| Party or group | 1st *duma* 1906 | 2nd *duma* 1907 | 3rd *duma* 1907–12 | 4th *duma* 1912–17 |
|---|---|---|---|---|
| SDs (Mensheviks) | 18 | 47 | – | – |
| SDs (Bolsheviks) | – | – | 19 | 15 |
| SRs | – | 37 | – | – |
| **Labourists** | 136 | 104 | 13 | 10 |
| Kadets | 182 | 91 | 54 | 53 |
| Octobrists | 17 | 42 | 154 | 95 |
| **Progressists** | 27 | 28 | 28 | 41 |
| **Rightists** | 8 | 10 | 147 | 154 |
| National parties | 60 | 93 | 26 | 22 |
| Others | – | 50 | – | 42 |
| Total | 448 | 502 | 441 | 432 |

**KEY TERMS**

**Labourists** The SRs as a party officially boycotted the elections to the first *duma*, but stood as Labourists.

**Progressists** A party of businessmen who favoured moderate reform.

**Rightists** Not a single party; they represented a range of conservative views from right of centre to extreme reaction.

**Bi-cameral** A parliament made up of two chambers, an upper and a lower.

## The first *duma*, April–June 1906

The high hopes the liberals had held that the *duma* marked a real constitutional advance were dashed even before it first met. Having survived the challenge of the 1905 Revolution, the tsarist regime quickly recovered its confidence. Early in 1906, it successfully negotiated a substantial loan from France. This lessened the likelihood of the *dumas* being able to exercise a financial hold over the government.

A still greater limitation on the *duma*'s influence was the tsar's issuing of the Fundamental Laws, which was timed to coincide with the opening of the *duma*. In addition to declaring that 'Supreme Autocratic Power belongs to the emperor of all Russia', the Laws announced that the *duma* would be **bi-cameral**; one chamber would be an elected lower house, the other would be a state council, the majority of whose members would be appointed by the tsar.

The existence of a second chamber with the right of veto deprived the elected *duma* of any real power. Taken together with the declaration that no law could come into being without the tsar's approval, these restrictions made it clear that the tsarist regime had no intention of allowing the concessions it had made in 1905 to diminish its absolute authority. The tsar had made this clear during ministerial discussions preceding the issuing of the Fundamental Laws.

? According to his statement in Source A, why was Nicholas II unwilling to consider any limitation on his power?

**SOURCE A**

**From the tsar's statement, April 1906, quoted in Marc Ferro, *Nicholas II: The Last of the Tsars*, Penguin, 1990, p. 107.**

*If I were convinced that Russia wanted me to abdicate my autocratic powers, I would do that, for the country's good. But I am not convinced this is so, and I do not believe that there is need to alter the nature of my supreme power. It is dangerous to change the way that power is formulated. I know, too, that if no change is made, this may give rise to agitation, to attacks. But where will these attacks come from? From so-called educated people, from the proletariat, from the Third Estate? Actually, I feel that eighty per cent of the people are with me.*

## *Duma* radicalism: the Vyborg appeal

The result was that the *duma* met in a mood of bitterness. The elections had returned an assembly that was dominated by the reformist parties, who immediately took a radical stance by voicing their anger at what they regarded as the government's reneging on its promises. They demanded that the rights and powers of the *duma* be increased. **Ivan Goremykin**, the chief minister, told them that their demands were 'inadmissible' and Nicholas II was reported as saying, 'Curse the *duma*. It is all Witte's doing.' After two months of bitter wrangling, the tsar ordered the *duma* to be dissolved on 9 July.

A day later, in frustration, 200 Kadet and Labourist deputies reassembled at Vyborg in Finland where they drew up an 'Appeal', urging the people of Russia to defy their government in two main ways by:

- refusing to pay taxes
- disobeying conscription orders.

The rebellious deputies who issued the appeal had made a serious tactical error. The response from the Russian people was not the widespread **passive disobedience** they had hoped for, but scattered violence. This provided the government with a ready excuse for retaliation. The tsar appointed Stolypin as chief minister to act as his strong man. The Vyborg group of deputies was arrested and debarred from re-election to the *duma*.

**KEY FIGURE**

**Ivan Goremykin (1839–1917)**

A committed monarchist and reactionary, he succeeded Witte as chief minister in 1906.

**KEY TERMS**

**Radicalism** The desire to change society fundamentally, literally at its roots.

**Passive disobedience** Opposing government not by violent challenge but by refusing to obey particular laws.

**Martial law** The placing of the population under direct military authority.

### Repression under Stolypin

The crushing of the Vyborg group was the prelude to Stolypin's introduction of a policy of fierce repression, which he sustained until his assassination in 1911. **Martial law** was proclaimed and a network of military courts, with sweeping powers, was used to quell disturbances wherever they occurred. Between 1906 and 1911 there were over 2500 executions in Russia, a grim detail that, in a piece of black humour, led to the hangman's noose being nicknamed 'Stolypin's necktie'.

The failure of the rebellious *duma* deputies in 1906 had serious long-term effects. Although the Kadet Party survived under the leadership of Milyukov, it never really recovered from its humiliation. The liberal cause had discredited itself, thus allowing both the left and the right to argue from their different standpoints that Russia's salvation could not be gained through moderate policies but only by revolution or extreme reaction.

## The second *duma*, February–June 1907

The immediate result of the Vyborg fiasco was that, in the elections for the second *duma*, the Kadets lost half their seats. These were filled by the SDs and the SRs, who between them returned over 80 deputies. This made the new assembly strongly radical and anti-government. Indeed, the SRs proclaimed dramatically that it was 'the *duma* of the people's wrath'. However, since the right-wing parties had also increased their numbers, there was considerable disagreement within the *duma*, as well as between it and the government.

Whatever the internal divisions among the parties, the mood of the *duma* was undeniably hostile to the government. Stolypin, who, despite his stern repression of social disorder, was willing to work with the *duma* in introducing necessary reforms, found his land programme strenuously opposed. The tsar was particularly incensed when the *duma* directed a strong attack on the way the imperial army was organised and deployed. The SD and SR deputies were accused of engaging in subversion; Nicholas ordered that the assembly be dissolved. Deputies scuffled and shouted out in protest as the session was duly brought to an end.

## The third *duma*, November 1907–June 1912

Despite the radicalism of the first two *dumas*, the tsar made no attempt to dispense with the *duma* altogether. There were two main reasons for this:

- The first related to foreign policy. The tsar was keen to project an image of Russia as a democratic nation. He was advised by his foreign ministers, who at this time were in trade talks with France and Britain, that Russia's new commercial allies were greatly impressed by his creation of a representative national parliament.
- The second reason was that the *duma* had been rendered docile by the government's doctoring of the electoral system. Stolypin introduced new laws that restricted the vote to the propertied classes. The peasants and industrial workers lost the franchise. The consequence was that the third and fourth *dumas* were heavily dominated by the right-wing parties (as Table 2.3 on page 48 shows), a reversal of the position in the first two *dumas* in which the radical parties had held a large majority. Any criticisms of tsardom were now much more muted.

With the balance of the parties redressed in this way, Stolypin found the third *duma* more co-operative, which enabled him to pursue his land reforms without opposition from the deputies. This is not to say that the *duma* was entirely subservient. It exercised its right to question ministers and to discuss state finances. It also used its **committee system** to make important proposals for modernising the armed services. Among the bills it approved were social-reform measures that included setting up schools for the children of the poor and **national insurance** for industrial workers.

### KEY TERMS

**Committee system**
A process in which the *duma* deputies formed various subgroups to consider particular issues.

**National insurance**
A system of providing workers with state benefits, such as unemployment pay and medical treatment, in return for the workers' contributing regularly to a central fund.

## The fourth *duma*, November 1912–August 1914

After 1917, it was usual for historians to follow the lead of the Bolsheviks in dismissing the later *dumas* as having been merely rubber stamps of government policy. However, modern scholars tend to be less dismissive. Although the fourth *duma* was less openly obstructive than the earlier ones had been, it still voiced criticism of the tsar's government. Interestingly, a Moscow *Okhrana* report in 1912 blamed the tension in Russia on the awkward and searching questions continually being asked in the *duma* about government policy.

**SOURCE B**

**From a Moscow *Okhrana* report in 1913, quoted in J.N. Westwood, *Endurance and Endeavour: Russian History 1812–1980*, Oxford University Press, 1985, p. 178.**

*People can be heard speaking of the government in the sharpest and most unbridled tones. Many say that the shooting of the Lena workers recalls the 'shooting' of the workers at the Winter palace of January 1905. Influenced by questions in the* duma *and the speeches which they called forth there, public tension is increasing still more. It is a long time since even the extreme left has spoken in such a way, since there have been references in the* duma *to the necessity of calling a Constituent Assembly and overthrowing the present system by the united strength of the proletariat.*

According to Source B, what influence has the *duma* had in increasing tension in Moscow in 1912?

Historians also emphasise the progressive work of the *duma* in providing the beginnings of state welfare, and suggest that it was only the blindness of the tsarist government that prevented the *dumas* from making a greater contribution to the development of Russia. This, indeed, was the essence of the plea made by the *duma* chairman, Mikhail Rodzianko, directly to the tsar in 1913, humbly requesting that the role of the *duma* should be clarified so that it could play a constructive role in Russian affairs.

**SOURCE C**

**From a report by Rodzianko of his audience of the tsar in 1913, quoted in Lionel Kochan, *Russia in Revolution*, Paladin, 1974, pp. 170–1.**

*We are accustomed to think that part of the executive power of the crown is delegated to the ministers and to the nominated members of the [State] council. [But] what do we see? Your Majesty will agree that the members of the government either do not wish to execute your will, or do not take the trouble to understand it. The population does not know where it is. Each minister has his own opinion. The cabinet is for the most part split into two parties, the state council form a third, the* Duma *a fourth, and your own will is unknown to the nation; this is not a government, it is anarchy.*

According to Rodzianko in Source C, why has the tsar's government descended into anarchy?

**Summary diagram: The *dumas* 1906–14**

| | *Character* | *Achievements* |
|---|---|---|
| 1st *duma* 1906 | Dominated by reformist parties | Short lived – little achieved |
| 2nd *duma* 1907 | Clash between revolutionaries and right-wing parties | Dissolved in disorder – little achieved |
| 3rd *duma* 1907–12 | Election rigged by Stolypin to produce more co-operative deputies from moderate parties | Committees did achieve effective work in social reform |
| 4th *duma* 1912–14 | Dominated by right-wing parties again willing to co-operate | Social reform work continued, but prepared to criticise government |

**The debate on the role of the *dumas***

- Were they ever more than a talking shop?
- How valuable was their committee work?
- How significant were they as critics of tsardom?

# 3 Growing tensions in Russia 1911–14

*Why was there mounting political and social strain in Russia between 1911 and 1914?*

## Urban unrest

Initially, during the 'great spurt' (see page 14), the peasants who had left the land to work in the urban areas were prepared to accept their grim factory conditions because of the higher wages they received. However, recurrent recessions caused widespread unemployment. The authorities found themselves facing large numbers of rootless workers who had had their expectations of a better life dashed by harsh economic realities. The regular presence of thousands of disaffected workers on the streets of St Petersburg and Moscow played an important part in the growth of serious social unrest in Russia between 1911 and 1914.

### Repression and disorder

Following Stolypin's assassination in 1911, the various ministers the tsar appointed were distinguished only by their ineptitude. Their only policy was further repression. Between 1911 and 1914 the regime's terror tactics were both cause and effect of a dramatic increase in public disorder. The number of strikes listed as 'political' by the Ministry of Trade and Industry rose from 24 in 1911 to 2401 in 1914, the year of a general strike. Trotsky's estimates put the number of political strikes even higher. This discrepancy was explained by the difficulty of distinguishing between a strike for better pay or conditions, and a strike as a political protest.

**Table 2.4** Trotsky's table of the numbers striking for political reasons, 1903–17 (from L. Trotsky, *The History of the Russian Revolution*, Sphere Books, 1967, p. 56)

| Date | No. of strikes | Date | No. of strikes |
|---|---|---|---|
| 1903 | 87 | 1910 | 4 |
| 1904 | 25 | 1911 | 8 |
| 1905 | 1843 | 1912 | 550 |
| 1906 | 651 | 1913 | 502 |
| 1907 | 540 | 1914 (1st half) | 1059 |
| 1908 | 93 | 1915 | 156 |
| 1909 | 8 | 1916 | 156 |
| | | 1917 (Jan./Feb.) | 575 |

## The Lena Goldfields incident 1912

The Moscow *Okhrana* report (Source B) that had referred to the role of the *duma* in creating tension went on to cite the 'shooting of the Lena workers' as the major reason why the 'people can be heard speaking of the government in the sharpest and most unbridled tones'. The mention of the Lena workers was a reference to the notorious incident that occurred in 1912 in the Lena Goldfields in Siberia. Demands from the miners there for better pay and conditions were resisted by the employers, who appealed to the police to arrest the strike leaders as criminals.

The issue thus became the much larger one of trade union rights in Russia. When the police moved into Lena, the strikers closed ranks and the situation rapidly deteriorated, resulting in troops firing on and killing or injuring a large number of miners. The *Okhrana* appeared to have acted as ***agents provocateurs*** in order to identify the organisers of the strike.

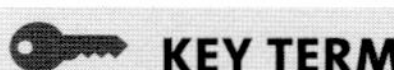

**KEY TERM**

***Agents provocateurs***
Government agents who infiltrated opposition movements to stir up trouble so that the ringleaders could be exposed.

It is important to note that an atmosphere of violence prevailed in Russia in the decade before 1914 which was not necessarily a product of government policies. There were 17,000 victims of acts of terrorism perpetrated by radicals and revolutionaries, not all of whom were inspired by high ideals. The modern Russian historian, Anna Geifman, has observed that a new type of brutal extremist entered the ranks of the revolutionary parties in the two decades before 1914. The new revolutionaries were little concerned with political or social theory; they often had a love of violence for its own sake. She writes that the new activists 'exhibited a considerably inferior level of intellectual and ideological awareness, as well as less inclination towards selfless idealism' than the older members. It was these pathological types, she concludes, who having infiltrated all the revolutionary groups, 'bore primary responsibility for the pervading atmosphere of anti-government violence and bloodshed in the empire in the first decade of the century'.

Anna Geifman (*Russia and the Last Tsar,* 1999) is quick to add that none of this exempts the tsarist government 'from a large share of the responsibility for the acute domestic crisis in the empire and the eventual collapse of its political order in 1917'.

## General strike 1914

Even the moderate liberal parties began to despair of the government's dealing effectively with the problems that confronted Russia. The Octobrist leader, Alexander Guchkov, told his party conference in 1913 that their attempts to achieve 'a peaceful, painless transition from the old condemned system to a new order' had failed. He warned that the blindness of the tsar's government was daily driving the Russian people closer to revolution. Guchkov's warning seemed to be closer to realisation in July 1914 when a general strike paralysed St Petersburg. Barricades were erected by the strikers which the police tried to break down; violence followed as the two sides clashed. Many of the progressive members of the *duma* openly supported the strikers. What finally prevented matters getting out of hand was Russia's entry later that month into the First World War.

**Summary diagram: Growing tensions in Russia 1911–14**

**Urban unrest**

- Disaffected workers took to the streets
- Strikes spread
- Repression the government's only response to disorder
- Violence also a product of revolutionary extremism

**The Lena Goldfields incident 1912**

- Revealed worker militancy and government brutality

**Even moderates despaired of government policies**

- General strike 1914 ended only by outbreak of war

# 4 Russia's foreign policy before 1914

- *By 1914, what factors had shaped Russia's attitude towards the outside world?*

## Russia's foreign concerns

As an empire covering a huge land mass, tsarist Russia had always been concerned for the security of its borders, but its greatest anxiety was in regard to its European frontiers. Russia believed that the greatest potential threat came from its neighbours in central and south-eastern Europe. Three particular developments in Europe in the second half of the nineteenth century had alarmed Russia:

- The growth of a united Germany. Russia feared that the unification of Germany in 1871 meant that central Europe was dominated by a powerful and ambitious nation, eager to expand eastwards.
- The formation of the Austro-Hungarian Empire in 1867. Russia was concerned that Austria would build on its new strength as a joint empire by an expansionist policy in south-east Europe.
- The decline of the Ottoman (Turkish) Empire. Russia's worry was that as Turkey weakened it would be increasingly challenged by aggressive national movements seeking independence from Turkish rule. This threatened Russian interests in the **Balkans**.

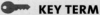

**KEY TERM**

**Balkans** The area of south-eastern Europe (fringed by Austria-Hungary to the north, the Black Sea to the east, Turkey to the south and the Aegean Sea to the west), which had largely been under Turkish control.

### Russia and the Balkans

Two main considerations influenced Russia's attitude towards the Balkans:

- The first had a long tradition attached to it. As a predominantly Slav nation, Russia had always believed it had a duty to protect the Slav Christian peoples of the Balkans from oppression by their Turkish Islamic masters.
- The second was a commercial concern. Seventy-five per cent of Russia's grain exports (which accounted for 40 per cent of its total foreign trade) were shipped through the Straits of the Dardanelles (see Figure 2.3). It was, therefore, necessary to ensure that the Straits did not come under the control of a hostile power capable of interrupting the passage of Russian ships from the Black Sea into the Mediterranean.

**Figure 2.2** Russia and its neighbouring western states on the eve of war in 1914.

## Russia's relations with Germany, France and Britain

In the quarter century before 1914, Russia's response to the shifts and turns of European diplomacy was consistently defensive. Russia was reluctant to take the diplomatic initiative, but was willing to enter into alliances that protected its western borders and possessions. In particular, it was concerned that its traditional control over Poland, a **buffer state** between Russia and Germany, should not be weakened.

**KEY TERM**

**Buffer state** An area that lies between two states, providing protection for each against the other.

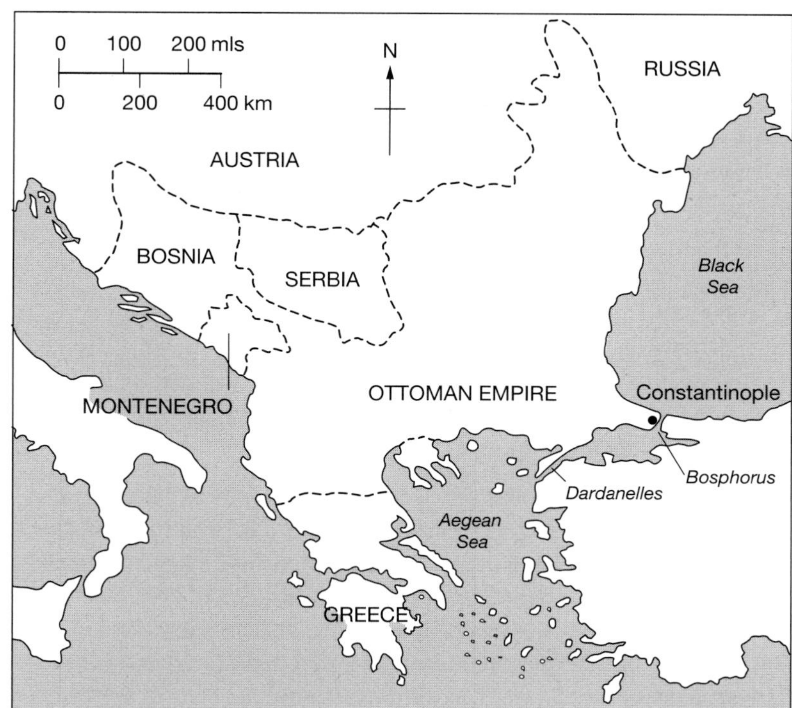


**Figure 2.3** The Dardenelles and the Balkans on the eve of war in 1914.

The unified Germany that came into being in 1871 dominated the European scene for a generation. Chancellor **Otto von Bismarck** achieved this largely by developing an alliance system. In order to encourage the European powers to make agreements with Germany, he played on their fears of becoming isolated. All the major powers came to accept the need for a diplomacy that guaranteed that they would not be left friendless should war threaten. However, in 1890, Bismarck was dismissed by the new German Kaiser, William II, who adopted a more aggressive form of diplomacy that hardened international attitudes and led eventually to the splitting of Europe into two opposed, armed camps. William II showed every intention of joining with Austria in asserting German influence in the Balkans and the Near East. This frightened the Russian government into looking for agreements with other powers so as to counter-balance the Austro-German threat.

**KEY FIGURE**

**Otto von Bismarck (1815–98)**

The Prussian chancellor who in 1871 brought the separate German states together in one united German empire under Prussian leadership.

## The Franco-Russian Convention 1892

To avoid isolation, Russia turned first to France. These two countries had not been on good terms, but a common fear of German aggression now outweighed their traditional dislike of each other. In the Franco-Russian Convention, signed in 1892, each partner promised to give military support to the other should it go to war with Germany. Economic co-operation also brought them closer. France was the major foreign investor in Russia's 'great spurt' in the 1890s (see page 14).

KEY TERMS

**Entente** An agreement to remain on friendly terms.

**Triple Entente** Not a formal alliance, but a declared willingness by three powers to co-operate.

### The Triple Entente 1907

The original **entente** between France and Russia expanded into a **Triple Entente** with the inclusion of Britain in 1907. This, too, was something of a diplomatic revolution. Anglo-Russian relations had been strained for decades. Imperial rivalries in Asia and Britain's resistance to what it regarded as Russia's attempts to dominate the eastern Mediterranean had aroused mutual animosity.

However, by the turn of the century Germany had embarked on an expansive naval programme that Britain interpreted as a direct threat to its own security and to its empire. Britain's response was to form an understanding with Germany's major western and eastern neighbours, France and Russia. In an earlier Anglo-French Entente (1904), Britain and France had already agreed to abandon their old rivalry. It made diplomatic sense for Russia and Britain to do the same.

Consequently, in 1907 they agreed to settle their past differences by recognising each other's legitimate interests in Afghanistan, Persia and Tibet. No precise agreement was reached regarding military co-operation but there was a general understanding that such co-operation would follow in the event of war. A key experience that had helped to convince Russia of the wisdom of entering into foreign alliances had been its defeat in the 1904–5 war against Japan. This strongly suggested that its plans for eastward expansion had been misplaced. It redirected its attention towards the west and became keener still to form protective agreements with friendly European powers.

## Russia's relations with Austria-Hungary

In 1908, Austria-Hungary made a startling move by annexing the Balkan state of Bosnia. When, Alexander Izvolski, the Russian foreign minister, protested, he was urged by his Austrian counterpart, Alois Aehrenthal, to accept the takeover as a means of creating greater stability in the Balkan region. Izvolski eventually agreed, in return for Austria-Hungary's promise that it would acknowledge Russia's unrestricted right to the use of the Dardanelles Straits (see page 57), and would persuade the other European powers to do the same. Russia kept its side of the bargain by recognising Austria-Hungary's takeover of Bosnia. The Austrians, however, did not honour their promise; they made no effort to encourage the international recognition of Russian rights in the Dardanelles.

### The question of Serbia

From this time onwards, relations between Russia and Austria-Hungary steadily deteriorated. A prominent issue dividing them was the position of Serbia. Bosnia contained many Serbs and its annexation by Austria-Hungary in 1908 aroused fierce Serbian nationalism. Russia, viewing itself as the special defender of Serbia and its Slav people, backed it in demanding compensation. Germany sided aggressively with Austria-Hungary and warned Russia not to interfere.

The crisis threatened for a time to spill over into war. However, in 1909 none of the countries involved felt ready to fight. Russia backed off from an open confrontation, while at the same time stating clearly that it regarded Germany and Austria-Hungary as the aggressors.

## The Balkan Wars

Between 1909 and 1914, Russia continued its involvement in the complexities of Balkan politics. The aim was to prevent Austria-Hungary from gaining a major advantage in the region. The tactic was to try to persuade the various nationalities in the area to form a coalition against Austria-Hungary. Russia had some success in this. Balkan nationalism led to a series of conflicts, known collectively as the Balkan Wars (1912–13). These were a confused mixture of anti-Turkish uprisings and squabbles between the Balkan states themselves over the division of the territories they had won from the Turks.

On balance, the outcome of these wars favoured Russian rather than Austro-Hungarian interests. Serbia had been doubled in size and felt itself more closely tied to Russia as an ally and protector. However, such gains as Russia had made were marginal. The international issues relating to Turkish decline and Balkan nationalism had not been resolved. The events of 1914 were to show how vulnerable Imperial Russia's status and security actually were.

**Summary diagram: Russia's foreign policy before 1914**

**Russia's chief concerns**
- The growth of a united Germany
- The formation of the Austro-Hungarian Empire
- The decline of the Ottoman (Turkish) Empire threatened Russian interests in the Balkans, where Russia saw itself as the defender of Slav nationalism

**Consequences of Russia's concerns**
Russia:
- drew away from Germany
- formed ententes with France and Britain
- competed with Austria-Hungary for influence in the Balkans

The Serbia question and the Balkan Wars heightened tension

**Critical factors that made the Balkans a flashpoint**
Russia's:
- role as champion of Slav culture
- commercial interests in the area

# The tsar's position at the outbreak of war in 1914

▶ *How stable was the tsar's position at the outbreak of war in 1914?*

In 1914, despite the continuing social unrest, there was no reason to consider that tsardom would collapse within three years. Indeed, 1913 had witnessed the celebration of the tricentenary of the Romanov dynasty. The pomp and pageantry that accompanied the occasion gave no hint of trouble to come. Rodzianko, the *duma* president, described (Source D) how the declaration of war in 1914 elevated Nicholas II's relationship with his people to mystical heights.

? How does Rozianko in Source D capture the 'moment of the union of the tsar with his people'?

**SOURCE D**

**From Rodzianko's account in 1914, quoted in David Christian, *Imperial and Soviet Russia*, Macmillan, 1997, p. 161.**

*On the day of the Manifesto [declaration] of the war with Germany a great crowd gathered before the Winter Palace. After a prayer for the granting of victory, the tsar spoke a few words ending with the solemn promise not to end the war while the enemy still occupied one inch of Russian soil. A loud 'hurrah' filled the palace and was taken up by an answering echo from the crowd on the square. After the prayer, the tsar came out onto the balcony to his people, the empress behind him. The huge crowd filled the square and the nearby streets, and when the tsar appeared it was as if an electric spark had run through the crowd, and an enormous 'hurrah' filled the air. Flags and placards with the inscription 'Long Live Russia and Slavdom' bowed to the ground, and the entire crowd fell to its knees as one man before the tsar. The tsar wanted to say something; he raised his hand; those in front began to sh-sh-sh; but the noise of the crowd, the unceasing 'hurrah', did not allow him to speak. He bowed his head and stood for some time overcome by the solemnity of this moment of the union of the tsar with his people.*

## Nicholas II's strengths in 1914

While it is true that Nicholas II had poor political judgement and lacked a sense of realism, he had legitimate reasons in 1914 to regard himself as being in a strong position as ruler:

- Tsardom had emerged stronger, not weaker, from the 1905 Revolution. Despite defeat in the Russo-Japanese war, the tsar's troops had remained loyal and had suppressed internal troubles (see page 37). The three groups who had caused problems in 1905, liberals, peasants and workers, had been placated or overcome.

- The October Manifesto had not been a relinquishing of power. This was clearly indicated by the tsar's issuing of the Fundamental Laws, which reaffirmed his autocratic powers.
- The *dumas* never became a threat to the tsar's power in the way that some had feared. Nicholas let them remain as a manageable parliamentary experiment that impressed international onlookers. In any case, Stolypin had so neutered the *dumas* that by the time of the fourth *duma*, which outlived him, it had been reduced to nothing more dangerous than a talking shop (a body that says much but does little).
- The liberals would not openly challenge the tsar even though, as their complaints in the *dumas* indicated, they had not been fully placated.
- The revolutionary parties were not considered, even by themselves, to be capable of mounting a successful assault on tsarist institutions or power. In 1914, they were on the fringe of the political scene. Indeed, most of the leading figures among them were in exile. Though they were to become prominent in 1917, it is reading history backwards to assume that they were poised to take power.
- Russia remained feared by the European nations. This was especially true for Germany, which regarded Russia as a great military power whose vast resources of labour made it a formidable force.
- The tsar was convinced that only a minority of industrial workers were opposed to his rule. His own estimate was that four-fifths of his people were dedicated and loyal. It was undeniable Russia had great problems of economic and social disparity and poverty, but, as Witte remarked to the tsar, 'these we have always had'. Their persistence did not mean that tsardom was doomed.
- Russia's potential for growth seemed enormous. While the Russian economy overall was some way behind its European rivals, it saw growth in the following areas:
  - Railways: the Trans-Siberian Railway was bringing Russia's distant provinces in touch with the centre. Migration and re-settlement offered the prospect of Russia utilising its untapped natural and human resources.
  - The economy in both the agriculture and industrial sectors had grown by six per cent by 1914. An interesting example of this was that Russia had become a major textile manufacturer, being fourth in world output behind the USA, Britain and Germany.

While it is arguable that Russia was in crisis in pre-war Russia, that was also the case in many other countries. Crises are a constant in most nations – but crisis does not always entail collapse. Until war came to Russia in 1914, there was no clear sign that its problems were of a magnitude that would lead unavoidably to revolution. In 1914, Nicholas II's throne was not at risk. The immediate impact on the position of Nicholas II personally when Russia went to war in July 1914 was a great increase in his personal standing. As tsar, he became the embodiment of the nation in its hour of need. Watching the great crowds cheering the tsar as he formally announced that Russia was at war, the French ambassador remarked: 'To those thousands the tsar really is the autocrat, the absolute master of their bodies and souls'.

**Summary diagram: The tsar's position at the outbreak of war in 1914**

**Tsardom had been strengthened by the outcome of 1905 Revolution**

- The October Manifesto had not weakened his authority
- The *dumas* never became a threat
- The liberals would not openly challenge the tsar
- Revolutionary parties incapable of mounting a successful challenge

**Tsar's position at the outbreak of war in 1914**

- Russia remained feared by the European nations
- Tsar convinced that only a minority of the people were opposed to his rule
- Russia's potential for growth seemed enormous
- These factors gave grounds for optimism rather than pessimism
- Nicholas II's status elevated by the outbreak of war

# 6 Key debate

► *Was tsardom already doomed in 1914?*

Armed with the knowledge that, three years after 1914, Russia would witness the downfall of the tsarist system, historians continue to discuss whether, but for the war, Russia would have progressed towards becoming a modern industrial state capable of turning its young parliamentary system into a constitutional monarchy. One could say that this debate was started as long ago as 1911 when Lenin, destined to take power in 1917 (see page 112), prophesised that Europe, beginning with Russia, was about 'to overthrow the rule of the bourgeoisie and establish the communist order'.

## The question of the Russian economy in 1914

However, there are those who regard Lenin as having been right, but premature. They suggest that, until the First World War intervened, Russia was in the process of developing into a modern industrial state. They cite the figures of increased industrial production, growth of the labour force and expansion of foreign investment. Other historians, while accepting these figures, argue that compared to developments in other countries, Russian growth was too limited to provide a genuine industrial base. They further stress that, in 1914, four-fifths of the population were still peasants, a fact that undermines the claim that there had been significant industrial development.

In the end, no final answer can be given to the question as to how the economy would have developed had the war and the revolution not occurred. There are too many ifs and buts. The comment of Alex Nove, an acknowledged Russian authority on the subject, is particularly telling in this context. He says that there are convincing arguments on either side of the question as to whether Russia would have modernised:

**EXTRACT 1**

**From Alex Nove, *An Economic History of the USSR*, Penguin, 1973, p. 17.**

*The question of whether Russia would have become a modern industrial state but for the war and the revolution is in essence a meaningless one. One may say that statistically the answer is in the affirmative. If the growth rates characteristic of the period 1890–1913 for industry and agriculture were simply projected over the succeeding 50 years, no doubt citizens would be leading a reasonable existence. However, this assumes that the imperial authorities would have successfully made the adjustment necessary to govern in an orderly manner a rapidly developing and changing society. But there must surely be a limit to the game of what-might-have-been.*

## The role of the tsar

The question turns on how the tsar's position in 1914 is assessed. American historian Leopold Haimson points to the strength of Nicholas II in 1914 even when he seemed to be assailed by problems.

**EXTRACT 2**

**From an article by L. Haimson, quoted in M. Cherniavsky, editor, *The Structure of Russian History*, Random House, 1970, p. 359.**

*No demonstrations, no public meetings, no collective petitions – no expressions of solidarity even comparable to those of bloody Sunday had evoked were now aroused. Thus, in the last analysis, the most important source of the political impotence revealed by the Petersburg strike was precisely the one that made for its monstrous revolutionary explosiveness: the sense of isolation, of psychological distance, that separated the Petersburg workers from educated, privileged society.*

Haimson is backed in this by Australian scholar David Christian:

**EXTRACT 3**

**From David Christian, *Imperial and Soviet Russia*, Macmillan, 1997, pp. 160–1.**

*Despite everything, traditions of loyalty to Tsarism survived among many sections of the population. These resurfaced immediately after the declaration of war, on 20 July 1914. In the first flush of enthusiasm the capital was renamed Petrograd instead of the Germanic St Petersburg. In the* duma *criticism of the government ceased. So did the demonstrations and strikes in the capital. Patriotic manifestations took their place.*

## Tsarist resistance to change

There is the added consideration that its blindness to the need for change made tsardom vulnerable to a major crisis. Despite some limited modifications to tsarist authority since 1906, Russia in 1914 was still essentially an autocratic state. A fundamental question remained unanswered in 1914. Was Russia capable of adopting or, indeed, willing to adopt the political and social changes necessary to become a modern industrial state comparable with those of Western Europe? The distinguished Marxist historian Christopher Hill had no doubt that the coming of war in 1914 simply exposed the underlying reality that the tsarist system had no possibility of surviving in a modern age:

**EXTRACT 4**

**From Christopher Hill, *Lenin and the Russian Revolution*, Penguin, 1971, p. 19.**

*Social change came with the rapid industrial development of the last three decades of the nineteenth century. But this was almost entirely financed by foreign capital, and had little effect on the position of the native middle class. Dependent on the West alike for capital, technicians and political ideas, the Russian bourgeoisie had to invoke the protection of the tsarist state against their economically more powerful rivals. They had no thought of challenging the political dominance of the monarchy until, in the twentieth century, the regime again revealed, under the stress of modern war, its utter incompetence and corruption, its inability even to maintain order and financial stability.*

The problem with which historians grapple in this key debate is often referred to as the 'the tsarist crisis' or 'the institutional crisis', which has been neatly summarised in question form by Robert Service, an outstanding modern Western scholar of Russia:

**EXTRACT 5**

**From Robert Service, *Lenin: A Biography*, Macmillan, 2000, p. 4.**

*It was a race against time. Would the tsarist system sustain its energy and authority for a sufficient period to modernise society and the economy? Would the revolutionaries accommodate themselves to the changing realities and avoid the excesses of violent politics? And would the tsarist system make concessions to bring this about?*

In what respects do the historians quoted in Extracts 1–5 agree or differ in their assessment of the strength of tsardom at the time of the outbreak of war in 1914? ?

## Chapter summary

In the aftermath of the 1905 Revolution, the tsarist government followed two lines of policy in which Peter Stolypin, as chief minister, took the lead. A political conservative, he was determined that the peasantry must not again become the threat they had been in 1905. His method for dealing with them was to construct an agricultural system that would provide them with security and create incentives for them to become increasingly productive. His 'wager on the strong' was an attempt to create a class of peasant proprietors, who would adopt progressive, profit-making methods, thus rewarding themselves and becoming a bulwark of support for the tsarist government. This policy was coupled with the sternest measures to suppress social disorder.

Stolypin followed the same approach in his relations with the *duma*. Wanting a quiescent parliament, he changed the critical character of the first two *dumas* by so manipulating membership qualifications that by the time of the fourth *duma* it had become dominated by the political right. Despite his best efforts, Russia at his death in 1911 was still a troubled land, as indicated by the unrest and industrial strikes of the period 1911–14. Meanwhile, troubles in the Balkans were threatening to draw Russia into an international crisis, which would test the strength of the tsar and tsardom. Whether it was war that brought down tsardom, or whether it was already doomed, is a question historians still debate.

## Refresher questions

Use these questions to remind yourself of the key material covered in this chapter.

**1** Why had a rural crisis developed in Russia by the first decade of the twentieth century?

**2** How did Stolypin intend to de-revolutionise the peasantry?

**3** What was Stolypin aiming to achieve by his wager on the strong?

**4** How strong had the Russian economy become by 1914?

**5** Why was the first *duma* unsuccessful?

**6** Why was the second *duma* even more critical of the government than the first had been?

**7** Why was the third *duma* less hostile to the government?

**8** Did the fourth *duma* serve any real purpose?

**9** What was at issue in the Lena Goldfields strike?

**10** Why were there mounting social and political strains in Russia between 1911 and 1914?

**11** What factors drew Russia away from Germany but closer to France and Britain?

**12** Why did Russia's relations with Austria-Hungary become increasingly strained?

# Question practice

## ESSAY QUESTIONS

1 How successful were the policies followed by Stolypin between 1906 and 1911?

2 'The four *dumas* which sat between 1906 and 1914 talked much but did little.' How far do you agree with this statement?

3 Which of the following was the greater problem for the tsarist government between 1906 and 1914? i) Opposition in the *dumas*. ii) Unrest among the workers. Explain your answer with reference to both i) and ii).

4 To what extent do you agree with the view that the tsar and his government were in a very strong position at home on the eve of war in 1914?

5 Which of the following was the more successful in dealing with the problems confronting Russia between 1894 and 1914? i) The policies of Sergei Witte. ii) The policies of Peter Stolypin. Explain your answer with reference to both i) and ii).

## INTERPRETATION QUESTION

1 Read the interpretation and then answer the question that follows. 'The outstanding feature of Russia in 1914 was its utter incompetence and corruption' (from Christopher Hill, *Lenin and the Russian Revolution*, 1971). Evaluate the strengths and limitations of this interpretation, making reference to other interpretations that you have studied.

CHAPTER 3

# From war to revolution 1914–17

At the outbreak of war, the Russian people rallied enthusiastically behind the tsar and his government, but, as the war progressed, poor military and political leadership led to mounting opposition. By 1917, continuous military failures and growing disorder revealed Nicholas's inability to handle crisis. Opposed by a rebellious *duma*, and despaired of by his high command, he chose to abdicate. In the power vacuum that followed, the remnant of the *duma* and the newly formed Petrograd soviet of soldiers and workers began to exercise a dual authority. The chapter examines four main themes:

★ Russia's entry into the war in 1914

★ The impact of war on Russia

★ The growth of opposition to tsardom

★ The February Revolution 1917

The key debate on *page 92* asks the question: Why was there a February Revolution?

## Key dates

| | | |
|---|---|---|
| **1914** | **June 28** | Assassination of Franz Ferdinand at Sarajevo |
| | **July 28** | Austria-Hungary declared war on Serbia |
| | **July 30** | Russian full mobilisation orders given |
| | **Aug. 1** | Germany declared war on Russia |
| | | Suspension of fourth *duma* |
| **1915** | **June–July** | Fourth *duma* reconvened |
| | **June 25** | The Progressive Bloc formed in the *duma* |
| | **Aug. 22** | Nicholas II made himself commander-in-chief of the Russian armies |
| **1916** | **Dec. 1** | Rasputin murdered |
| **1917** | **Feb. 18** | Strike began at Putilov factories in Petrograd |
| | **Feb. 23** | International Women's Day |
| | | Widespread workers' demonstrations |
| | **Feb. 25** | General strike began |
| | **Feb. 27** | Unofficial meeting of *duma* |
| | | First meeting of the Petrograd soviet |
| | **Feb. 28** | Nicholas II prevented from returning to Petrograd |
| | **March 2** | Provisional Government formed from the *duma* committee |
| | | Tsar signed abdication decree |
| | **March 4** | Tsar's abdication publicly proclaimed |

# Russia's entry into the war in 1914

 *Why was Russia drawn into war in 1914?*

**KEY TERMS**

**Central Powers** Germany, Austria-Hungary and Turkey.

**Serbian nationalists** Activists struggling for Serbia's independence from Austria-Hungary.

**Bosphorus** The narrow waterway linking the Black Sea with the Dardanelles.

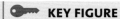

**KEY FIGURE**

**Sergei Sazonov (1860–1927)**

Russian foreign secretary from 1910 to 1916.

Russia's anxieties in foreign affairs predisposed it to regard Germany and Austria-Hungary with deep suspicion (see page 58). When crises occurred, therefore, they were more likely to lead to conflict. But this is not to say that the tsarist government was looking for war in 1914. Russia's experience ten years earlier against Japan had made it wary of putting itself at risk again, and its foreign policy after 1905 had been essentially defensive. Russia had joined France and Britain in the Triple Entente as a means of safeguarding itself against the alliance of the **Central Powers**. However, the events that followed the assassination in June 1914 of Franz Ferdinand, the heir to the Austro-Hungarian throne, by **Serbian nationalists** made it virtually impossible for Russia to avoid being drawn into a European conflict.

A critical factor at this point was Russia's perception of itself as the protector of the Slav peoples of the Balkans. **Sazonov**, the tsar's foreign minister in 1914, claimed that 'Russia's sole and unchanging object was to see that those Serbian peoples should not fall under the influence of hostile powers.' He added that the basic aim of Russian policy was 'to obtain free access to the Mediterranean, and to be in a position to defend its Black Sea coasts against the threat of the irruption of hostile naval forces through the **Bosphorus**' (see the map on page 57).

On 28 July 1914, a month after Franz Ferdinand's murder by a Bosnian-Serb nationalist on 28 June, Austria-Hungary, with German encouragement, declared war on Serbia. Russia still expected to be able to force the Austrians to withdraw, without itself having to go to war. Russia hoped that, if it mobilised, this would act as a deterrent to Austria. This was not unrealistic. Despite Russia's defeat by Japan, its armies were still regarded as formidable. German generals often spoke of 'the Russian steamroller', a reference to the immense reserves of manpower on which it was judged that Russia could draw.

With tension building, Nicholas II made a personal move to avoid war with Germany. In July he exchanged a series of personal telegrams with his cousin, Kaiser William II, regretting the growing crisis in Russo-German relations and hoping that conflict could be avoided. But although these 'Willy–Nicky' exchanges, written in English, were friendly, there was a sense in which the two emperors were being carried along by events beyond their control.

## Russia's mobilisation plans

It was at this stage that the great length of Russia's western frontier proved to be of momentous significance. The Russian military high command had two basic mobilisation schemes:

- Partial – based on plans for a limited campaign in the Balkans against Austria-Hungary.
- Full – based on plans for a full-scale war against both Germany and Austria-Hungary.

Both forms of mobilisation depended on detailed and precise railway timetabling aimed at transporting huge numbers of men and vast amounts of *matériel*. The complexity of the timetables meant that the adoption of one type of mobilisation ruled out the use of the other. Horse-drawn wagons and marching men can change direction quickly; trains cannot. Russia's fear in July 1914 was that if it mobilised only partially it would leave it defenceless should Austria's ally, Germany, strike at its Polish borders (see the map on page 56).

On the other hand, full mobilisation might well appear to Germany as a deliberate provocation. The German government did, indeed, warn Sazonov that if Russia mobilised Germany would have to do the same.

**SOURCE A**

How does the cartoon in Source A illustrate Austrian and German fears of Russia's strength?

RUSSIA
"THE STEAM-ROLLER."
AUSTRIA. "I SAY, YOU KNOW, YOU'RE EXCEEDING THE SPEED LIMIT!"


**British cartoon of 1914 showing Franz Joseph, the Austro-Hungarian emperor, fleeing from the chasing Russian 'steamroller'. In pre-1914 Germany and Austria-Hungary, the image of Russia as a steamroller that could crush their armies was a powerful and frightening one.**

**KEY TERM**

**Schlieffen Plan** A strategy entailing a lightning knockout blow against France, which would then enable German forces to turn fully on Russia.

## Germany's mobilisation plans

Here a vital fact intervened and made war unstoppable. Germany had no room for manoeuvre. According to German contingency plans, if Russia mobilised, Germany would have to go to war. There would no longer be a choice. German strategy was based on the **Schlieffen Plan**, which aimed at avoiding a two-front war against France and Russia. Speed was of the essence. Germany could not play a game of diplomatic bluff; it had to strike first.

When, therefore, on 30 July 1914, after a long hesitation, Nicholas chose to sign the Russian full mobilisation order, he had taken a more fateful decision than he realised. What had been intended as a diplomatic move that would leave Russia free to hold back from war was the step that precipitated war. On 31 July Germany demanded that the Russians cease their mobilisation. On 1 August, having received no response, Germany declared war on Russia. Four days later Austria-Hungary did the same.

### Key sequence of events

- 28 July 1914: Austria-Hungary declared war on Serbia.
- 30 July 1914: Tsar signed full Russian mobilisation order.
- 1 August 1914: Germany declared war on Russia.

**Summary diagram: Russia's entry into the war in 1914**

**Line-up of opposed alliances**

| *Central Powers* | *Triple Entente* |
|---|---|
| • Germany | • Russia |
| • Austria-Hungary | • France |
| • Turkey | • Britain |

**Events in Serbia**

Austro-Hungarian ultimatum to Serbia, following Franz Ferdinand's assassination in June 1914, resisted by Russia

Germany backed Austria-Hungary

The crisis did not make war unavoidable, but Russian and German mobilisation plans did

**Mobilisation plans**

| **Russia** | **Germany** |
|---|---|
| Choice between partial and full mobilisation | Schlieffen Plan ruled that if it mobilised it went to war |

**Consequence**

When tsar signed full mobilisation order, Germany had no choice but to declare war on Russia

# The impact of war on Russia

*How was Russian morale affected during the course of the war?*

Whatever the tsar's previous uncertainties may have been, once war was declared, he became wholly committed to it. By 1917 the war would prove to be the undoing of tsardom, but in 1914 the outbreak of hostilities greatly enhanced the tsar's position. At a special session of the *duma*, all the deputies, save for the five Bolshevik representatives, cheered for the tsar and fervently pledged themselves to the national struggle.

## Setback for the Bolsheviks

It was a similar story in all the warring countries. The socialist parties abandoned their policies and committed themselves to the national war effort. Lenin was bitter in his condemnation of 'these class traitors'. He called on all true revolutionaries 'to transform the imperialist war everywhere into a civil war'. But the prevailing mood in Russia and Europe was all against him.

The early stages of the war were dark days for Lenin's Bolsheviks. Vilified as traitors and German agents for their opposition to the war, they were forced to flee or go into hiding. Lenin, who was already in exile in Poland, made his way with Austrian help to neutral Switzerland. Had the war gone well for Russia there is every reason to think that the Bolshevik Party would have disappeared as a political force. But the war did not go well for Russia, and the reason was only partly military.

## Russia's problems

The basic explanation for Russia's decline and slide into revolution in 1917 was an economic one. Three years of **total war** were to prove too great a strain for the Russian economy to bear. War is a time when the character and structure of a society are put to the test in a particularly intense way. The longer the war lasts, the greater the test. During the years 1914–17, the political, social and economic institutions of Russia proved increasingly incapable of meeting the demands that war placed on them.

**KEY TERM**

**Total war** A struggle in which the whole nation, people, resources and institutions, is involved.

This does not prove that Russia was uniquely incompetent. The pressure of total war on all countries was immense, and it should be remembered that of the six empires engaged in the First World War – Germany, Austria, Turkey, Russia, France and Britain – only the last two survived.

Differing estimates have been made of Russia's potential for growth in 1914. But however that is assessed, the fact remains that the demands of the 1914–17 struggle eventually proved too heavy for Russia to sustain. The impact of the war on Russia can be conveniently studied under a number of headings:

- inflation
- food and transport
- living conditions
- the army
- prohibition.

## Inflation

Russia had achieved remarkable financial stability by 1914. Its currency was on the gold standard (see page 15) and it had the largest gold reserves of any European country. This happy position was destroyed by the war. Between 1914 and 1917 government spending rose from 4 million to 30 million roubles. Increased taxation at home and heavy borrowing from abroad were only partially successful in raising the capital Russia needed. The gold standard was abandoned, which allowed the government to put more notes into circulation. This was what is now known as **quantitative easing (QE)**. In the short term this enabled wages to be paid and commerce to continue, but in the long term it made money practically worthless. The result was severe inflation, which became particularly acute in 1916. In broad terms, between 1914 and 1916 average earnings doubled while the price of food and fuel quadrupled.

**KEY TERM**

**Quantitative easing (QE)** The printing of extra currency notes to meet the demand for ready money; a risky process since the money is not tied to an actual increase in genuine wealth.

**Table 3.1** Wartime inflation in Russia 1914–17

| Prices (to a base unit of 100) | | Notes in circulation (to a base of 100) | |
|---|---|---|---|
| July 1914 | 100 | July 1914 | 100 |
| January 1915 | 130 | January 1915 | 146 |
| January 1916 | 141 | January 1916 | 199 |
| January 1917 | 398 | January 1917 | 336 |

**Table 3.2** The cost of the war 1914–17

| Year | Cost (in millions of roubles) |
|---|---|
| 1914 | 1,655 |
| 1915 | 8,818 |
| 1916 | 14,573 |
| 1917 (up to August) | 13,603 |

## Food and transport

Initially, many of the peasant farmers benefited from the war, since the demand for food and increased agricultural production enabled them to charge higher prices and make profits. During the first two years of the war, Russia's grain yield was higher than it had been between 1912 and 1914. But in 1916 it began to fall. There were four main reasons for this:

- Inflation made trading unprofitable, so the peasants stopped selling food and began hoarding their stocks.

- The **requisitioning** of horses and fertiliser by the military for the war effort made it difficult for peasants to sustain agricultural output.
- The army had first claim on the more limited amount of food being produced.
- The military also had priority in the use of the transport system. It commandeered the railways and the roads, with the result that food supplies to civilian areas became difficult to maintain.

**Requisitioning** State authorised takeover of property or resources

**Petrograd** For patriotic reasons, soon after the war began, the German name for the capital, St Petersburg, was changed to the Russian form, Petrograd.

Transport dislocation meant food supplies could not be distributed effectively. Hunger bordering on famine became a constant reality for much of Russia. Shortages were at their worst in the towns and cities. **Petrograd** suffered particularly badly because of its remoteness from the food-producing regions and because of the large number of refugees who swelled its population and increased the demand on its dwindling resources. By early 1917, bread rationing meant that Petrograd's inhabitants were receiving less than a quarter of the amount that had been available in 1914.

It was the disruption of the transport system rather than the decline in food production that was the major cause of Russia's wartime shortages. The growth of the railways, from 13,000 to 44,000 miles between 1881 and 1914 (see page 15), had been an impressive achievement, but it did not meet the demands of war. The attempt to transport millions of troops and masses of supplies to the war fronts created unbearable pressures. The signalling system on which the railway network depended broke down; blocked lines and steam trains stranded by engine failure or lack of coal became commonplace.

Less than two years after the war began, the Russian railway system had virtually collapsed. By 1916, some 575 stations were no longer capable of handling freight. A graphic example of the confusion was provided by Archangel, the northern port through which the bulk of the Allied aid to Russia passed. So great was the pile-up of undistributed goods that they sank into the ground beneath the weight of new supplies. Elsewhere there were frequent reports of food rotting in railway trucks that could not be moved. One of the tsar's wartime prime ministers later admitted: 'There were so many trucks blocking the lines that we had to tip some of them down the embankments to move the ones that arrived later.' Russia began to suffer serious shortages:

- By 1916, Petrograd and Moscow were receiving only a third of their food and fuel requirements.
- Before the war Moscow had received an average of 2200 wagons of grain per month; by February 1917 this figure had dropped to below 700.
- The figures for Petrograd told a similar story; in February 1917 the capital received only 300 wagon-loads of grain instead of the 1000 it needed.

## Living conditions

Unsurprisingly, the disruption to food supplies made living and working conditions increasingly difficult. An insight into the war's impact on Russia's

? What picture of the workers' conditions emerges from Source B?

workers was provided by an *Okhrana* report from the capital Petrograd, written in October 1916 and recording the statistics relating to workers' conditions.

**SOURCE B**

**From an *Okhrana* report, October 1916, in G. Vernadsky, editor, *A Source Book for Russian History from Early Times to 1917*, volume 3, Yale University Press, 1973, pp. 867–8.**

| **Daily income** | | |
|---|---|---|
| **Type of worker** | **pre-war wages** | **present [1916] wages** |
| Unskilled | 1 to 1.25 roubles | 2.5 to 3 roubles |
| Metalworker | 2 to 2.5 roubles | 4 to 5 roubles |
| Electrician | 2 to 3 roubles | 5 to 6 roubles |
| **Expenses** | | |
| **Item** | **pre-war cost** | **present [1916] cost** |
| Monthly rent (for a shared room) | 2 to 3 roubles | 8 to 12 roubles |
| Dinner | 0.15 to 0.2 roubles | 1 to 1.2 roubles |
| Tea | 0.07 roubles | 0.35 |
| Boots | 5 to 6 roubles | 20 to 30 roubles |
| Shirt | 0.75 to 0.9 roubles | 2.5 to 3 roubles |

*Even if we estimate the rise in earnings at 100 per cent, the prices of products have risen on the average, 300 per cent. The impossibility of even buying many food products and necessities, the time wasted standing idle in queues to receive goods, the increasing incidence of disease due to malnutrition and unsanitary living conditions (cold and dampness because of lack of coal and wood), and so forth, have made the workers as a whole, prepared for the wildest excesses of a 'hunger riot'.*

*If in the future grain continues to be hidden, the very fact of its disappearance will be sufficient to provoke in the capitals and in the other most populated centers of the empire the greatest disorders, attended by pogroms and endless street rioting.*

## Prohibition

Drink was not a trivial matter in Russia. The consumption of alcohol, particularly vodka, was an integral part of Russian social tradition. The primary purpose was not sensual enjoyment but a method of putting up with the grimness of life. It has been described as Russia's alternative to religion. Both provided a way of making life endurable. Periodically, tsarist governments had introduced anti-drink measures in order to control the disorder associated with drunkenness, but these were dropped for two reasons:

- Taxes on vodka sales were a source of government revenue.
- To deprive Russians of alcohol was likely to cause more, not less, social unrest.

Nicholas II, however, in one of his major errors, took the moralistic and short-sighted decision at the very beginning of the war to introduce **prohibition**. His aim was to stimulate the war effort by removing a potent distraction from the people. What he had overlooked was that the government derived nearly a third of its revenue from the taxes on alcohol sales. The result was that at a critical point in its destinies, the Russian state had deprived itself of an irreplaceable source of income. By 1916, the damage being done was so evident that prohibition was repealed. But by then it was too late to recover what had been lost. Nor was it merely a matter of lost revenue. Prohibition had proved a social disaster. Since alcohol was no longer legally available, deprived drinkers turned to illegal ways of obtaining it. Production of ***samogon*** became a nationwide undercover industry, supplying towns and villages across Russia.

**KEY TERMS**

**Prohibition** The state's banning of the production and sale of alcohol.

***Samogon*** Illicitly distilled vodka, the equivalent of 'moonshine' or 'hooch', Western forms of unlicensed alcohol.

**SOURCE C**

**From D.N. Voronov, *O Samagone [Oh, Vodka!]*, Izdatel'stro Z-oe, 1929, p. 6.**

*At first, instead of vodka, they tried to use various other substances containing alcohol – eau-de-cologne, varnish, or denatured alcohol. But these were hard to get hold of, they were expensive, and they were unpleasant tasting and obviously dangerous to the health of the consumers. Then people turned to domestic beers and* braga *[a strong domestic ale], trying to make them as strong as possible, but these couldn't get you drunk enough. Finally … they learnt how to extract spirits by distilling fermented grains or sugary substances.*

According to Source C, to what extremes were Russian drinkers prepared to go to obtain alcohol?

## The army

A striking detail of the First World War is that Russia, in proportion to its population, put fewer than half the troops into the field than either Germany or France (see Table 3.3).

**Table 3.3** Numbers and percentages of the population mobilised

| State | 1914 | 1918 | Total population | % of population mobilised |
|---|---|---|---|---|
| Russia | 5.3 million | 15.3 million | 180 million | 8.8 |
| Germany | 3.8 million | 14.0 million | 68 million | 20.5 |
| France | 3.8 million | 7.9 million | 39 million | 19.9 |
| Britain | 0.6 million | 5.7 million | 45 million | 12.7 |

Yet, in total numbers the Russian army was still a formidable force. It was by far the largest army of all the countries that fought in the war. Its crippling weakness, which denied it the military advantage that its sheer size should have given it, was lack of equipment. This was not a matter of Russia's military underspending. Indeed, until 1914, Russia led Europe in the amount and the proportions it spent on defence (see Figure 3.1, overleaf).

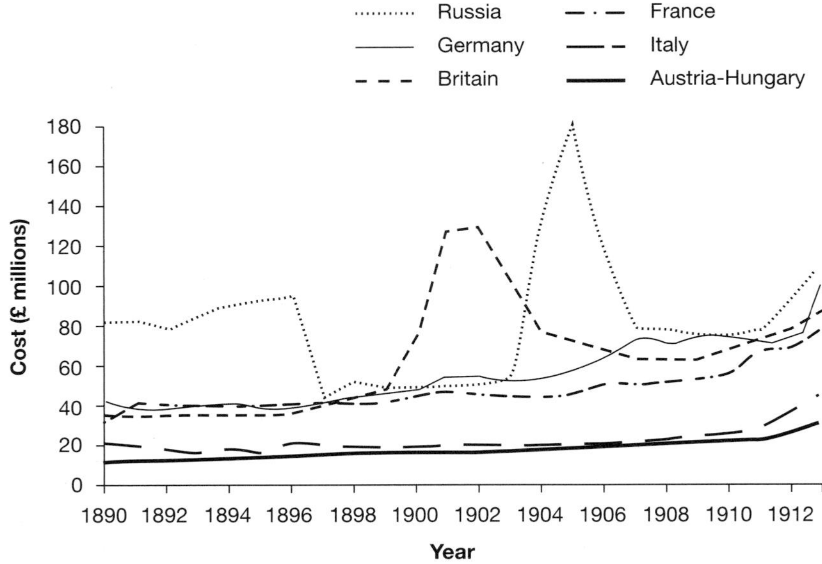


**Figure 3.1** Graph showing the comparative defence expenditures of the European powers 1890–1913 (in £ million).

The problem was not the lack of resources but poor administration and ineffective liaison between the government departments responsible for supplies. Despite its commandeering of the transport system, the military was as much a victim of the poor distribution of resources as the civilian population. In the first two years of the war, the army managed to obtain its supply needs, but from 1916 serious shortages began to occur. Rodzianko, the president of the *duma*, who undertook a special fact-finding study in 1916 of conditions in the army, reported to the *duma* on the widespread disorganisation and its dismal effects. He described as a 'great evil' the lack of direction and organisation by the government, which left Russia's gallant soldiers desperately short of food, ammunition and medical supplies.

**Table 3.4** Russian casualty figures 1914–17 (to nearest thousand)

| | |
|---|---|
| **Killed in action** | 1,200,000 |
| **Missing in action** | 440,000 |
| **Died of wounds** | 240,000 |
| **Gassed** | 11,000 |
| **Died from disease** | 155,000 |
| **Deaths among prisoners of war in captivity** | 190,000 |
| **Deaths due to accidents** | 19,000 |
| **Total war dead** | **2,255,000** |
| **Wounded** | 3,749,000 |
| **Prisoners of war** | 3,342,900 |
| **Civilian deaths** | 1,500,000 |

## Nicholas II as a war leader

Conscious, like Rodzianko, of the military situation, Alexander Naumov, minister of agriculture, made a similar visit to the front. Afterwards, he wrote to the tsar attempting to impress on him the desperate need for effective government direction (see Source D).

**SOURCE D**

**From a report by Alexander Naumov recording his meeting with Nicholas II, June 1916, quoted in Dominic Lieven, *Nicholas II*, Pimlico, 1993, p. 229.**

*I tried to tell His Majesty about the situation of the food supply … The Emperor kept interrupting me with questions that related not to the business side of my official journey but rather to everyday trivia that interested him … I must admit that this kind of attitude from the Emperor towards matters of fundamental national importance discouraged me greatly … I became clearly aware of a certain characteristic of the monarch which I attribute to general nervous exhaustion brought about by all the adversities attending his reign and the extraordinary complications he has encountered in governing the country since the outbreak of war in 1914.*

What impression of the tsar as leader is conveyed in Source D?

### The tsar's decision to become commander-in-chief, August 1915

The clear implication in the accounts of both Rodzianko and Naumov was that the strong central leadership, which the war effort desperately needed, was not being provided. This was a view that became increasingly widespread and it was against the tsar that criticisms began to mount. Much of this resulted from a huge error of judgement Nicholas II had made. In August 1915, he had formally taken over the direct command of Russia's armed services. This was a momentous decision. The intention was to rally the nation around him as Tsar of Russia. But it also made him a hostage to fortune. Nicholas II was now personally responsible for Russia's performance in the war. If it went well he took the credit, but if it went badly he was to blame. Lack of success could no longer be attributed solely to his appointees.

### Nicholas II's limitations as a war leader

Although trained as a soldier, the tsar was a not a natural commander. A major biographer, Dominic Lieven (1994), points out that although Nicholas had been in a prestigious cavalry regiment, 'This was not a real training in the military art … the most exclusive regiments of the Guards came closer to being a pleasant and sociable finishing school for wealthy young aristocrats than a serious professional training for a military career.' The result was that, despite his nominal position as commander-in-chief, he had to rely wholly on his generals. He had nothing original to offer in the planning of campaigns and merely followed what he was told. In no real sense could he offer military leadership since he did not know enough about military matters; of actual fighting, he had no experience. He treated Mogilev, the military headquarters, as a retreat from the politics of Petrograd rather than as a place from which he could direct the war. At the headquarters he gave an air of detachment, not commitment. An authoritative modern historian describes the tsar's non-involvement in the real world: Stephen Kotkin, *Stalin Paradoxes of Power 1878–1928* (Allen Lane, 2014, pp. 158–9):

> *Nicholas II took long walks with his English setters [dogs], rode into the countryside in his Rolls-Royce [car], listened to music, played dominoes and solitaire, and watched motion pictures. The Tsar occasionally had Alexei brought to Mogilev for visits, and the heir 'marched about with his rifle and sang loudly', interrupting the war councils. True, although Nicholas loved the romance of military pageantry, he knew next to nothing of strategy and tactics.*

The tsar's military appointees, like his political ones, were not men of high ability. He played safe, appointing officers according to their social standing rather than their military prowess. When he did give preferment to those of ability, such as Generals Mikhail Alekseev and Aleksei Brusilov, he did not give them consistent support and allowed the personal rivalries among the high command to undermine morale. It is interesting to note the range of comments made about him by people who knew Nicholas II personally, all of which help to explain his inability to provide leadership in the time of crisis. Sergei Witte said of him: 'His character is the source of all our misfortunes. His outstanding weakness is a lack of willpower.' Rasputin, who was a sharp observer of the royal family, remarked, 'The tsar can change his mind from one minute to the next; he's a sad man; he lacks guts.' Pobedonostsev, the man who had trained Nicholas as tsar commented, 'He only grasps the significance of a fact in isolation without its relationship to other facts.'

Perhaps the most significant observation was made by the empress, his wife. Alexandra pointed out that as tsar Nicholas was rarely told the full truth by those who served him. His elevated position detached him from them: 'My poor Nick's cross is heavy, all the more so as he has nobody on whom he can thoroughly rely. The lack of what I call "real" men is great. Of course they must exist somewhere, but it is difficult to get to them.' The tsar's political and military failings, which all derived from the same source – his lack of realism – were a potent factor in the decline and collapse of imperial Russia between 1914 and 1917.

## Morale

The suffering that the food shortages and the dislocated transport system brought to both troops and civilians might have been bearable had the news from the war front been encouraging or had there been inspired leadership from the top. There were occasional military successes, such as those achieved on the south-western front in 1916 when a Russian offensive under General Brusilov killed or wounded half a million Austrian troops, and brought Austria-Hungary to the point of collapse. But the gains made were not followed up and were never enough to justify the appalling casualty lists. The enthusiasm and high morale of August 1914 had turned by 1916 into pessimism and defeatism. Ill-equipped and under-fed, the 'peasants in uniform' who composed the Russian army began to desert in increasing numbers.

## How broken were the Russian armies?

Care should be taken not to exaggerate the effect of the breakdown in morale. Modern research, such as that undertaken by historians Evan Mawdsley and Norman Stone, has shown that the Russian army was not on the verge of collapse in 1917. Mutinies had occurred but these were not exclusive to Russia. The strains of war in 1917 produced mutinies in all the major armies, including the French and British. Stone dismisses the idea of a disintegrating Russian army as a Bolshevik 'fabrication'. With all its problems the Russian armies were still intact as a fighting force in 1917.

Stone also emphasises the vital role that Russia played as an ally of Britain and France in tying down the German army for over three years on the Eastern Front. An interesting detail, indicating how far Russia was from absolute collapse in 1916, is that in that year Russia managed to produce more shells than Germany. To quote these findings is not to deny the importance of Russia's military crises, but it is to recognise that historians have traditionally tended to overstate Russia's military weakness in 1917.

### Summary diagram: The impact of war on Russia

**Immediate effect**
Enhanced the popularity and status of the tsar
Weakened the anti-war Bolsheviks

**BUT**
'Total war' created major problems for Russia

1. **Inflation** – value of money sharply declined, creating instability and high prices
2. **Food supplies** – dwindled as result of requisitioning and transport disruption – urban areas suffered acute shortages
3. **Transport system** – broke down under stress of war
4. **The army** – fought well but was undermined by poor organisation and lack of supplies
5. **Role of the tsar** – Nicholas II's fateful decision to become commander-in-chief made survival of tsardom dependent on military success
6. **Morale** – high at the start among army and civilians but was damaged by lengthening casualty lists at the front and declining supplies at home, particularly of prohibited vodka

# The growth of opposition to tsardom

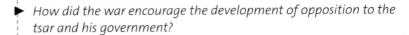

▶ *How did the war encourage the development of opposition to the tsar and his government?*

By 1916 the basic patriotism of the Russian people remained intact but among all important sections of the population a common view had developed that the tsar was an inept political and military leader, incapable of providing the inspiration that the nation needed. It is significant that the first moves in the February Revolution in 1917, the event that led to the fall of tsardom, were not made by the revolutionary parties. The revolution was set in motion by those members of Russian society who, at the outbreak of the war in 1914, had been the tsar's strongest supporters, but, by the winter of 1916, were too wearied by his incompetence to wish to save him or the barren system he represented.

## The *duma* recalled

In August 1914, the *duma* had shown its total support for the tsar by voting for its own suspension for the duration of the war. But within a year Russia's poor military showing led to the *duma* demanding its own recall. Nicholas II bowed before the pressure and allowed the *duma* to reassemble in July 1915.

**KEY TERMS**

**Union of *Zemstvos*** A set of patriotic rural local councils.

**Union of Municipal Councils** A set of patriotic urban local councils.

***Zemgor*** The joint body that devoted itself to helping Russia's war wounded.

One major political mistake of the tsar and his ministers was their refusal to co-operate fully with the non-governmental organisations such as the **Union of *Zemstvos*** and the **Union of Municipal Councils**, which at the beginning of the war had been wholly willing to work with the government in the national war effort. These elected bodies formed a joint organisation, ***Zemgor***. The success of this organisation both highlighted the government's own failures and hinted that there might be a workable alternative to tsardom.

## Formation of a 'Progressive Bloc'

A similar political blindness characterised the tsar's dismissal of the *duma*'s appeal to him to replace his inept cabinet with 'a ministry of national confidence' whose members would be drawn from the *duma*. Nicholas rejected this proposal, and in doing so destroyed the last opportunity he would have of retaining the support of the politically progressive parties. Paul Milyukov, the Kadet leader, complained that the tsar and his advisers had 'brushed aside the hand that was offered them'.

Denied a direct voice in national policy, 236 of the 422 *duma* members formed themselves into a 'Progressive Bloc' composed of Kadets, Octobrists and Progressists. The SRs did not formally join the bloc but voted with it in all the *duma* resolutions that criticised the government's handling of the war. Initially, the bloc did not directly challenge the tsar's authority, but tried to persuade him

## Nicholas II

| | |
|---|---|
| 1868 | Born into the Romanov house |
| 1894 | Became tsar |
| | Married Alexandra, the German grand-daughter of Queen Victoria |
| 1905 | Granted the October Constitution |
| 1906 | Opened the first *duma* |
| 1913 | Led the celebrations of 300 years of Romanov rule |
| 1914 | Signed the general mobilisation order |
| 1915 | Became commander-in-chief of the Russian armed forces |
| 1917 | Advised by military high command and *duma* to stand down |
| | Abdicated on behalf of the Romanov dynasty |
| 1918 | Murdered with his family in Ekaterinburg |

The character of Nicholas II is important in any analysis of revolutionary Russia. The evidence suggests that, though he was far from being as unintelligent as his detractors asserted, his limited imagination prevented him from fully grasping the nature of the events in which he was involved. As with many basically ineffectual monarchs, when he attempted to be decisive, he simply appeared obdurate. Pobedonostsev said of him, 'he only grasps the significance of a fact in isolation without its relationship to other facts', while Witte observed, 'His character is the source of all our misfortunes. His outstanding weakness is a lack of willpower.' **Alexander Kerensky** asserted, 'His mentality kept him wholly out of touch with his people. From his youth he had been trained to believe that his welfare and the welfare of Russia were one and the same thing.'

The tsar made a number of crucial errors in his handling of the war, the most significant being his decision in 1915 to take direct command of Russia's armed forces. This in effect tied the fate of the Romanov dynasty to the success or otherwise of Russia's armies. There are good grounds for arguing that the war had offered tsardom its last great opportunity to identify itself with the needs of modern Russia and so consolidate itself beyond challenge as the legitimate ruling system. That opportunity was squandered. In 1914 there had been a very genuine enthusiasm for the tsar as representative of the nation. Within three years that enthusiasm had wholly evaporated, even among dedicated tsarists. The fall of Nicholas was the result of poor leadership rather than of savage oppression. He was not helped by his wife's German nationality or by court scandals, of which Rasputin's was the most notorious. But these would not by themselves have been sufficient to bring down a dynasty.

to make concessions. Nicholas, however, was not willing to listen. It was part of that stubbornness that he mistook for firmness.

One of the bloc's leading members, **Vasily Shulgin**, pointed out despairingly how short-sighted the tsar was in viewing the bloc as an enemy not a friend: 'The whole purpose of the Progressive Bloc was to prevent revolution so as to enable the government to finish the war.' The tragedy for the tsar was that as he and his government proved increasingly incapable of running the war, the bloc, from having been a supporter, became a source of political resistance. It was another of tsardom's self-inflicted wounds.

The government continued to shuffle its ministers in the hope of finding a successful team. In the year 1915–16, there were four prime ministers, three foreign secretaries, three ministers of defence and six interior ministers. It was all to no avail. None of them was up to the task. The description by the British ambassador in Petrograd of one of the prime ministers, Boris Sturmer, was applicable to all the tsar's wartime ministers: 'Possessed of only a second-class

 **KEY FIGURES**

**Alexander Kerensky (1881–1970)**

A lawyer and leading member of the SR Party, he was to be prime minister of the Provisional Government from July until its fall in October 1917.

**Vasily Shulgin (1878–1976)**

The leader of the Progressists and an ardent monarchist.

mind, and having no experience of statesmanship, he owed his appointment to the fact that he was a friend of Rasputin and enjoyed the support of the crowd of intriguers around the empress.'

## The role of Rasputin

Gregory Efimovich Rasputin (1872–1916) was the individual on whom much of the hatred of the tsarist system came to be focused. By any measure his rise to prominence in Russia was an extraordinary story, but its true significance lay in the light it shed on the nature of tsarist government. Rasputin was a self-ordained holy man from the Russian steppes, who was notorious for his sexual depravity. (By an interesting coincidence, the word *rasputin* in Russian also means lecher.) This made him fascinating to certain women, who threw themselves at him. Many fashionable ladies in St Petersburg, including the wives of courtiers, boasted that they had slept with him. That Rasputin seldom washed or changed his clothes seemed to add to the attraction.

Rasputin's behaviour made him bitterly hated at the imperial court to which he was officially invited. Outraged husbands and officials detested this upstart from the steppes. But they could not get rid of him; he enjoyed royal favour. As early as 1907 Rasputin had gained himself a personal introduction to the tsar and his wife. The Empress Alexandra was desperate to cure her son, Alexei, the heir to the throne, of his **haemophilia**. Hearing that Rasputin had extraordinary gifts of healing, she invited him to court. Rasputin did, indeed, prove able to help Alexei, whose condition eased considerably when the ***starets*** was with him.

### KEY TERMS

**Haemophilia** A genetic condition in which the blood does not clot, leaving the sufferer with painful bruising and internal bleeding, which can be life threatening.

***Starets*** Russian for holy man, the name given to Rasputin by the impressionable peasants who believed he had superhuman powers.

***Confidant*** A person in whom another places a special trust and to whom one confides intimate secrets.

Rasputin did not, of course, have the magical or devilish powers that the more superstitious claimed for him, but he was a very good amateur psychologist. He realised that the prodding to which Alexei was invariably subjected when being examined by his doctors only made the boy more anxious and feverish. Rasputin's way was to speak calmly to him, stroking him gently so that he relaxed. This lowered Alexei's temperature and lessened his pain. It was not a cure but it was the most successful treatment he had ever had. Alexandra, a deeply religious woman, believed it was the work of God and that Rasputin was His instrument. She made the 'mad monk', as his enemies called him, her ***confidant***.

Scandal inevitably followed. Alexandra's German nationality had made her suspect and unpopular since the outbreak of war, but she had tried to ride out the storm. She would hear no ill of 'our dear friend', as she called Rasputin in letters to Nicholas, and obliged the tsar to maintain him at court. Since Nicholas was away at military headquarters for long periods after 1915, it was no great exaggeration by opponents to charge that Alexandra and Rasputin effectively became the government of Russia. Even the staunchest supporters of tsardom found it difficult to defend a system that allowed a nation in the hour of its greatest trial to fall under the sway of a debauched monk and the 'German woman', as Alexandra was disparagingly called by anti-tsarists.

Alexandra was, indeed, German, being born to the house of Hesse Darmstadt. However, after marrying Nicholas, she had made sincere efforts to make Russia her adopted country. She converted to the Orthodox Church, and endeavoured to adopt Russian customs and conventions. This counted for little after 1914, when, despite her undoubted commitment to the Russian cause, her enemies portrayed her as a German agent.

## Death of Rasputin

In December 1916, in a mixture of spite, resentment and a genuine wish to save the monarchy, a group of aristocratic conspirators murdered Rasputin. His death was as bizarre as his life. Poisoned with arsenic, shot at point-blank range, battered over the head with a steel bar, he was still alive when he was thrown, trussed in a heavy curtain, into the River Neva. His post-mortem showed that he had water in lungs, evidence that he had still been breathing when finally sucked below the icy waters.

**SOURCE E**

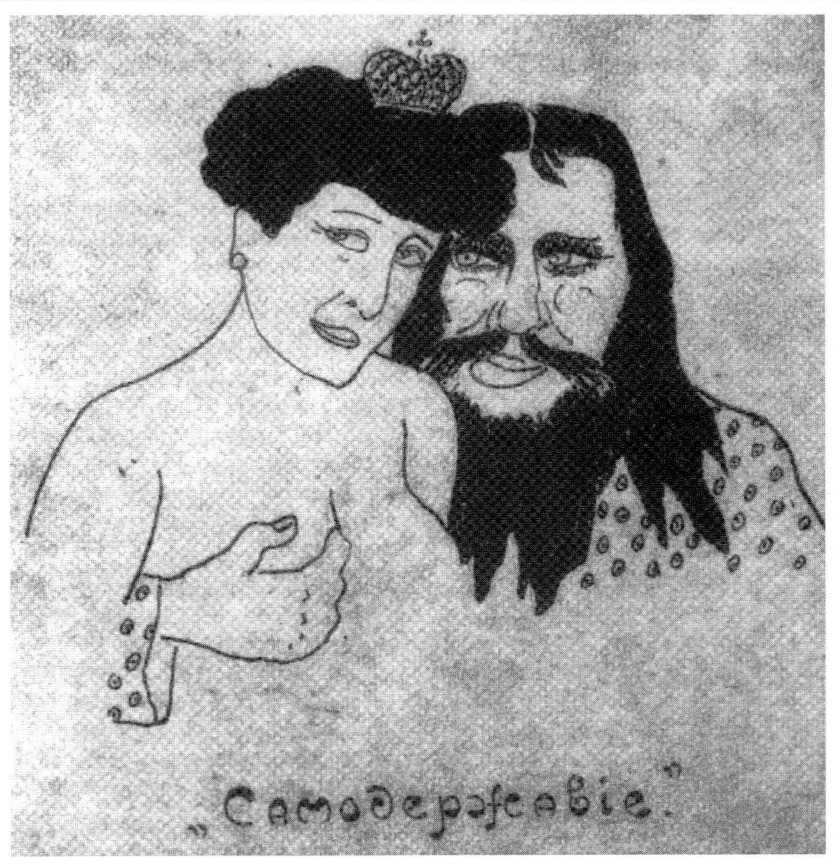


**One of the many pornographic postcards circulating in Petrograd in 1916. The word *samoderzhavie* means 'holding'. It is used here as a pun to suggest Rasputin's hold on Russia as well as on the empress. Despite this cartoon and the rumours about Rasputin and Alexandra, it is unlikely that they were ever lovers in a physical sense.**

How reliable is Source E as evidence for a historian researching the nature of the relationship between Rasputin and Alexandra?

## Rasputin's importance

From time to time there have been various attempts to present Rasputin in a more sympathetic light by drawing attention, for example, to his achievement in reorganising the army's medical supplies system. In doing this, he showed the common sense and administrative skill that Russia so desperately needed and that his aristocratic superiors in government so markedly lacked. Ironically, it was his competence rather than his supposedly corrupting influence that infuriated many of those who wanted him out of the way. Yet, no matter how much the reactionaries in the court and government might rejoice at the death of the upstart, Rasputin's extraordinary life at court and his murder by courtiers were but symptoms of the fatal disease affecting the tsarist system. The truth was that by the end of 1916 it was already too late to save tsardom. Its traditional supporters had abandoned it. This was clear from the ferocity of the *duma* denunciations of the government, as shown in Source F.

? In what ways does Source F indicate that tsardom has lost the support of its traditional supporters?

**SOURCE F**

**From a speech made by Paul Milyukov, the leader of the Kadet Party, to the fourth *duma* on 1 November 1916, quoted in G. Vernadsky, editor, *A Source Book for Russian History*, volume 3, Yale University Press, 1972, p. 870.**

*This present government has sunk beneath the level on which it stood during normal times in Russian life. And now the gulf between us and that government has grown wider and become impassable. Today we are aware that with this government we cannot legislate, and we cannot, with this government, lead Russia to victory. We are telling this government, as the declaration of the [Progressive Bloc] stated: We shall fight you, we shall fight you with all legitimate means until you go.*

*When the Duma declares again and again that the home front must be organized for a successful war and the government continues to insist that to organize the country means to organize a revolution, and consciously chooses chaos and disorganization – is this stupidity or treason? We have many reasons for being discontented with the government. But all these reasons boil down to one general one: the incompetence and evil intentions of the present government. We shall fight until we get a responsible government. Cabinet members must agree unanimously as to the most urgent tasks. They must agree and be prepared to implement the programme of the Duma majority. They must rely on this majority, not just in the implementation of this programme, but in all their actions.*

**Summary diagram: The growth of opposition to tsardom**

Rasputin and Alexandra became the focal point of the growing hatred of tsardom. The very fact of Rasputin's becoming so prominent within the tsarist system convinced many that the system was not worth saving

- The most significant opposition came from those who had been the tsar's keenest supporters in 1914
- *Duma* recalled in August 1915 but tsar not willing to co-operate with it
- Government also declined to work with patriotic non-government organisations, e.g. *Zemgor*, which called for a united national war effort
- Tsar rejected notion of working with the Progressive Bloc
- Tsar's ministers staggeringly incompetent
- Tsar's limited powers of judgement blinded him to the need to make an accommodation with his natural supporters
- Key significance of Nicholas II's character – mixture of naïvety, stubbornness and political myopia – the wrong man in the wrong time

# The February Revolution 1917

▶ *Were the events of February 1917 a revolution from below or a collapse at the top?*

In the year preceding February 1917, there had been a number of challenges to the tsar and his government. The Kadets in the *duma* had frequently demanded the removal of unwanted ministers and generals. What made February 1917 different was the range of the opposition to the government and the speed with which events turned from a protest into a revolution. Rumours of the likelihood of serious public disturbances breaking out in Petrograd had been widespread since the beginning of the year. An *Okhrana* report in January 1917 provides an illuminating summary of the situation:

**SOURCE G**

**From an *Okhrana* report, January 1917, quoted in Lionel Kochan, *Russia in Revolution*, Paladin, 1974, p. 189.**

*The mass of industrial workers are quite ready to let themselves go to the wildest excesses of a hunger riot ... The working masses, led in their actions and sympathies by the more conscious and already revolutionary-minded*

How does Source G indicate the coming together of political and economic grievances in Russia in early 1917? ?

*elements, are violently hostile to the authorities and protest with all means and devices against a continuation of the war … Thus left wing – revolutionary – circles are firmly convinced that a revolution will begin very soon, that its undoubted forerunners have already appeared and that the government will at once show itself powerless in the struggles with the revolutionary masses, who will be all the more dangerous because they consist two-thirds of present soldiers … the internal source of Russian state life is at present threatened by the unrelenting approach of a grave shock.*

On 14 February, Rodzianko, the *duma* president, warned the tsar that 'very serious outbreaks of unrest' were imminent. He added ominously, 'there is not one honest man left in your entourage; all the decent people have either been dismissed or left'. It was this desertion by those closest to the tsar that unwittingly set in motion what proved to be a revolution.

**KEY TERM**

**System of dating** Until February 1918 Russia used the Julian calendar, which was thirteen days behind the Gregorian calendar, the one used in most Western countries by this time. That is why different books may give different dates for the same event. This book uses the older dating for the events of 1917.

According to the **system of dating** in Imperial Russia, the revolution occupied the period from 18 February to 4 March 1917. A full-scale strike was started on 18 February by the employees at the Putilov steel works, the largest and most politically active factory in Petrograd. During the next five days, the Putilov strikers were joined on the streets by growing numbers of workers, who had been angered by rumours of a further cut in bread supplies. It is now known that these were merely rumours and that there was still enough bread to meet the capital's basic needs. However, in times of acute crisis rumour often has the same power as fact.

### Key steps in the February Revolution

- 18 February: strike began at the Putilov factories in Petrograd.
- 23 February: International Women's Day, a demonstration organised by socialist groups to demand female equality.
- 25 February: a general strike began.
- 26 February: desertion of Petrograd garrison.
- 27 February: breakaway members of the *Duma* formed a Provisional Committee. Petrograd soviet formed.
- 28 February: Nicholas II prevented from returning to Petrograd.
- 2 March: Provisional Committee declared itself a Provisional Government. Tsar signed abdication decree.
- 3 March: Provisional Government declared a revolution had taken place.
- 4 March: tsar's abdication publicly proclaimed.

## The course of events

It also happened that 23 February was International Women's Day. This brought thousands of women on to the streets to join the protesters in demanding food and an end to the war. By 25 February, Petrograd was paralysed by a city-wide strike. Factories were occupied and attempts by the authorities to disperse the workers were hampered by the growing sympathy among the police for the demonstrators. There was a great deal of confusion and little clear direction at the top. Events that were later seen as having had major political significance took place in an atmosphere in which political protests were indistinguishable from the general outcry against food shortages and the miseries brought by war.

## The breakdown of order

The tsar, at his military headquarters at Mogilev, 400 miles from Petrograd, relied for news largely on the letters received from the tsarina, who was still in the capital. When he learned from her about the disturbances, Nicholas ordered the commander of the Petrograd garrison, General Khabalov, to restore order. Khabalov cabled back that, with the various contingents of the police and militia either fighting each other or joining the demonstrators, and his own garrison troops disobeying orders, the situation was uncontrollable.

Khabalov had earlier begged the government to declare martial law in Petrograd, which would have given him the power to use unlimited force against the demonstrators. But the breakdown of ordinary life in the capital meant that the martial law proclamation could not even be printed, let alone enforced. More serious still, by 26 February all but a few thousand of the original 150,000 Petrograd garrison troops had deserted. Desertions also seriously depleted a battalion of troops sent from the front under General Ivanov to reinforce the garrison.

**SOURCE H**

**Some of the demonstrators at the 1917 International Women's Day. On the banner is written: 'As long as women are slaves, there will be no freedom. Long live equal rights for women'.**

What wartime conditions have led the women in Petrograd to make the protests expressed on their banners in Source H?

## Provisional Committee formed

Faced with this near-hopeless situation, Rodzianko on behalf of the *duma* informed the tsar that only a major concession on the government's part offered any hope of preserving the imperial power. Nicholas, again with that occasional stubbornness that he mistook for decisiveness, then ordered the *duma* to dissolve. It did so formally as an assembly, but a group of twelve members disobeyed the order and remained in session as a 'Provisional Committee'. This marked the first open unconstitutional defiance of the tsar. It was immediately followed by the boldest move so far, when Alexander Kerensky, a lawyer and a leading SR member in the *duma*, called for the tsar to stand down as head of state or be deposed.

### KEY FIGURE

**Alexander Shlyapnikov (1885–1937)**

Later became a Bolshevik, one of the few major revolutionaries to be in Petrograd during the February Revolution.

## Petrograd soviet formed

On the same day, 27 February, another event took place that was to prove as significant as the formation of the Provisional Committee. This was the first meeting of the 'Petrograd Soviet of Soldiers', Sailors' and Workers' Deputies', which gathered in the Tauride Palace, the same building that housed the Provisional Committee. The moving force behind the setting up of the soviet was the Mensheviks, who, under their local leader, **Alexander Shlyapnikov**, had grown in strength in Petrograd during the war.

These two self-appointed bodies – the Provisional Committee, representing the reformist elements of the old *duma*, and the Soviet, speaking for the striking workers and rebellious troops – became the ***de facto*** government of Russia. This was the beginning of what Lenin later called the **Dual Authority**, an uneasy alliance that was to last until October. On 28 February, the soviet published the first edition of its newspaper *Izvestiya* (*The News*), in which it declared its determination 'to wipe out the old system completely' and to summon a **Russian constituent assembly**, elected by **universal suffrage**.

### KEY TERMS

***De facto*** 'By the very fact' – a term used to denote the real situation, as compared to what it should or might be in theory or in law.

**Dual Authority** Lenin first coined this term to describe the balance of power between the Provisional Government and the Petrograd soviet.

**Russian constituent assembly** A full gathering of the elected representatives of the Russian people.

**Universal suffrage** An electoral system in which all adults have the right to vote.

***Stavka*** The high command of the Russian army.

## The tsar abdicates

The remaining ministers in the tsar's cabinet were not prepared to face the growing storm. They used the pretext of an electricity failure in their government offices to abandon their responsibilities and to slip out of the capital. Rodzianko, who up to this point had struggled to remain loyal to the official government, then advised Nicholas that only his personal abdication could save the Russian monarchy. On 28 February, Nicholas decided to return to Petrograd, apparently in the belief that his personal presence would have a calming effect on the capital. However, the royal train was intercepted on its journey by mutinous troops who forced it to divert to Pskov, 190 miles from Petrograd. It was at Pskov that a group of generals from ***stavka***, together with the representatives of the old *duma*, met the tsar to inform him that the seriousness of the situation in Petrograd made his return both futile and dangerous. They, too, advised abdication.

Nicholas tamely accepted the advice. His only concern was whether he should also renounce the throne on behalf of his son, Alexei. This he eventually decided to do. The decree of abdication that Nicholas signed on 2 March nominated his brother, the Grand Duke Michael, as the new tsar. However, the Grand Duke, unwilling to accept the poisoned chalice, refused the title on the pretext that it had not been offered to him by a Russian constituent assembly.

By default, the Provisional Committee, which had renamed itself the Provisional Government, thus found itself responsible for governing Russia. On 3 March, the new government officially informed the rest of the world of the revolution that had taken place. On the following day, Nicholas II's formal abdication was publicly announced. The house of Romanov, which only four years earlier in 1913 had celebrated its tricentenary as a divinely appointed dynasty, came to an end not with a bang but with a whimper.

## The role of the Bolsheviks

It would be more accurate to speak of the 'non-role'. The Bolsheviks, absent from the 1905 Revolution, were also missing when the February Revolution took place. Practically all their leaders were in exile. Lenin, who was himself in Switzerland at the time, had not been in Russia for over a decade. With so many of the leading Bolsheviks out of the country for so long before 1917, and given the difficulties of communication in wartime, their knowledge of the situation in Petrograd in 1917 was fragmentary and unreliable. It is small wonder, therefore, that the events of February took them by surprise. This is borne out by a statement of Lenin's to a group of students in Zurich in December 1916, only two months before the February Revolution. He told his audience of youthful Bolshevik sympathisers that although they might live to see the proletarian revolution, he, at the age of 46, did not expect to do so.

## The role of Petrograd

One remarkable feature of the revolution was that it had been overwhelmingly the affair of one city, Petrograd. Another was the willingness of the rest of Russia to accept it. Trotsky observed:

**SOURCE I**

**From Leon Trotsky, *The History of the Russian Revolution*, Pluto Press, 1985, p. 158.**

*It would be no exaggeration to say that Petrograd achieved the February Revolution. The rest of the country adhered to it. There was no struggle anywhere except in Petrograd. Nowhere in the country were there any groups of the population, any parties, institutions, or military units ready to put up a fight for the old regime. Neither at the front nor at the rear was there a brigade or regiment prepared to do battle for Nicholas II. The revolution was carried out upon the initiative and by the strength of one city, constituting approximately 1/75 of the population of the country.*

According to Source I, how significant does Trotsky consider Petrograd's role to have been in the February Revolution?

## The character of the February Revolution

The February Revolution was not quite the bloodless affair that some of the liberal newspapers in Petrograd claimed. Modern estimates suggest that between 1500 and 2000 people were killed or wounded in the disturbances. But, by the scale of the casualties regularly suffered by Russian armies in the war, this figure was small, which further supported Trotsky's contention that the nation was unwilling to fight to save the old regime.

It is difficult to see the events of 18 February to 3 March as an overthrow of the Russian monarchy. What does stand out is the lack of direction and leadership at the top, and the unwillingness at the moment of crisis of the tsarist generals and politicians to fight to save the system. Tsardom collapsed from within. Revolutionary pressure from outside had no direct effect. It should be re-emphasised that it was among tsardom's hitherto most committed supporters that the earliest rejection of the tsar occurred. It was the highest ranking officers who first intimated to Nicholas that he should stand down. It was the aristocratic members of the *duma* who took the lead in refusing to disband on the tsar's orders. It was when the army and the police told Nicholas that they were unable to carry out his command to keep the populace in order that his position became finally hopeless.

The strikes and demonstrations in Petrograd in February 1917 did not in themselves cause the revolution. It was the defection of the tsar's previous supporters at the moment of crisis, compounded by Nicholas II's own failure to resist, that brought about the fall of the Romanov dynasty. Lenin once observed that a true revolution can occur only when certain preconditions exist; one essential is that the ruling power loses the will to survive. Some time before he formally abdicated, Nicholas had given up the fight. It was not the fact but the speed and completeness of the collapse of tsardom in February 1917 that was so remarkable.

## The importance of the war 1914–17

What ultimately destroyed tsardom was the length of the war. A short war, even if unsuccessful, might have been bearable, as Russia's defeat by Japan twelve years earlier had shown. But the cumulative effect of a prolonged struggle proved overwhelming. The key factors were:

- 3 million deaths
- soaring inflation
- a dislocated communications system
- hunger and deprivation
- a series of increasingly bewildered and ineffectual ministries under an incompetent tsar.

These were the lot of the Russian people between 1914 and 1917. The consequence was a loss of morale and a sense of hopelessness that fatally undermined the once-potent myth of the tsar's God-given authority. By 1917, the tsarist system had forfeited its claim to the loyalty of the Russian people.

**Summary diagram: The February Revolution 1917**

**Background**

A general unrest and anger in Petrograd, but this was not led or directed

|

The revolution began as a challenge not by revolutionaries but by traditional supporters of tsardom

**Course**

Strikes in major factories

|

International Women's Day protest became a riot for bread

|

Disorder spread throughout the city

|

Police and garrison troops declared the situation uncontrollable

|

12 rebellious *duma* members created the Provisional Committee

|

Mensheviks set up the Petrograd soviet

|

Nicholas tried to return to Petrograd but was prevented by mutinous troops

|

Army high command advised tsar to abdicate

|

Nicholas tamely abdicated

|

Dual Authority became *de facto* government

**Character**

Not a revolution from below

|

Bolsheviks played no part

|

Revolution started by tsardom's traditional supporters

|

A failure of leadership and nerve at the top

|

A revolution of one city – Petrograd

|

Not the result of a social or political movement but a consequence of war

|

An institutional crisis?

# 5 Key debate

> Why was there a February Revolution?

The February Revolution was the first in a series of events in 1917 that changed the character of Russia, and impacted on the whole world. Because of its importance, its causes have been debated by historians ever since.

An appropriate starting point is the view of the Russian revolutionary, Leon Trotsky. In his classic account, *The February Revolution* (Berlin, 1931), he laid down what was to become the received Bolshevik interpretation that dominated the thinking of the Soviet Union throughout its existence. Trotsky's premise was 'that the revolution was begun from below' by workers who had been educated in revolutionary ways by Lenin and the Bolsheviks. He added, however, that while the Bolshevik teaching had guaranteed the victory of the uprising, circumstances had not allowed the Bolsheviks to lead the revolution itself at this point. That would come later.

Trotsky's view was accepted and expanded in 1935 by a pro-Soviet, American writer W.H. Chamberlin, in *The Russian Revolution 1917–1921* (1935). He described the events of February 1917 as 'leaderless and spontaneous', and stressed that 'no one, even among the revolutionary leaders, realized that the strikes and bread riots which broke out in Petrograd on February 23 would culminate in the overthrow of the government four days later'.

Another writer with basic sympathy for the Soviet Union was the celebrated British historian E.H. Carr, who also accepted Trotsky's interpretation:

**EXTRACT 1**

**From E.H. Carr, *The Bolshevik Revolution*, volume 1, Penguin, 1973, p. 81.**

*The February revolution of 1917 which overthrew the Romanov dynasty was the spontaneous outbreak of a multitude exasperated by the privations of the war and by manifest inequality in the distribution of burdens. It was welcomed and utilized by a broad stratum of the bourgeoisie and the official class, which had lost confidence in the autocratic system of government and especially in the persons of the Tsar and of his advisers; it was from this section of the population that the first Provisional Government was drawn. The revolutionary parties played no part in the making of the revolution. They did not expect it, and were at first nonplussed by it. The creation at the moment of the revolution of a Petrograd Soviet of Workers Deputies was a spontaneous act of groups of workers without central direction.*

However, George Katkov, a Russian exile and stern critic of the Soviet Union, resurrected the notion that the February Revolution, far from being a spontaneous people's rising, was the work of conspirators in the pay of German agents eager to knock Russia out of the war.

**EXTRACT 2**

**From G. Katkov, *Russia 1917: The February Revolution*, Prentice-Hall, 1967, p. 422.**

*The belief that German agents were behind it is as old as the events themselves – indeed older, for the Russian government had suspected and indeed known of the German wartime influence on the labour movement in Russia long before the Petrograd rising. We know now for certain that from the very beginning of the war the German government consistently pursued in Russia a* Revolutionierungspolitik *[a strategy aimed at creating revolution], an essential element of which was the support of an economic strike movement capable, so it was hoped, of gradually escalating into a political revolution. The German government expended considerable sums on fostering the [Russian] strike movement.*

Richard Pipes, a Polish-American scholar, whose first-hand experience of the USSR made him a formidable critic of Soviet-style history, rejects the idea that February was a revolt by a bitter, war-weary people. His contention is that Russians wanted the war not to end but to be fought more effectively until victory was gained. What ultimately doomed the tsar was his abandonment by Russia's military and political establishment.

**EXTRACT 3**

**From R. Pipes, *Three Whys of the Russian Revolution*, Pimlico, 1998, pp. 28–9.**

*Having studied in minute detail the massive information regarding the steps leading up to the abdication of Nicholas II, I have not the slightest doubt that he faced no popular pressures to abdicate; the pressure stemmed exclusively from the ranks of politicians and generals who thought the Crown's removal essential to victory. The fact that the tsar's abdication had the opposite effect of that intended tells nothing of his motives in so doing.*

*[The tsar's] power, however dazzling its external glitter, was internally weak and quite unable to cope effectively with the strains – political, economic, and psychological – which the war brought in its wake. In my opinion, the principal causes of the downfall in 1917 were political and not economic or social … In 1917, you had intellectuals gathered in political parties that had well formulated programs for drastic change.*

Australian historian David Christian also accepts that the role of the established class around the tsar was highly significant, but he regards Nicholas II's lack of political judgement as being the decisive factor. He writes, 'The February Revolution could have been avoided. There remained, even in 1916, a willingness within the upper classes to rally around the tsar, if only he could bring himself to create a genuinely constitutional government.' But 'by February 1917, he had alienated the only groups in the empire who might have been able to rescue him'.

While not dismissing the importance of individuals and groups in the events of February 1917, many historians now interpret the rising as the climax of an 'institutional crisis' in Russia. They suggest that what produced the 1917 crisis in Russia was the failure of its *institutions*, that is, its political, social and economic systems, to cope with the problems it faced. Norman Stone is a leading proponent of this concept. His essential argument is that Russia's institutions were too undeveloped to cope with the problems which Russia's attempts to modernise had brought. This was made evident by the war of 1914–17, which created economic chaos. 'But', Stone adds, 'economic backwardness did not alone make for revolution. The economic chaos came more from a contest between the old and the new in the Russian economy. There was a crisis, not of decline but rather of growth.'

It was an outstanding feature of the major wars of the twentieth century that they put immense pressures on the nations that fought them. The war that Russia entered in 1914 intensified all the problems from which it had traditionally suffered. Russia's institutional crisis showed up the tsarist system as being politically as well as economically bankrupt. While this line of thought does not absolve the tsar and his ministers from all responsibility for the collapse of Imperial Russia, it does lessen their blame. If the institutions of which they were a part were inadequate to meet the challenges, then no matter what efforts they might have had made, the problems would have overwhelmed them.

? How do the historians quoted in Extracts 1–3 or referred to above differ in their explanation of the February Revolution?

## Chapter summary

Tsar Nicholas II had never been more revered than when Russia went to war on 1 August 1914. As the embodiment of Russian pride, the nation was behind him. But, within three years, all the goodwill had dissipated. By taking personal command of the Russian armies, he tied his dynasty's fate to the outcome of the war. Poorly led and equipped, his troops fought valiantly but unavailingly. A barely broken series of military defeats created deep disillusion to add to the privations of wartime. The tsar's political incompetence was even more marked than his military shortcomings. He appeared to let government slip into the hands of his unpopular German wife and her confidant, Rasputin, a lascivious upstart whom the court detested.

Unwilling to extend authority to the Progressive Bloc, Nicholas continued to rely on blundering ministers. The result was that when serious disorder occurred in Petrograd early in 1917, he had no one to whom he could turn. His officials and his high command advised him that abdication was the only way of preventing civil war. He duly abdicated, to be succeeded by a Dual Authority composed of the Provisional Government and the Petrograd soviet. The causes of these events have become the subject of continuous historical debate.

## Refresher questions

Use these questions to remind yourself of the key material covered in this chapter.

1. What circumstances led Russia into war in 1914?
2. How did Russia respond to the demands of war?
3. How was Russia's financial position damaged by the war?
4. How did the war disrupt the supply of food?
5. Why did the Russian transport system prove inadequate in wartime?
6. How well did the organisation of the Russian army adapt to the needs of war?
7. How did Nicholas respond to the war?
8. Why did Rasputin prove such an influential figure in the build-up to revolution?
9. What led to the emergence of the Dual Authority?
10. Were the events of February 1917 a collapse at the top or a revolution from below?

## Question practice

### ESSAY QUESTIONS

1. 'The tsar's decision in 1915 to become commander-in-chief of the Russian armies was a mistake from which he never recovered.' How far do you agree with this statement?
2. To what extent was the growth of opposition in the fourth *duma* the result of Nicholas II's policies and actions?
3. Which of the following was the greater threat to the tsarist government by 1917? i) Opposition in the *duma*. ii) Social unrest in Petrograd. Explain your answer with reference to both i) and ii).
4. How far was Rasputin responsible for the unpopularity of the tsarist government by the end of 1916?
5. 'The tsarist government was not overthrown in February 1917; it collapsed from within.' How far do you agree with this statement?

# 1917: From Provisional Government to October Revolution

The February Revolution was followed by an eight-month period in which the Provisional Government, initially in co-operation with the Petrograd soviet, struggled to resolve Russia's major problems. Led by Lenin, the Bolsheviks strove to exploit the government's difficulties. After a thwarted attempt to seize power in July, they were again in a position in October to challenge for power. Kerensky's government, deprived of support, caved in and fled. Carried to power in this bloodless way, Lenin proceeded to claim authority in the name of the soviets and establish a Bolshevik government. This chapter examines these developments under the following themes:

- ☆ The Dual Authority
- ☆ The return of the Bolsheviks
- ☆ The Provisional Government and its problems
- ☆ The October Revolution
- ☆ Reasons for the Bolshevik success

The key debate on *page 123* of this chapter asks the question: What was the true character of the October Revolution?

## Key dates

| | | |
|---|---|---|
| **1917** | **March 1** | Petrograd soviet issued Order No. 1 |
| | **March 2** | Provisional Government claimed authority |
| | **April 3** | Lenin returned to Petrograd |
| | **April 4** | Lenin issued his *April Theses* |
| | **July 3–6** | Failure of the Bolshevik 'July Days' uprising |
| | **July 8** | Kerensky became prime minister |
| | **Sept. 1** | Kornilov's abortive march on Petrograd |
| | **Sept. 25** | Bolsheviks gained majority in Petrograd soviet |
| **1917** | **Oct. 9** | Petrograd soviet set up Military Revolutionary Committee |
| | **Oct. 24–25** | Bolsheviks took control of Petrograd |
| | **Oct. 25–26** | Kerensky fled from Petrograd |
| | **Oct. 26** | Bolsheviks established *Sovnarkom*, with Lenin as chairman |
| | **Oct. 27** | Lenin informed the Congress of Soviets that the Bolsheviks had taken power in their name |

# 1 The Dual Authority

*What were the basic weaknesses of the Provisional Government?*

**KEY FIGURE**

**Prince Lvov (1861–1925)**

A prominent landowner and progressive reformer, he headed the Provisional Government from March to July 1917.

The Provisional Government, led by **Prince Lvov**, which picked up the reins of authority after the tsar's abdication (see page 88), was really the old *duma* in a new form. When, on 2 March, Paul Milyukov, the foreign minister, read out the list of ministers in the newly-formed government someone in the listening crowd called out, 'Who appointed you lot, then?' Milyukov replied, 'We were appointed by the Revolution itself.' In that exchange were expressed the two crippling weaknesses of the Provisional Government throughout the eight months of its existence:

- It was not an elected body, having come into being as a rebellious committee of the old *duma*, refusing to disband at the tsar's order. As a consequence, it lacked legitimate authority and had no constitutional claim on the loyalty of the Russian people. Lacking this, it would be judged entirely on how well it dealt with the nation's problems.
- Its authority was limited by its unofficial partnership with the Petrograd soviet.

## Role of the Petrograd soviet

The soviet did not set out initially to be an alternative government. It regarded its role as supervisory, checking that the interests of the soldiers and workers were fully understood by the new government. However, in the uncertain times that followed the February Revolution, the Provisional Government often seemed unsure of its own authority. This uncertainty tended to give the soviet greater prominence.

In addition, there was the impressive fact that in the aftermath of the February Revolution, soviets were rapidly set up in all the major cities and towns of Russia. Yet, although the soviets were to play an increasingly important role in the development of the revolution, in the early stages the Bolsheviks did not dominate them. The soviets were not, therefore, necessarily opposed to the Provisional Government. Indeed, at first, there was considerable co-operation between them. Some individuals were members of both bodies. For example, Alexander Kerensky, the SR leader, was for a time chairman of the soviet as well as a minister in the Provisional Government.

It was significant, however, that even before the Bolshevik influence became dominant, the ability of the Petrograd soviet to restrict the Provisional Government's authority had been clearly revealed. On 1 March, in one of its first moves as an organisation, it had issued its 'Soviet Order Number 1', which declared that, in military matters, the orders of the Provisional Government were to be obeyed 'only when they do not contradict the orders and decrees of the soviet'.

**SOURCE A**

**An overflowing meeting of the Petrograd soviet in March 1917. Huge numbers of soldiers and workers, sometimes as many 3000, attended the early meetings. By the autumn, this had dropped to a few hundred but the Bolsheviks kept up their numbers, which gave them a disproportionate influence in the soviet.**

? Study Source A. Why was the presence of the Bolsheviks in Petrograd soviet meetings so politically important between March and October 1917?

## Importance of Soviet Order Number 1

The order meant that the decrees of the Provisional Government were not binding unless they were approved by the Petrograd soviet. History shows that unless a government has control of its army it does not hold real power. Order Number 1 made it clear that the Provisional Government did not have such power. It had, therefore, to compromise with the soviet. Between February and April 1917 this arrangement worked reasonably well; there were no serious disputes between the two bodies in the 'Dual Authority'.

## Early political co-operation

An important factor promoting co-operation was the widespread elation in Petrograd in the weeks following the February Revolution. Excitement was in the air; people on the streets greeted each other with enthusiasm as if a new era had dawned. This encouraged a genuine feeling across all the political groups that Russia had entered a period of real freedom. For a time, co-operation between opposing parties became much easier to achieve.

**KEY TERMS**

**Anarchy** Absence of government or authority, leading to disorder.

**Monarchists** Reactionaries who wanted a restoration of tsardom.

**People's militia** A new set of volunteer law-enforcement officers drawn from ordinary civilians.

There was also a general acceptance that the new liberty that had come with the collapse of tsardom should not be allowed to slip into **anarchy**. This created a willingness to maintain state authority at the centre of affairs. Furthermore, at the beginning, both the Provisional Government and the Petrograd soviet contained a wide range of political representation. In the first meetings of the soviet, moderates had a bigger influence than the SRs or SDs. In addition, all parties, apart from the Bolsheviks and the **monarchists**, were represented in the Provisional Government during its early weeks. As the year wore on and the problems mounted, the Provisional Government moved increasingly to the right and the soviet to the left. But before that shift occurred there had been considerable harmony.

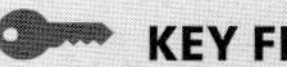

**KEY FIGURE**

**Nicolai Sukhanov (1882–1940)**

An SD activist who wrote an insider's account of 1917; he was tried under Stalin and shot in 1940.

A further fact was that Bolsheviks were not yet in a position to influence matters, while the other main socialist parties, the SRs and the Mensheviks, were reluctant to demand too much, too soon. They judged that their international isolation limited how far they could go and that they had to rely on the administrators from the old regime. **Nicolai Sukhanov**, a leading Menshevik member of the Petrograd soviet, later defined this attitude: 'the soviet democracy had to entrust the power to the propertied classes, its class enemy, without whose participation it could not now master the technique of administration in the desperate conditions of disintegration'.

## Early achievements of the Provisional Government

The fruits of the early harmony between the soviet and the government were shown in a set of progressive measures adopted by the Provisional Government. These included:

- amnesty for political prisoners
- legal recognition of trade unions
- an eight-hour day for industrial workers
- replacement of the tsarist police with a **people's militia**
- granting of full civil and religious freedoms
- preparations for the election of a constituent assembly.

Noticeably, however, these changes did not touch on the critical issues of the war and the land. It would be these that would destroy the always tenuous partnership of the Dual Authority, and it would be Lenin who would begin the process of destruction.

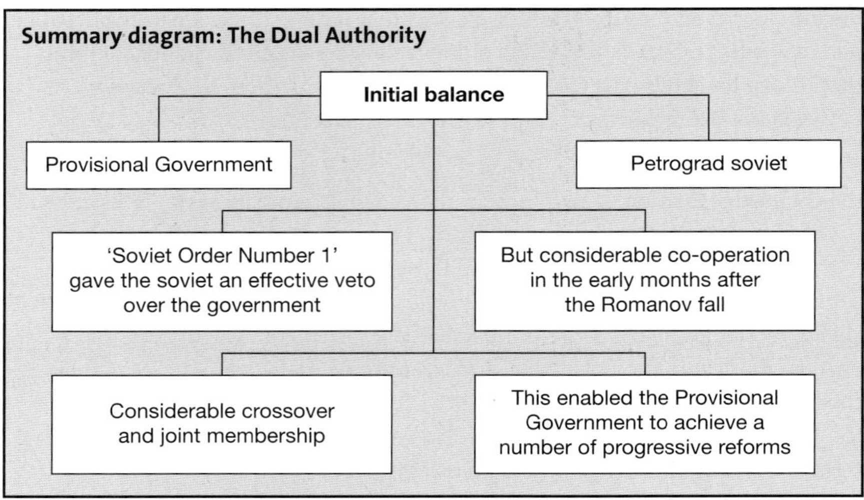
Summary diagram: The Dual Authority
Initial balance
Provisional Government
Petrograd soviet
'Soviet Order Number 1' gave the soviet an effective veto over the government
But considerable co-operation in the early months after the Romanov fall
Considerable crossover and joint membership
This enabled the Provisional Government to achieve a number of progressive reforms

# 2 The return of the Bolsheviks

▶ *What impact did Lenin's return have on the situation in Petrograd?*

## The impact of Stalin and Kamenev

KEY FIGURE

**Lev Kamenev (1883–1936)**

Returned from Siberian exile to hold various key positions under Lenin between 1917 and 1924; he became a victim of Stalin's purges and was executed in 1936.

Once the exiled Bolsheviks learned of Nicholas II's abdication, they rushed back to Petrograd. Those, like Stalin, who had been in Siberia were the first to return in March. Stalin's return was significant. Because of their standing in the party, he and his fellow returnee, **Lev Kamenev**, became the leading voices among the Petrograd Bolsheviks. Initially, this duo took an anti-Lenin line. Lenin, who did not reach Petrograd until nearly a month later, still tried to direct things from exile. In his 'Letters from Afar', he urged that the war Russia was fighting should be turned into a class war; Bolsheviks should infiltrate the armies of the warring nations and encourage the soldiers to turn their weapons against their officers as the first move towards overthrowing their governments. Lenin also instructed the Bolsheviks not to co-operate with the Provisional Government or with the other parties.

Stalin and Kamenev ignored Lenin's instructions. On the war issue, they argued that the best policy was to press for international negotiations to be started. Stalin wrote to the Bolsheviks in Petrograd, telling them to 'put pressure on the Provisional Government to announce its willingness to start peace talks at once'. On the question of the Bolsheviks' relations with the Provisional Government, Kamenev insisted that circumstances made co-operation with it essential, at least for the time being, since the government was 'genuinely struggling against the remnants of the old regime'.

As to the other parties, Kamenev believed co-operation with them made perfect sense. He backed a proposal that it was 'possible and desirable' for the Bolsheviks to restore links with the Mensheviks. Clearly at this juncture, there was a wide divergence of view between Lenin and the other two men. Interestingly, Kamenev appears to have been the major partner in his relations with Stalin, who later admitted that, in the period before Lenin arrived, Kamenev dominated Bolshevik discussions in Petrograd. What Kamenev was advancing and what Stalin went along with was what is often referred to as **accommodationism**. It was an approach that Lenin would totally reject once he was back in Petrograd.

KEY TERM

**Accommodationism**
The idea that the Bolsheviks should co-operate with the Provisional Government and work with the other revolutionary and reforming parties.

## Lenin's return in April 1917

Lenin arrived in Petrograd on 3 April. The manner of his return from Switzerland was a remarkable story in itself. His wife, Krupskaya, recorded it:

**SOURCE B**

**From K.K. Krupskaya, *Reminiscences of Lenin*, Lawrence & Wishart, 1959, pp. 336–67**

*The moment the news of the February Revolution was received, Ilyich [Lenin] was all eagerness to get back to Russia. As there were no legal ways of travelling, illegal ways would have to be used. But what ways? From the moment the news of the Revolution was received, Ilyich had no sleep. His nights were spent building the most improbable plans. Naturally the Germans gave us permission to travel through Germany in the belief that Revolution was a disaster to a country, and that by allowing emigrant internationalists [Russian revolutionaries in exile] to return to their country they were helping to spread the Revolution in Russia. The Bolsheviks, for their part, considered it their duty to bring about a victorious proletarian revolution. They did not care what the German bourgeois government thought about it.*

According to Krupskaya in Source B, in what way did the attitudes of the Bolsheviks and the Germans coincide?

Krupskaya's account is instructive. In the hope that the tsar's fall would be the prelude to the collapse of the Russian armies, the German government arranged for Lenin to return to Russia in a sealed train across occupied Europe. British historian Norman Stone waggishly referred to it as 'the first no-smoking train in history', Lenin being a fanatical anti-smoker.

Since the outbreak of war in 1914, Lenin's opponents had continually accused him of being in the pay of the German government. Their charge had weight. Between 1914 and 1917, the German Foreign Office gave regular financial support to Lenin and the Bolsheviks, in the hope that if they achieved their revolutionary aims they would pull Russia out of the war. As Krupskaya observed, Lenin did not really care what the attitude of the Germans was. It just so happened that, for quite different reasons, what they wanted – the withdrawal of the Russian armies from the war – was precisely what he wanted. However, it made no difference to anti-Bolsheviks that the German reasons were military and Lenin's were political. They considered the German government and the Bolshevik Party to be co-operating in a common cause, the defeat of Russia.

## Lenin's impact

There is no doubting the great significance of Lenin's return to Petrograd in April 1917. A German official likened it to the transporting of a deadly virus in a test-tube. Once safely arrived in Russia, the test-tube was broken, releasing the lethal germ to infect the Russian body politic. It was an apt simile. Up to the time of Lenin's arrival, the Bolsheviks, led by Kamenev and Stalin, had accepted the formation of the Dual Authority as part of a genuine revolution. They had been willing to work with the other reformist parties. Lenin changed all that. In his speech on his arrival at Petrograd's Finland Station on 3 April, he declared that the events of February, far from giving Russia political freedom, had created a **parliamentary-bourgeois republic**. He condemned the Provisional Government and called for its overthrow in a genuine revolution.

**KEY TERM**

**Parliamentary-bourgeois republic** Lenin's contemptuous term for the Provisional Government, which he dismissed as an unrepresentative mockery that had simply replaced the rule of the tsar with the rule of the reactionary *duma*.

## The *April Theses*

The following day Lenin issued his *April Theses*, in which he spelt out future Bolshevik policy. To the bewilderment of those Bolsheviks who had been in Petrograd since February and expected to be congratulated for their efforts in working with the other revolutionary groups, Lenin condemned all that had happened since the fall of the tsar. He insisted that, since the Bolsheviks were the only truly revolutionary proletarian party, they must:

- abandon co-operation with all other parties
- work for a true revolution entirely by their own efforts
- overthrow the Provisional Government, which was simply the old, class-ridden *duma* in a new garb
- struggle, not to extend freedom to all classes, but to transfer power to the workers
- demand that authority pass to the soviets.

Lenin had ulterior motives in demanding the soviets take over government. Although he rejected much of what the soviets had done, he saw them as a power base. Circumstances had made them an essential part of the structure of post-tsarist government. Lenin calculated that the soviets – the Petrograd soviet in particular – offered his small Bolshevik Party the means by which it could obtain power in the name of the **proletariat**. By infiltrating and dominating the soviets, the Bolshevik Party would be in a position to take over the state.

The essence of Lenin's argument was summed up in two provocative Bolshevik slogans that he coined: 'Peace, Bread and Land' and 'All Power to the Soviets'.

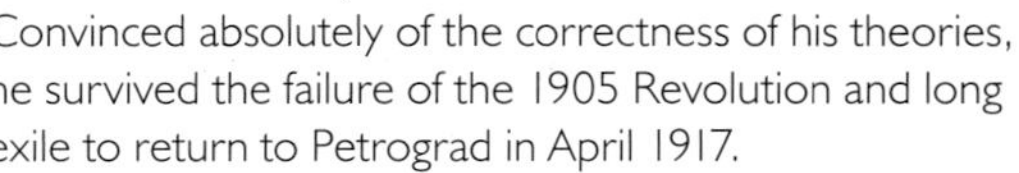

## V.I. Lenin

| | |
|---|---|
| 1870 | Lenin born, as Vladimir Ilyich Ulyanov, to a minor aristocratic family of Jewish ancestry |
| 1897 | Exiled to Siberia, took the alias Lenin |
| 1900 | Joined the SD Party |
| 1903 | Led the Bolshevik breakaway movement in the SDs |
| 1906–17 | In exile abroad |
| 1917 | Returned to Petrograd to lead the Bolsheviks in the October Revolution |
| 1917–22 | Led the Bolsheviks in consolidating their hold on Russia |
| 1921 | Introduced the New Economic Policy |
| 1924 | Died after being incapacitated for two years by strokes |

A natural contrarian, Lenin was confirmed in his hatred of tsardom by the execution of his brother in 1887 for an attempted assassination of the tsar. On the authorities' list of 'dangerous persons' from the age of seventeen, Lenin became a powerful revolutionary writer. In 1903, he led the Bolsheviks in a breakaway movement from the Marxist SD Party which he had joined five years earlier.

Lenin's greatest single achievement as a revolutionary was to reshape Marxist theory to make it fit Russian conditions. The instrument that he chose for this was the Bolshevik Party. Because the party was the vehicle of historical change, its role was not to win large-scale backing, but to direct the revolution from above, regardless of the scale of popular support. 'No revolution', Lenin wrote, 'ever waits for formal majorities'. Convinced absolutely of the correctness of his theories, he survived the failure of the 1905 Revolution and long exile to return to Petrograd in April 1917.

After a desperate six months of preparation, during which the Bolsheviks were almost destroyed, Lenin was the inspiration behind the successful coup in October which saw his party take power from the ineffectual Provisional Government.

Over the next five years, Lenin, against great odds, proceeded to create a new Soviet state, overcoming his internal opponents in a savage civil war and resisting the attempts of a number of foreign powers to crush Bolshevism. He showed ruthless determination in transforming Russia into a Communist state. Thwarted in his plans to develop a socialist economy, Lenin was forced to return to capitalist methods in his New Economic Policy (NEP) in 1921. Already weakened by an attempt on his life in 1918, he suffered a number of strokes which, from 1922, left him increasingly incapable of direct government. Having given no clear indication as to who should follow him as leader, he left the way open for a power struggle over the succession. At his death in 1924, Lenin bequeathed the Soviet state a legacy of totalitarianism, economic experimentation and Soviet hostility towards the outside world.

But these were more than slogans. They were Lenin's way of presenting in simple, dramatic headings the basic problems confronting Russia:

- 'peace' – the continuing war with Germany
- 'bread' – the chronic food shortage
- 'land' – the disruption in the countryside.

Lenin asserted that as long as the Provisional Government stayed in power these problems could not be solved because the ministers governed only in the interests of their own class. They had no wish to end the war, which brought them profits, or supply food to the Russian people, whom they despised, or reform the land-holding system, which guaranteed their property rights and privileges. That is why Lenin demanded 'All Power to the Soviets'. The current ministers must be swept aside and replaced with a government of the soviets. Only then would the people's needs be addressed.

Lenin's analysis was shrewd and prophetic; the Provisional Government's failure to deal with the three principal issues he had identified would lead to its eventual downfall.

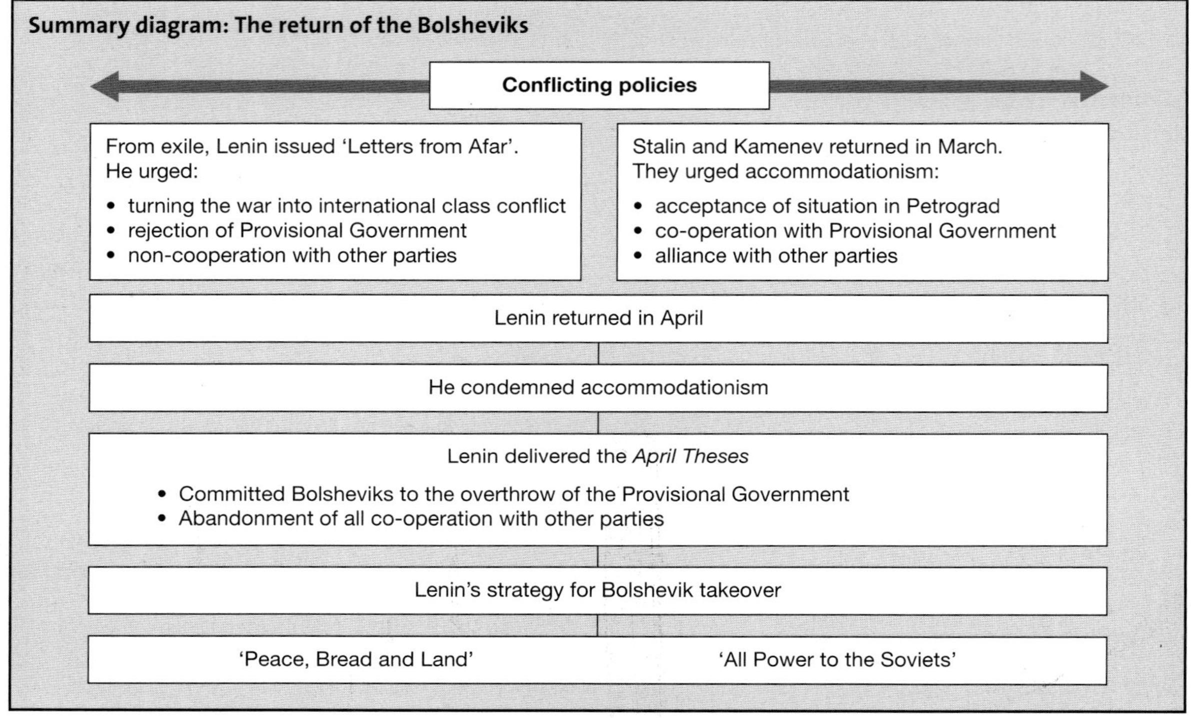

Summary diagram: The return of the Bolsheviks
Conflicting policies
From exile, Lenin issued 'Letters from Afar'. He urged:
• turning the war into international class conflict
• rejection of Provisional Government
• non-cooperation with other parties
Stalin and Kamenev returned in March. They urged accommodationism:
• acceptance of situation in Petrograd
• co-operation with Provisional Government
• alliance with other parties
Lenin returned in April
He condemned accommodationism
Lenin delivered the *April Theses*
• Committed Bolsheviks to the overthrow of the Provisional Government
• Abandonment of all co-operation with other parties
Lenin's strategy for Bolshevik takeover
'Peace, Bread and Land'
'All Power to the Soviets'

# 3 The Provisional Government and its problems

▶ *What particular difficulties beset the Provisional Government?*

From the outset, the Provisional Government was confronted by a set of daunting problems: the war, financial difficulties, food shortages and ministerial crises.

**KEY TERM**

**War-credits** Money loaned on easy repayment terms to Russia to finance its war effort.

## The war

The most persistent problem was the war. For the Provisional Government after February 1917 there was no choice but to fight on. The reason was not idealistic but financial. Unless it did so, it would no longer receive the supplies and **war-credits** from the Western allies on which it had come to rely. Tsardom had left Russia virtually bankrupt. No government could have carried on without large injections of capital from abroad. Foreign bankers were among the first to visit Russia after Nicholas's abdication to ensure that the new regime would carry on the war.

The strain that this obligation imposed on the Provisional Government finally proved unsustainable. Its preoccupation with the war prevented it from dealing with Russia's social and economic problems. This was a paradox: in order to survive, the Provisional Government had to keep Russia in the war, but in doing so it destroyed its own chances of survival.

## Ministerial crisis

The question of the war brought about the first serious rift between the Petrograd soviet and the Provisional Government. On 14 March, the soviet had issued an 'Address to the people of the whole world', calling for 'peace without annexations or **indemnities**'. The government declared that it accepted the address, but this appeared meaningless when it became known that Milyukov, the foreign minister, had made a pledge to the Allies that Russia would fight on until Germany was defeated.

**Indemnities** Payment of war costs demanded by the victors from the defeated.

Late in April, a series of violent demonstrations occurred in Petrograd, directed against Milyukov. These produced a ministerial crisis. Milyukov and Alexander Guchkov, the war minister, resigned early in May. These resignations were an illustration of the divisions within the government as well as of the outside pressures it faced. In the reshuffled cabinet, Alexander Kerensky become the war minister and places were found for leading Mensheviks and SRs.

It was hoped that this apparent leftward shift of the Provisional Government would ease its relationship with the soviet. But the opposite happened. The socialists in the government tended to become isolated from the soviet. This was because in joining the government they had to enter into coalition with the Kadets, which opened them to the charge that they were compromising with the bourgeoisie. Lenin wrote of 'those despicable socialists who have sold out to the government'.

## Emergence of Kerensky

Some individuals within the Provisional Government had misgivings about continuing the war, but at no time did the government as a body contemplate withdrawing from it. This would have mattered less had the Russian armies been successful, but the military situation continued to deteriorate, eroding the support the government had initially enjoyed.

Lvov stayed as nominal head of the government but it was Kerensky who became the major influence. As war minister, he campaigned for Russia to embrace the conflict with Germany as a crusade to save the revolution, requiring the total dedication of the nation. He made a number of personal visits to the front to deliver passionate speeches to the troops, appealing to them to be prepared to lay down their lives for Russia. 'Forward to the battle for freedom. I summon you not to a feast but death.'

### Government troubles increase

The attempt to turn the war into a national crusade took no account of the real situation. The truth was that Russia had gone beyond the point where it could fight a successful war. Yet Kerensky persisted. In June, a major offensive was launched on the south-western front. It failed badly. With their already low morale further weakened by Bolshevik agitators who encouraged them to disobey orders, the Russian forces were no match for the Austrians, who easily repulsed them and inflicted heavy losses. Whole Russian regiments mutinied or deserted. **General Kornilov**, the commander on the south-western front, called on the Provisional Government to halt the offensive and direct its energies to crushing the 'political subversives' at home, by which he meant the SDs and SRs. This appeal for a tougher policy was taken up by the government. On 8 July, Lvov stood down as prime minister, to be replaced by Kerensky. Kornilov became commander-in-chief.

**KEY FIGURE**

**General Kornilov (1870–1918)**

Distinguished by his bravery as a soldier, he was a fierce patriot who hated Russia's revolutionaries.

### Kronstadt

The government's troubles were deepened by events on the island of Kronstadt, the naval base situated fifteen miles west of Petrograd in the Bay of Finland. Sailors and workers there defied the central authorities by setting up their own separate government. Such developments tempted a number of revolutionaries in Petrograd into thinking that the opportunity had come for them to bring down the Provisional Government. The attempt to do so became known as the 'July Days'.

## The 'July Days': 3–6 July 1917

By the summer of 1917 a number of developments suggested that the government was no longer in full control of events. The most threatening were:

- the spread of soviets
- worker control of the factories
- widespread seizure of land by the peasants
- internal government disputes.

### Crisis in Ukraine

An especially pressing problem was that a number of Russia's ethnic peoples had exploited the Provisional Government's difficulties by setting up their own national minority governments and claiming independence of central control.

The most notable example of a breakaway national minority government was Ukraine. It was this that helped to provoke the July Days' crisis. Ukraine, in southern Russia, contained the largest number of non-Russian people (23 million) in the empire. It was also the nation's largest food-producing region and, therefore, vital to the Russian state. When the Kadet ministers in the government learned in late June that a Provisional Government deputation had offered independence to Ukraine, they resigned, protesting that only an all-Russian constituent assembly could properly decide such matters.

## Failure of the July Days

The ministerial clash over Ukraine coincided with large-scale street demonstrations in Petrograd. Public protests were not uncommon; they had been almost a daily occurrence since February. But, in the atmosphere created by the news of the failure of the south-western offensive and the government's mounting problems, the demonstrations of 3–6 July turned into a direct challenge to the Provisional Government.

It is not entirely clear who started the July Days. A month before, at the first **All-Russian Congress of Soviets**, Lenin had declared that the Bolshevik Party was ready to take power, but the delegates had regarded this as a general intention rather than a specific plan. There were also a number of SRs and other non-Bolshevik revolutionaries in the soviet who, for some time, had been demanding that the Petrograd soviet take over from the Provisional Government. The July Days' uprising itself was a confused, disorderly affair. In the course of the three days the demonstrators fell out amongst themselves; those members of the soviet who seemed reluctant to make a real bid for power were physically attacked. The disunity made it relatively easy for the Provisional Government to crush the rising. Troops loyal to the government were rushed from the front. They duly scattered the demonstrators and restored order.

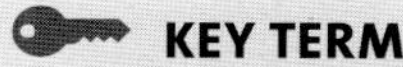
KEY TERM

**All-Russian Congress of Soviets** A gathering of representatives from all the soviets formed in Russia since February.

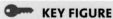

Trotsky later referred to the July Days as a 'semi-insurrection', and argued that it had been started by the Mensheviks and SRs. In saying this, he was trying to absolve the Bolsheviks from the blame of having begun a rising that failed. The explanation offered afterwards by the Bolsheviks was that they had come heroically to the aid of the workers of Petrograd and their comrades-in-arms, the sailors of Kronstadt, who had risen spontaneously against the government. The opposite point of view was put at the time by **Nikolai Chkheidze**, who argued that the Bolsheviks, having been behind the rising from the beginning, later tried to disclaim responsibility for its failure.

KEY FIGURE

**Nikolai Chkheidze (1864–1926)**

The Menshevik chairman of the Petrograd soviet.

## The consequences of the July Days

While the origins of the July Days may have been uncertain, the results were not. The failed uprising revealed a number of important facts:

- The opposition movement was disunited.
- The Bolsheviks were still far from being the dominant revolutionary party.
- The Provisional Government still had sufficient strength to put down an armed insurrection.

This last revelation did much to raise the spirits of the Provisional Government and brought particular credit to Kerensky as war minister. On 8 July, two days after the rising had been crushed, he became prime minister. He immediately put the Bolsheviks under pressure. *Pravda* was closed down and many of the Bolshevik leaders, including Trotsky and Kamenev, were arrested. Lenin fled to Finland. Kerensky also launched a propaganda campaign in which Lenin and his party were branded as traitors and agents in the pay of the German high command. A fortnight after the July Days, the Bolshevik Party appeared to have been broken as a political force in Russia. What enabled the Bolsheviks to survive, as the next two sections show, were the critical misjudgements by the Provisional Government over the land question and the Kornilov affair.

**SOURCE C**

? What evidence does Source C provide regarding the Provisional Government's response to the July Days?

**Anti-government protesters scattering under rifle-fire during the suppression of the July Days.**

**SOURCE D**

? Why did Lenin regard it necessary to disguise himself, as shown in Source D?

**Photo of Lenin, clean-shaven and bewigged, in hiding in Petrograd in 1917. Throughout the period April–October 1917, Lenin went in constant fear of being arrested and executed by the Provisional Government. He adopted various disguises, kept continually on the move and frequently fled to Finland. Yet, oddly, as Kerensky later regretfully admitted, the authorities made little concerted effort to capture their chief opponent. This raises the interesting question of whether Lenin exaggerated, or the government underestimated, his powers of disruption.**

## The land question

The Provisional Government had misread the public attitude towards the war. It similarly failed to appreciate the common view on the land question. Land shortage was a chronic problem in Russia. It had been a chief cause of peasant unrest since the emancipation of the serfs in 1861 (see page 7). The February Revolution had led the peasants to believe that they would soon benefit from a major land redistribution which the government would introduce after taking over the landowners' estates. When the government made no such moves, the peasants in many parts of Russia took the law into their own hands and seized the property of local landlords. Disturbances in the countryside occurred daily throughout 1917 in what amounted to a national peasants' revolt.

The Provisional Government had no real answer to the land problem. While it was true that it had set up a Land Commission with the ultimate aim of redistributing land, this body made little progress in handling a massive task. It was doubtful, moreover, whether the government's heart was ever really in land reform. The majority of its members came from the landed and propertied classes. They were unlikely to be enthusiasts for a policy that would threaten their own interests. They had supported the February Revolution as a political change, not as a social upheaval. They were quite willing for the estates of the fallen monarchy to go to the peasants, but they had no intention of losing their own possessions in a state land grab. This had been the strength of Lenin's assertion in the *April Theses* that tsardom had been replaced not by a revolutionary but by a bourgeois regime.

### The Bolshevik position on the land question

Interestingly, the land issue was equally difficult for the Bolsheviks. They simply did not have a land policy. As a Marxist party, they had dismissed the peasantry as, in Trotsky's words, 'the pack horse' of history, lacking true revolutionary initiative. By definition, the proletarian revolution was an affair of the industrial working class. Lenin, on his return in April, had declared that it would be pointless for the Bolsheviks, the party of the workers, to make an alliance with the backward peasantry. However, faced with the fact of peasant land seizures throughout Russia, Lenin was quite prepared to make a tactical adjustment. Appreciating that it was impossible to ignore the disruptive behaviour of four-fifths of the Russian population, he asserted that the special circumstances of post-tsarist Russia had produced a situation in which the peasants were acting as a truly revolutionary force. This adaptation of Marxist theory thus allowed Lenin to add the Russian peasants to the proletarian cause.

Lacking a land policy of his own, Lenin simply stole one from the SRs. 'Land to the Peasants', a slogan lifted straight from the SR programme, became the new Bolshevik catchphrase. What this meant in mid-1917 was that the Bolsheviks

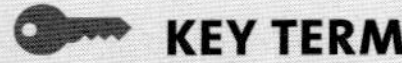

**KEY TERM**

**Left SRs** Social revolutionaries who sided with the Bolsheviks in their recognition of the legitimacy of the peasant land seizures and in their demand that Russia withdraw from the war.

recognised the peasant land seizures as perfectly legitimate. This produced a considerable swing to the Bolsheviks in the countryside. It had the further effect of splitting the SRs, a significant number of whom began to align themselves with the Bolsheviks. Known as **Left SRs**, they sided with the Bolshevik Party on all major issues.

## The Kornilov affair

In August 1917, Kerensky's government became involved in the Kornilov affair, a crisis that undermined the gains it had made from its handling of the July Days, and allowed the Bolsheviks to recover from their humiliation. Parts of the story have been obscured by the conflicting descriptions later given by some of the participants, but there was little doubt as to the intentions of the chief figure in the episode, General Kornilov, the new commander-in-chief.

Kornilov was the type of army officer who had never accepted the February Revolution. He believed that before Russia could fulfil its national duty of defeating Germany, it must first destroy the socialist enemies within. 'It's time', he said, 'to hang the German supporters and spies, with Lenin at their head, and to disperse the Petrograd soviet.' By late August, the advance of German forces deeper into Russia began to threaten Petrograd itself. Large numbers of refugees and deserters flocked into the city, heightening the tension there and increasing the disorder. Kornilov declared that Russia and the government stood in grave danger of a socialist-inspired insurrection. He informed Kerensky that he intended to bring his loyal troops to Petrograd to save the Provisional Government from being overthrown.

Accounts tend to diverge at this point in their description of Kerensky's response. Those who believe that he was involved in a plot with Kornilov to destroy the Petrograd soviet and set up a dictatorship argue that Kerensky had at first fully supported this move. It was only afterwards, when he realised that Kornilov also intended to remove the Provisional Government and impose military rule, that he turned against him.

Other commentators, sympathetic to Kerensky, maintain that he had not plotted with Kornilov and that his actions had been wholly consistent. They also emphasise that a special Commission of Enquiry into the affair in 1917 cleared Kerensky of any complicity. But, however the question of collusion is decided, it was certainly the case that Kerensky publicly condemned Kornilov's advance. He ordered him to surrender his post and placed Petrograd under martial law. Kornilov reacted by sending an open telegram (Source E, opposite).

**SOURCE E**

**From Kornilov's appeal, 26 August 1917, quoted in R. Pipes, *The Russian Revolution*, Collins Harvill, 1990, p. 460.**

*People of Russia! Our great motherland is dying. The moment of death is near. I, General Kornilov, declare that the Provisional Government, under pressure from the Bolshevik majority in the Soviet, acts in full accord with the plans of the German General Staff, and concurrently with the imminent landings of the enemy forces on the coast of Riga, destroys the army and convulses the country from within.*

*I, General Kornilov, declare to each and all that I personally desire nothing but to save Great Russia. I swear to lead the people through victory over the enemy to the Constituent Assembly, where it will decide its own destiny and choose its new political system.*

What motives, other than those stated in Source E, might Kornilov have had in planning to march on Petrograd?

## Kerensky's response

Fearful that Kornilov would attack, Kerensky called on all loyal citizens to take up arms to defend the city. The Bolsheviks were released from prison or came out of hiding to collect the weapons issued by the Provisional Government to all who were willing to fight. By this strange twist in the story of 1917, the Bolsheviks found themselves being given arms by the very government they were pledged to overthrow.

In the event, the weapons were not needed against Kornilov. The railway workers refused to operate the trains to bring Kornilov's army to Petrograd. When he learned of this and of a mass workers' militia formed to oppose him, Kornilov, on 1 September, abandoned the advance and allowed himself to be arrested. He was to die early in April 1918, killed by a stray shell at the start of the Russian Civil War (see page 139).

## Bolshevik gains

It was the Bolsheviks who benefited most from the failure of the attempted coup. They had been able to present themselves as defenders of Petrograd and the revolution, thereby diverting attention away from their failure in the July Days. What further boosted the Bolsheviks was that, despite the obvious readiness of the people of Petrograd to defend their city, this could not be read as a sign of their belief in the Provisional Government. Indeed, the episode had damaged the Provisional Government by revealing its political weakness and showing how vulnerable it was to military threat. Kerensky later admitted that the Kornilov affair had been 'the prelude to the October Revolution'.

**Summary diagram: The Provisional Government and its problems**

| The war | National minorities question |
| --- | --- |
| Government obliged to continue the war in order to maintain loans from the Allies<br>Caused first serious split between Soviet and Provisional Government<br>Prevented resources being spent on other needs<br>Kerensky emerged as committed supporter of the war | Caused ministerial crisis which led to the July Days, which saw the near extinction of Bolsheviks |
| **The land question** | **The Kornilov affair** |
| Provisional Government not genuinely committed to land reform<br>Enabled Bolsheviks to steal a march and gain peasant support | Provisional Government survived but gravely weakened<br>Bolsheviks began recovery<br>The prelude to the October Revolution |

# The October Revolution

▶ *What factors put the Bolsheviks in a position to bid for power by October 1917?*

## The political shift in Petrograd

The measure of the Bolsheviks' recovery from the July Days and of their gains from the Kornilov affair was soon apparent. By the middle of September they had gained a majority in both the Petrograd and Moscow soviets. However, this should not be seen as indicating a large swing of opinion in their favour, but rather as a reflection of the changing character of the soviets.

In the first few months after the February Revolution the meetings of the soviets had been fully attended. Over 3000 deputies had packed into the Petrograd soviet at the Tauride Palace. But as the months passed enthusiasm waned. By the autumn of 1917 attendance was often down to a few hundred. This was a major advantage to the Bolsheviks. Their political dedication meant that they continued to turn up in force while the members of the other parties attended only occasionally. The result was that the Bolshevik Party exerted an influence out of proportion to its numbers. This was especially the case in regard to the composition of the various soviet sub-committees.

Broadly what happened in Petrograd following the Kornilov affair was that the Petrograd soviet moved to the left, wanting a greater say in government, while the Provisional Government shifted to the right, wishing to prevent Soviet encroachment on its power. This made some form of clash between the two bodies increasingly likely. Lenin put it as a matter of stark choice: 'Either a soviet government or Kornilovism. There is no middle course.'

## Lenin's strategy

From his exile in Finland, Lenin constantly appealed to his party to prepare for the immediate overthrow of Kerensky's government. He claimed that his earlier prediction had proved wholly correct: the Provisional Government, incapable of solving the war and land questions, was becoming increasingly reactionary. This left the soviet as the only hope of true revolutionaries. He further argued that the Bolsheviks could not wait; they must seize the moment while the government was at its most vulnerable. In a sentence that was to become part of Bolshevik legend, Lenin wrote on 12 September: 'History will not forgive us if we do not assume power.'

Lenin's sense of urgency arose from his concern over two events that were due to take place in the autumn, and which, he calculated, would seriously limit the Bolsheviks' freedom of action:

- the meeting of the All-Russian Congress of Soviets in late October
- the election for the Constituent Assembly in November

Lenin was convinced that the Bolsheviks would have to take power before these events occurred. If, under the banner 'All Power to the Soviets', the Bolsheviks could topple the Provisional Government before the Congress of Soviets met, they could then present their new authority as a ***fait accompli*** which the Congress would have no reason to reject since it had been carried out in their name and, in theory, had handed them power.

The elections to the Constituent Assembly presented a different problem. The assembly was the body on which all **progressives** and reformers had set their hopes. Once it came into being, its moral authority would be difficult to challenge. Lenin told his party that since it was impossible to forecast how successfully the Bolsheviks would perform in the elections, they would have to be in power before the results were announced. This would provide them with the authority to undermine the results should they go against them.

***Fait accompli*** An established situation that cannot be changed.

**Progressives** Those who believed in parliamentary government for Russia.

## The 'pre-parliament'

At the same time as Lenin pressed this policy on his party, Kerensky tried to make his government less exposed by announcing plans for the creation of a 'pre-parliament'. This was to be a body with the authority to advise the government. Drawn from a variety of parties and thus representative of a range of political opinion, it was intended to fill the interim before the Constituent Assembly came into being. Lenin immediately condemned the pre-parliament as a manoeuvre not to broaden the government's base but to strengthen its grip on power. Acting on his orders, the Bolshevik members of the soviet who were entitled to attend the pre-parliament mocked it loudly and derisively and then walked out.

## Lenin urges a rising

Emboldened by the Bolsheviks' success in undermining the pre-parliament, Lenin began urging his party to prepare to overthrow the Provisional Government. However, despite the intense conviction with which Lenin put his arguments to his colleagues, there were Bolsheviks on the Central Committee of the party who doubted the wisdom of striking against the Provisional Government at this point.

In an effort to enforce his will, Lenin slipped back into Petrograd on 7 October. His personal presence stiffened Bolshevik resolve, but did not produce total unity. During the next two weeks he spent exhausting hours at a series of Central Committee meetings trying to convince the waverers. On 10 October, the Central Committee pledged itself to an armed insurrection, but failed to agree on a specific date. In the end, by another quirk of fate, it was Kerensky and the government, not the Bolsheviks, who initiated the actual rising.

 **KEY FIGURE**

**Grigor Zinoviev (1883–1936)**

A close colleague of Lenin since the formation of the Bolshevik Party in 1903; he would be executed in the Stalin purges.

? In what ways might Source F have propelled Kerensky into taking action against the Bolsheviks?

## Kerensky makes the first move

Rumours of an imminent Bolshevik coup had been circulating in Petrograd for some weeks, but it was not until an article, written by two members of the Bolshevik Central Committee, appeared in a journal on 11 October that the authorities felt they had sure proof. The writers of the article, **Grigor Zinoviev** and Lev Kamenev, argued that it would be a mistake to attempt to overthrow the government in the current circumstances.

**SOURCE F**

**From an article of 11 October 1917, written by Lev Kamenev and Grigor Zinoviev, quoted in M. McCauley, *The Russian Revolution & the Soviet State 1917–21 Documents*, Macmillan, 1984, p. 115.**

*A current is forming and growing in workers' groups which see the only way out in an immediate declaration of an armed uprising. Now all the timescales have coincided so that if one is to speak of such an uprising, one has plainly to fix a date and moreover for the immediate future. This question is already being debated in one form or another in all the periodical press, in workers' meetings and is occupying the minds of a wide circle of party workers. We, in our turn, regard it as our duty and our right to speak out on this question with full frankness.*

*We are most profoundly convinced that to declare at once an armed uprising would mean to stake not only the fate of our party, but also the fate of the Russian and international revolution. There is no doubt that there are such historical situations that an oppressed class has to acknowledge that it is better to join battle and lose than to surrender without a fight. Is the Russian working class in such a position now?* No, and a thousand times no.

Kerensky interpreted this as indicating that a date had already been set. Rather than wait to be caught off guard, he ordered a pre-emptive attack on the

Bolsheviks. On 23 October, the Bolshevik newspapers, *Pravda* and *Izvestiya*, were closed down by government troops and an attempted round-up of the leading Bolsheviks began. The Bolsheviks no longer had a choice; Lenin ordered the planned insurrection to begin.

### Key steps in the Bolshevik Revolution 1917

- September 25: Bolsheviks gained a majority in the Petrograd soviet.
- October 9: Petrograd soviet set up Military Revolutionary Committee (MRC).
- October 11: Kamenev and Zinoviev publicly opposed the idea of an uprising.
- October 23: Kerensky moved to close down *Pravda* and *Izvestiya*. Lenin instructed the Bolsheviks to begin the rising against Kerensky's government.
- October 24: First session of the Congress of Soviets.
- October 24–25: Bolsheviks took control of Petrograd.
- October 25–26: Kerensky fled from Petrograd after failing to raise troops. Bolsheviks seized the Winter Palace.
- October 26: Bolsheviks established *Sovnarkom*.
- October 27: Lenin claimed power in the name of the Congress of Soviets.

### Trotsky's role

That the Bolsheviks had a plan at all was the work not of Lenin but of Trotsky. While it was Lenin who was undoubtedly the great influence behind the October Rising, it was Trotsky who actually organised it. The key to Trotsky's success in this was his chairmanship of the Petrograd soviet, to which he had been elected in September. On 9 October, the soviet set up the Military Revolutionary Committee (MRC) to organise the defence of Petrograd against a possible German attack or another Kornilov-type assault from within Russia. It proved a critical decision. Realising that, if the Bolsheviks could control the MRC, they would control Petrograd, Trotsky used his influence to have himself accepted as one of the three-man inner team appointed to run the MRC. This meant he had at his disposal the only effective military force in Petrograd. Moreover, it was a legitimate force since, theoretically, it acted on the authority of the soviet. Trotsky was now in a position to draft the plans for the overthrow of the Provisional Government. When Lenin gave the order for the uprising to begin, it was Trotsky who directed the **Red Guards** in their seizure of the key vantage points in Petrograd, such as the bridges and the telegraph offices.

**Red Guards** A force, some 10,000 in number, largely made up at this time of elderly men recruited from the workers in the factories.

## Collapse of the Provisional Government

In the three days (25–27 October) that it took for the city to fall under Bolshevik control there was remarkably little fighting. There were only six deaths during the whole episode and these were all Red Guards, most probably accidentally

**KEY TERMS**

**Cossacks** The remnants of the elite cavalry regiment of the tsars.

**Amazons** A special corps of female soldiers recruited by Kerensky to show the patriotism of Russia's women in the anti-German struggle.

? In what ways might Source G be regarded as an example of myth becoming more powerful than fact?

shot by their own side. The simple fact was that the Provisional Government had hardly any military forces on which to call. The Petrograd garrison which had turned out to defend the government on previous occasions did not come to its aid now. The truth was that desertions had reduced the garrison to a few loyal officer-cadets, a small group of **Cossacks** and a unit known as the **Amazons**.

When the Red Guards approached the Winter Palace, which housed the Provisional Government, they expected stiff resistance, but there was none. A black-and-white film of the dramatic, death-defying storming of the palace gates often appears in television documentaries about the October Revolution. This is very misleading since there was no such event. What modern programme makers invariably use are the powerful but fictional images from the feature film *October*, made in 1927 on the tenth anniversary of the Russian Revolution by the celebrated Bolshevik film maker, Sergei Eisenstein. Interestingly, more damage was done to the Winter Palace in making the film than had actually occurred at the time.

**SOURCE G**

**A still from *October*, a brilliant but unhistorical feature film shot in 1927 by Sergei Eisenstein, purporting to show the Red Guards attacking the Winter Palace.**

**SOURCE H**

**A contingent of Amazons under instruction in 1917. Kerensky had specially recruited these female soldiers, also known as 'the Women's Battalion of Death', as an example of the fighting spirit of the Russian people.**

The Bolshevik forces did not need to storm the gates; there was nobody defending them. The Winter Palace was a vast building, many times larger than London's Buckingham Palace. The Red Guards simply entered through the back doors. This was enough to make the defenders give up. The Cossacks declined to fight and made off when confronted by the Red Guards. After that, it did not take much pressure to persuade the cadets and the Amazons that it was better for them to lay down their arms and go home rather than die in a futile struggle.

Look at Source H. From where would the Amazons in this photo probably have been recruited? ?

The sounding of its guns in a pre-arranged signal by the pro-soviet crew of the cruiser *Aurora*, moored in the River Neva, convinced the remaining members of the government that their position was hopeless. As many as were able escaped unnoticed out of the building. Kerensky, having earlier left the city in a vain effort to raise loyal troops, fled to the US embassy. He later slipped out of Petrograd, disguised as a female nurse, and made his way to the USA, where he eventually became a professor of history.

## The Bolsheviks take power

The Bolsheviks did not seize power; it fell into their hands. The speed and ease with which it had happened surprised even Lenin. In the early hours of 27 October, he said to Trotsky 'from being on the run to supreme power makes one dizzy'. He then rolled himself up in a large fur coat, lay down on the floor, and went to sleep.

On the following evening, the All-Russian Congress of Soviets began their first session. The opening formalities had barely been completed when the chairman, who happened to be Lev Kamenev, the Bolshevik who had originally opposed the rising, informed the delegates that they were now the supreme authority in Russia; the Petrograd soviet had seized power in their name and had formed a new government. Kamenev then read out to the bewildered delegates the list of fourteen names of the new government they had supposedly just appointed. The fourteen were all Bolsheviks or Left SRs. At the head of the list of **Commissars** who made up the new ***Sovnarkom*** was the name of the chief minister – Vladimir Ilyich Lenin.

**KEY TERMS**

**Commissars** Russian for ministers: Lenin chose the word because he said 'it reeked of blood'.

***Sovnarkom*** Russian for government or cabinet.

The SRs and the Mensheviks walked out, protesting that it was not a taking of power by the soviets but a Bolshevik coup. Trotsky jeered after them that they and their kind had 'consigned themselves to the garbage heap of history'. Lenin then announced to the Bolshevik and the Left SR delegates who had remained that they would now proceed 'to construct the towering edifice of socialist society'.

**Summary diagram: The October Revolution**

| Political left | Political centre | Political right |
|---|---|---|
| • Petrograd soviet<br>• By October moved to the left and dominated by Trotsky | • Dual Authority | • Provisional Government<br>• By October moved to the right and deserted by socialists<br>• Kerensky left without allies |

**The building blocks of revolution**

| | | |
|---|---|---|
| • Soviet Order No. 1 | • Lenin's return | • *April Theses* |
| • 'Peace, Bread and Land' | • Failure of Summer Offensive | • 'All Power to the Soviets' |
| • July Days | • Kornilov affair | • Trotsky and the MRC |

# Reasons for the Bolshevik success

- *Why was there so little resistance to the Bolshevik coup in October 1917?*

Trotsky later said that there were two principal factors that explained the Bolshevik success in October 1917:

- the failure of the Petrograd garrison to resist
- the existence of the Military Revolutionary Committee (MRC).

He claimed that the Soviet decision to create the MRC had sounded the death-knell of the Provisional Government. The Bolsheviks' control of the MRC gave them 'three-quarters if not nine-tenths' of their victory in the October Revolution. Since Trotsky was a major player in the drama played out in October 1917, his views demand respect. But his analysis was largely concerned with the immediate events of October. The success of the coup had as much to do with government weakness as Bolshevik strength, a weakness that was built into the Provisional Government from the start.

## Provisional Government weaknesses

The collapse of tsardom left a power vacuum. Although the Provisional Government held office between February and October 1917, it never held power. It lacked the ruthlessness which the desperate situation demanded. Furthermore, from the first, its authority was weakened by the existence of the Petrograd soviet. Unable to fight the war successfully and unwilling to introduce the reforms that might have given it popular support, the Provisional Government tottered towards collapse. When it was challenged in October 1917 by the Bolsheviks, who themselves had been on the point of political extinction in July, it was friendless. It gave in with scarcely a show of resistance.

The failure of the Provisional Government to rally effective military support in its hour of need followed from its political failure over the previous eight months. It was not that the Provisional Government was bitterly rejected by the Russian people. It was more a matter of its inability to arouse genuine enthusiasm. Kerensky's government had come nowhere near to solving Russia's problems. Its support had evaporated. Dependent on foreign loans and largely deserted by its militarily forces, the Provisional Government was not considered worth struggling to save. In October 1917, the Bolsheviks were pushing against an already open door.

An important consideration is that the Provisional Government had never been meant to last. As its very title suggested, it was intended to be an interim government. Along with its partner in the Dual Authority, the Petrograd soviet, its role was to provide a caretaker administration until an All-Russian Constituent Assembly was formed after the autumn election. The assembly was the ultimate dream of all liberals and democrats; it would be the first fully elected, nationwide, democratic parliament in Russia. All parties, including the Bolsheviks, were committed to it.

As a consequence, the Provisional Government was always open to the charge that as an unelected, self-appointed body it had no right to exercise the authority that properly belonged to the Constituent Assembly alone. Such limited strength as the Provisional Government had rested on its claim to be the representative of the February Revolution. Lenin had made it his task to undermine that claim.

## The weakness of the non-Bolshevik parties

An obvious question is why none of the other parties was able to mount a serious challenge to the Bolsheviks for the leadership of the revolution between February and October. One answer is that they had all accepted February as a genuine revolution. Consequently, it made sense for them to co-operate with the Provisional Government, which reputedly represented all the progressive forces in Russia. The result was that the revolutionary parties, such as the SRs, were prepared to enter into coalition with the Kadets, the dominant party in the government, and await the convening of the Constituent Assembly. This gave the Bolsheviks a powerful propaganda weapon, which Lenin exploited. He charged the socialists with having sold out to the bourgeoisie.

Another explanation is that the other parties were weakened by their support for the war. None of them opposed the continuation of the struggle against Germany with the consistency that Lenin's Bolsheviks did after April 1917. The non-Bolshevik parties regarded it as Russia's duty to defeat the enemy. The SRs, the Mensheviks and, indeed, some individual Bolsheviks believed wholeheartedly in a revolutionary war against bourgeois Germany. On the left of the Menshevik Party there was a vociferous wing of international revolutionaries who saw the war as the ideal opportunity for beginning the worldwide class struggle.

## The Menshevik position

As committed Marxists, the Mensheviks had good reason for co-operating with the Provisional Government rather than opposing it. They saw the February Revolution as marking a critical stage in the class war, when the bourgeoisie had overthrown the old feudal forces represented by the tsar. This stage of the dialectic, as Marx had argued, was the necessary prelude to the revolution of the proletariat. However, the Mensheviks judged that since Russia did not yet possess a proletariat large enough to be a truly revolutionary force, it was their immediate task to align themselves with the other parties and work for the consolidation of the bourgeois revolution. When this had been achieved, the Mensheviks could turn to the ultimate objective of a proletarian rising. One of the interesting paradoxes of the Russian Revolution is that, in strictly theoretical terms, the Mensheviks were always better, that is to say more consistent, Marxists than were Lenin and his Bolsheviks.

## Bolshevik ruthlessness

A key factor was that none of the contending parties was as determined as the Bolsheviks to exploit the crises facing Russia in 1917. **Tseretelli**, a prominent Menshevik, admitted: 'Everything we did at that time was a vain effort to hold back a destructive elemental flood with a handful of insignificant chips'. Peter Struve, a liberal ***émigré***, observed: 'Only Bolshevism was logical about revolution and true to its essence, and therefore in the revolution it conquered.' Milyukov, the Kadet leader, shared Struve's view of the Bolsheviks: 'They knew where they were going, and they went in the direction which they had chosen once and for all toward a goal which came nearer with every new, unsuccessful, experiment of compromise.'

**KEY FIGURE**

**Iraklii Tseretelli (1882–1959)**
A Georgian revolutionary and a leading member of the Petrograd soviet before its domination by the Bolsheviks.

**KEY TERM**

***Émigré*** One who flees from his own country; in the Russian case, *émigrés* were those who left after October 1917 from fear or a desire to plan a counter-strike against the Bolsheviks.

Lenin's Bolsheviks were a new breed of politician: utterly self-confident and scornful of all other parties and ideas. Their drive and conviction came from the belief that they were an unstoppable force of history. As Trotsky put it: 'The party in the last analysis is always right, because the party is the only historical instrument given to the proletariat to resolve its fundamental tasks.' The ruthlessness of the Bolsheviks did not guarantee their success, but it did mean that no other party could hope to gain or hold power unless it was able to overcome the challenge of these dedicated revolutionaries. In the event, none of the other parties was ever in a position to do this.

## The role of mutual misunderstanding

An irony of the pre-October situation was that both the Provisional Government and the Bolsheviks overestimated each other's power, each delaying their moves against the other for fear of overplaying their hand. Historians have often wondered why the Provisional Government did not make a more sustained effort to destroy the Bolsheviks politically. It is true that some arrests were made, but the government's efforts at suppression were half-hearted.

One reason for this, odd though it seems in retrospect, is that Kerensky's government was more frightened of an attack from the right than from the left. Fear of a tsarist reaction against the revolution preoccupied the thoughts of many in the government. For much of 1917, Kornilov was regarded as a bigger threat than Lenin. This was not entirely unrealistic. The Bolsheviks were not militarily strong. Nicolai Sukhanov, a Menshevik eyewitness of the events of 1917, calculated that so limited was Bolshevik strength at the time of the October

**KEY TERMS**

**Smolny** The Bolshevik headquarters in Petrograd, housed in what had been a young ladies' finishing school.

**Radicalisation** A movement towards more sweeping or revolutionary ideas.

Rising that 'a good detachment of 500 men would have been enough to liquidate **Smolny** and everybody in it'. Trotsky agreed, but asked mockingly: 'And just where would the Provisional Government find 500 good men to fight for it?'

## Lenin's importance

It says much for Lenin's forcefulness as leader that, despite his frequent absences from Petrograd between February and October, he continued to dominate the actions of the Bolshevik Party. Trotsky later made an interesting assessment of the part played by Lenin in the October Revolution: 'Had I not been present in 1917 in Petersburg, the October Revolution would still have taken place – on the condition that Lenin was present and in command. If neither Lenin nor I had been present in Petersburg, there would have been no October Revolution.' However, most historians are now careful not to overstate Lenin's power to dictate events in 1917. In the standard Bolshevik version of what happened, Lenin was portrayed as having fulfilled his plans for revolution along the lines he had laid down in such writings as his 1902 pamphlet, *What Is To Be Done?* This had visualised the development of a tightly knit, disciplined Bolshevik Party that would seize power in the name of the masses at the opportune moment (see page 23). Yet, the evidence of the many disputes within the Bolshevik ranks over policy between February and October 1917 suggests that the party was by no means as disciplined or centrally controlled as it later claimed it to have been.

Part of the reason for this was that the composition of the party had changed in ways that Lenin and the Central Committee had not originally planned. After the February Revolution there had been a large increase in membership. The following figures indicate the remarkable transformation that the Bolshevik Party underwent in 1917.

**Table 4.1** Membership of the Bolshevik Party in 1917

| | |
|---|---|
| **February** | 24,000 |
| **April** | 100,000 |
| **October** | 340,000 (60,000 in Petrograd) |

Modern commentators view this influx of party members as an aspect of the general **radicalisation** of Russian politics that occurred as the Provisional Government got into increasing difficulties. What had helped to prepare the ground for the successful Bolshevik coup in October was the growth in the Petrograd factories of workers' committees that, while not necessarily pro-Bolshevik, were certainly not pro-government. One result of the anti-government agitation of these committees was that, when the open challenge to the Provisional Government came in October, Kerensky's desperate appeal for support from the people of Petrograd went unheeded.

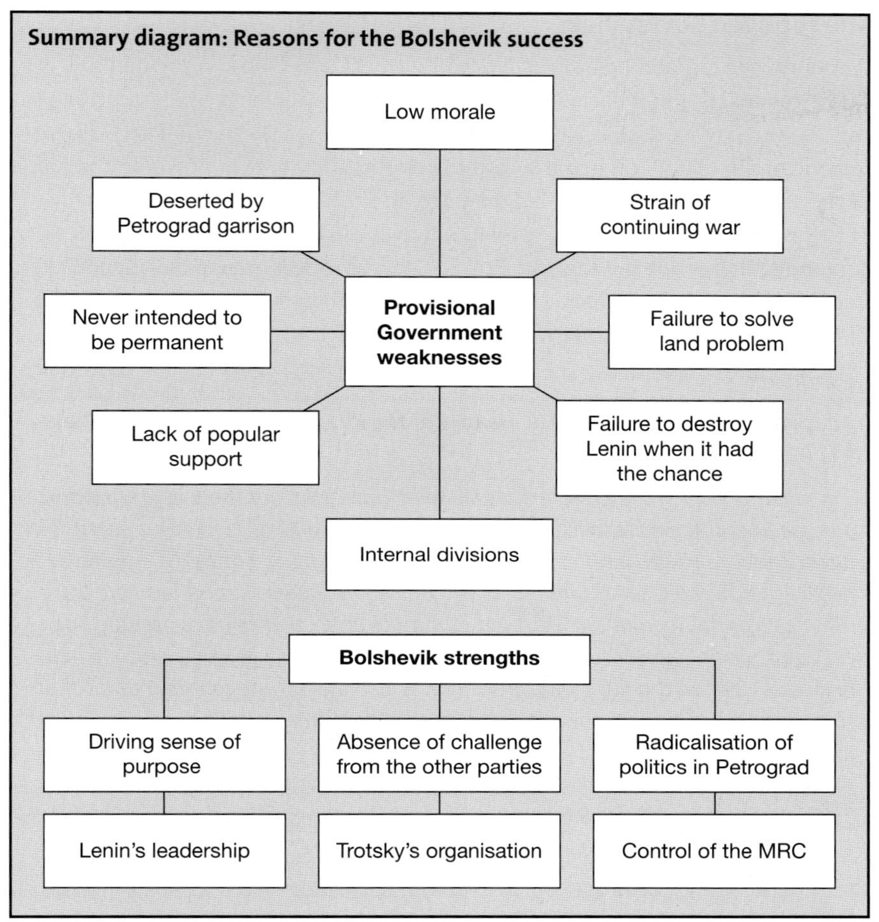


# 6 Key debate

▶ *What was the true character of the October Revolution?*

Since 1917, there has been continuous debate and disagreement over the October Revolution. The official version maintained by the Soviet Communist Party was that Lenin, backed by the Russian people, had led his Bolshevik Party to power and had then gone on to create a workers' state. Critics of this view, however, have challenged this interpretation as an over-simplification and a distortion. The following indicates some of the major contributions to the debate.

## The received Soviet view

Although he was later disgraced in Stalin's time, Leon Trotsky provided the historical analysis that became the official interpretation of events. According to this, Lenin, having developed a tightly knit, disciplined Bolshevik Party, steered it to victory in October when it seized the opportunity to take power in the name of the masses. Lenin had thus led the party in fulfilling the Marxist prophecy of the inevitable triumph of the proletariat over the bourgeoisie. Trotsky later contended that while the Russian Revolution was indeed inevitable, it needed Lenin's particular dynamism to make it happen when it did. Lenin was a great historical force, the vital link in the dialectical chain.

**EXTRACT 1**

**Adapted from Leon Trotsky, *The History of the Russian Revolution*, Pluto Press, 1977, pp. 343–44.**

*The dictatorship of the proletariat was to be inferred from the whole situation, but it had still to be established. It could not be established without a party. The party could fulfil its mission only after understanding it. For that Lenin was needed. Until his arrival, not one of the Bolshevik leaders dared to make a diagnosis of the revolution. Without Lenin the crisis would have assumed an extraordinarily sharp and protracted character. The role of personality arises before us here on a truly gigantic scale. It is necessary only to understand that role correctly, taking personality as a link in the historic chain. Lenin was not an accidental element in the historical development, but a product of the whole past of Russian history.*

A number of Western sympathisers accepted the Soviet line in its essentials. Prominent among these was the British Marxist scholar Eric Hobsbawm, who in the 1990s, described Lenin's essential achievement in 1917 as having been to convince 'the hesitant elements in his party that power would escape them … if not seized by planned action during the short time it was within their grasp'.

## Opposition to the received view

Other historians, mainly those on the right, challenged the notion that Lenin led a popular movement to success in October 1917. Richard Pipes argued that Lenin headed a minority-party coup in October that violently wrenched the revolution away from its popular roots.

**EXTRACT 2**

**From R. Pipes, *Three Whys of the Russian Revolution*, Pimlico, 1998, pp. 60–1.**

*[W]hat occurred in October 1917 was a classical* coup d'état *accomplished without mass support. It was a surreptitious seizure of the nerve centre of the modern state, carried out under false slogans in order to neutralize the population at large, the true purpose of which was revealed only after the new claimants were firmly in the saddle.*

*The population at large offered little resistance at a time when resistance would have made all the difference because it believed that the new regime could not last. The so-called Soviet government was seen as made up of crazy utopians who would be swept from the scene as suddenly as they had appeared. When Bolshevik policies began to affect adversely the interests of workers and peasants they rebelled.*

**KEY TERM**

**Non-determinist approach** Rejection of the idea that history follows a fixed, inevitable course.

While Pipes differs in points of detail and emphasis from Robert Service, the major authority on Lenin, what the two historians share is a **non-determinist approach**. They concur in suggesting that in 1917 Russia nothing was pre-ordained, nothing absolutely had to happen the way it did. Politics was crucial. Things occurred the way they did because of the decisions made by the participants. Lenin was pivotal. Service stresses that at the time of the actual October takeover Lenin acted essentially practically, giving little attention to ideology or theory.

**EXTRACT 3**

**From R. Service, *Lenin*, Macmillan, 2000, p. 315.**

*Not once did Lenin mention Marxism in his various speeches of 25–27 October. He referred to 'socialism' only very fleetingly. Nor did he explain that his immediate objective was the establishment of a class-based dictatorship and that ultimately he aimed at the realisation of a communist, classless society. He was keeping his political cards close to his chest. He was a party boss and wanted Bolshevism to be attractive to those workers, soldiers, peasants and intellectuals who had not yet supported it. And so terms such as dictatorship, terror, civil war and revolutionary war were again quietly shelved ... His emphasis was skewed more sharply in favour of a revolution from below ... His wish was for the Bolsheviks to appear as a party that would facilitate the making of Revolution by and for the people.*

## The 'unfinished' revolution

This theory is associated particularly with the later followers of Trotsky. It argues that a genuine workers' revolution had indeed occurred in 1917, but it had then been betrayed by Lenin's successors. According to this school of thought, which was powerfully represented in the West by such writers as Isaac Deutscher and Adam Ulam, the initial revolutionary achievement of the workers was perverted by the deadening rule of Stalin. That was why Lenin's October Revolution was 'unfinished'.

## The 'optimist' view

An extension of the 'unfinished' theory is the 'optimistic' notion advanced by Russian *émigré* historians, such as George Katkov. The optimism lay in their claim that Imperial Russia had been successfully transforming itself into a modern, democratic, industrial society, until it was weakened by the First World War. However, at that point, Lenin's Bolsheviks, who were in the pay of the German government, had unscrupulously exploited the nation's difficulties to seize power in an illegal coup which diverted Russia from the path of progress.

### The 'pessimist' view

In the 1960s, Leopold Haimson, an American scholar, had a major impact on studies of the revolution. He suggested that, far from moving towards modernisation, Imperial Russia by 1914 was heading towards revolutionary turmoil, even before war came. Hence the term 'pessimist'. He argued that Russia was suffering an 'institutional crisis'; an unbridgeable gap had developed between the reactionary tsarist establishment and the progressive professional classes and urban workers. So great was the divide that violent revolution was the unavoidable outcome. Lenin and the Bolsheviks exploited the crisis, but they did not create the revolution; it was created for them.

## Revisionism

Certain modern commentators, often termed revisionists, veered back towards the notion that the 1917 October Revolution may have indeed been at its base a popular movement. The ground for this argument was that in 1917 a radicalisation of Russian politics had occurred as a result of the mistakes made by the Provisional Government. Angry soldiers and frustrated workers began to agitate against Kerensky's government, which became friendless. In October 1917, the Bolsheviks did not seize power; they simply picked it up.

### 1917 as a cultural revolution

An interesting line of interpretation has developed among revisionist historians, involving less concentration on individuals and a greater emphasis on the broad social shifts occurring in late Imperial Russia. The claim is not that Lenin and the Bolsheviks were unimportant but that they were representatives (rather than initiators) of the revolutionary movement associated with them. In simplified form, the argument is that late tsarist society was undergoing a profound cultural revolution, brought about by modernisation. Although Russian conservatives tried to resist change, change was occurring nonetheless; industrialisation and contact with Western countries fundamentally altered the character of society to the point where it fractured.

So, although Lenin and the Bolsheviks were a minority, fringe party working to take power, their real significance was that, without knowing it, they represented a deeper driving force for change within society. This view is expressed by American historian Robert C. Williams:

**EXTRACT 4**

**From R.C. Williams, 'The Bolsheviks', in Anna Geifman, editor, *Russia and the Last Tsar: Opposition and Subversion 1894–1917*, Blackwell, 1999, p. 49.**

*Over the course of the twentieth century Bolshevism has ceased to mean the Marxist ideology of one individual, Lenin, and has come to mean the cultural transformation of an entire society. Bolshevism before 1917 appears in retrospect more internally divided and disputatious, more popular and less conspiratorial, linked more with society and less with ideology, than imagined. Of all the political parties of imperial Russia, Bolshevism may have seemed the most unlikely to seize power in 1917. Yet a deeper and more extensive knowledge of Russian society and culture has made it possible for historians to discover roots of social support and cultural resonance in a movement previously associated with raw political power. We now know that Bolshevism was more supported from below by workers and peasants, and more embedded in the deep structure of Russian culture than we thought.*

How do the historians quoted in Extracts 1–4 differ or agree in their interpretation of the Russian Revolution? ?

The view of the 'cultural revolutionists' has not won universal acceptance among historians, though it has added another dimension to the ongoing debate about one of modern history's most controversial issues.

## Chapter summary

The February Revolution was followed by the establishment of a Dual Authority, which saw initial co-operation between the Provisional Government and the Petrograd soviet. This harmony had broken down by the summer months and, prompted by Lenin, who had returned in April to demand the end of the Bolsheviks' co-operation with the other parties, his party began to consider rising against the government. An attempt to do so in July proved premature and brought the Bolsheviks to the verge of destruction. They were saved only by the government's mishandling of the Kornilov affair, which enabled the Bolsheviks to act as defenders of Petrograd against tsarist reaction.

Unable to deal with the major problems facing Russia – disastrous war losses, food shortages and a rebellious peasantry – Kerensky's government by the autumn had forfeited popular support. To avoid arrest, Lenin was only intermittently in Petrograd but, such was his influence from afar, that by late October he had persuaded his followers to strike against the government. Trotsky, in the name of the soviet, whose chairman and military chief he had become, organised the October Revolution which overthrew a barely resistant government. The reasons for the Bolshevik success are the subject of continuing debate.

##  Refresher questions

Use these questions to remind yourself of the key material covered in this chapter.

1 Why, initially, was there so little political conflict between the Provisional Government and the Petrograd soviet?
2 What did Stalin and Kamenev think Bolshevik policy should be after the February Revolution?
3 What were the essential arguments in Lenin's *April Theses*?
4 How were the Bolsheviks able to survive their failure in the July Days?
5 How real a threat was the Kornilov affair to the Provisional Government?
6 Why was land such a contentious issue in revolutionary Russia?
7 Why did the Provisional Government continue the war against Germany?
8 Why was it the Bolsheviks, and not any of the other parties, who took power in October 1917?
9 In what ways did the Bolsheviks and the Provisional Government overestimate each other's strength?
10 What roles did Lenin and Trotsky play in the October Rising?

##  Question practice

### ESSAY QUESTIONS

1 How important was the return of Lenin to Petrograd in April 1917?
2 To what extent did the character and composition of the Petrograd soviet change between February and October 1917?
3 How far were the problems faced by the Provisional Government in 1917 a consequence of the continuing war with Germany?
4 'The weakness of the Provisional Government, not the strength of the revolutionaries, explains why the Bolshevik Rising of October 1917 succeeded.' How far do you agree with this statement?

CHAPTER 5

# Lenin's government of Russia 1917–24

The successful Bolshevik coup of October 1917 marked the beginning rather than the end of the Russian Revolution. The big test was whether the Bolsheviks could retain their power and build upon it. Their fraught but successful efforts to do so are studied in this chapter under the following headings:

- ★ The Bolsheviks in power
- ★ Dissolution of the Constituent Assembly 1918
- ★ Treaty of Brest-Litovsk 1918
- ★ Russian Civil War 1918–20
- ★ Foreign interventions 1918–21
- ★ Lenin's methods of imposing control 1917–21
- ★ War Communism 1918–21
- ★ Kronstadt Rising 1921
- ★ New Economic Policy
- ★ Lenin's legacy

The key debate on *page 178* asks the question: Was the authoritarianism of Lenin's rule, 1917–24, a response to circumstances or an essential feature of Soviet Communism?

## Key dates

| | | |
|---|---|---|
| **1917** | **Oct.** | Decree on Peace |
| | **Nov.** | Decrees on Land and Workers' Control |
| **1918–20** | | Russian Civil War and foreign interventions |
| **1918–21** | | War Communism |
| **1918** | **Jan.** | Bolsheviks forcibly dissolved the Constituent Assembly |
| | | Red Army established |
| | **March** | Treaty of Brest-Litovsk |
| | **June** | Decree on Nationalisation |
| **1918** | **July** | Forced grain requisitions began |
| | | Murder of tsar and his family |
| | **Sept.** | Red Terror |
| **1919** | **March** | Comintern established |
| | | Bolshevik Party renamed the Communist Party |
| **1920** | **April** | Invading Red Army driven from Poland |
| **1921** | **March** | Kronstadt Rising |
| | | Introduction of the New Economic Policy |
| **1924** | **Jan.** | Death of Lenin |

# The Bolsheviks in power

- *How did the Bolsheviks tackle the problems confronting them after they had taken power in 1917?*
- *What were Lenin's Decrees intended to achieve?*

From the beginning, Lenin's Bolsheviks were engaged in a desperate struggle for survival. In their government of Russia, they were working from hand to mouth. They had few plans to help them. This was because before 1917 they had spent their time in preparing for revolution. They had given little thought to the details of how affairs would be organised once this had been achieved. It had always been a Marxist belief that after the triumph of the proletariat the state would 'wither away'. Trotsky had expressed this simple faith at the time of his appointment in October 1917 as **commissar for foreign affairs** when he said 'all we need to do is issue a few decrees, then shut up shop and go home'. But circumstances were not to allow such a relaxed approach to government.

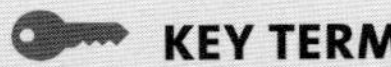

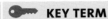

**KEY TERM**

**Commissar for foreign affairs** Equivalent to the secretary of state in the USA or the foreign secretary in Britain.

## The distribution of power

Lenin claimed that the October Revolution had been the taking of power by the soviets. In fact, it had been a seizure of power by the Bolshevik Party. Nevertheless, Lenin persisted with the notion that *Sovnarkom* had been appointed to govern by the Congress of Soviets. According to this view, the distribution of power in revolutionary Russia took the form of a pyramid, with *Sovnarkom* at the top, drawing its authority from the Russian people who expressed their will through the soviets at the base (see Figure 5.1).

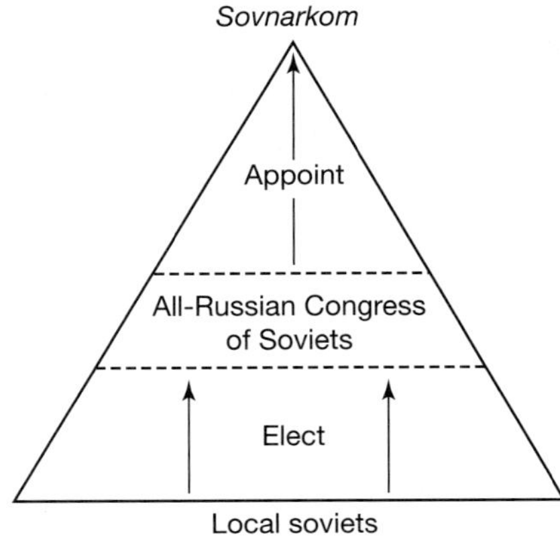


**Figure 5.1** The distribution of power in revolutionary Russia.

The reality was altogether different. Traditional forms of government had broken down in 1917 with the fall of tsardom and the overthrow of the Provisional Government. This meant the Bolsheviks were in a position to make up their own rules. The notion that it was the soviets who had taken power and now ruled was simply a convenient cover. From the beginning, whatever the claims may have been about the soviets' being in authority, it was in fact the Bolsheviks who held power. The key body here was the Central Committee of the Bolshevik party. It was this organisation, under Lenin's direction, that provided the members of the government. In a sense, *Sovnarkom* was a wing of the Bolshevik Party.

The Central Committee supposedly derived its authority from the All-Russian Congress of the Bolshevik Party, whose locally elected representatives voted on policy. However, in practice, the Congress and the local parties did as they were told. This was in keeping with Lenin's demand that the Bolshevik Party operate according to the principle of democratic centralism (see page 24), a formula that guaranteed that power was exercised from the top down, rather than the bottom up.

## Lenin's Decrees

Before the October Revolution, Lenin had written powerfully against landlords and grasping capitalists, but he had produced little by way of a coherent plan for their replacement. It is understandable, therefore, that his policy after taking power in 1917 was a pragmatic one. He argued that the change from a bourgeois to a proletarian economy could not be achieved overnight. The Bolshevik government would continue to use the existing structures until the transition had been completed and a fully fledged socialist system could be adopted. This transitional stage was referred to as 'state capitalism' (see page 14).

Lenin was aware that there were many Bolsheviks who wanted the immediate introduction of a sweeping revolutionary policy, but he pointed out that the new regime simply did not possess the power to impose this. Its authority did not run much beyond Petrograd and Moscow. Until the Bolsheviks could exercise a truly national control, their policies would have to fit the prevailing circumstances. The war against Germany and Austria had brought Russia huge problems. Chief among these were:

- a shortage of raw materials
- rocketing inflation
- a fractured transport system
- hunger gripped large areas of Russia – grain supplies were over 13 million tons short of the nation's needs
- within a few months of the October Revolution, the food crisis had been further deepened by the ceding to Germany of Ukraine, Russia's richest grain-producing region (see page 141).

To tackle these problems, three decrees were issued that were meant to define the government's approach to national policy: Decrees on Peace, Land and Workers' Control, and Nationalisation.

### Decree on Peace, October 1917

Issued in October, this was not so much a decree as an appeal to the warring nations to enter into talks for 'a democratic peace without annexations'. Despite its apparent idealism, this was Lenin's hard-headed first step towards making peace with Germany, something which he knew the Bolshevik government had to do if it was to survive (see page 136).

### Decree on Land, November 1917

The key part of this measure is quoted in Source A. In truth, the decree simply gave Bolshevik approval to the reality of what had been happening in the countryside since the February Revolution: in many areas the peasants had overthrown their landlords and occupied their property.

? To which section of Russian society was the decree in Source A aimed to appeal?

**SOURCE A**

**From 'The Decree on Land' (available from www.marxists.org/archive/lenin/works/1917/oct/25-26/26d.htm).**

*(1) Private ownership of land shall be abolished forever; land shall not be sold, purchased, leased, mortgaged, or otherwise alienated. All land, whether state, crown, monastery, church, factory, entailed, private, public, peasant, etc., shall be confiscated without compensation and become the property of the whole people, and pass into the use of all those who cultivate it. Persons who suffer by this property revolution shall be deemed to be entitled to public support only for the period necessary for adaptation to the new conditions of life.*

*(2) All mineral wealth ore, oil, coal, salt, etc., and also all forests and waters of state importance, shall pass into the exclusive use of the state. All the small streams, lakes, woods, etc., shall pass into the use of the communes, to be administered by the local self-government bodies.*

*(3) Lands on which high-level scientific farming is practised, orchards, tree-farms, seed plots, nurseries, hothouses, etc. shall not be divided up, but shall be converted into model farms, to be turned over for exclusive use to the state or to the communes, depending on the size and importance of such lands.*

### Decree on Workers' Control, November 1917

This measure, too, was also largely concerned with authorising what had already occurred. During 1917 a large number of factories had been taken over by the workers. However, the workers' committees that were then formed seldom ran the factories efficiently. The result was a serious fall in industrial output. The decree accepted the workers' takeover, but at the same time it instructed the workers' committees to maintain 'the strictest order and discipline' in the workplace.

## *Vesenkha*

Although Lenin's government did not yet exercise full control over Russia, it pressed on with a scheme for establishing state direction of the economy. In December 1917, ***Vesenkha*** (*Gosplan*) was set up 'to take charge of all existing institutions for the regulation of economic life'. Initially, *Vesenkha* was unable to exercise the full authority granted to it. However, it did preside over a number of important developments:

- Banks and railways were nationalised.
- Foreign debts were cancelled (see page 150).
- The transport system was improved.

These were important practical achievements, which suggested how effective centralised control might become were the Bolsheviks able to gain complete power.

**KEY TERM**

***Vesenkha*** The Supreme Council of the National Economy, later known as *Gosplan*.

## Decree on Nationalisation, June 1918

This measure laid down a programme for the takeover by the state of the larger industrial concerns. Within two years, it had brought practically all the major industrial enterprises in Russia under central government control.

**Summary diagram: The Bolsheviks in power**

**Problems confronting the Bolsheviks**

- Bolsheviks controlled only Petrograd and Moscow
- Low industrial production
- High inflation
- Severe food shortages
- Occupation by Germany

**Measures to tackle problems**

***Economic***

*Adoption of state capitalism* – a compromise measure to achieve the transition to a socialist economy

*Decree on Land* – abolished private property – recognised peasant takeovers

*Decree on Workers' Control* – an attempt to assert government authority over the factories which had been seized by workers

*Vesenkha* – body to oversee economic development

# Dissolution of the Constituent Assembly 1918

▶ *What did this event reveal about Lenin's attitude towards the exercise of power?*

As a revolutionary, Lenin had never been particularly concerned about how many people supported the Bolsheviks. Mere numbers did not interest him. He had no faith in democratic elections, which he dismissed as tricks by which the bourgeoisie kept itself in power. His primary objective was not to win mass support, but to create a party capable of seizing power when the opportune moment came. After the successful October coup in 1917, Lenin was even more determined not to allow elections to undermine the Bolsheviks' newly won power. However, there was an immediate problem. The October events had come too late to prevent the elections to the All-Russian Constituent Assembly from going ahead in November as planned. When the results came through by the end of the year they did not make pleasant reading for the Bolsheviks:

- they had been outvoted by nearly two to one by the Social Revolutionaries (SRs)
- they had won only 24 per cent of the total vote
- they had gained barely a quarter of the seats in the assembly.

**Table 5.1** Results of the election for the Constituent Assembly, November 1917

| Parties | Votes | Seats |
|---|---|---|
| SRs | 17,490,000 | 370 |
| Bolsheviks | 9,844,000 | 175 |
| National minority groups | 8,257,000 | 99 |
| Left SRs (pro-Bolshevik) | 2,861,000 | 40 |
| Kadets | 1,986,000 | 17 |
| Mensheviks | 1,248,000 | 16 |
| Total | 41,686,000 | 717 |

## Lenin's motives for destroying the assembly

Lenin had originally supported the idea of a Constituent Assembly since it offered a way of further weakening the authority of the Provisional Government. Now, however, with his party in power, he had no need of an assembly. Furthermore, since it was overwhelmingly non-Bolshevik it would almost certainly make life difficult for his government. One possibility was that he could have tried to work with the new assembly. But that was not how Lenin operated. He was not a democrat; he did not deal in compromise. He was a revolutionary who believed that the only way to govern was not by compromise but by crushing opposition. Hence, his response to the Constituent Assembly, when it gathered in January 1918, was simple and ruthless. After only one day's session, it was dissolved at gunpoint by the Red Guards. A few members tried to protest, but, with rifles trained on their heads, their resistance soon evaporated. It was a bitter end to the dreams of liberals and reformers. There would not be another democratic body in Russia until after the collapse of Soviet communism over 70 years later.

Lenin's act of violence in January 1918 has to be viewed in context. The Bolsheviks' hold on power was precarious. Indeed, the prospects of Bolshevik survival at all seemed slim. There was strong and widespread opposition to them inside the country. Moreover, Russia was still at war with Germany, which meant that the Allies, France and Britain, were all set to interfere should the new Russian government make a separate peace. In such an atmosphere, the Bolsheviks were not prepared to consider power sharing.

Lenin justified the Bolshevik action by arguing that the original reason for electing an assembly, the establishing of an all-Russian representative body, had already been achieved by the creation of a Soviet government in October 1917. The people's will had expressed itself in the October Revolution. The Constituent Assembly was, therefore, superfluous. More than that, it was corrupt. The elections, he asserted, had been rigged by the SRs and the Kadets; consequently, the results did not truly reflect the wishes of the Russian people. In such circumstances, Lenin declared, to hand over power to the Constituent Assembly would be 'to compromise with the malignant bourgeoisie. Nothing in the world will induce us to surrender the Soviet power.'

Commenting on Lenin's attitude, Trotsky noted that Lenin was always ready to back his theories with force by using 'sharpshooters'. He recorded a remark Lenin had made to him in private: 'The dissolution of the Constituent Assembly by the Soviet government means a complete and frank liquidation of the idea of democracy by the idea of dictatorship.'

## Reactions to the crushing of the assembly

Lenin's ruthlessness caused unease among some of his own supporters. **Maxim Gorky**, one of the Bolshevik Party's leading intellectuals, likened it to Bloody Sunday 1905 (see page 32) and described Lenin as 'a cold-blooded trickster who spares neither the honour nor the life of the proletariat'. Many foreign Communists were similarly appalled by Lenin's behaviour. Rosa Luxemburg, a German socialist, condemned 'the elimination of democracy' in Russia. She complained bitterly that the 'remedy' provided by Lenin and Trotsky was 'worse than the disease it is supposed to cure'.

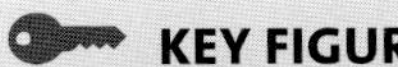
**KEY FIGURE**

**Maxim Gorky (1868–1936)**

Internationally celebrated Russian social and political commentator.

Such criticisms did not move Lenin. As he saw it, the desperately vulnerable position the Bolsheviks were in – attempting to impose themselves on Russia while surrounded by enemies on all sides – demanded the sternest of measures. Nor was he short of theory to justify his actions. The concept of democratic centralism, which required the absolute obedience of party members to the leaders, perfectly fitted the situation in which the Bolsheviks found themselves.

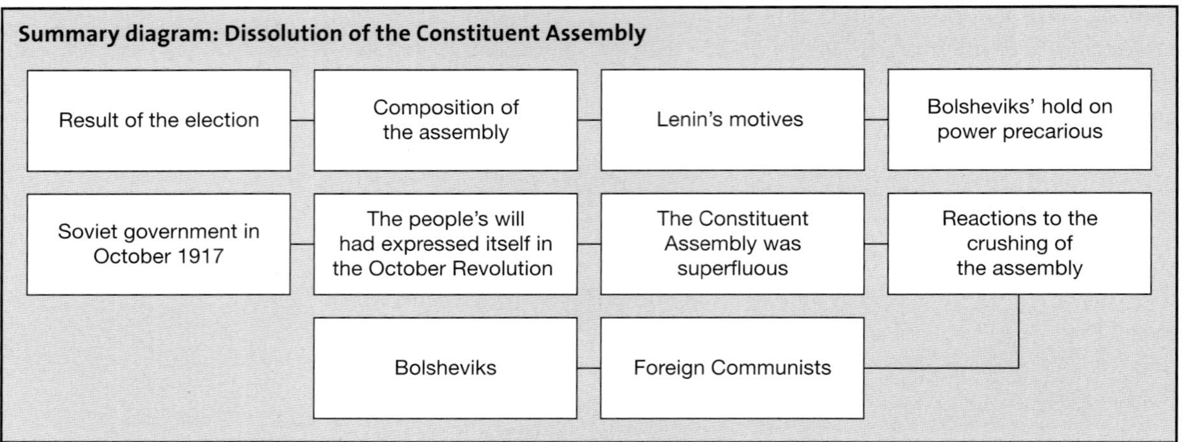


# 3 Treaty of Brest-Litovsk 1918

► *Why were the Bolsheviks willing to accept the humiliation of Russia in the Treaty of Brest-Litovsk?*

Lenin and Trotsky were united in their suppression of the Constituent Assembly. However, there was a marked difference of attitude between them over the issue of the war with Germany. Both wanted it ended but they disagreed on how this could best be achieved. Lenin wanted an immediate peace; Trotsky wanted a delay.

## Lenin's view

Lenin's thinking ran along the following lines. Russia's military exhaustion made it impossible for it to fight on successfully. If Germany eventually won the war on both fronts it would retain the Russian territory it now possessed. But if Germany lost the war against the Western Allies, Russia would regain its occupied lands. In the first eventuality, Russia would not be worse off; in the second it would actually gain. It was, therefore, pointless for Bolshevik Russia to continue to fight.

An interesting aspect of Lenin's readiness to make peace with Germany was that it was not wholly ideological. Between 1914 and 1917 the German Foreign Office had given substantial amounts of money to Lenin and the Bolsheviks in the hope that if they succeeded in their revolution they would pull Russia out of the war (see page 101). Germany continued to finance Lenin even after the October Revolution and the armistice of December 1917. A settlement with Germany was, therefore, very much in Lenin's interests since it was the best guarantee against the drying up of this lucrative source of Bolshevik revenue.

## Trotsky's view

Trotsky took a middle position between Lenin, who wanted a peace straightaway, and those Bolsheviks and Left Revolutionaries who pressed for the continuation of the war as a revolutionary crusade against imperialist Germany. Trotsky shared Lenin's view that Bolshevik Russia had no realistic chance of successfully continuing the military struggle against Germany. However, in the hope that within a short time the German armies would collapse on the Western Front and revolution would follow in Germany, Trotsky was determined to make the peace talks a protracted affair. He wanted to buy time for Bolshevik agitators to exploit the mutinies in the Austro-German armies.

## Bolshevik tactics at Brest-Litovsk

Trotsky's approach, for which he coined the slogan 'neither peace, nor war', was intended to confuse and infuriate the German delegation at Brest-Litovsk, the Polish town where the Germans and Russians gathered to discuss peace terms. Trotsky showed his contempt for what he called 'bourgeois propriety' by consistently flouting the traditional etiquette of European diplomacy. He would yawn loudly while German representatives were speaking and start private conversations with his Bolshevik colleagues rather than listen to what was being said. When he did join in the formal negotiations, he would ignore the point under discussion and launch into revolutionary speeches praising the October coup in Russia and calling on Germany to overthrow its corrupt bourgeois government.

Germany's chief negotiator, Field-Marshal Hindenburg, complained that Trotsky and Lenin 'behaved more like victors than vanquished'. What Hindenburg had failed to grasp was that Trotsky and Lenin did indeed see themselves as victors – potential if not actual. They were not perturbed by the thought of national defeat. Their conviction was that time and history were on their side. They believed that a great international political victory was imminent. It is important to remember that Lenin and Trotsky were **international revolutionaries**. They had only a limited loyalty towards Russia as a nation. Their first concern was to spread the proletarian revolution.

This readiness to subordinate Russian national interests explains why, to the dismay of most Russians and many Bolsheviks, the Soviet delegation at Brest-Litovsk was eventually willing to sign a devastating peace treaty as soon as it became clear that the exasperated Germans were seriously considering marching on Petrograd to overthrow Lenin's government.

Trotsky's outlook as an international revolutionary did not prevent him from scoring a sharp nationalist propaganda point. Before signing the treaty on 3 March 1918, Sokolnikov, the Soviet representative, declared, under instructions from Trotsky, that it was not a freely negotiated settlement but a German ***Diktat*** imposed on a helpless Russia. Backing was given to this claim

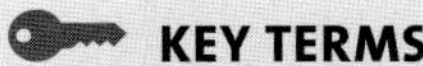

**KEY TERMS**

**International revolutionaries** Those Marxists who were willing to sacrifice mere national interests in the cause of the worldwide rising of the workers.

***Diktat*** A settlement imposed on a weaker nation by a stronger one.

by the terms of the treaty, which could hardly have been more humiliating for Russia:

- A huge slice of territory, amounting to a third of European Russia, stretching from the Baltic to the Black Sea and including Ukraine, Russia's major grain source, was ceded to Germany or its allies.
- The land lost by Russia – about 386,000 square miles (a million square kilometres) – contained a population of 45 million.
- Russia was required to pay three billion roubles in war **reparations**.

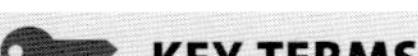

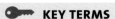

**KEY TERMS**

**Reparations** Payment of war costs by the loser to the victor.

**Finance-capital** The resource used by stronger countries to exploit weaker ones. By investing heavily in another country, a stronger power made that country dependent on it.

**'Left Communists'** Those Bolsheviks who were convinced that their first task was to consolidate the October Revolution by driving the German imperialist armies from Russia.

## Lenin's reasons for signing the treaty

Aware that the signing of the treaty would be resented by many Bolsheviks, who were still pressing for a revolutionary struggle against Germany, Lenin stressed that his policy was the only realistic one: 'Russia can offer no physical resistance because she is materially exhausted by three years of war.' He acknowledged that there were Russians willing to fight on in a great cause. But they were, he said, 'romanticists' who did not understand the situation. Wars were not won by idealism alone; resources and technical skills were needed. The plain truth was that Bolshevik Russia did not yet have these in sufficient quantity to match Germany. Therefore, 'the Russian Revolution must sign the peace to obtain a breathing space to recuperate for the struggle'.

Lenin added that he expected that Russia would soon be in a position to reclaim its lost territories, since in the aftermath of the war a violent conflict would soon develop among the capitalist powers. The main struggle would be between 'English and German **finance-capital**'. In Lenin's view, the First World War had been caused by the rivalry between the imperialist powers, France, Germany and Britain, competing for the dwindling markets in which to invest their surplus capital. His rallying cry was, therefore, 'Let the Revolution utilise this struggle for its own ends'. Lenin's argument was a powerful one, yet he still experienced great difficulty in convincing his colleagues. The matter was debated bitterly in the Central Committee. In the end, Lenin gained his way by a majority of only one in a crucial committee division.

A profound issue lay at the base of Bolshevik disagreements. To understand this, it has to be re-emphasised that Lenin and Trotsky were primarily international revolutionaries. They expected workers' risings, based on the Russian model, to sweep across Europe. Purely national conflicts would soon be superseded by the international class struggle of the workers. Lenin and Trotsky regarded the crippling terms of the Treaty of Brest-Litovsk as of small account when set against the great sweep of world revolution.

## The 'Left Communists'

Not all Bolsheviks shared this vision. A number, known as **'Left Communists'**, condemned the signing of the Treaty at Brest-Litovsk. In the end, after days of wrangling, it was only Lenin's insistence on the absolute need for party loyalty in a time of crisis that finally persuaded them reluctantly to accept the treaty. Even then, serious opposition to Lenin's leadership might well have persisted had not the turn of military events in Western Europe saved the day.

What eventually destroyed the argument of the Left Communists was the collapse of Germany's Western Front in August 1918, followed by the almost total withdrawal of German forces from Russia. Lenin's gamble that circumstances would soon make the Treaty of Brest-Litovsk meaningless had paid off. It strengthened his hold over the party and provided the opportunity to expel the Left SRs from the government and to outlaw them politically.

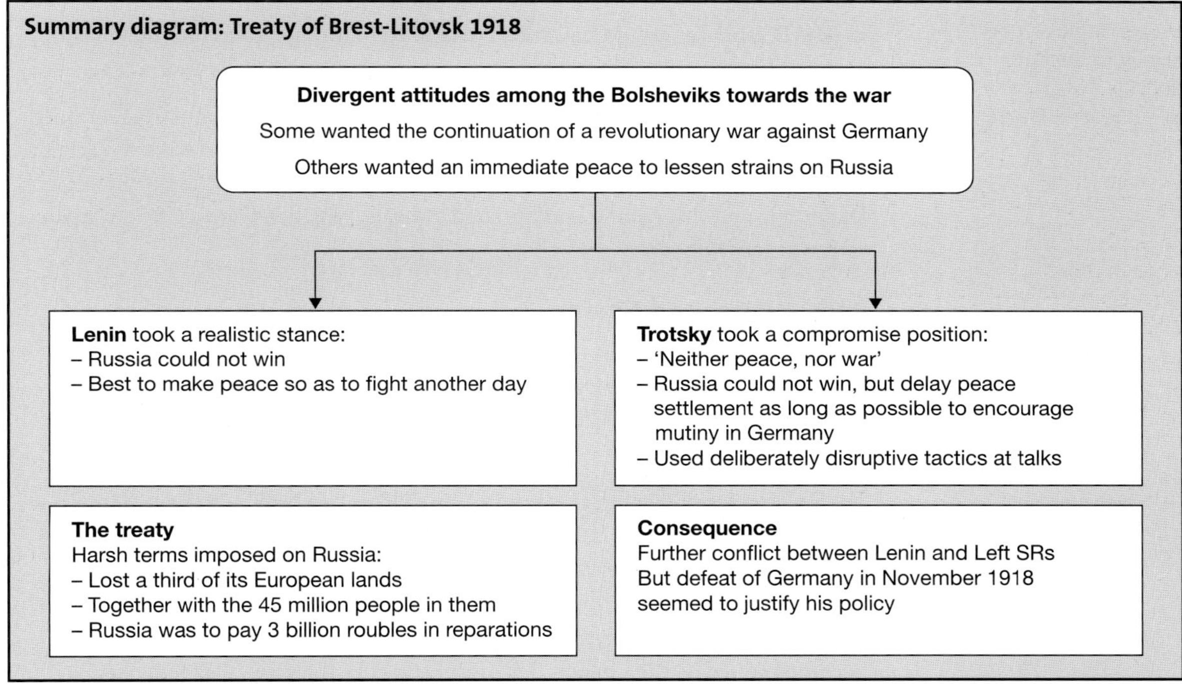

Summary diagram: Treaty of Brest-Litovsk 1918
Divergent attitudes among the Bolsheviks towards the war
Some wanted the continuation of a revolutionary war against Germany
Others wanted an immediate peace to lessen strains on Russia
Lenin took a realistic stance:
– Russia could not win
– Best to make peace so as to fight another day
Trotsky took a compromise position:
– 'Neither peace, nor war'
– Russia could not win, but delay peace settlement as long as possible to encourage mutiny in Germany
– Used deliberately disruptive tactics at talks
The treaty
Harsh terms imposed on Russia:
– Lost a third of its European lands
– Together with the 45 million people in them
– Russia was to pay 3 billion roubles in reparations
Consequence
Further conflict between Lenin and Left SRs
But defeat of Germany in November 1918 seemed to justify his policy

## 4 Russian Civil War 1918–20

▶ *How far was Lenin personally responsible for the Civil War?*

The Bolsheviks' crushing of the Constituent Assembly in January 1918, followed by their outlawing of all other parties, showed that they were not prepared to share power. This bid for absolute authority made civil war highly likely, given that the Bolsheviks had only a limited grip on Russia in their early years in power. They were bound to face military opposition from their wide range of opponents who were not prepared to accept being subjected to the absolute rule of a minority party.

Modern research strongly suggests that Lenin truly wanted a destructive civil war. Although it involved obvious dangers to the Bolsheviks, Lenin was convinced that his forces could win and in the process wipe out all their opponents, military and political. Better to have a short, brutal struggle than face many years of being harassed and challenged by the anti-Bolsheviks who were a large majority in Russia, as the Constituent Assembly election results had shown (see page 134). Lenin feared that, had the Bolsheviks chosen to co-operate in a coalition of all the revolutionary parties in 1918, it would have had two consequences:

- A successful counter-revolution would be easier to mount since the socialist parties would have had a popular **mandate** to govern.
- The Bolsheviks would have been unable to dominate government since they were very much a minority compared with the Social Revolutionaries.

**KEY TERM**

**Mandate** The authority to govern granted by a majority of the people through elections.

It was the second consequence that Lenin refused to contemplate. As Dominic Lieven, an outstanding modern scholar, observes: 'Some Bolsheviks would have accepted a socialist coalition but Lenin was not one of them. The Bolshevik leader rejected this course and pursued policies, which, as he well knew, made civil war inevitable.'

## Reds, Whites and Greens

The conflict that began in the summer of 1918 was not just a matter of the Bolsheviks (Reds) facing their political enemies (Whites) in military struggle. From the start the Civil War was a more complex affair. It involved yet another colour – the Greens.

The Bolsheviks presented the struggle as a class war, but it was never simply this. The sheer size of Russia often meant that local or regional considerations predominated over larger issues. Significantly, a number of Russia's national minorities, such as the Ukrainians and the Georgians, fought in the war primarily to establish their independence from Russia. These national forces became known as the Greens. The best known of the Green leaders was Makhno, a one-time Bolshevik, who organised a guerrilla resistance to the Reds in Ukraine.

- Reds: the Bolsheviks and their supporters, red being the colour traditionally associated with revolution.
- Whites: the Bolsheviks' opponents, including monarchists looking for a tsarist restoration, and those parties who had been outlawed or suppressed by the new regime. White was the colour traditionally associated with Russian monarchy.
- Greens: groups from the national minorities, struggling for independence from central Russian control. For nationalists, green was a colour symbolising freedom.

It was ironic that, although most of the leading Bolsheviks were non-Russian, having been born in other provinces of the empire, their rule was seen by many as yet another attempt to reassert Russian authority over the rest of the country – the very situation that had prevailed under the tsars. An additional complication was that, as in all civil wars, the disruption provided a cover for settling old scores and pursuing personal vendettas, and it was not uncommon for villages or families to be divided against each other.

## A war about food

On occasion, the fighting was simply a desperate struggle for food. Famine provided the backdrop to the Civil War. The breakdown in food supplies that had occurred during the war against Germany persisted. Until this was remedied whole areas of Russia remained hungry.

The failure of the new regime to end hunger was a factor in the forming of the initial military opposition to the Bolsheviks in 1918. In addition to the problems of a fractured transport system, Lenin's government was faced with the loss to Germany of Russia's main wheat-supply area, Ukraine. In March 1918, the month in which the Brest-Litovsk Treaty was signed, the bread ration in Petrograd reached its lowest ever allocation of 50 grams per day. Hunger forced many workers out of the major industrial cities. By June 1918 the workforce in Petrograd had shrunk by 60 per cent and the overall population had declined from 3 million to 2 million. A visitor to the city at this time spoke of 'entering a metropolis of cold, of hunger, of hatred, of endurance'. The Bolshevik boast that October 1917 had established worker control of Russian industry meant little now that the workers were deserting the factories in growing numbers.

## Challenge from the SRs

The desperate circumstances encouraged open challenges to the Bolsheviks from both left and right. The SRs, who had been driven from the government following their refusal to accept the Brest-Litovsk settlement, organised an anti-Bolshevik coup in Moscow, which for security reasons had replaced Petrograd as Russia's capital. The Civil War could be said, therefore, to have begun not as a counter-revolution but as an effort by one set of revolutionaries to take power from another. In that sense it was an attempted act of revenge by a majority party, the SRs, against a minority party, the Bolsheviks, for having usurped the authority that they claimed was properly theirs. In their bitterness at being denied any say in government, the SRs joined the Whites in their struggle against Lenin's Reds. In the event, the SR challenge in Moscow was violently crushed. The climax came on 7 July 1918, when, after a four-hour battle, the 2000 troops that the SRs were able to muster were eventually scattered by Bolshevik artillery units.

### Attempted assassination of Lenin

The SRs' military rising in Moscow failed, but their terrorism came closer to success. Lenin narrowly survived two attempts on his life, in July and August 1918. The second attempt, by Dora Kaplan, an SR fanatic, left him with a bullet lodged in his neck, an injury that contributed to his death six years later.

### The Czech Legion

Armed resistance to the Bolsheviks had occurred sporadically in various parts of Russia since October 1917. What gave focus to this struggle was the behaviour in the summer of 1918 of one of the foreign armies still in Russia. Forty thousand Czechoslovak troops who had volunteered to fight on the Russian side in the First World War as a means of gaining independence from Austria-Hungary, found themselves isolated after the Treaty of Brest-Litovsk. They reformed themselves into the Czech Legion and decided to make the long journey eastwards to Vladivostok. Their aim was eventually to rejoin the Allies on the Western Front in the hope of winning international support for the formation of an independent Czechoslovak state. The Bolsheviks resented the presence of this well-equipped foreign army making its way arrogantly across Russia. Local soviets began to challenge the Czech Legion and fierce fighting accompanied its progress along the Trans-Siberian Railway.

? How does Source B help to explain why the presence of the Czech Legion in Russia was such a problem for the Bolsheviks?

**SOURCE B**

**Well armed and supplied, the troops of the Czech Legion aboard an armoured train in 1918.**

### White resistance

All this encouraged the Whites, and the revolutionary and liberal groups who had been outlawed by the Bolsheviks, to come out openly against Lenin's regime. Among the key areas of conflict were the following:

- The SRs organised a number of uprisings in central Russia and established an anti-Bolshevik Volga 'Republic' at Samara.
- A White 'Volunteer Army', led by **General Denikin**, had already been formed in the Caucasus region of southern Russia from tsarist loyalists and outlawed Kadets.
- In Siberia, the presence of the Czech Legion encouraged the formation of a White army under **Admiral Kolchak**, the self-proclaimed 'Supreme Ruler of the Russian State'.
- In Estonia, **General Yudenich** began to form a White army of resistance.
- In Ukraine, **Baron Wrangel** led a 'Caucasus Volunteer Army' against the Bolsheviks.
- White units appeared in many regions elsewhere. The speed with which they arose indicated just how limited Bolshevik control was outside the cities of western Russia.

**KEY FIGURES**

**General Anton Denikin (1872–1947)**

An ex-tsarist general who had supported Kornilov in 1917.

**Admiral Alexander Kolchak (1873–1920)**

Former Commander of the Russian Black Sea fleet.

**General Nicolai Yudenich (1862–1933)**

An ex-tsarist general who had distinguished himself in the Russo-Japanese War.

**Baron Pyotr Wrangel (1878–1928)**

Served in the imperial army in the Russo-Japanese War and the First World War; decorated for bravery.

The patchwork of political, regional and national loyalties inside Russia made the Civil War a confused affair. It is best understood as a story of the Bolsheviks' resisting attacks on four main fronts, and then taking the initiative and driving back their attackers until they eventually withdrew or surrendered. Unlike the First World War, the Civil War was a war of movement, largely dictated by the layout of Russia's railway system. It was because the Bolsheviks were largely successful in their desperate fight to maintain control of the railways that they were able to keep themselves supplied, while denying the Whites the same benefit.

## Reasons for Bolshevik victory

The reasons for the final victory of the Reds in the Civil War are not difficult to determine.

### White weaknesses

- The various White armies fought as separate detachments.
- Apart from their obvious desire to overthrow the Bolsheviks, they were not bound together by a single aim.
- The Whites were unwilling to sacrifice their individual interests in order to form a united anti-Bolshevik front. This allowed the Reds to pick off the White armies separately.
- In the rare cases in which the Whites did consider combining, they were too widely scattered geographically to be able to bring sufficient pressure to bear on the enemy.

- The Whites were too reliant on supplies from abroad, which seldom arrived in sufficient quantities, in the right places, at the right time.
- The Whites lacked leaders of the quality of Trotsky.

## Red strengths

The Reds, in contrast, had a number of overwhelming advantages:

- They remained in control of a concentrated central area of western Russia, which they were able to defend by maintaining their inner communication and supply lines.
- The two major cities, Petrograd and Moscow, the administrative centres of Russia, remained in their hands throughout the war, as did most of the railway network.
- The Reds also possessed a key advantage in that the areas where they had their strongest hold were the industrial centres of Russia. This gave them access to munitions and resources denied to the Whites.
- The dependence of the Whites on supplies from abroad appeared to prove the Red accusation that they were in league with the foreign interventionists (see page 148). The Civil War had produced a paradoxical situation in which the Reds were able to stand as champions of the Russian nation as well as proletarian revolutionaries.
- The Red Army was brilliantly organised and led by Trotsky.

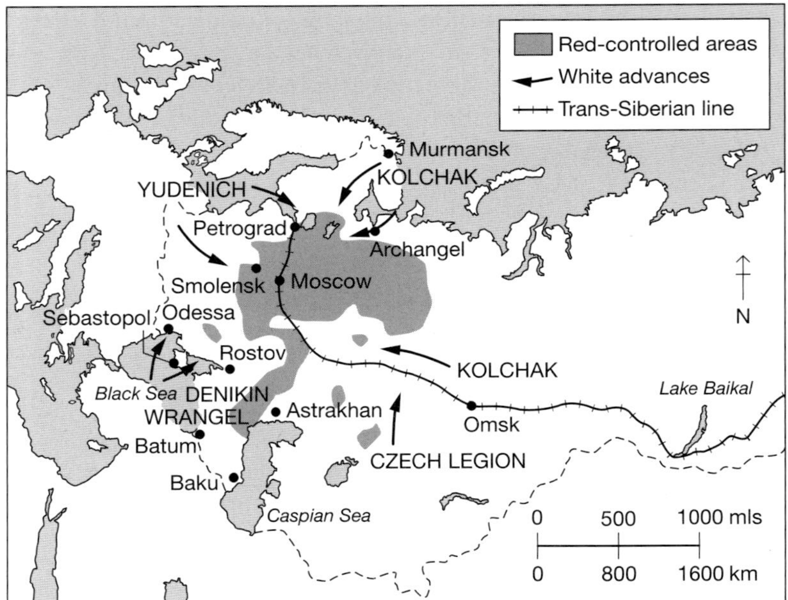


**Figure 5.2** The Russian Civil War 1918–20. The names of the principal White opponents of the Reds are in capitals.

## Trotsky's role

Trotsky's strategy was simple and direct:

- To defend the Red Army's internal lines of communication.
- To deny the Whites the opportunity to concentrate large forces in any one location.
- To prevent the Whites maintaining regular supplies.

The basis of this strategy was control of Russia's railways. Trotsky viewed the function of the railways as equivalent to that of the cavalry in former times. They were the means of transporting troops swiftly and in large numbers to the critical areas of defence or attack. That was why the decisive confrontations between Reds and Whites took place near rail junctions and depots. Trotsky's broad strategy was successful. Once the Reds had established an effective defence of their main region around Petrograd and Moscow, they were able to exhaust the enemy as an attacking force and then drive them back on the major fronts until they scattered or surrendered.

## Red brutality

As in most civil wars, the Reds and Whites continually accused each other of committing atrocities. Both sides did undoubtedly use terror to crush opposition in the areas they seized. The actual fighting was not unduly bloody; it was in the aftermath, when the civilian population had been cowed, that the savagery usually occurred. The Reds gained recruits by offering defeated enemy troops and neutral civilians the stark choice of enlistment or execution.

Although the Reds imposed a reign of terror, the Whites' own record in ill-treating local populations was equally notorious. A White general wrote revealingly of how the atrocities committed by his side provided a propaganda gift to the Reds:

**SOURCE C**

**From the diary of General Alexei Budberg, 3 May 1919, quoted in E. Acton, editor, *The Soviet Union: A Documentary History*, volume 1, University of Exeter Press, 2005, p. 80.**

*The lads think that, if they have killed and tortured a few hundred or thousand Bolsheviks and beaten up a certain number of commissars, then they have done a great job, inflicted a decisive blow on Bolshevism and brought the restoration of the old order nearer … The lads do not seem to realise that if they rape, flog, rob, torture and kill indiscriminately and without restraint, they are thereby instilling such hatred for the government they represent that the swine in Moscow must be delighted at having such diligent, valuable and beneficial collaborators.*

What ironic consequence of White Terror does the writer of Source C foresee?

To the ordinary Russian there was little to choose between the warring sides in the matter of brutality. By the end of the Civil War, any initial sympathy gained by the Reds from the peasants was lost by the severity of their grain-requisitioning methods. However, the Whites were unable to present themselves as a better alternative. All they could offer was a return to the pre-revolutionary past. This was particularly damaging to them in relation to the land question. The Reds continually pointed out that all the lands that the peasants had seized in the revolutions of 1917 would be forfeit if ever the Whites were to win the war. It was this fear more than any other that stopped the peasants from giving their support to the Whites.

### The importance of morale

Waging war is not just a matter of resources and firepower. Morale and dedication play a vital role. Throughout the struggle, the Reds were sustained by a driving sense of purpose. Trotsky, as the Bolshevik war commissar, may have been extreme in his methods, but he created an army that proved capable of fighting with an unshakable belief in its own eventual victory. Set against this, the Whites were never more than an uncoordinated group of forces, whose morale was seldom high. They were a collection of dispossessed socialists and liberals, whose political differences often led them into bitter disputes among themselves. Save for their hatred of Bolshevism, the Whites lacked a common purpose. Throughout the Civil War, the White cause was deeply divided by the conflicting interests of those who were fighting for national or regional independence and those who wanted a return to strong central government. Furthermore, no White leader emerged of the stature of Trotsky or Lenin around whom an effective anti-Bolshevik army could unite.

## The effects of the Civil War on the Bolsheviks

The war had a number of formative influences on the character of the Bolshevik Party (renamed the Communist Party in 1919).

### Toughness

The Bolsheviks' efforts to consolidate their hold on Russian government took place during a period of conflict in which their very survival was at stake. The development of the party and the government has to be set against this background. The revolution had been born in war, and the government had been formed in war. Of all the members of the Communist Party in 1927, a third had joined in the years 1917–20 and had fought in the Red Army. This had created a tradition of military obedience and loyalty. The Bolsheviks of this generation were hard men, forged in the fires of war.

### Authoritarianism

A number of modern analysts have emphasised the central place that the Civil War had in shaping the character of Communist rule in Soviet Russia.

Historian Robert Tucker stresses that it was the military aspect of early Bolshevik government that left it with a 'readiness to resort to coercion, rule by **administrative fiat**, centralised administration and summary justice'. No regime placed in the Bolshevik predicament between 1917 and 1921 could have survived without resorting to authoritarian measures.

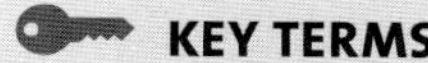

**KEY TERMS**

**Administrative fiat** Strict command from above.

**Politburo** The Political Bureau, responsible for major policy decisions.

**Orgburo** Organisation Bureau, which turned the policies into practice.

**Secretariat** A form of civil service that administered policies.

## Centralisation

The move towards centralism in government increased as the Civil War dragged on. The emergencies of war required immediate day-to-day decisions to be made. This led to effective power moving away from the Central Committee of the Communist (Bolshevik) Party, which was too cumbersome, into the hands of the two key sub-committees, the **Politburo** and the **Orgburo**, set up in 1919, that could act with the necessary speed. In practice, the authority of *Sovnarkom*, the official government of Soviet Russia, became indistinguishable from the rule of these party committees, which were served by the **Secretariat**.

## The war's end

Since the Civil War had not been formally declared, it followed that there was no formal date for its ending. No Red–White peace treaties were signed. The war in a sense petered out in 1920 as the leaders of the disparate White armies accepted that they had no realistic chance of militarily defeating their Red enemies.

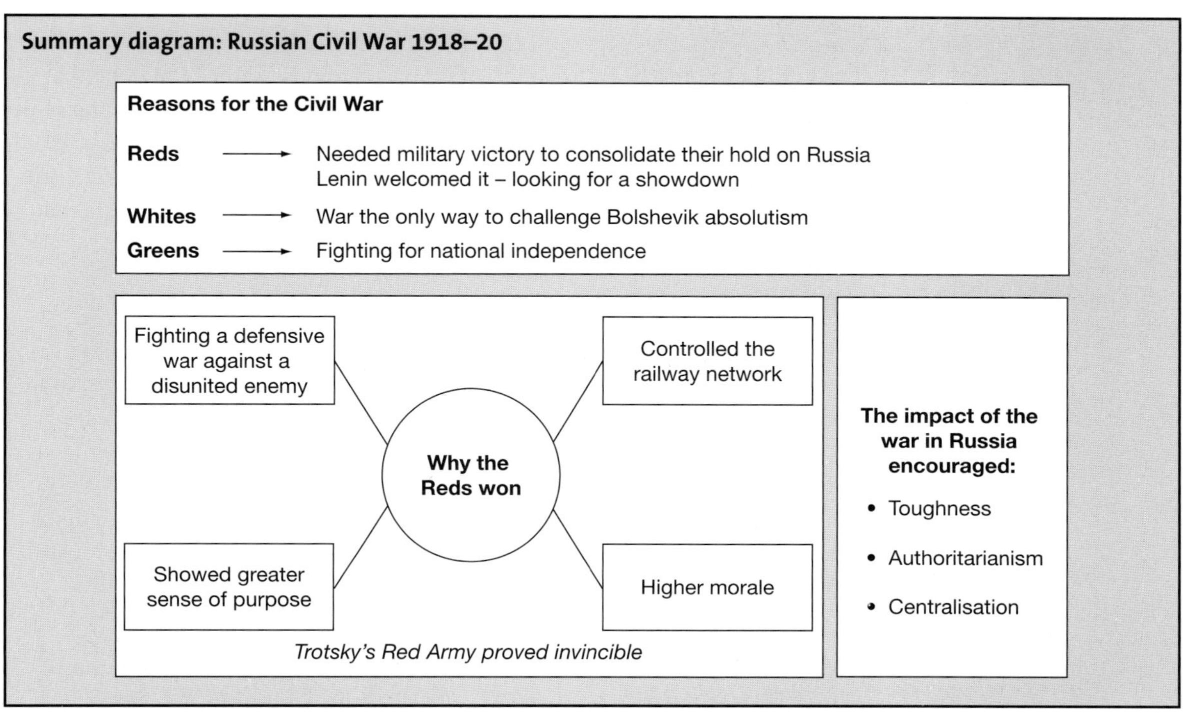

Summary diagram: Russian Civil War 1918–20
Reasons for the Civil War
Reds
Needed military victory to consolidate their hold on Russia
Lenin welcomed it – looking for a showdown
Whites
War the only way to challenge Bolshevik absolutism
Greens
Fighting for national independence
Fighting a defensive war against a disunited enemy
Controlled the railway network
Why the Reds won
Showed greater sense of purpose
Higher morale
Trotsky's Red Army proved invincible
The impact of the war in Russia encouraged:
• Toughness
• Authoritarianism
• Centralisation

#  Foreign interventions 1918–21

▶ *What led foreign powers to intervene in Russia?*

## Russia and the Western Allies

When tsardom collapsed in 1917, the immediate worry for the Western Allies was whether the new regime would keep Russia in the war. If revolutionary Russia made a separate peace, Germany would be free to divert huge military resources from the Eastern to the Western Front. To prevent this, the Allies offered large amounts of capital and military supplies to Russia to keep it in the war. The new government eagerly accepted the offer; throughout its eight months in office from February to October 1917 the Provisional Government remained committed to the war against Germany in return for Allied war-credits and supplies.

This produced an extraordinary balance. On one side stood Lenin and his anti-war Bolsheviks, financed by Germany; on the other the pro-war Provisional government, funded by the Allies. However, the October Revolution destroyed the balance. The collapse of the Provisional Government and the seizure of power by the Bolsheviks had precisely the effect hoped for by Germany and feared by the Allies. Within weeks, an armistice had been agreed between Germany and the new government, and fighting on the Eastern Front stopped in December 1917.

The initial response of France and Britain was cautious. In the faint hope that the Bolsheviks might be persuaded to continue the fight against Germany, the same support was offered to them as to their predecessors. David Lloyd George, the British prime minister, declared that he was neither for nor against Bolshevism, but simply anti-German. He was willing to side with any group in Russia that would continue the war against Germany.

### Allied and Bolshevik attitudes harden

The Treaty of Brest-Litovsk in March 1918 ended all hope of Lenin's Russia renewing the war against Germany. From now on, any help given by Britain to anti-German Russians went necessarily to anti-Bolshevik forces. It appeared to the Bolsheviks that Britain and its allies were intent on destroying them. This was matched by the Allies' view that in making a separate peace with Germany the Bolsheviks had betrayed the Allied cause. The result was a fierce determination among the Allies to prevent their vital war supplies, previously loaned to Russia and still stockpiled there, from falling into German hands.

Soon after the signing of the Treaty of Brest-Litovsk, British, French and US troops occupied the ports of Murmansk in the Arctic and Archangel in the White Sea (see the map on page 144). This was the beginning of a two-year

**SOURCE D**

What influence might images such as the one in Source D have in shaping British attitudes towards Bolshevik Russia?

**'The Peril Without'. A cartoon published in *Punch*, a British satirical magazine, in April 1919. The cartoon shows the Bolsheviks as ravenous wolves preparing to attack a peaceful Europe. Britain and France were among the leading Western countries who feared that revolutionary Bolshevism would spread across Europe.**

period during which armed forces from a large number of countries occupied key areas of European, central and far-eastern Russia.

Once the First World War had ended in Europe in November 1918, the attention of the major powers turned to the possibility of a full offensive against the Bolsheviks. Among those most eager for an attack were Winston Churchill, the British cabinet minister, and Marshal Foch, the French military leader. They were alarmed by the creation of the **Comintern** and by the spread of revolution in Germany and central Europe. Among the principal attempts at establishing Communist revolutions were the following:

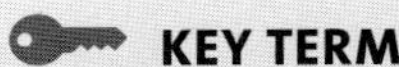

**KEY TERM**

**Comintern** The Communist International, a body set up in Moscow in March 1919 to organise worldwide revolution.

**KEY TERM**

**Spartacists** Named after Spartacus, the leader of a slave rebellion in ancient Rome.

- In January 1918, the **Spartacists**, a Communist movement in Germany, tried unsuccessfully to mount a coup in Berlin.
- In 1919, a short-lived Communist republic was established in Bavaria.
- In March 1919, in Hungary, a Marxist government was set up under Bela Kun, only to fall five months later.

## The interventions spread

There was also a strong financial aspect to anti-Bolshevism in Western Europe. One of the first acts of the Bolshevik regime had been to declare that the new government had no intention of honouring the foreign debts of its predecessors. In addition, it nationalised a large number of foreign companies and froze all foreign assets in Russia. The bitter reaction to what was regarded as international theft was particularly strong in France, where many financiers had invested in tsarist Russia. It was the French who now took the lead in proposing an international campaign against the Reds:

- In 1918 British land forces entered Transcaucasia in southern Russia and also occupied part of central Asia.
- British warships entered Russian Baltic waters and the Black Sea, where French naval vessels joined them.
- The French also established a major land base around the port of Odessa.
- In April 1918, Japanese troops occupied Russia's far-eastern port of Vladivostok.
- Four months later, units from France, Britain, the USA and Italy joined them.
- Czech, Finnish, Lithuanian, Polish and Romanian forces crossed into Russia.
- In 1919, Japanese and US troops occupied parts of Siberia.

These were not co-ordinated attacks. There was little co-operation between the occupiers. The declared motive of Britain, France, Germany, Italy, Japan and the USA was the legitimate protection of their individual interests. The objective of Czechoslovakia, Finland, Lithuania, Poland and Romania, all of whom directly bordered western Russia, was to achieve their separatist aim, going back to tsarist times, of gaining independence from Russia.

## The failure of the interventions

Despite the preaching of an anti-Bolshevik crusade by influential voices in Western Europe, no concerted attempt was ever made to unseat the Bolshevik regime. This was shown by the relative ease with which the interventions were resisted. The truth was that after four long years of struggle against Germany the interventionists had no stomach for a prolonged campaign. There were serious threats of mutiny in some British and French regiments ordered to embark for Russia. Trade unionists who were sympathetic towards the new 'workers' state' refused to transport military supplies bound for Russia.

**Figure 5.3** Foreign interventions 1918–21. © Sir Martin Gilbert

**KEY TERM**

**Baltic States** Estonia, Latvia and Lithuania.

After the separate national forces had arrived in Russia, there was seldom effective contact between them. Furthermore, such efforts as the foreign forces made to liaise with the White armies were half-hearted and came to little. The one major exception to this was in the **Baltic States** where the national forces, backed by British warships and troops, crushed a Bolshevik invasion and obliged Lenin's government to recognise the independence of Estonia, Latvia and Lithuania, a freedom which they maintained until taken over by Stalin in 1940.

Such interventionist success was not repeated elsewhere. After a token display of aggression, the foreign troops began to withdraw. By the end of 1919, all French and American troops had been recalled, and by the end of 1920, all other Western forces had left. It was only the Japanese who remained in Russia for the duration of the Civil War, not finally leaving until 1922.

### Propaganda success for the Bolsheviks

In no real sense were the foreign withdrawals a military victory for the Bolsheviks, but that was exactly how they were portrayed in Soviet propaganda. Lenin's government presented itself as the saviour of the nation from foreign conquest; all the interventions had been imperialist invasions of Russia intent on overthrowing the revolution. This apparent success over Russia's enemies helped the Bolshevik regime to recover the esteem it had lost over its 1918 capitulation to Germany. It helped to put resolve into the doubters in the party and it lent credibility to the Bolshevik depiction of the Whites as agents of foreign powers, intent on restoring reactionary tsardom.

### War against Poland

The failure of the foreign interventions encouraged the Bolsheviks to undertake what proved to be a disastrous attempt to expand their authority outside Russia. In 1920, the Red Army marched into neighbouring Poland, expecting the Polish workers to rise in rebellion against their own government. However, the Poles saw the invasion as traditional Russian aggression and drove the Red Army back across the border. Soviet morale was seriously damaged, which forced Lenin and the Bolsheviks to rethink the whole question of international revolution.

## Lenin's approach to foreign affairs

Lenin adopted an essentially realistic approach. He judged that the Polish reverse, the foreign interventions in Russia, and the failure of the Communist risings in Germany and Hungary all showed that the time was not ripe for world revolution. The capitalist nations were still too strong. The Bolsheviks would, therefore, without abandoning their long-term revolutionary aims, adjust their foreign policy to meet the new situation. The Comintern would continue to call for world revolution, but Soviet Russia would soften its international attitude.

Lenin's concerns were very much in the tradition of Russian foreign policy. Western encroachment into Russia had been a constant fear of the tsars. That long-standing Russian worry had been increased by the hostility of European governments towards the October Revolution and by their support of the Whites during the Civil War. Lenin's reading of the international situation led him to conclude that discretion was the better part of valour. Under him, Soviet foreign policy was activated not by thoughts of expansion but by the desire to avoid conflict.

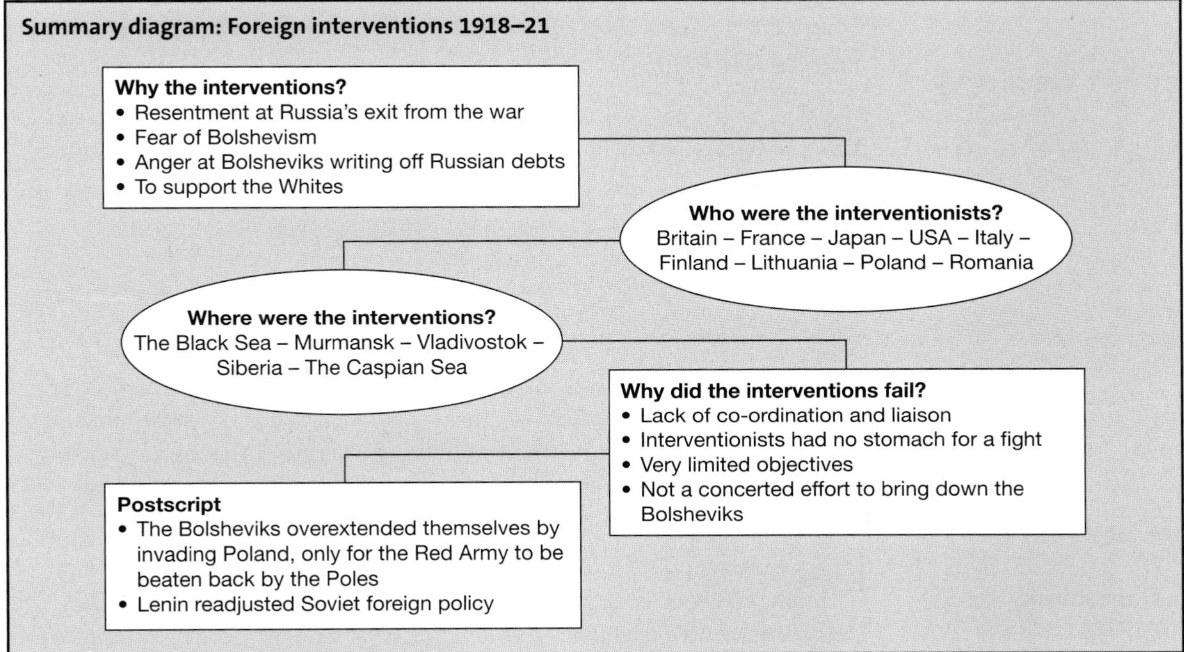

Summary diagram: Foreign interventions 1918–21
Why the interventions?
• Resentment at Russia's exit from the war
• Fear of Bolshevism
• Anger at Bolsheviks writing off Russian debts
• To support the Whites
Who were the interventionists?
Britain – France – Japan – USA – Italy – Finland – Lithuania – Poland – Romania
Where were the interventions?
The Black Sea – Murmansk – Vladivostok – Siberia – The Caspian Sea
Why did the interventions fail?
• Lack of co-ordination and liaison
• Interventionists had no stomach for a fight
• Very limited objectives
• Not a concerted effort to bring down the Bolsheviks
Postscript
• The Bolsheviks overextended themselves by invading Poland, only for the Red Army to be beaten back by the Poles
• Lenin readjusted Soviet foreign policy

# Lenin's methods of imposing control 1917–21

*Why did Lenin resort to authoritarian methods in consolidating Bolshevik control of Russia?*

The repression that accompanied the spread of Bolshevik control over Russia between 1918 and 1921 became known as the Red Terror. Whether the terror was necessary or justified remains a controversial question. One argument is that the extreme measures that Lenin's government adopted were the only response possible to the problems confronting the Bolsheviks after the October Revolution, in particular the need to win a desperate civil war.

An opposing view is that repression was not a reaction to circumstances but was a defining characteristic of **Marxism–Leninism**, a creed that regarded itself

**Marxism–Leninism** The notion that Marx's scientific analysis of class war had been developed by Lenin into a practical, workable programme.

as uniquely superior to all other ideologies. An extension of this argument is that there was something essentially totalitarian about Lenin himself. He did not know how to act in any other way. He had always accepted the necessity of terror as an instrument of political control. Before 1917 he had often made it clear that a Marxist revolution could not survive if it were not prepared to smash its enemies: 'Coercion is necessary for the transition from capitalism to socialism. There is absolutely no contradiction between Soviet democracy and the exercise of dictatorial powers.'

## The Red Terror

The chief instruments by which the Bolsheviks exercised their policy of terror were the ***Cheka*** and the Red Army, both of which played a critical role during the civil war.

**KEY TERM**

***Cheka*** 'The All-Russian Extraordinary Commission for Fighting Counter-Revolution, Sabotage and Speculation', a long title for what was essentially a secret police force, modelled on the tsarist *Okhrana*.

### The *Cheka*

Lenin was determined to impose absolute Bolshevik rule by the suppressing of all political opposition. A development that gave the Bolsheviks muscle in dealing with their opponents was the creation, in the weeks following the October coup, of the *Cheka*. In essentials, the *Cheka* was a better organised and more efficient form of the *Okhrana*, the tsarist secret police, at whose hands nearly every Bolshevik activist had suffered. Its express purpose was to destroy 'counter-revolution and sabotage', terms that were so elastic they could be stretched to cover anything of which the Bolsheviks disapproved.

This state secret police force, often likened historically to the *Gestapo* in Nazi Germany, had been created in December 1917 under the direction of **Felix Dzerzhinsky**, a Polish intellectual and aristocrat who pathologically despised his own class and wanted them to suffer. Lenin found him the ideal choice to lead the fight against the enemies of the revolution. Dzerzhinsky never allowed finer feelings or compassion to deter him from the task of destroying the opponents of Bolshevism. His remorseless attitude was shown in his first address as head of the *Cheka*:

**KEY FIGURE**

**Felix Dzerzhinsky (1877–1926)**

Head of the *Cheka*; of Polish aristocratic background, he sought to atone for his privileged origins by absolute dedication to Bolshevism.

**SOURCE E**

**From Dzerzhinsky's address, 20 December 1917, quoted in N. Zubov, *Dzerzhinsky*, Moscow, 1933, p. 9.**

*This is no time for speech-making. Our Revolution is in serious danger. We are ready to do all to defend the attainments of our Revolution. Do not think that I am on the look-out for forms of revolutionary justice. We have no need for justice now. Now we have need of a battle to the death! I propose, I demand the use of the revolutionary sword, which will put an end to all counter-revolutionaries. We must act not tomorrow, but today, at once. Do not demand evidence to prove that the prisoner has opposed the Soviet government; your first duty is to ask him to which class he belongs, what are his origins. These questions should decide the fate of the prisoner.*

? In Source E, what does Dzerzhinsky mean by saying, 'We have no need for justice'?

The *Cheka*, which was to change its title several times over the years (for example, GPU, OGPU, KGB) but never its essential character, remains the outstanding expression of Bolshevik ruthlessness. Operating as a law unto itself, and answerable only to Lenin, it was granted unlimited powers of arrest, detention and torture, which it used in the most arbitrary and brutal way. It was the main instrument by which Lenin and his successors terrorised the Russian people into subservience and conformity.

### The murder of the Romanovs, July 1918

In July 1918, a group of SRs assassinated the German ambassador as a protest against the Treaty of Brest-Litovsk. A month later an attempt was made on Lenin's life (see page 142), followed by the murder of the Petrograd chairman of the *Cheka*. These incidents were made the pretext for a Bolshevik reign of terror across the greater part of Russia. It was in this atmosphere that a local *Cheka* detachment, on Lenin's personal order, executed the ex-tsar and his family in Ekaterinburg in July 1918.

### The *Cheka* wages class war

The summary shooting of the Romanovs without benefit of trial was typical of the manner in which the *Cheka* went about its business throughout Russia. In accordance with Dzerzhinsky's instructions, all pretence of legality was abandoned; the basic rules relating to evidence and proof of guilt no longer applied. Persecution was directed not simply against individuals, but against whole classes. This was class war of the most direct kind. Some Bolsheviks were uneasy about the relentless savagery of the *Cheka* but there were no attempts to restrict its powers. The majority of party members accepted that the hazardous situation they were in justified the severity of the repression. The foreign interventions and the Civil War, fought out against the background of famine and social disorder, threatened the existence of the Communist Party and the government. This had the effect of stifling criticism of the *Cheka*'s methods. Dzerzhinsky declared that the proletarian revolution could not be saved except by 'exterminating the enemies of the working class'.

### Labour camps

One particularly notable move was the setting up under Dzerzhinsky of forced labour camps in which 'enemies of the Revolution', a blanket term for all those the Bolsheviks considered to be actual or potential enemies, were incarcerated. By the time of Lenin's death there were 315 such camps. Developed as part of the Red Terror, they held White prisoners of war, uncooperative peasants, and political prisoners, such as SRs, who were considered a threat to Soviet authority. The regime in the camps was deliberately harsh; acute hunger and beatings were the everyday lot of the prisoners.

### Show trials

The *Cheka* was also involved in the arrest of those subsequently prosecuted in a series of show trials. On Lenin's instruction, between April and August 1922, leading members of the Soviet Union's outlawed parties and of the Moscow clergy were put on humiliating public trial, before being sentenced to imprisonment. Lenin's authority was also behind an accompanying campaign to politicise the law. Under the new regime, the law was operated not as a means of protecting society and the individual but as an extension of political control. Lenin declared that the task of the courts was to apply revolutionary justice. 'The court is not to eliminate terror but to legitimise it.'

## The Red Army

Dzerzhinsky's methods of asserting Bolshevik control were complemented by the activities of Trotsky as war commissar, a post he took after the signing of the Treaty of Brest-Litovsk. Trotsky's outstanding achievement as commissar for war was his creation of the Red Army, which more than any other factor explains the survival of the Bolshevik government. This has obvious reference to the Reds' triumph in the Civil War, but the Red Army also became the means by which the Bolsheviks imposed their authority on the population at large.

? What does Source F suggest about the public relationship between Lenin and Trotsky?

**SOURCE F**

**Lenin addressing a crowd in Moscow in May 1920. Trotsky and Kamenev are on the steps of the podium. This photo later became notorious when in Stalin's time it was airbrushed to remove Trotsky from it. Despite such later attempts to deny Trotsky's role in the revolution, he had undoubtedly been Lenin's right-hand man.**

## Trade unions crushed

Trotsky used his powers to end the independence of the trade unions, which had first been legalised in 1905. Trotsky dismissed the unions as 'unnecessary chatterboxes' and told them: 'The working classes cannot be nomads. They must be commanded just like soldiers. Without this there can be no serious talk of industrialising on new foundations.' Early in 1920, the workers were brought under military discipline on the same terms as soldiers. Among the restrictions put into effect were:

- A total ban was placed on the questioning of orders and instructions.
- Rates of pay or conditions were no longer negotiable.
- Severe penalties were imposed for poor workmanship or not meeting production targets.

## Organisation of the Red Army

Lenin showed his complete trust in Trotsky by giving him a totally free hand in military matters. From his heavily armed special train, which served as his military headquarters and travelled vast distances, Trotsky supervised the development of a new fighting force in Russia. He had inherited 'The Workers' and Peasants' Red Army', formed early in 1918. Within two years he had turned an unpromising collection of tired Red Guard veterans and raw recruits into a formidable army of 3 million men. Ignoring the objections of many fellow Bolsheviks, he enlisted large numbers of ex-tsarist officers to train the rank and file into efficient soldiers. As a precaution, Trotsky attached **political commissars** to the army. These became an integral part of the Red Army structure. No military order carried final authority unless a commissar countersigned it.

**KEY TERM**

**Political commissars** Party officials who accompanied the officers and reported on their political correctness.

Trotsky tolerated no opposition within the Red Army from officers or men. The death sentence was imposed for desertion or disloyalty. In the heady revolutionary days before Trotsky took over, the traditional forms of army discipline had been greatly relaxed. Graded ranks, special uniforms, saluting and deferential titles were dropped as belonging to the reactionary past. Trotsky, however, had no truck with such fanciful experiments. He insisted that the demands of war meant that discipline had to be tighter, not looser.

Although 'commander' replaced the term 'officer', in all other key respects the Red Army returned to the customary forms of rank and address, with the word 'Comrade' usually prefixing the standard terms, as in 'Comrade Captain'. The practice of electing officers, which had come into favour in the democratic atmosphere of the February Revolution, was abandoned, as were soldiers' committees.

**SOURCE G**

? What does Source G illustrate about the scope of Trotsky's activities as war commissar?

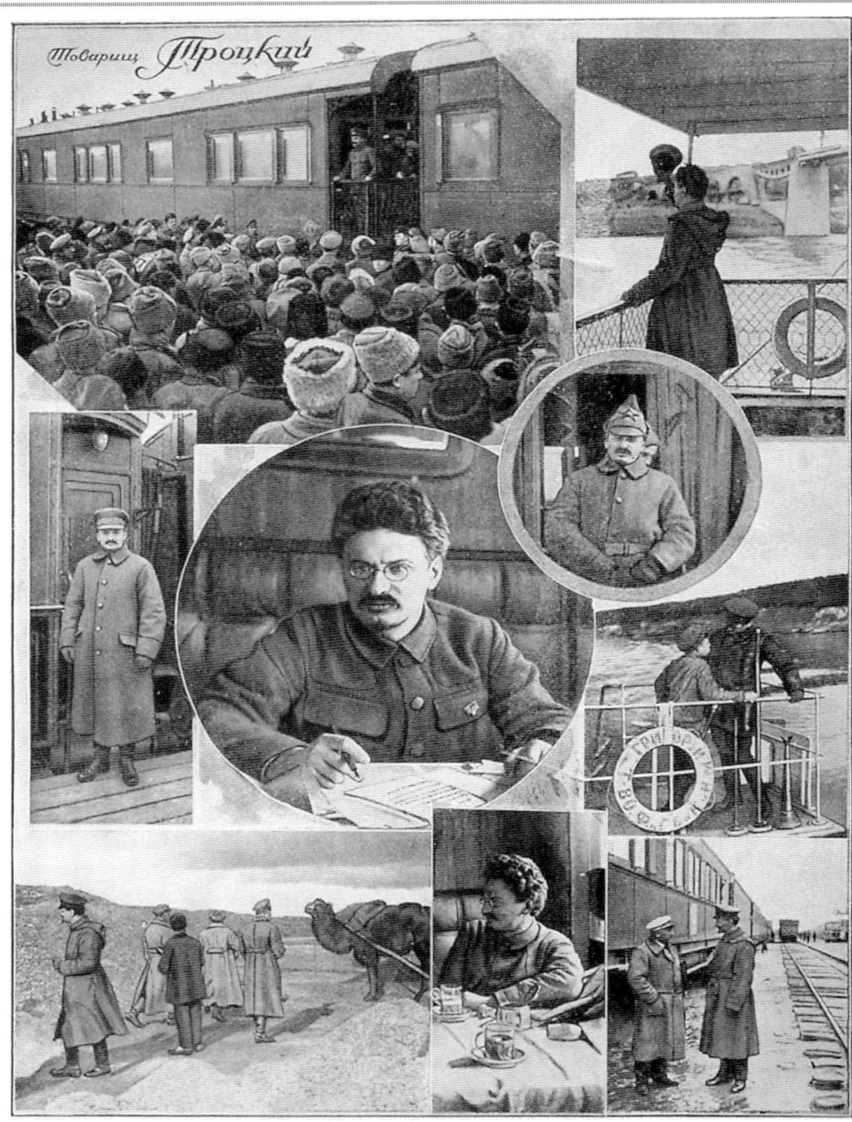


**A montage showing the enormous efforts Trotsky put into his work as commissar of war. One of the most remarkable features of Trotsky's activities was the use of his special train in which he travelled over 100,000 km (63,000 miles) during the Civil War. It was not just a train. It was a town on wheels, serving as mobile command post, military headquarters, troop transporter, radio station, court martial, propaganda unit, publishing centre, arsenal and administrative office. In Trotsky's own words: 'The train linked the front with the base, solved urgent problems on the spot, educated, appealed, supplied, rewarded and punished.'**

## Conscription

Trotsky responded to the Civil War's increasing demand for manpower by enforcing conscription in those areas under Bolshevik control. (The Whites did the same in their areas.) Under the slogan 'Everything for the Front', Trotsky justified the severity of the Red Army's methods by referring to the dangers that Russia faced on all sides. Those individuals whose social or political background made them suspect as fighting-men were nevertheless conscripted, being formed into labour battalions for back-breaking service behind the lines, such as digging trenches, loading ammunition and pulling heavy guns.

Most of the peasants who were drafted into the Red Army proved reluctant warriors, and were not regarded as reliable in a crisis. Desertions were commonplace, in spite of the heavy penalties. The Bolsheviks judged that the only dependable units were those drawn predominantly from among the workers. Such units became in practice the elite corps of the Red Army. Heroic stories of the workers as defenders of the revolution quickly became legends.

## Red Army idealism

Not everything was achieved by coercion; there were idealists among the troops who believed sincerely in the Communist mission to create a new proletarian world. Theirs was a vital contribution to the relatively high morale of the Reds. Although, by the standards of the European armies of the time, the Red Army was short of equipment and expertise, within Russia it soon came to outstrip its White opponents in its efficiency and sense of purpose.

Despite Trotsky's military triumphs, his authority did not go unchallenged. He met opposition from local Red commanders and commissars over tactics. His most notable dispute was with Josef Stalin, whom Lenin had appointed People's Commissar for Nationalities in 1917 (see page 186). In this key post, Stalin was in charge of the officials in the many regions and republics that were to form the USSR, the official title of the Soviet state after 1922. The legendary personal hostility between Trotsky and Stalin (see page 190) dates from the Civil War days. Nonetheless, whatever the disputes in which Trotsky was involved, there was no doubting that his organisation and leadership of the Red Army was the major factor in the survival of Bolshevik Russia.

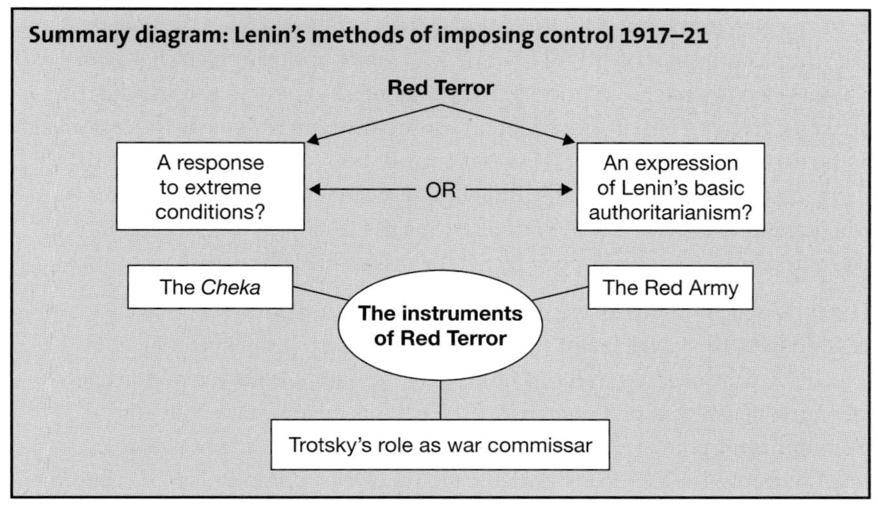

#  War Communism 1918–21

▶ *What was the impact of War Communism on the economy?*

In the summer of 1918, Lenin began to introduce a series of harshly restrictive economic measures, which were collectively known as War Communism. The chief reason for the move away from the system of state capitalism, which had operated up to then, was the desperate situation created by the Civil War. Lenin judged that the White menace could be met only by an intensification of authority in those regions that the Reds controlled (approximately 30 of the 50 provinces of European Russia). The change in economic strategy has to be seen, therefore, as part of the terror that the Bolsheviks operated in these years. Every aspect of life, social, political and economic, had to be subordinated to the task of winning the Civil War.

## Impact on industry

The first step towards War Communism as a formal policy was taken in June 1918. The existence of the *Cheka* and the Red Army enabled Lenin to embark on a policy of centralisation, knowing that he had the means of enforcing it. By that time also, there had been a considerable increase in Bolshevik influence in the factories. This was a result of the infiltration of the workers' committees by political commissars. This development helped to prepare the way for the issuing of the Decree on Nationalisation in June, which by 1920 had imposed government control over all major industrial enterprises in Russia (see page 133).

Nationalisation by itself did nothing to increase production. It was imposed at a time of severe industrial disruption, which had been caused initially by the strains of the war of 1914–17 but which worsened during the Civil War. Military needs were given priority, thus denying resources to those industries not considered essential. The situation was made more serious by the factories' being deprived of manpower. This was a result both of conscription into the Red Army and of the flight from the urban areas of large numbers of inhabitants, who left either in search of food or to escape the Civil War. The populations of Petrograd and Moscow dropped by a half between 1918 and 1921.

The problems for industry were deepened by hyperinflation. The scarcity of goods and the government's policy of continuing to print currency notes effectively destroyed the value of money. By the end of 1920, the rouble had fallen to one per cent of its worth in 1917. All this meant that while War Communism tightened the Bolshevik grip on industry it did not lead to economic growth. Table 5.2 shows the failure of War Communism in economic terms.

**Table 5.2** A comparison of industrial output in 1913 and in 1921

| Output | 1913 | 1921 |
|---|---|---|
| Index of gross industrial output | 100 | 31 |
| Index of large-scale industrial output | 100 | 21 |
| Electricity (million kW hours) | 2039 | 520 |
| Coal (millions of tonnes) | 29 | 8.9 |
| Oil (millions of tonnes) | 9.2 | 3.8 |
| Steel (millions of tonnes) | 4.3 | 0.18 |
| Imports (at 1913 rouble value, millions) | 1374 | 208 |
| Exports (at 1913 rouble value, millions) | 1520 | 20 |

## Impact on agriculture

For Lenin, the major purpose of War Communism was to tighten government control over agriculture and force the peasants to provide more food. But the peasants proved difficult to bring into line. As a naturally conservative class, they were resistant to central government, whether tsarist or Bolshevik. The government blamed the resistance on the ***kulaks*** who, it was claimed, were hoarding their grain stocks in order to keep prices artificially high. This was untrue. There was no hoarding. The plain truth was that the peasants saw no point in producing more food until the government, which had become the main grain purchaser, was willing to pay a fair price for it. Moreover, the existence of a *kulak* class was a myth. Rather than being a class of exploiters, the *kulaks* were simply the more efficient farmers who were marginally more prosperous.

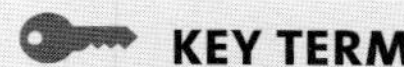
**KEY TERM**

***Kulaks*** The Bolshevik term for the class of allegedly rich, exploiting peasants.

### Grain requisitioning

Exasperated by the peasants' refusal to conform, the government condemned them as counter-revolutionaries and resorted to coercion. Beginning in July 1918, *Cheka* requisition units were sent into the countryside to take the grain by force. In August 1918, the people's commissar for food issued the following orders:

**SOURCE H**

**From 'Instructions for Requisitioning Grain', 20 August 1918, quoted in M. McCauley, editor, *The Russian Revolution and the Soviet State*, Macmillan, 1975, p. 184.**

*A commander is to head each detachment. The tasks of the requisition detachments are to: harvest winter grain in former landlord-owned estates; harvest grain on the land of notorious* kulaks*; every food requisition detachment is to consist of not less than 75 men and two or three machine guns. The political commissar's duties are to ensure that the detachment carries out its duties and is full of revolutionary enthusiasm and discipline. The food requisition detachments shall be deployed in such a manner as to allow two or three detachments to link up quickly. Continuous cavalry communication shall be maintained between the various food requisition detachments.*

What explains the severity of the measures laid down in Source H?

Between 1918 and 1921, the requisition squads systematically terrorised the countryside. The *kulaks* were targeted for particularly brutal treatment. Lenin ordered that they were to be 'mercilessly suppressed'. In a letter of 1920, he gave instructions that 100 *kulaks* were to be hanged in public in order to terrify the population 'for hundreds of miles around'.

Yet, the result was largely the reverse of the one intended. Even less food became available. Knowing that any surplus would simply be confiscated, the peasant produced only the barest minimum to feed himself and his family. Nevertheless, throughout the period of War Communism, the Bolsheviks persisted in their belief that grain hoarding was the basic problem. Official reports continued to speak of 'concealment everywhere, in the hopes of selling grain to town speculators at fabulous prices'.

### Famine

By 1921, the combination of requisitioning, drought and the general disruption of war had created a national famine. The grain harvests in 1920 and 1921 produced less than half that gathered in 1913. Even *Pravda*, the government's propaganda newspaper, admitted in 1921 that one in five of the population was starving. Matters became so desperate that the Bolsheviks, while careful to blame the *kulaks* and the Whites, were prepared to admit there was a famine and to accept foreign assistance. A number of countries supplied Russia with aid. The outstanding contribution came from the USA, which through the **ARA**, provided food for some 10 million Russians.

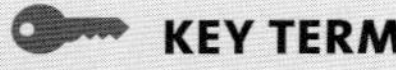

**KEY TERM**

**ARA** The American Relief Association, formed to provide food and medical supplies for post-war Europe.

Despite such efforts, foreign help came too late to prevent mass starvation. Of the 10 million fatalities of the Civil War period, over half starved to death. Lenin resented having to accept aid from the ARA and ordered it to withdraw from Russia in 1923 after two years, during which time it had spent over $60 million in relief work.

## Enforcing War Communism

It is now known that Lenin positively welcomed the famine as providing an opportunity to pursue his destruction of the Orthodox Church. In a letter of 1922, he ordered the Politburo to exploit the famine by shooting priests, 'the more, the better'. He went on: 'It is precisely now when in the starving regions people are eating human flesh and thousands of corpses are littering the roads that we can (and therefore must) carry out the confiscation of the church valuables with the most savage and merciless energy.'

By 1921, the grim economic situation had undermined the original justification for War Communism. During its operation, industrial and agricultural production had fallen alarmingly. Yet, this did not mean that the policy necessarily became unpopular among the Bolsheviks themselves. Indeed, there were many in the party who, far from regarding it as a temporary measure to meet an extreme situation, believed that it represented true revolutionary

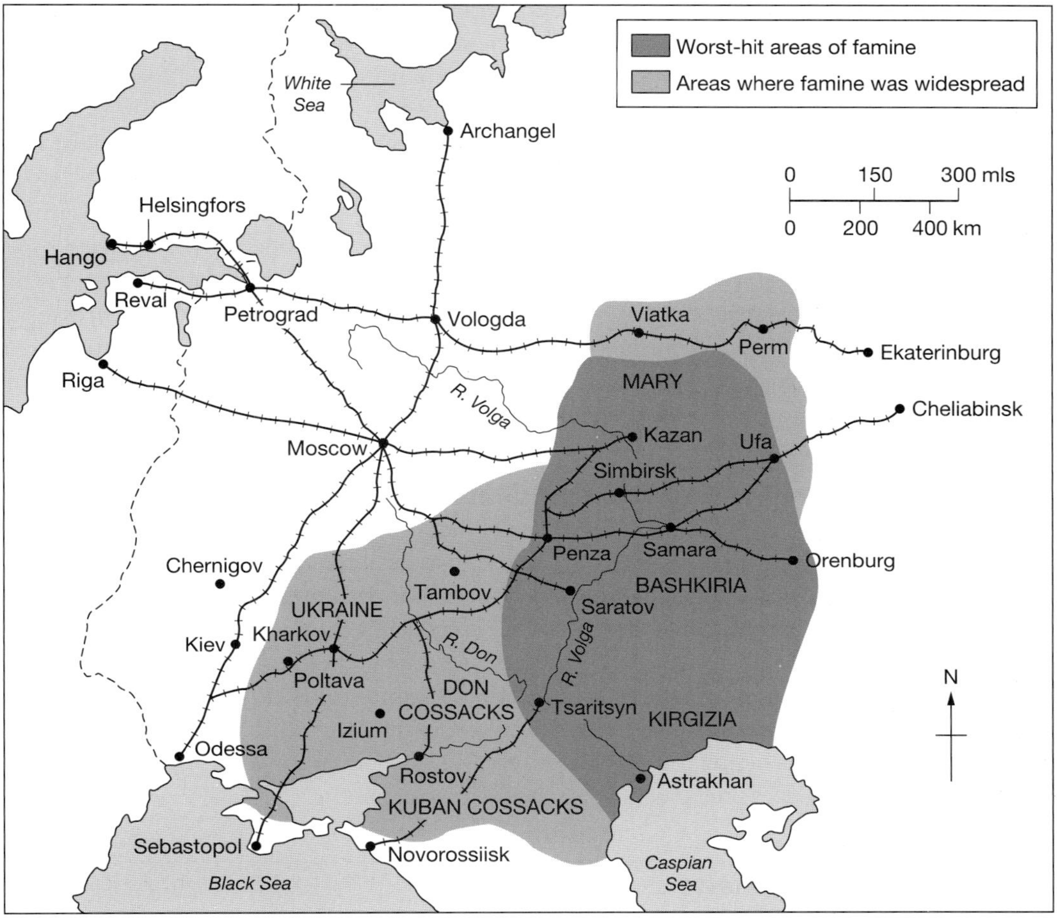

**Figure 5.4** Areas of Russia worst hit by famine in 1932–3. © Sir Martin Gilbert

Communism. The party's leading economists, **Nikolai Bukharin** and **Yevgeny Preobrazhensky**, urged that War Communism should be retained as the permanent economic strategy of the Bolshevik government. They saw it as true socialism in action since it involved:

- the centralising of industry
- the ending of private ownership
- the squeezing of the peasants.

The policy of War Communism was maintained even after the victory of the Red Army in the Civil War. The systematic use of terror by the *Cheka*, the spying on factory workers by political commissars and the enforced requisitioning of peasant grain stocks all continued. As a short-term measure the policy had produced the results Lenin wanted, but its severity had increased Bolshevik unpopularity. Throughout 1920 there were outbreaks of resistance, the scale of the disturbances being evident in a *Cheka* admission that they had been involved

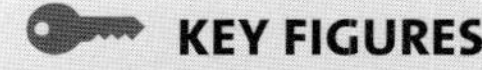

**KEY FIGURES**

**Nikolai Bukharin (1888–1938)**

Ally of Lenin since 1906, later executed under Stalin.

**Yevgeny Preobrazhensky (1886–1937)**

A Bolshevik since 1903, later executed under Stalin.

in suppressing 120 separate uprisings. Ukraine witnessed many of these but the most serious trouble occurred in the central province of Tambov.

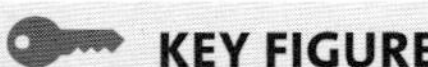


**Alexander Antonov (1888–1922)**

A former SR member, he had been imprisoned by the tsarist authorities for robbery and political crimes. He initially supported the Reds during the Civil War but turned against them because of their repression of the peasants.

## The Tambov Rising

In Tambov, what were, in effect, peasant armies, were formed. The principal leader of these was **Alexander Antonov**, a Social Revolutionary. The peasants attacked the requisition squads, seized their weapons, including machine guns, and took over whole areas and regions in the countryside. In retaliation for the past ill-treatment they had received from the requisition detachments, the peasants hunted down Red sympathisers, venting their anger with particular savagery on any officials they captured. Execution by shooting, bayonetting or beheading, was often preceded by torture which included the victims' being branding with irons. Even after death, the vengeance continued with bodies being mutilated.

By the end of 1920, Antonov commanded a guerrilla army of some 20,000. It was only with the greatest difficulty that sufficient Red Army detachments were gathered and sent into Tambov to re-establish government control. The Reds then resorted to the same vicious tactics that the peasants had used. Mass arrests, deportations and summary executions continued the cycle of violence. Whole families were taken hostage and their houses burnt to the ground. Such measures eventually worked and by the summer of 1921 peasant resistance had been broken. Antonov himself eluded capture for another year but in June 1922, after his hiding place had been revealed by a former supporter, he was cornered by a *Cheka* unit and killed in an exchange of gunfire.

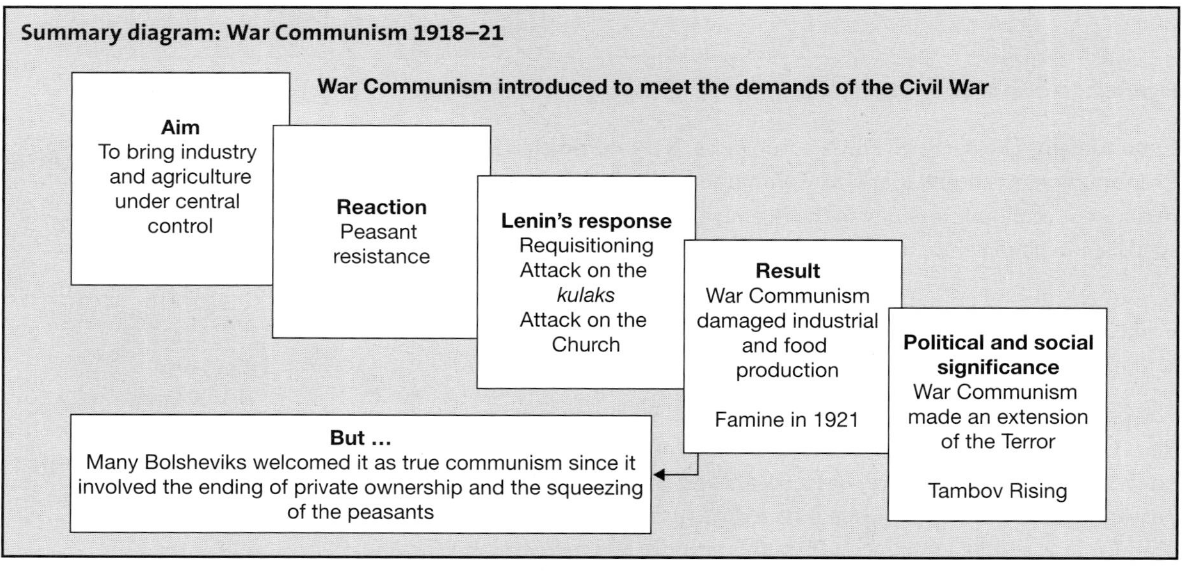

Summary diagram: War Communism 1918–21
War Communism introduced to meet the demands of the Civil War
Aim
To bring industry and agriculture under central control
Reaction
Peasant resistance
Lenin's response
Requisitioning
Attack on the kulaks
Attack on the Church
Result
War Communism damaged industrial and food production
Famine in 1921
Political and social significance
War Communism made an extension of the Terror
Tambov Rising
But …
Many Bolsheviks welcomed it as true communism since it involved the ending of private ownership and the squeezing of the peasants

# 8 Kronstadt Rising 1921

▶ *Why was the Kronstadt Rising such a threat to Lenin's government?*

Lenin himself clung to War Communism as long as he could. However, the failure of the economy to recover and the scale of the famine led him to consider possible alternative policies. He was finally convinced of the need for change by widespread anti-Bolshevik risings in 1920–1. These were a direct reaction against the brutality of requisitioning. One in particular, the Kronstadt Rising of 1921, was the most serious challenge to Bolshevik control since the October Revolution.

## The 'Workers' Opposition'

As long as unrest was confined to the peasants and to the Bolsheviks' political enemies it was a containable problem. What became deeply worrying to Lenin in 1921 was the development of opposition to War Communism within the party itself. Two prominent Bolsheviks, Alexander Shlyapnikov, the labour commissar, and **Alexandra Kollontai**, the outstanding woman in the party, led a 'Workers' Opposition' movement against the excesses of War Communism. Kollontai produced a pamphlet in which she accused the party leaders of losing touch with the proletariat. Speaking for the workers, she asked rhetorically, 'Are we really the prop of the class dictatorship, or just an obedient flock that serves as a support for those, who, having severed all ties with the masses, carry out their own policy without any regard to our opinions?'

**KEY FIGURE**

**Alexandra Kollontai (1872–1952)**

The outstanding female intellectual and agitator in the Bolshevik Party.

Picking up the cue given by the 'Workers' Opposition', groups of workers in Petrograd went on strike early in 1921, justifying their actions in an angrily worded proclamation:

**SOURCE I**

**From the Kronstadt workers' proclamation, 'What are we fighting for?' February 1921, quoted in R. Pipes, *Russia Under the Bolshevik Regime 1919–24*, Harvill, 1994, pp. 384–5.**

*It has become ever more clear, and is now self-evident, that the Russian Communist Party is not the protector of the working people that it claims to be, that the interests of the working people are foreign to it, and that having gained power, its only fear is of losing it, and hence that all means are permissible to that end: slander, violence, deception, murder, revenge on the families of those who have revolted. The long suffering of the toilers has drawn to an end. The current revolt finally offers the toilers a chance to have their freely elected, functioning soviets, free of violent Party pressures, to refashion the state-run trade unions into free associations of workers, peasants, and the working intelligentsia. At last the police baton of the Communist autocracy is smashed.*

According to Source I, why have the workers become disillusioned with the Soviet central government?

In February 1921, thousands of Petrograd workers crossed to the naval base on Kronstadt. There they linked up with the sailors and dockyard workers to demonstrate for greater freedom. They demanded that in a workers' state, which the Bolshevik government claimed Soviet Russia to be, the workers should be better, not worse, off than in tsarist times. In an attempt to pacify the strikers, Lenin sent a team of political commissars to Kronstadt. They were greeted with derision. Stephen Petrechenko, a spokesman for the demonstrators, rounded bitterly on the commissars at a public meeting:

? In Source J, whom does Petrechenko identify as 'false Communists'?

**SOURCE J**

**From Petrechenko's speech in February 1921, quoted in D. Shub, *Lenin*, Penguin, 1976, p. 408.**

*You are comfortable; you are warm; you commissars live in the palaces … Comrades, look around you and you will see that we have fallen into a terrible mire. We were pulled into this mire by a group of Communist bureaucrats, who, under the mask of Communism, have feathered their nests in our republic. I myself was a Communist, and I call on you, Comrades, drive out these false Communists who set worker against peasant and peasant against worker. Enough shooting of our brothers!*

## The Kronstadt manifesto

Early in March, the sailors and workers of Kronstadt elected Petrechenko as Chairman of a fifteen-man Revolutionary Committee, responsible for representing their grievances to the government. This committee produced a manifesto that included the following demands:

- New elections to the soviets, to be held by secret ballot.
- Freedom of speech and of the press.
- Freedom of assembly.
- Rights for trade unions and release of imprisoned trade unionists.
- Ending of the right of Communists to be the only permitted socialist political party.
- Ending of special food rations for Communist Party members.
- Freedom for individuals to bring food from the country into the towns without confiscation.
- Withdrawal of political commissars from the factories.
- Ending of the Communist Party's monopoly of the press.

It was not the demands themselves that frightened the Bolsheviks; it was the people who had drafted them: the workers and sailors of Kronstadt. They had been the great supporters of the Bolsheviks in 1917. Trotsky had referred to them as 'the heroes of the Revolution'. It was these same heroes who were now insisting that the Bolshevik government return to the promises that had inspired the revolution. For all the efforts of the Bolshevik press to brand the Kronstadt protesters as White agents, the truth was that they were genuine socialists who had previously been wholly loyal to Lenin's government, but who had become appalled by the regime's betrayal of the workers' cause.

## The rising crushed

Angered by the growing number of strikers and their increasing demands, Trotsky ordered General Tukhachevsky to direct his Red Army across the late-winter ice linking Kronstadt to Petrograd and crush 'the tools of former tsarist generals and agents of the interventionists'. An ultimatum (Source K) was issued to the demonstrators.

**SOURCE K**

**From a Decree of 6 March 1921, issued by Trotsky and distributed by General Tukhachevsky, quoted in D. Shub, *Lenin*, Penguin, 1976, pp. 408–9.**

*To the garrison and population of Kronstadt and the rebel forts. The Workers' and Peasants' Government has decided that Kronstadt and the naval ships should all at once be turned over to the Soviet Republic and therefore I order all those who raise their hands against the Socialist Fatherland to lay down their arms immediately. Those who refuse must be immediately disarmed and surrendered to the Soviet officials. The arrested commissars must be released at once. Only those who surrender unconditionally can hope for the mercy of the Soviet Republic. Simultaneously I also gave an order to prepare for the suppression of the rebellion and the destruction of the rebels by armed forces. The responsibility for all the misfortune that will fall on the peaceable elements will be on the heads of the White Guard rebels. This warning is the last one.*

*Signed, Chairman of the Revolutionary Military Council of the Republic, TROTSKY.*

Why does the ultimatum in Source K leave so little room for negotiation?

When the ultimatum was rejected, Tukhachevsky gave the signal for his force, made up of Red Army units and *Cheka* detachments, to attack. After an artillery bombardment, 60,000 Red troops stormed the Kronstadt base. The sailors and workers resisted fiercely. Savage fighting occurred before they were finally overcome. Tukhachevsky reported back to Trotsky that 'the sailors fought like wild beasts. I cannot understand where they found the might for such rage. Each house where they were located had to be taken by storm. They seemed half-dead, but they snatched their revolvers and gasped, "Too little did we shoot at you scoundrels".'

? Study Source L. Why did Alexandra Kollontai oppose Lenin over the Kronstadt affair?

**SOURCE L**

**Alexandra Kollontai, the leading female in the ranks of the Bolsheviks and a consistent supporter of Lenin from the time of his return to Petrograd in April 1917 until the Kronstadt Rising. Photographed here *c*.1934.**

## Aftermath of the rising

Immediately after the rising had been suppressed, the ringleaders who had survived were condemned as White reactionaries and shot. In the succeeding months the *Cheka* hunted down and executed those rebels who had escaped from Kronstadt. Lenin justified the severity on the grounds that the rising had been the work of the bourgeois enemies of the October Revolution: 'Both the Mensheviks and the Socialist Revolutionaries declared the Kronstadt movement to be their own.' However, as well as being a propagandist, Lenin was a realist. He took the lesson of Kronstadt to heart. To avoid the scandal and embarrassment of another open challenge to his party and government, he decided it was time to soften the severity of War Communism. At the tenth conference of the Communist Party, which opened in March 1921, Lenin declared that the Kronstadt Rising had 'lit up reality like a lightning flash'. This was the prelude to his introduction of the New Economic Policy (NEP), a move intended to tackle the famine and in doing so to lessen the opposition to Bolshevism. However, this was to be a purely economic adjustment. Lenin was not prepared to make political concessions: Communist control was to be made even tighter.

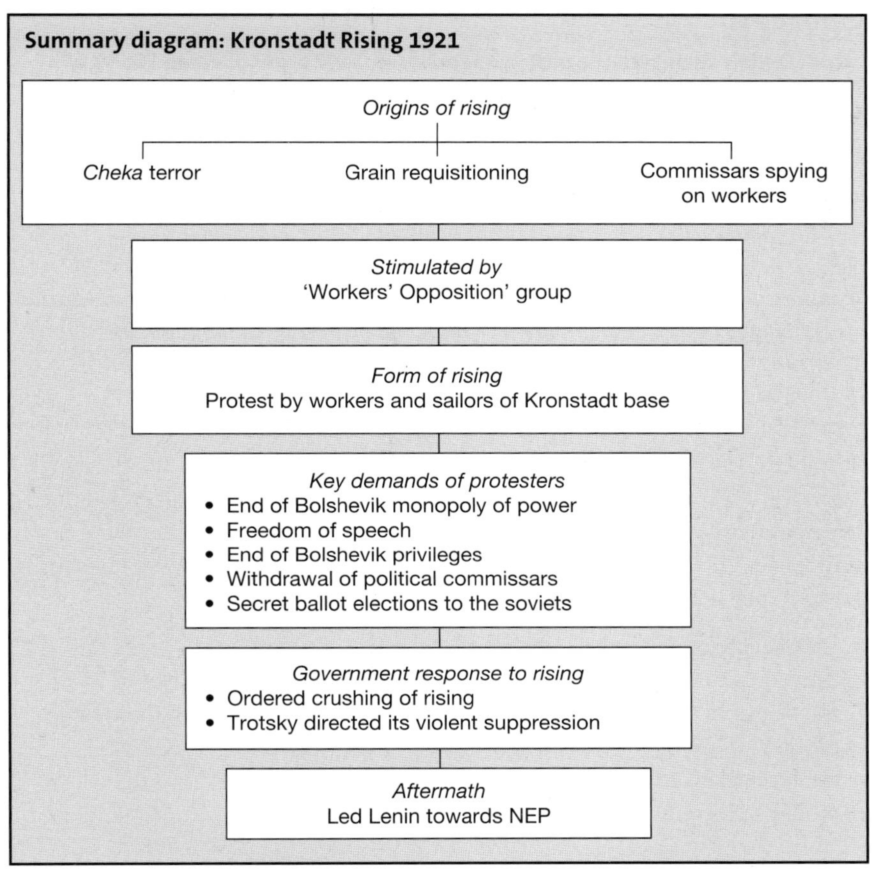

Summary diagram: Kronstadt Rising 1921
Origins of rising
Cheka terror
Grain requisitioning
Commissars spying on workers
Stimulated by
'Workers' Opposition' group
Form of rising
Protest by workers and sailors of Kronstadt base
Key demands of protesters
• End of Bolshevik monopoly of power
• Freedom of speech
• End of Bolshevik privileges
• Withdrawal of political commissars
• Secret ballot elections to the soviets
Government response to rising
• Ordered crushing of rising
• Trotsky directed its violent suppression
Aftermath
Led Lenin towards NEP


# 9 New Economic Policy (NEP)

► *What were Lenin's reasons for introducing the New Economic Policy in 1921?*

As with the policy it replaced, the New Economic Policy (NEP) was intended by Lenin primarily to meet Russia's urgent need for food. Whatever the purity of the revolutionary theory behind War Communism, it had clearly failed to deliver the goods. State terror had not forced the peasants into producing larger grain stocks. Pragmatic as ever, Lenin judged, that, if the peasants could not be forced, they must be persuaded. The stick had not worked so now was the time to offer the carrot. He told the delegates at the 1921 party congress:

? According to Lenin in Source M, what measures are necessary to preserve the regime from danger?

**SOURCE M**

**From Lenin's speech to the party congress, April 1921, in *Collected Works of Lenin*, volume XXXII, Lawrence & Wishart, 1959, p. 341.**

*We must try to satisfy the demands of the peasants who are dissatisfied, discontented, and cannot be otherwise. In essence the small farmer can be satisfied with two things. First of all, there must be a certain amount of freedom for the small private proprietor; and, secondly, commodities and products must be provided ... The effect will be the revival of the petty bourgeoisie and of capitalism [but] the proletarian regime is in no danger as long as the proletariat firmly holds power in its hands. We must not be afraid of Communists 'learning' from bourgeois specialists, including merchants, small capitalist co-operators and capitalists.*

Despite the deep disagreements that were soon to emerge within the Bolshevik Party over NEP, the famine and the grim economic situation in Russia led the delegates to give unanimous support to Lenin's proposals when they were first introduced. The decree making NEP official government policy was published in the spring of 1921. Its essential features were:

- central economic control to be relaxed
- the requisitioning of grain to be abandoned and replaced by a **tax in kind**
- the peasants to be allowed to keep their food surpluses and sell them for a profit
- public markets to be restored
- money to be reintroduced as a means of trading.

**KEY TERM**

**Tax in kind** The peasant surrendering a certain amount of his produce, equivalent to a fixed sum of money.

Lenin was aware that the new policy marked a retreat from the principle of state control of the economy. It restored a mixed economy in which certain features of capitalism existed alongside socialism. Knowing how uneasy this made many Bolsheviks, Lenin stressed that NEP was only a temporary concession to capitalism. He emphasised that the party still retained control of 'the commanding heights of the economy', by which he meant large-scale industry, banking and foreign trade. He added: 'we are prepared to let the peasants have their little bit of capitalism as long as we keep the power'.

The adoption of NEP showed that the Bolshevik government since 1917 had been unable to create a successful economy along purely ideological lines. Lenin admitted as much. He told party members that it made no sense for Bolsheviks to pretend that they could pursue an economic policy that took no account of the circumstances.

## Bolshevik objections to NEP

Lenin's realism demanded that political theory take second place to economic necessity. It was this that troubled the members of the party, such as Trotsky and Preobrazhensky, who had regarded the repressive measures of War Communism as the proper revolutionary strategy for the Bolsheviks to follow.

To their mind, bashing the peasants was exactly what the Bolsheviks should be doing since it advanced the revolution. It disturbed them that the peasants were being given in to and that capitalist ways were being tolerated. Trotsky described NEP as 'the first sign of the degeneration of Bolshevism'.

A main complaint of the objectors was that the reintroduction of money and private trading was creating a new class of profiteers whom they derisively dubbed **Nepmen**. It was the profiteering that Victor Serge, a representative of the Left Bolsheviks, had in mind when he described the immediate social effects of NEP: 'the cities we ruled over assumed a foreign aspect; we felt ourselves sinking into the mire. Money lubricated and befouled the entire machine just as under capitalism'.

KEY TERMS

**Nepmen** Those who stood to gain from the free trading permitted under NEP: the rich peasants, the retailers, the traders and the small-scale manufacturers.

**Factionalism** The forming within the party of groups with a particular complaint or grievance.

## Lenin's ban on factionalism

NEP became such a contentious issue among the Bolsheviks that Lenin took firm steps to prevent the party being torn apart over it. At the tenth party congress in 1921, at which NEP had been formally announced, he introduced a resolution 'On Party Unity'. The key passage read: 'Congress orders the immediate dissolution of all groups that have been formed on the basis of some platform or other, and instructs all organisations to be very strict in ensuring that no **factionalism** of any sort be tolerated.' Members were warned that non-compliance with the resolution would lead to immediate expulsion.

The object of Lenin's ban on factionalism was to prevent criticism of government or Central Committee decisions. An accompanying resolution condemned the 'Workers' Opposition', the group that had opposed the brutalities of War Communism and had been involved in the Kronstadt Rising. The two resolutions on party loyalty provided a highly effective means of stifling criticism of the NEP.

At the same time as Lenin condemned factionalism, he also declared that all socialist parties other than the Bolsheviks were now outlawed in Soviet Russia. 'Marxism teaches that only the Communist Party is capable of training and organising a vanguard of the proletariat and the whole mass of the working people'. This was the logical climax of the policy, begun in 1918, of suppressing all opposition to Bolshevik rule. Lenin's announcements at this critical juncture made it extremely difficult for doubting members to come out and openly challenge NEP, since this would appear tantamount to challenging the party itself.

## Bukharin's role

A further boost to Bolshevik unity was the decision by Nikolai Bukharin, the outstanding party economist, to abandon his opposition to NEP and become its most enthusiastic supporter. His new approach was expressed in his appeal to the peasants: 'Enrich yourselves under NEP'. Bukharin believed that the greater amount of money the peasants would now have, after selling their surplus grain, would stimulate industry since their extra income would be spent on buying manufactured goods. It is significant that during the final two years of Lenin's life, when he became increasingly exhausted by a series of crippling strokes, it was Bukharin who was his closest colleague. The last two articles published under Lenin's name, *On Co-operation* and *Better Fewer, But Better*, were justifications of NEP. Both were the work of Bukharin.

## Economic results of NEP

In the end, the most powerful reason for the party to accept NEP proved to be a statistical one. The production figures suggested that the policy worked. By the time of Lenin's death in 1924, the Soviet economy had begun to make a marked recovery. Table 5.3 indicates the scale of this.

**Table 5.3** Growth under NEP

| Output | 1921 | 1922 | 1923 | 1924 |
|---|---|---|---|---|
| Grain harvest (millions of tonnes) | 37.6 | 50.3 | 56.6 | 51.4 |
| Value of factory output (millions of roubles) | 2004 | 2619 | 4005 | 4660 |
| Electricity (millions of kW hours) | 520 | 775 | 1146 | 1562 |
| Average monthly wage of urban worker (roubles) | 10.2 | 12.2 | 15.9 | 20.8 |

Lenin's claim that under the NEP the Bolsheviks would still control 'the commanding heights of the economy' was shown to be substantially correct by the census of 1923. Table 5.4 and Figure 5.5 indicate that, in broad terms, the NEP had produced an economic balance: while agriculture and trade were largely in private hands, the state dominated Russian industry.

NEP was not a total success. Its opponents criticised it on the grounds that the balance it appeared to have achieved was notional rather than real. The fact was that industry failed to expand as rapidly as agriculture. The Nepmen may have done well, but there was high unemployment in the urban areas. NEP would continue to be a matter of dispute and division among the Bolsheviks long after Lenin's death.

**Table 5.4** Balance between main types of enterprise

| Enterprise | Proportion of industrial workforce | Average number of workers in each factory |
|---|---|---|
| Private | 12% | 2 |
| State | 85% | 155 |
| Co-operative | 3% | 15 |

**KEY TERM**

**Co-operatives** Groups of workers or farmers working together on their own enterprise.

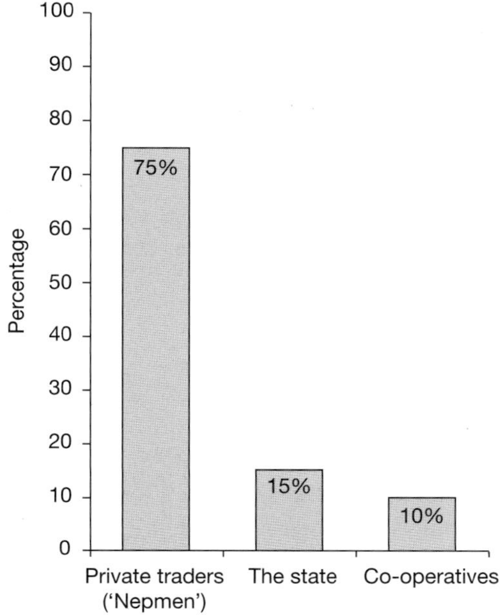


**Figure 5.5** Share of trade under NEP, 1923.

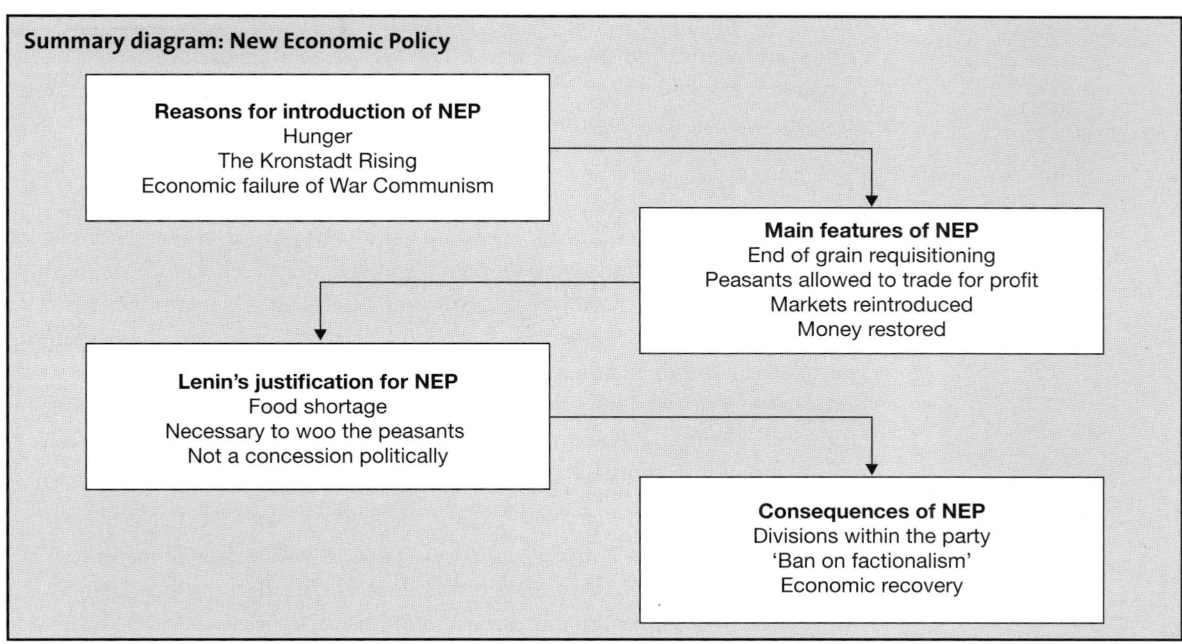

Summary diagram: New Economic Policy
Reasons for introduction of NEP
Hunger
The Kronstadt Rising
Economic failure of War Communism
Main features of NEP
End of grain requisitioning
Peasants allowed to trade for profit
Markets reintroduced
Money restored
Lenin's justification for NEP
Food shortage
Necessary to woo the peasants
Not a concession politically
Consequences of NEP
Divisions within the party
'Ban on factionalism'
Economic recovery

# 10 Lenin's legacy

▶ *What were Lenin's main strengths and weaknesses as leader?*

In name, it was the soviets which took power in October 1917, but in reality it was the Bolsheviks, who proceeded to turn Russia into a one-party state. It took them three years of bitter civil war to do it, but they alone of all the political parties in post-tsarist Russia had the necessary willingness under Lenin to destroy whatever stood in their way.

## Lenin exploits Russia's authoritarian tradition

Although Lenin rejected the Russian past, he remained very much its inheritor. He had as little time for democracy as the tsars had. The rule of the Bolsheviks was a continuation of the absolutist tradition in Russia. The Civil War and the foreign interventions, by intensifying the threat to the Bolshevik government, provided it with the pretext for demanding total conformity from the masses and the party members as the price of the Revolution's survival.

Yet it is doubtful whether, even without that threat, Bolshevism could have developed other than as an oppressive system. Its dogmatic Marxist creed, as interpreted by Lenin, made it as intolerant of other political ideas as tsardom had been. The forcible dissolution of the Constituent Assembly in 1918, the Red Terror and the crushing of the Kronstadt Rising in 1921 were clear proof of the absolutism of Bolshevik control. The 1917 Revolution did not mark a complete break with the past. Rather, it was the replacement of one form of state authoritarianism with another.

## Lenin's Marxism

Lenin's greatest single achievement as a revolutionary was to reshape Marxist theory to make it fit Russian conditions. The instrument which he chose for this was the Bolshevik Party. Although Lenin was careful always to describe his policies as democratic, for him the term had a particular meaning. Democracy was not to be reckoned as a matter of numbers but as a method of party rule. Because the party was the vehicle of historical change, its role was not to win large-scale backing, but to direct the revolution from above, regardless of the scale of popular support. 'No revolution', Lenin wrote, 'ever waits for formal majorities'.

Since authority flowed from the centre outwards, it was the role of the leaders to lead, the role of the party members to follow. The special term describing this was 'democratic centralism' (see page 24). Lenin defined it in these terms: 'Soviet socialist democracy is not in the least incompatible with individual rule and dictatorship. What is necessary is individual rule, the recognition of the dictatorial powers of one man. All phrases about equal rights are nonsense.'

## Lenin's view of the Russian proletariat

Lenin's political certainties followed logically from his view of the contemporary Russian working class. Its small size and limited political awareness meant that it could not achieve revolution unaided. It was, therefore, the historical mission of the enlightened Bolshevik Party to use its unique understanding of how human society worked to guide the proletariat towards its revolutionary destiny. As a realist, Lenin knew that the peasants could not be ignored since they were the food producers in the state. Nevertheless, the function of the peasantry was to serve the needs of the proletariat. The rules of the dialectic taught that true revolution could come only from the industrial workers.

### The 'telescoped revolution'

A marked feature of Lenin as a revolutionary was his ability to adjust theory to fit circumstances. This pragmatic approach often led him to diverge from the strict pattern of the Marxist dialectic with its clear-cut stages of class revolution (see page 21), but it made him and his followers infinitely adaptable. In his writings and speeches he always insisted that his ideas were wholly in accordance with those of Marx. However, in practical terms, Lenin's role in Russia after April 1917 was that of a skilled opportunist who outmanoeuvred a collection of opponents who never matched him in sense of purpose and sheer determination.

**KEY TERM**

**'Telescoped revolution'** The notion that the final two stages of revolution, bourgeois and proletarian, could be compressed into one.

It was Lenin's concept of the **'telescoped revolution'** that had justified the Bolsheviks' revolution against the Provisional Government in October 1917 without their having to wait for the Russian proletariat to grow substantially in size. It was not necessary for the Russian workers to initiate the revolution; it was enough that it was carried out in their name by the Bolsheviks, the special agents of historical change and the true voice of the proletariat.

This readiness to make Marxist theory conform to practical necessity was very evident in Lenin's economic policies. A basic premise of Marxism was that political systems were determined by the economic structure on which they rested. Lenin turned this idea upside down. His government after 1917 used its political power to determine the character of the economy. His flexible approach was then shown in 1921 when he introduced NEP, a policy that entailed the abandonment of War Communism and a reversion to capitalism.

Lenin was perfectly clear about what his ultimate objectives were but he was wholly pragmatic in the methods he used to achieve them. The end justified the means. This approach was consistent with his interpretation of the scientific nature of Marxism. Once the concept of the historical inevitability of the proletarian revolution had been accepted, it followed that the binding duty of revolutionaries was to work for that end by whatever means necessary. The Bolsheviks' belief that they were the special agents of historical change led logically to their destruction of all other political parties. Since history was on their side, the Bolsheviks had the right to absolute control.

## Lenin the international revolutionary

A vital factor to stress when assessing Lenin's role is that he regarded himself primarily as an international revolutionary. Originally, he had expected that the successful Bolshevik seizure of power in October 1917 would be the first stage in a worldwide proletarian uprising. When this proved mistaken, he had to adapt to a situation in which Bolshevik Russia became an isolated revolutionary state, beset by internal and external enemies.

Lenin responded by making another major adjustment of Marxist theory. Marx had taught that proletarian revolution would be an international class movement. Yet the 1917 Revolution had been the work not of a class but of a party, and had been restricted to one nation. Lenin explained this in terms of a delayed revolution; the international rising would occur at some point in the future; in the interim Soviet Russia must consolidate its own individual revolution.

This placed the Bolshevik government and its international agency, the Comintern, in an ambiguous position. What was their essential role to be? At Lenin's death in 1924, this question – whether Soviet Russia's primary aim was world revolution or national survival – was still unresolved.

## Lenin's strengths

In purely political terms, Lenin's strengths far outweighed his weaknesses. Those strengths were aspects of his character and personality. Consumed by politics, such private life as he had was merely an adjunct to his public career. Among his outstanding attributes were:

- A total ruthlessness in pursuit of his revolutionary objectives.
- An ability to inspire dedicated support from party members and intense loyalty from government and party colleagues.
- A remarkable sense of political opportunism, which enabled him to lead his minority party into power in 1917 and then establish a Communist state.
- A driving sense of self-belief that allowed him to overcome opposition within and outside his party.
- A gift for interpreting abstract ideas and turning them into a meaningful ideology. He shaped Marxist notions in such a way that he made communism one of the dominant ideologies of the twentieth century.
- An accompanying gift for turning ideology into a workable programme.
- A refusal to be deterred by reversal and failure which saw him survive exile, civil war, economic collapse, famine and foreign invasion.

## Lenin's weaknesses

It has to be said that it is equally logical to regard the list above not as strengths but as failings. One would need to be sympathetic to Lenin's politics to be sympathetic to his methods. That is why he remains a controversial figure. It is possible to acknowledge his talents but to argue that they were put to oppressive use in an unworthy cause. Among the charges made on these grounds are:

- Conviction and commitment led him to disregard the human cost of his methods.
- His ruthless approach led to unnecessary suffering and created a set of grim precedents.
- Exploiting the authoritarianism he inherited from the tsarist system, Lenin made the Bolshevik state more oppressive than its predecessor.
- Refusing to acknowledge the legitimacy of any other political viewpoint than his own, Lenin stifled any possibility of genuine democracy developing in Russia.
- By outlawing all other parties, Lenin made violent conflict unavoidable.
- While he was occasionally willing to adjust economic policy for expediency's sake, Lenin's basic hostility to capitalism denied Soviet Russia the opportunity to achieve sustained growth.
- By politicising all aspects of life in Russia, Lenin prevented the nation from becoming an open, progressive society.

Lenin's greatest legacy to Soviet Russia was authoritarianism. He returned Russia to the absolutism that it had known under the tsars. In that sense, Soviet communism was a continuation of, not a break with, Russia's past. To help in estimating the impact Lenin had on Russia it is worth listing the main features of his legacy. At his death in 1924 the Soviet Union exhibited the following characteristics:

- The one-party state – all parties other than the Bolsheviks had been outlawed.
- The bureaucratic state – despite the Bolsheviks' original belief in the withering away of the state, central power increased under Lenin and the number of government institutions and officials grew.
- The police state – the *Cheka* was the first of a series of secret police organisations in Soviet Russia whose task was to impose government control over the people.
- The ban on factionalism – prevented criticism of leadership within the party, in effect a prohibition of free speech.
- The destruction of the trade unions – with Lenin's encouragement, Trotsky had destroyed the independence of the trade unions with the result that the Russian workers were entirely at the mercy of the state.
- The politicising of the law – under Lenin the law was operated not as a means of protecting society and the individual but as an extension of political control. He declared that the task of the courts was to apply revolutionary justice. 'The court is not to eliminate terror but to legitimise it.'
- The system of purges and show trials, which were to become a notorious feature of Stalinism (see page 225), had first been created under Lenin. Outstanding examples of these were the public trials of the Moscow clergy between April and July 1922 and of the SRs between June and August of the same year.
- Concentration camps – at the time of Lenin's death there were 315 such camps. Developed as part of the Red Terror, they held White prisoners of

war, rebel peasants, *kulaks* and political prisoners, such as SRs, who were considered a threat to Soviet authority.
- Prohibition of public worship – the Orthodox churches had been looted, then closed, their clergy arrested or dispersed and atheism adopted as a replacement for religious belief.
- The USSR, the only Communist state, had strained relations with the outside world.

The apparatus of the tyranny that Stalin was later to exercise over the Soviet state was already in place at the time of Lenin's death.

## Key debate

*Was the authoritarianism of Lenin's rule, 1917–24, a response to circumstances or an essential feature of Soviet Communism?*

The character of Soviet rule under Lenin between 1917 and 1924 has long been a matter of debate among historians. Trotsky had in a sense set the terms of the debate when in 1904 he had written: 'Lenin's methods lead to this: the party organization first substitutes itself for the party as a whole: then the central committee substitutes itself for the organization; and finally a single "dictator" substitutes himself for the central committee.'

The British historian A.J.P. Taylor, provocatively remarked that the way to view Lenin and his ideas was 'not as a political philosophy but as a guide to political practice in the era of gangster warfare'. This notion that Lenin's importance lay not in his ideas but in his pragmatism and skill as a political operator is one of the main elements in the discussion among historians about the nature of Lenin's impact.

Sympathisers with Lenin argue that, given the extreme situation in which the USSR found itself between 1917 and 1924, particularly during the civil war years, there was no alternative to the imposed terror. The extended argument is that Lenin's policy was vindicated by the success of the Reds in the civil war, the repelling of the foreign interventions, and the establishment of a degree of social and political stability that Russia had not experienced since at least 1914.

Geoffrey Hosking, an acknowledged British authority, considers that it was the pressures of civil war that prevented the Communist Party moving towards democracy after it took power in 1917.

**EXTRACT 1**

**From Geoffrey Hosking, *Russia and the Russians*, Allen Lane, 2001, p. 415.**

*The civil war permanently marked Soviet society. It completed the work, begun by the revolution, of destroying the old society, so that almost no ancient regime [tsarist] institutions of social classes survived in a recognizable form.*

*The institutions of the new society could be created anew by any force which could control it. That force was the Communist party, which had itself changed considerably during the civil war. From being a party of oppositional intellectuals, engaged in constant debate and open to the opinion of workers soldiers and peasants, it became a party of power.*

Lenin's particular contribution to applied Marxism was the development of the party as the essential instrument of revolution. This was essentially a practical achievement. He was, of course, a major theoretician and left a corpus of significant political writings. Yet these would have remained a set of abstract analyses had he not also been a man of action who ruthlessly exploited his times, first, to lead his party in a seizure of power and then to consolidate its hold over Russia. Lenin's Russian biographer, Dmitri Volkogonov, wrote of Lenin: 'it was not his writings, but his ability to convert Marx's concept of class struggle into a tool for the achievement of his main goal, the seizure of power, that made Lenin a giant in history'.

Lenin's abiding belief was that the Marxism he adopted was not simply a set of political theories but was a truly scientific analysis which explained the human condition and provided a programme for action. Basic to his understanding was the conviction that all history was a dialectical struggle between the powerful and powerless, the exploiters and the exploited. Since no class ever gives up its power willingly, progress by the exploited can only be made through violent revolution in which they seize power. However, that is not the end of the process; the dispossessed class fights tenaciously to regain its lost control. To prevent this, the revolutionaries have to resort to every means at their disposal to prevent the reactionaries winning back what they have lost. The whole struggle was necessarily violent. Indeed, violence was its dynamic.

It is by reference to Lenin's belief in dialectical process that some historians explain the severity of the repression that characterised the Bolshevik rule between 1917 and 1924. They suggest that the violence was not a reaction to the troubled situation but was implicit in the form of Communism that Lenin had developed.

A representative of this point of view is the historian Harold Shukman, born into a family of Russian-Jewish *émigrés* who had fled the 1917 Revolution.

**EXTRACT 2**

**From Harold Shukman, *The Russian Revolution*, Sutton Publishing, 1998, p. 78.**

*Lenin thought of the organisation of the state as an organisation controlled by a single and single-minded operator. And society, which must be made to function classlessly and harmoniously, would similarly only do so if a single intelligence, i.e., Lenin and his like-minded party, were in full control.*

*Lenin closed down the non-Bolshevik press; through the Cheka he hounded then banned other political parties, imprisoning, exiling or deporting their members; he used public hangings, not merely as punishment, but as examples to the rest of the local population; he emasculated the trade unions and enforced labour discipline by exploiting the food shortages … Workers left their factories to forage in the surrounding village, to buy or barter food from the peasants. The Bolsheviks banned this form of self-help which they labelled black marketing or speculation and set up road blocks to search men venturing to town, confiscating the produce and prosecuting the culprits.*

Dietrich Geyer, a leading German scholar, suggests that Lenin's authoritarianism was a consequence of his and his party's inability to mature from their secret society origins.

**EXTRACT 3**

**From Dietrich Geyer, *The Russian Revolution*, Berg Publishers, 1987, p. 134.**

*Lenin had developed organisational centralism when the Bolshevik party was still an underground conspiracy directed against tsarism, but this centralist approach survived 1917 and became the norm in the post-revolutionary period. The organisation suited to a secret society of professional revolutionaries was replaced not by a democratic party but by a bureaucratic oligarchy which endeavoured to exercise supervision and control. Most party members were removed from decision-making roles and reduced to functionaries.*

The British Marxist historian, Eric Hobsbawm, emphasises that Lenin's move towards authoritarianism has to be understood in the context of the problems confronting the new Soviet government.

**EXTRACT 4**

**From Eric Hobsbawm, *Age of Extremes*, Michael Joseph, 1994, p. 187.**

*Whatever the pre-revolutionary attitude of the Bolsheviks to democracy in and outside the party, to free speech, civil liberties and toleration, the circumstances of the years 1917–21 imposed an increasingly authoritarian mode of government on (and within) a party committed to any action that was (or seemed) necessary to maintain the fragile and struggling Soviet power. It had not actually begun as a one-party government, nor one rejecting opposition, but it won the Civil War as a single-party dictatorship buttressed by a powerful security apparatus, and using terror against counter-revolutionaries. Equally to the point, the party itself abandoned internal democracy … The 'democratic centralism' which governed it in theory became mere centralism.*

A modern British authority, S.A. Smith offers a neatly balanced analysis of the various arguments:

**EXTRACT 5**

**From S.A. Smith, *The Russian Revolution*, Oxford University Press, 2002, p. 97.**

*Historians debate the extent to which the party-state came into being as the result of ideology or the pressure of civil war. Some argue that the seeds of*

*Bolshevik tyranny lay in the Marxist notion of the dictatorship of the proletariat; others in Lenin's notion of the vanguard party with its implication that the party knew what was best for the working class. Yet the civil war was as much about certain principles being jettisoned as about others being confirmed. The fact that ideology evolved in this way suggests that it was not the sole or even paramount driving force behind the creation of the party dictatorship. If the seeds of dictatorship lay in ideology, they only came to fruition in the face of the remorseless demands placed on party and state by civil war and economic collapse.*

*The Bolshevik ethos had always been one of ruthlessness, authoritarianism and class hatred, but in the context of civil war these qualities transmogrified into cruelty, fanaticism, and absolute intolerance of those who thought differently.*

How far do the historians quoted in Extracts 1–5 agree or differ in their interpretation of Soviet rule between 1917 and 1924?

It is unlikely that there will ever be a complete consensus among historians concerning the character of Lenin's rule between 1917 and 1924. This is because, while there is little dispute among them over the facts, they differ in their evaluation of Lenin as a party leader and of the nature of communism as a political and social movement.

## Chapter summary

Faced with major domestic and foreign problems, it was questionable whether Lenin's Bolsheviks could retain power. But a combination of their ruthlessness, which included the forcible dissolution of the Constituent Assembly, and their opponents' weaknesses enabled the new regime to survive. Lenin's acceptance of the punitive peace treaty imposed by Germany left his government free to concentrate on internal consolidation. A savage civil war (1918–20) ended with Bolshevik victory and the repulsing of a series of foreign interventions. It was with a resounding yes that Lenin had answered the question of whether the Bolshevik regime could survive.

The oppressive political methods (the Red Terror) by which Lenin governed were extended into the economic field in the form of War Communism, a programme of centralised control aimed at providing the resources for war. However, such was the disruption that famine set in. Deprivation and state oppression stimulated a resistance movement from within the Bolsheviks' own ranks. The most threatening challenge came at Kronstadt in 1921, when workers previously loyal to the party rose in protest. Trotsky crushed the movement bloodily, but it had taught Lenin that the rigidities of War Communism had to be eased. His did this by introducing NEP, a policy of concessions, which aroused opposition from some party members, a development which Lenin immediately repressed by his ban on factionalism.

Lenin's legacy was to leave the Soviet Union as a one-party, centralised, bureaucratised state, committed to a single ideology and equipped with the political and legal apparatus to suppress all internal opposition. It was an inheritance on which Stalin would build. The character of Lenin's rule is the subject of the key debate.

##  Refresher questions

Use these questions to remind yourself of the key material covered in this chapter.

**1** What measures did Lenin introduce to establish Bolshevik governmental control?
**2** Why did Lenin dissolve the Constituent Assembly in 1918?
**3** Was the Treaty of Brest-Litovsk a humiliation or a triumph for the Bolsheviks?
**4** Was the Bolshevik victory in the Civil War the result of Red strength or White weakness?
**5** What strategy did Trotsky follow as War Commissar?
**6** What influence did the Civil War have on the character of Bolshevism?
**7** Why did the foreign interventions of 1918–21 fail?
**8** What roles did the *Cheka* and the Red Army play in the Red Terror?
**9** What was the impact of War Communism on the economy?
**10** In what ways was War Communism an extension of the Red Terror?
**11** Why was the Kronstadt Rising so disturbing for Lenin and the Bolsheviks?
**12** What problems was NEP intended to resolve?
**13** How did Lenin preserve party unity over NEP?
**14** What were the main achievements of Lenin as a revolutionary?
**15** What were Lenin's main strengths and weaknesses as a leader?

##  Question practice

### ESSAY QUESTIONS

**1** How important was the dissolution of the Constituent Assembly in 1918 in the consolidation of Bolshevik power?
**2** To what extent were Lenin and the Bolsheviks responsible for the outbreak of the Russian Civil War in 1918?
**3** 'The Kronstadt Rising in 1921 was a clear sign that War Communism had failed.' How far do you agree with this statement?
**4** The introduction by Lenin of NEP in 1921 was more important as a political move than as an economic one.' How far do you agree?

### INTERPRETATION QUESTION

**1** Read the interpretation and then answer the question that follows. 'Whatever the pre-revolutionary attitude of the Bolsheviks to democracy, it was the circumstances of the years 1917–21 that led them to adopt an authoritarian mode of government.' (From Eric Hobsbawm, *Age of Extremes*, 1994.) Evaluate the strength and limitations of this interpretation, making reference to other interpretations that you have studied.

# Stalin's rise to power 1924–9

When Lenin, the Bolshevik leader, died he left many problems but no obvious successor. Few Russian Communists gave a thought to Stalin as a likely leader. Yet five years later, after a bitter power struggle, it was Stalin who had outmanoeuvred his rivals and established his authority over the party and the nation. How he achieved this is the subject of this chapter, the main themes of which are:

★ Stalin's character and background

★ The power struggle within the Communist Party

★ 'Permanent Revolution' versus 'Socialism in One Country'

★ Stalin's defeat of Trotsky and the Left

★ Stalin's defeat of the Right

## Key dates

| | |
|---|---|
| **1924** | Death of Lenin |
| | Politburo opted for collective leadership |
| **1925** | Trotsky lost his position as war commissar |
| | Kamenev and Zinoviev headed United Opposition |
| **1926** | Trotsky joined Kamenev and Zinoviev in bloc |
| **1926–7** | Stalin defeated the Left |
| **1927** | Trotsky expelled from the Communist Party of the Soviet Union |
| **1928** | Stalin attacked the Right |
| **1929** | The Right finally defeated by Stalin |
| | Trotsky exiled from the USSR |

## 1 Stalin's character and background

▶ *How had Stalin's career before 1924 put him in a strong position to bid for power after Lenin's death?*

Stalin, meaning 'man of steel', was not his real name. It was simply the alias he adopted in 1912, the last in a series of 40 that Josef Vissarionovich Djugashvili had used to avoid detection as a revolutionary. He was born in Georgia, in a poverty-stricken province in the south of the Russian Empire. His drunken father eked out a miserable existence as a cobbler. There have been suggestions that both Stalin's admiration of all things Russian and his contempt for middle-class intellectuals derived from a sense of resentment over his humble non-Russian origins.

## Stalin's early revolutionary career

Stalin's mother was a particularly devout woman and it was largely through her influence that her son was enrolled as a student in a Georgian-Orthodox seminary in Tiflis (Tbilisi), the capital of Georgia. This did not indicate religious fervour on his part; the fact was that at this time in Imperial Russia attendance at a Church academy was the only way to obtain a Russian-style education, an essential requirement for anyone from the provinces who had ambition. In the event, Stalin soon showed that he was attracted less by theology than by the revolutionary ideas with which he came into contact outside the seminary.

Stalin's involvement in the Georgian resistance movement, agitating against tsarist control, led to his expulsion from the seminary in 1899. His anti-government activities drew him into the Social Democratic Workers' Party. From the time he left the seminary to the Revolution of 1917 Stalin was a committed follower of Lenin. He threw himself into the task of raising funds for the Bolsheviks; his specialities were bank hold-ups and train robberies. With Lenin's backing, he had risen by 1912 to become one of the six members of the Bolshevik Central Committee. He had also helped to found the party's newspaper, *Pravda*. By 1917 Stalin had been arrested eight times and had been sentenced to various periods of imprisonment and exile. Afterwards, he tended to despise those revolutionaries who had escaped such experiences by fleeing to the relative comfort of self-imposed exile abroad.

There was once a common view among historians that Stalin's pre-1924 career was unimportant. They tended to accept Nicolai Sukhanov's 1922 description of him as a 'dull, grey blank'. But researches into the Soviet archives over the last 25 years have indicated that the notion of Stalin as a nonentity before 1924 is the opposite of the truth. Stalin was very highly regarded by Lenin and played a central role in the Bolshevik Party. Far from being a grey blank, he was an indispensable Bolshevik activist before 1917. Lenin once described Stalin as 'that wonderful Georgian', a reference to his work as an agitator among the non-Russian peoples.

## The October Revolution and Civil War

Having spent the war years, 1914–17, in exile in Siberia, Stalin returned to Petrograd in March 1917. His role in the October Revolution is not wholly clear. Official accounts, written after he had taken power, were a mixture of distortion and invention, with any unflattering episodes totally omitted. What is reasonably certain is that Stalin was loyal to Lenin after the latter had returned to Petrograd in April 1917 and instructed the Bolsheviks to abandon all co-operation with other parties and devote themselves to preparing for a seizure of power. As a Leninist, Stalin was opposed to the **'October deserters'**, such as Kamenev and Zinoviev (see page 113).

During the period of crisis and civil war that accompanied the efforts of the Bolsheviks to consolidate their authority after 1917, Stalin's non-Russian background proved invaluable. His knowledge of the minority peoples of the old Russian Empire led to his being appointed **commissar for nationalities**. Lenin believed that Stalin's toughness qualified him well for this role. As commissar, Stalin became the ruthless Bolshevik organiser for the whole of the Caucasus region (see the map on page 2) during the Civil War from 1918 to 1920. This led to a number of disputes with Trotsky, the Bolshevik commissar for war. Superficially, the quarrels were about strategy and tactics, but at a deeper level they were a clash of personalities and proved to be the beginning of a deep rivalry between the two men.

**KEY TERMS**

**'October deserters'** Those Bolsheviks who in October 1917, believing that the party was not yet strong enough, had advised against a Bolshevik rising.

**Commissar for nationalities** Minister responsible for liaising with the non-Russian national minorities.

**'Testament'** A set of reflections and comments that Lenin made on his fellow Communist leaders.

## Lenin's testament

Although Stalin had been totally loyal to Lenin, there were two particular occasions when he had aroused Lenin's anger. After the Civil War had ended, Stalin had been off-hand in discussions with the representatives from Georgia. Lenin, anxious to gain the support of the national minorities for the Bolshevik regime, had to intervene personally to prevent the Georgians leaving in a pique. On another occasion, in a more directly personal matter, Lenin learned from his wife, Krupskaya, that in a row over the Georgian question Stalin had subjected her to 'a storm of the coarsest abuse', telling her to keep her nose out of state affairs, and calling her a 'whore'. The very day that Lenin was informed of this, 22 December 1922, he dictated his **'testament'**, in which he urged comrades to think of ways of removing Stalin from his position as general secretary (see Source A).

Despite this warning, nothing was done. Lenin was too ill during the final years of his life to be politically active. At his death in January 1924, he had still not taken any formal steps to remove Stalin, and the testament had not been made public (see page 191).

**SOURCE A**

**From Lenin's testament, January 1923, quoted in S. Hendel, *The Social Crucible*, Van Nostrand, 1959, pp. 281–2.**

*Comrade Stalin, having become General Secretary of the Party, has concentrated enormous power in his hands; and I am not sure that he always knows how to exercise that power with sufficient caution. Stalin is too rude; and this fault, entirely bearable in relations amongst us Communists, ourselves becomes insupportable in the office of General Secretary. I therefore propose to the comrades to find a way to remove Stalin from that position and to appoint to it another man who in all respects differs from Stalin only in superiority – namely more patient, more loyal, more polite and more attentive to comrades, less capricious, etc.*

?

What problems did Lenin's comments in Source A raise for Stalin in his bid for leadership after Stalin's death?

## Stalin's position in 1924

In the uncertain atmosphere that followed Lenin's death, a number of pieces of luck helped Stalin to promote his own claims, but it would be wrong to ascribe his success wholly to good fortune. The luck had to be used. Stalin may have lacked brilliance, but he had great ability. His particular qualities of perseverance and willingness to undertake laborious administrative work were ideally suited to the times. The government of Soviet Russia, as it had developed by 1924, had two main features: the **Council of People's Commissars**, and the Secretariat. Both these bodies were staffed and controlled by the Bolshevik Party. The vital characteristic of this governmental system was that the party ruled. By 1922, Soviet Russia was a one-party state. Membership of that one party was essential for all who held government posts at whatever level.

As government grew in scope, certain posts, which initially had not been considered especially significant, began to provide their holders with the levers of power. This had not been the intention, but was the unforeseen result of the emerging pattern of Bolshevik rule. It was in this context that Stalin's previous appointments to key posts in both government and party proved vital. These had been:

- People's commissar for nationalities (appointed 1917, see page 185). In this post, Stalin was in charge of the officials in the many regions and republics that made up the USSR (the official title of the Soviet state after 1922).
- Liaison officer between Politburo and Orgburo (appointed 1919). This post placed Stalin in a unique position to monitor both the party's policy and the party's personnel.
- Head of the workers' and peasants' inspectorate (appointed 1919). This position entitled Stalin to oversee the work of all government departments.
- General secretary of the Communist Party (appointed 1922). In this position, Stalin recorded and conveyed party policy. This enabled him to build up personal files on all the members of the party. Nothing of note happened that Stalin did not know about.

Stalin became the indispensable link in the chain of command in the Communist Party and the Soviet government. What these posts gave him above all was the power of **patronage**. He used this authority to put his own supporters in top positions. Since they then owed their place to him, Stalin could count on their support in the voting in the various committees which made up the organisation of the party and the government. Such were the levers in Stalin's possession during the party infighting over the succession to Lenin. No other contender came anywhere near matching Stalin in his hold on the party machine. Whatever the ability of the individuals or groups who opposed him, he could always outvote and outmanoeuvre them.

### KEY TERMS

**Council of People's Commissars** A cabinet of ministers, responsible for creating government policies.

**Patronage** The right to appoint individuals to official posts in the party and government.

## The Lenin enrolment

Stalin had also benefited politically from recent changes in the structure of the Communist Party. Between 1923 and 1925, the party had set out to increase the number of true proletarians in its ranks. This was known as the 'Lenin enrolment'. It resulted in the membership of the **CPSU** rising from 340,000 in 1922 to 600,000 by 1925. The new members were predominantly poorly educated and politically unsophisticated, but they were fully aware that the many privileges which came with party membership depended on their being loyal to those who had first invited them into the Bolshevik ranks. The task of vetting the 'Lenin enrolment' had fallen largely to the officials in the Secretariat who worked directly under Stalin as general secretary. In this way, the expansion of the party added to his growing power of patronage. It provided him with a reliable body of votes in the various party committees at local and central level.

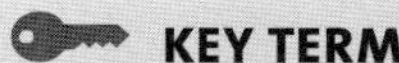

**KEY TERM**

**CPSU** The Communist Party of the Soviet Union, the new name for the Bolshevik Party from 1918 onwards.

## The attack on factionalism

Another lasting feature of Lenin's period in government that proved of great value to Stalin was what had become known as the 'attack on factionalism'. This referred to Lenin's condemnation in 1921 of divisions within the party (see page 171). The effect of this rejection of 'factionalism' was to frustrate any serious attempt to criticise party decisions or policies. It became extremely difficult to mount any form of legitimate opposition within the CPSU. Stalin gained directly from the ban on criticism of the party line. The charge of 'factionalism' provided him with a ready weapon for resisting challenges to the authority he had begun to exercise.

## The Lenin legacy

There was an accompanying factor that legitimised Stalin's position. Stalin became heir to the 'Lenin legacy', the tradition of authority and leadership that Lenin had established during his lifetime, and the veneration in which he was held after his death. It is barely an exaggeration to say that in the eyes of the Communist Party, Lenin became a god. His actions and decisions became unchallengeable, and all arguments and disputes within the party were settled by reference to his statements and writings. Lenin became the measure of the correctness of Soviet theory and practice. Soviet communism became Leninism. After 1924, if a party member could assume the mantle of Lenin and appear to carry on Lenin's work, he would establish a formidable claim to power. This is exactly what Stalin began to do.

**Summary diagram: Stalin's character and background**

| Background |
| --- |
| • Stalin had worked closely and loyally with Lenin<br>• Stalin had been a major worker for the Bolsheviks<br>• Lenin regarded him as 'that wonderful Georgian' |

| Key posts taken by Stalin during Lenin's time |
| --- |
| • People's commissar for nationalities<br>• Liaison officer between Politburo and Orgburo<br>• Head of the Workers' and Peasants' Inspectorate<br>• Secretary of the Communist Party |

| Key moment, January 1923 |
| --- |
| • Lenin's death prevented his 'testament' from being published. This saved Stalin from being dismissed as general secretary |

| Key benefits to Stalin from developments during Lenin's last years |
| --- |
| • The Lenin enrolment<br>• The attack on factionalism<br>• Lenin's legacy |

# The power struggle within the Communist Party

► *What were Stalin's advantages in the power struggle following Lenin's death?*

Following Lenin's death, a period of political manoeuvring began. This took the form of disputes between Left and Right Communists, terms which were not very precise but broadly referred to those in the party who wanted the New Economic Policy (NEP) to be modified or abandoned (Left) and those who wanted it to continue (Right). Although his position on NEP was not clear at this stage, Stalin came to be regarded as the dominant figure of the Right opposed to Trotsky on the Left. However, in this early period of manoeuvring the differences between the two rivals had as much to do with personality as policy.

## Lenin's funeral

Immediately after Lenin's death, the Politburo, whose members were Stalin, Trotsky, **Rykov**, **Tomsky**, Kamenev and Zinoviev, publicly proclaimed their intention to continue as a collective leadership. However, behind the scenes the competition for individual authority had already begun. In the manoeuvring, Stalin gained an advantage by being the one to deliver the oration at Lenin's funeral. The sight of Stalin as leading mourner suggested a continuity between him and Lenin, an impression heightened by the contents of his speech in which, in the name of the party, he humbly dedicated himself to follow in the tradition of the departed leader (see Source B).

**KEY FIGURES**

**Aleksei Rykov (1881–1938)**

Chairman of the Central Committee of the CPSU.

**Mikhail Tomsky (1880–1937)**

Minister responsible for representing (in practice, controlling) the trade unions.

**SOURCE B**

**From Stalin's address at Lenin's funeral, January 1924, quoted in *Stalin's Works*, volume 6, Lawrence & Wishart, 1955, p. 47.**

*In leaving us, Comrade Lenin commanded us to hold high and pure the great calling of Party Member. We swear to thee, Comrade Lenin, to honour thy command. In leaving us, Comrade Lenin commanded us to keep the unity of our party as the apple of our eye. We swear to thee, Comrade Lenin, to honour thy command.*

*In leaving us, Comrade Lenin ordered us to maintain and strengthen the dictatorship of the proletariat. We swear to thee, Comrade Lenin, to exert our full strength in honouring thy command.*

*In leaving us, Comrade Lenin ordered us to strengthen with all our might the union of workers and peasants. We swear to thee Comrade Lenin, to honour your command.*

*In leaving us, Comrade Lenin enjoined us to be faithful to the Communist International. We swear to thee Comrade Lenin, that we shall dedicate our lives to the enlargement and reinforcement of the union of the workers of the world.*

In Source B, what effect is Stalin trying to achieve by the constant repetition of his commitment to Lenin's commands?

Since Stalin's speech was the first crucial move to promote himself as Lenin's successor, it was to be expected that Leon Trotsky, his chief rival, would try to counter it. Yet Trotsky was not even present at the funeral. It was a very conspicuous absence, and it is puzzling why Trotsky did not appreciate the importance of appearances following Lenin's death in January 1924. Initially he, not Stalin, had been offered the opportunity of making the major speech at the funeral. But not only did he decline this, he also failed to attend the ceremony itself. His excuse was that Stalin had given him the wrong date, but this simply was not true. Documents show that he learned the actual date early enough for him to have reached Moscow with time to spare. Instead, he continued his planned journey and was on holiday on the day of the funeral. This was hardly the image of a dedicated Leninist.

What makes Trotsky's behaviour more inexplicable is that he was well aware of the danger that Stalin represented. In 1924 he prophesied that Stalin would become 'the dictator of the USSR'. He also gave a remarkable analysis of the basis of Stalin's power in the party (see Source C).

? In Source C, what political gifts does Trotsky acknowledge that Stalin possesses?

**SOURCE C**

**From a comment made by Trotsky in 1924, quoted in Leon Trotsky, *Stalin, An Appraisal of the Man and His Influence*, Hollis & Carter, 1966, pp. 392–3.**

*The dialectics of history have already hooked him and will raise him up. He is needed by all of them; by the tired radicals, by the bureaucrats, by the Nepmen, the upstarts, by all the worms that are crawling out of the upturned soil of the manured revolution. He knows how to meet them on their own ground, he speaks their language and he knows how to lead them. He has the deserved reputation of an old revolutionist, which makes him invaluable to them as a blinder on the eyes of the country. He has will and daring. He will not hesitate to use them and to move against the party. He has already started doing this. Right now he is organising around himself the sneaks of the party, the artful dodgers.*

Trotsky's description was a bitter but strikingly accurate assessment of how Stalin had made a large part of the party dependent on him. But logically, such awareness on Trotsky's part should have made him eager to prevent Stalin from stealing an advantage. His reluctance to act is a fascinating feature of Trotsky's enigmatic character.

## Trotsky's character

Trotsky had a complex personality. He was one of those figures in history who may be described as having been their own worst enemy. Despite his many talents and intellectual brilliance, he had serious flaws that undermined his chances of success. At times, he was unreasonably self-assured; at other critical times, he suffered from diffidence and lack of judgement. An example of this had occurred earlier, at the time of Stalin's mishandling of the Georgian question (see page 185). Lenin's anger with Stalin had offered Trotsky a perfect opportunity to undermine Stalin's position, but for some reason he had declined to attack.

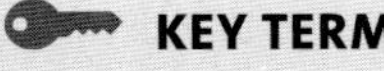

**KEY TERM**

**Anti-Semitism** Hatred of the Jewish race; for centuries Russia had been notorious for its vicious treatment of the Jews.

A possible clue to his reluctance is that he felt inhibited by his Jewishness. Trotsky knew that, in a nation such as Russia with its deeply ingrained **anti-Semitism**, his race made him an outsider. A remarkable example of his awareness of this occurred in 1917, when Lenin offered him the post of deputy chairman of the Soviet government. Trotsky rejected it on the grounds that his appointment would be an embarrassment to Lenin and the government. 'It would', he said, 'give enemies grounds for claiming that the country was ruled by a Jew.' It may have been similar reasoning that allowed Stalin to gain an advantage over him at the time of Lenin's funeral. It may have been, of course, that Trotsky simply did not want the responsibility of party leadership, but this does not accord with his worries over the dangers of Stalin taking the position or his own subsequent bid for power.

## Suppression of Lenin's testament

A dangerous hurdle in Stalin's way was Lenin's testament. If it were to be published, Stalin would be gravely damaged by it contents. However, here, as so often during this period, fortune favoured him. Had the document been made public, not only would Lenin's criticisms of Stalin have been revealed, but also those concerning Trotsky, Zinoviev and Kamenev. Nearly all the members of the Politburo had reason for suppressing the testament. When the Central Committee was presented with the document in May 1924, they realised that it was too damning broadly to be used exclusively against any one individual. They agreed to its being shelved indefinitely. Trotsky, for obvious personal reasons, went along with the decision, but in doing so he was declining yet another opportunity to challenge Stalin's right to power. In fact it was Trotsky, not Stalin, whom the Politburo regarded as the greater danger.

## Party members' attitudes towards Trotsky

The attitude of party members towards Trotsky was an important factor in the weakening of his position. Colleagues tended to regard Trotsky as dangerously ambitious and his rival Stalin as reliably self-effacing. This was because Trotsky was flamboyant and brilliant, while his rival was unspectacular and methodical. Trotsky was the type of person who attracted either admiration or distaste, but seldom loyalty. That was why he lacked a genuine following. It is true that he was highly regarded by the Red Army, whose creator he had been, but this was never matched by any comparable political support. Trotsky failed to build a power base within the party. This invariably gave him the appearance of an outsider.

Adding to his difficulties in this regard was the doubt about his commitment to Bolshevism. Until 1917, as Lenin had noted in his testament, Trotsky had belonged to the Mensheviks. This led to the suspicion that his conversion had been a matter of expediency rather than conviction. Many of the old-guard Bolsheviks regarded Trotsky as a Menshevik turncoat who could not be trusted. Kamenev and Zinoviev joined Stalin in an unofficial **triumvirate** within the Politburo. Their aim was to isolate Trotsky by exploiting his unpopularity with large sections of the party. The 'Lenin enrolment' helped them in this. The new proletarian members were hardly the type of men to be impressed by the cultured Trotsky. The seemingly down-to-earth Stalin was much more to their liking.

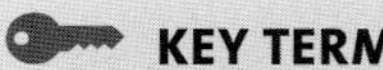

**KEY TERM**

**Triumvirate** A ruling or influential bloc of three people.

## Leon Trotsky

| | |
|---|---|
| 1879 | Born, Leon Bronstein, into a Ukrainian Jewish family |
| 1905 | Became chairman of St Petersburg soviet |
| 1907–17 | Lived in various European countries and in the USA |
| 1917 | Principal organiser of the October coup |
| 1918 | Negotiated the Treaty of Brest-Litovsk |
| 1918–20 | Created the Red Army |
| 1924–27 | Outmanoeuvred in the power struggle with Stalin |
| 1940 | Assassinated in Mexico on Stalin's orders |

As a young revolutionary, Trotsky was drawn to Menshevism and it was as a Menshevik that he became chairman of the St Petersburg soviet during the 1905 Revolution. His activities led to his arrest and exile. Between 1906 and 1917 he developed his theory of 'Permanent Revolution', the notion that revolution was not one event but a continuous process of international class warfare.

Following the February Revolution, Trotsky returned to Petrograd and immediately joined the Bolshevik Party. He became chairman of the Petrograd soviet, a position that he used to organise the Bolshevik Rising, which overthrew the Provisional Government in October 1917. In the Bolshevik government that then took over, Trotsky became commissar for foreign affairs. He was the chief negotiator in the Russo-German talks that resulted in Russia's withdrawal from the war in 1918. Then, as war commissar, he achieved the greatest success of his career, the victory of the Red Army in the Civil War of 1918–20. As a hardliner, Trotsky fully supported Lenin's repressive policy of War Communism. He plotted the destruction of the Russian trade unions, and in 1921 ordered the suppression of the rebellious Kronstadt workers.

Never fully accepted by his fellow Bolsheviks, despite his brilliance, Trotsky lost to Stalin in the power struggle that followed Lenin's death. Trotsky's concept of Permanent Revolution was suppressed in favour of 'Socialism in One Country', Stalin's term for the consolidation of Communist rule in the USSR.

In 1929 Trotsky was exiled from the USSR. In 1939 he founded the vocal but ineffectual anti-Stalin Fourth International. Trotsky's end came in 1940 in Mexico City, when a Soviet agent, acting on Stalin's direct orders, killed him by driving an ice-pick into his head.

**KEY TERMS**

**Bureaucratisation**
The growth in power of the Secretariat, which was able to make decisions and operate policies without reference to ordinary party members.

**'Party democracy'**
The right of all party members to express their opinion on policy.

## Bureaucratisation

Despite the attacks on him, Trotsky attempted to hold his ground. The issue he chose to fight on was **bureaucratisation**, which he linked with the abandonment of genuine discussion within the party. He had good reason to think he had selected a powerful cause. Lenin himself in his last writings had warned the party against the dangers of creeping bureaucracy. Accordingly, Trotsky pressed his views in the Central Committee, in the Politburo and at party congresses. His condemnation of the growth of bureaucracy was coupled with an appeal for a return to '**party democracy**'. He expanded his arguments in a series of essays, the most controversial of which was *Lessons of October*, in which he criticised Kamenev and Zinoviev for their past disagreements with Lenin. The assault was ill judged, since it invited retaliation in kind. Trotsky's Menshevik past and his divergence from Leninism were highlighted in a number of books and pamphlets, most notably Kamenev's *Leninism or Trotskyism?*

As a move in the power struggle, Trotsky's campaign for greater party democracy was misjudged. His censures on bureaucracy left Stalin largely unscathed. Moreover, Trotsky had overlooked the essential fact that Bolshevik rule since 1917 had always been bureaucratic. Indeed, it was because the Soviet state functioned as a bureaucracy that party members received privileges in political and public life. Trotsky's line was unlikely to gain significant support from party members who had a vested interest in maintaining the party's bureaucratic ways.

## Disputes over NEP

Trotsky's reputation was further damaged by the issue of NEP. When introducing NEP, Lenin had admitted that it was a relaxing of strict socialism, but had emphasised that it was a temporary, stop-gap measure. However, at the time of his death in 1924 the question was already being asked as to how long in practice NEP was meant to last. Was it not becoming a permanent policy? The party members who were unhappy with it saw its continuation as a betrayal of revolutionary principle. They objected to a policy which, in effect, allowed the peasants to dictate the pace of Soviet Russia's advance towards full communism. A serious division had developed between Left Communists and Right Communists.

## Stalin's exploitation of the NEP question

Although fierce disputes were to arise over the issue, initially the disagreement was simply about timing: how long should NEP be allowed to run? However, in the power struggle of the 1920s these minor differences deepened into questions of political correctness and party loyalty. A rival's attitude towards NEP might be a weakness to be exploited; if it could be established that his views indicated deviant Marxist thinking it would be possible to destroy his position in the party.

Stalin did precisely this. He used Trotsky's attitude towards NEP as a way of undermining him. Trotsky had backed Lenin in 1921, but there were strong rumours that his support had been reluctant and that he regarded NEP as a deviation from true socialism. It was certainly the case that in 1923 Trotsky had led a group of party members in openly criticising ***Gosplan*** for its 'flagrant radical errors of economic policy'. Trotsky's charge was that the government had placed the interests of the Nepmen above those of the revolution and the Russian people. He urged a return to a much tighter state control of industry and warned that under NEP the revolutionary gains made under War Communism would be lost.

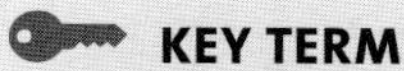

**KEY TERM**

***Gosplan*** The government body responsible for national economic planning.

Stalin was quick to suggest to party members who already looked on Trotsky as a disruptive force that he was, indeed, suspect. The interesting point here is that Stalin's own view of NEP was far from clear at this stage. He had loyally supported Lenin's introduction of it in 1921, but had given little indication as to whether, or how long, it should be retained after Lenin's death. He preferred to keep his own views to himself and play on the differences between his colleagues.

## The issue of modernisation

The NEP debate was one aspect of the question that remained unanswered at Lenin's death. How should the Soviet Union plan for the future? This would have been a demanding issue regardless of whether or not there had been a power struggle. What the rivalry for leadership did was to intensify the argument. The USSR was a poor country. To modernise and overcome its poverty, it would have to industrialise. Recent history had shown that a strong industrial base was an absolute essential for a modern state, and there was common agreement among Soviet Communists about that. The quarrel was not over whether the USSR should industrialise, but over how and at what speed.

History had further shown that the industrial expansion which had taken place in the previous century, in such countries as Germany and Britain, had relied on a ready supply of resources and the availability of capital for investment. Russia was rich in natural resources, but these had yet to be effectively exploited, and it certainly did not possess large amounts of capital. Nor could it easily borrow any, since, after 1917, the Bolsheviks had rejected **capitalist methods of finance**. Moreover, even if the Bolsheviks had been willing to borrow, there were few countries after 1917 willing to risk the dangers of investing in revolutionary Russia.

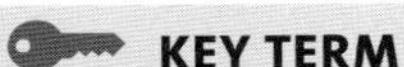


**Capitalist methods of finance** The system in which the owners of private capital (money) increase their wealth by making loans on which interest has to be paid later by the borrower.

The only usable resource, therefore, was the Russian people themselves, 80 per cent of whom were peasants. To achieve industrialisation, it was necessary that the peasants be persuaded or forced into producing a food surplus which could then be sold abroad to raise capital for industrial investment. Both Left and Right agreed that this was the only solution, but, whereas the Right were content to rely on persuasion, the Left demanded that the peasantry be forced into line. It was Trotsky who most clearly represented the view of the Left on this. He wanted the peasants to be coerced into co-operating. However, for him the industrialisation debate was secondary to the far more demanding question of Soviet Russia's role as the organiser of international revolution.

**Summary diagram: The power struggle within the Communist Party**

**Stalin's advantages**

- Held key posts in party and government
- Took initiative on Lenin's death

**Trotsky's disadvantages**

- Strange diffidence allowed Stalin to make the running
- Lacked a power base in the party

**Triumvirate (Stalin, Kamenev, Zinoviev) versus Trotsky**

**Issues on which Trotsky attempted to fight**

Bureaucratisation | NEP | Modernisation of USSR

# 'Permanent Revolution' versus 'Socialism in One Country'

▶ *What were the main ideas dividing Trotsky and Stalin in their attitude towards the role of the USSR as a revolutionary nation?*

The ideological divide between Trotsky and Stalin was expressed as a clash between their opposing notions of 'Permanent Revolution' and 'Socialism in One Country'.

## 'Permanent Revolution'

Trotsky's politics were inspired by his belief in 'Permanent Revolution', which was made up of a number of key ideas:

- Revolution was not a single event but a permanent (continuous) process in which risings took place from country to country.
- The events in Russia since 1917 were simply a first step towards a worldwide revolution of the proletariat.
- Individual nations did not matter. The interests of the international working class were paramount.
- True revolutionary socialism could be achieved in the USSR only if an international uprising took place.

Trotsky believed that the USSR could not survive alone in a hostile world. With its vast peasant population and undeveloped proletariat, it would prove 'incapable of holding its own against conservative Europe'. He contended that the immediate task of the USSR was 'to export revolution'. That was the only way to guarantee its survival. It should be stressed that at no point did Trotsky call for the Soviet Union to be sacrificed to some theoretical notion of world revolution. His argument was an opposite one; unless there was international revolution the Soviet Union would go under. Stalin, however, ignored the subtlety of his opponent's reasoning. He chose to portray Trotsky as someone intent on damaging the Soviet Union.

## 'Socialism in One Country'

Stalin countered Trotsky's notion of 'Permanent Revolution' with his own concept of 'Socialism in One Country'. He meant by this that the nation's first task was to consolidate Lenin's Revolution and the rule of the CPSU by turning the USSR into a modern state, capable of defending itself against its internal and external enemies. The Soviet Union, therefore must work to:

- Overcome its present agricultural and industrial problems by its own unaided efforts.
- Build a modern state, the equal of any nation in the world.

- Make the survival of the Soviet Union an absolute priority, even if this meant suspending efforts to create international revolution.

Stalin used the contrast between this programme and Trotsky's to portray his rival as an enemy of the Soviet Union. Trotsky's ideas were condemned as an affront to Lenin and the Bolshevik Revolution. An image was created of Trotsky as an isolated figure, a posturing Jewish intellectual, whose vague notions of international revolution threatened the security of the Soviet Union. Trotsky's position was further weakened by the fact that throughout the 1920s the Soviet Union went in fear of invasion by the combined capitalist nations. It was a constant theme in Soviet public propaganda. Although this fear was ill-founded, the tense atmosphere it created made Trotsky's notion of the USSR's engaging in foreign revolutionary wars appear even more irresponsible. A number of historians, including E.H. Carr and Isaac Deutscher, have remarked on Stalin's ability to rally support and silence opponents at critical moments by assuming the role of the great Russian patriot, concerned to save the nation from the grave dangers with which it was threatened.

**Summary diagram: 'Permanent Revolution' versus 'Socialism in One Country'**

| 'Permanent Revolution' | 'Socialism in One Country' |
|---|---|
| **Trotsky's ideas**<br>• Revolution a continuous process<br>• Russian Revolution only a first step<br>• Goal was international proletarian revolution<br>• Individual nations did not matter<br>• USSR safe only if international rising occurred | **Stalin's ideas**<br>• Modernisation by USSR's own efforts<br>• Survival of USSR an absolute priority<br>• Suspension of efforts at international revolution |

# Stalin's defeat of Trotsky and the Left

*What were the basic weaknesses of the Left in its challenge to Stalin?*

**KEY TERMS**

**'To deliver the votes'** To use control of the party machine to gain majority support in key divisions.

**Leningrad** Petrograd had been renamed in Lenin's honour.

Trotsky's failure in the propaganda war of the 1920s meant that he was in no position to persuade either the Politburo or the Central Committee to vote for his proposals. Stalin's ability **'to deliver the votes'** in the crucial divisions was decisive. Following a vote against him in the 1925 party congress, Trotsky was relieved of his position as commissar for war. Lev Kamenev and Grigory Zinoviev, the respective chairmen of the Moscow and **Leningrad** soviets, played a key part in this. They used their influence over the local party organisations to ensure that it was a pro-Stalin, anti-Trotsky, congress that gathered.

## Kamenev and Zinoviev

With Trotsky weakened, Stalin turned to the problem of how to deal with two key figures, whom he now saw as potential rivals. Kamenev and Zinoviev had been motivated by a personal dislike of Trotsky, who at various times had tried to embarrass them by reminding the party of their failure to support Lenin in October 1917. Now it was their turn to be ousted. As it happened, they had already created a trap for themselves. In 1925 Kamenev and Zinoviev, worried by the USSR's economic backwardness, publicly stated that it would require the victory of proletarian revolution in the capitalist nations in order for the Soviet Union to achieve socialism. Zinoviev wrote: 'When the time comes for the revolution in other countries and the proletariat comes to our aid, then we shall again go over to the offensive. For the time being we have only a little breathing space.'

Zinoviev and Kamenev called for NEP to be abandoned, for restrictions to be reimposed on the peasants, and for enforced industrialisation. It was understandable that Kamenev and Zinoviev, as respective party bosses in the Soviet Union's only genuinely industrial areas, Moscow and Leningrad, should have thought in these terms. Their viewpoint formed the basis of what was termed the **United Opposition**, but it appeared to be indistinguishable from old Trotskyism. It was no surprise, therefore, when Trotsky joined his former opponents in 1926 to form a 'Trotskyite–Kamenevite–Zinovievite' opposition bloc.

Again, Stalin's control of the party machine proved critical. The party congress declined to be influenced by pressure from the United Opposition. Stalin's chief backers among the Right Communists were Rykov, Tomsky and Bukharin. They and their supporters combined to outvote the United Opposition. Kamenev and Zinoviev were dismissed from their posts as soviet chairmen, to be replaced by two of Stalin's staunchest allies, **Molotov** in Moscow and **Kirov** in Leningrad. It was little surprise that soon afterwards, Trotsky was expelled from both the Politburo and the Central Committee.

## Trotsky exiled

Trotsky still did not admit defeat. In 1927, on the tenth anniversary of the Bolshevik Rising, he tried to rally support in a direct challenge to Stalin's authority. But even fewer members of congress than before were prepared to side with him and he was again outvoted. His complete failure led to congress's accepting Stalin's proposal that Trotsky be expelled from the party altogether. An internal exile order against him in 1927 was followed two years later by his total exile from the USSR.

Stalin's victory over Trotsky was not primarily a matter of ability or principle. Stalin won because Trotsky lacked a power base. Trotsky's superiority as a speaker and writer, and his greater intellectual gifts, counted for little when set

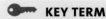

### KEY TERM

**United Opposition**
The group led by Kamenev and Zinoviev, sometimes known as the New Opposition, who called for an end to NEP and the adoption of a rapid industrialisation programme.

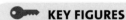

### KEY FIGURES

**Vyacheslav Molotov (1890–1986)**

A prominent Bolshevik agitator in 1917, he became a dedicated supporter of Stalin in home and foreign affairs. Winston Churchill, the British statesman, regarded him as an 'automaton'.

**Sergei Kirov (1886–1934)**

An able and popular individual who rose quickly in the party, holding a number of key posts; he was murdered in mysterious circumstances in 1934, possibly at Stalin's instigation.

against Stalin's grip on the party machine. It is difficult to see how, after 1924, Trotsky could have ever mounted a serious challenge to his rival. Even had his own particular failings not stopped him from acting at vital moments, Trotsky never had control of the political system as it operated in Soviet Russia. Politics is the art of the possible. After 1924 all the possibilities belonged to Stalin, and he used them.

**Summary diagram: Stalin's defeat of Trotsky and the Left**

Local party bosses, Kamenev and Zinoviev, used their influence to create a pro-Stalin, anti-Trotsky, CPSU congress in 1925

**Result**
*Congress voted against Trotsky – he was dismissed as commissar for war*

Stalin then turned on Kamenev and Zinoviev, who formed 'United Opposition'

↓

Policies of United Opposition on NEP and modernisation matched Trotsky's

**Result**
*Kamenevite–Zinovievite–Trotskyite bloc formed*

↓

Stalin used the Right Communists to deliver the votes in 1926 congress

**Results**
- *Left United Opposition defeated*
- *Kamenev and Zinoviev dismissed as Soviet chairmen*
- *Trotsky expelled from both the Politburo and Central Committee*

Trotsky fought on, but 1927 Congress expelled him from the party

↓

**1929 Trotsky exiled from Soviet Union**

# 5 Stalin's defeat of the Right

*How did Stalin exploit the attitude of the Right towards NEP and industrialisation?*

Although the victory of Stalin over the Right opposition is best studied as a feature of his industrialisation programme (see page 213), it is important also to see it as the last stage in the consolidation of his authority over the party and over the USSR. The defeat of the Right marked the end of any serious attempt to limit his power. From the late 1920s to his death in 1953 he would become increasingly dictatorial.

The major representatives of the Right were Rykov, Tomsky and Bukharin, the three who had loyally served Stalin in his outflanking of Trotsky and the Left. Politically, the Right were by no means as challenging to Stalin as the Trotskyite bloc had been. What made Stalin move against them was that they stood in the way of the industrial and agricultural schemes that his growing strength by 1928 put him in a position to begin implementing.

## Collectivisation and industrialisation

Historians are uncertain as to when Stalin finally decided that the answer to the Soviet Union's growth problem was to impose **collectivisation** and **industrialisation**. It is unlikely to have been an early decision; the probability is that it was another piece of opportunism. Having defeated the Left politically he may then have felt free to adopt their economic policies.

Some scholars have suggested that in 1928 Stalin became genuinely concerned about the serious grain shortage and decided that the only way to avoid a crisis was to resort to the drastic methods of collectivisation. It no longer mattered that this had been the very solution that the Left had advanced, since they were now scattered. For some time it had been the view of Bukharin and the Right that it was unnecessary to force the pace of industrialisation in the USSR. They argued that it would be less disruptive to let industry develop its own momentum. The state should assist, but it should not direct. Similarly, the peasants should not be controlled and oppressed; this would make them resentful and less productive.

The Right agreed that it was from the land that the means of financing industrialisation would have to come, but they suggested that, by offering the peasants the chance to become prosperous, far more grain would be produced for sale abroad. Bukharin argued in the Politburo and at the party congress in 1928 that Stalin's aggressive policy of **state grain procurements** was counter-productive. He declared that there were alternatives to these repressive policies. Bukharin was prepared to state openly what everybody knew, but was afraid to admit: that Stalin's programme was no different from the one that Trotsky had previously advocated.

**KEY TERMS**

**Collectivisation** The taking over by the Soviet state of the land and property previously owned by the peasants, accompanied by the requirement that the peasants now live and work communally.

**Industrialisation** The introduction of a vast scheme for the building of factories, which would produce heavy goods such as iron and steel.

**State grain procurements** Enforced collections of fixed quotas of grain from the peasants.

### Weaknesses of the Right

The Right suffered from a number of weaknesses, which Stalin was able to exploit: these related to their ideas, their organisation and their support.

#### Ideas

- Their economic arguments were not unsound, but in the taut atmosphere of the late 1920s, created by fear of invasion, they appeared timid and unrealistic.
- Their plea for a softer line with the peasants was unacceptable to the party hardliners around Stalin, who argued that the threatening times required a dedicated resistance to the enemies of revolution both within the USSR and outside it.

- Stalin was able to suggest that the Right were guilty of underestimating the crisis facing the party and the Soviet Union. He declared that it was a time for closing the ranks, in keeping with the tradition of 1917.

Stalin showed a shrewd understanding of the mentality of party members. The majority were far more likely to respond to the call for a return to a hardline policy, such as had helped them survive the desperate days of the Civil War, than they were to risk the revolution itself by untimely concessions to a peasantry that had no real place in the proletarian future. The party of Marx and Lenin, they asserted, would not be well served by the policies of the Right.

### Organisation

- Forming an organised opposition against Stalin was fast approaching an impossibility. The difficulty experienced by the Right in advancing their views was the same as that which had confronted the Left. How could they impress their ideas on the party while Stalin remained master of the party machine?
- Bukharin and his colleagues wanted to remain good party men and it was this sense of loyalty that weakened them in their attempts to oppose Stalin. Fearful of creating 'factionalism', they hoped that they could win the party round to their way of thinking without causing deep divisions. On occasion they were sharply outspoken, Bukharin particularly so, but their basic approach was conciliatory.

All this played into Stalin's hands. Since it was largely his supporters who were responsible for drafting and distributing party information, it was not difficult for Stalin to belittle the Right as a weak and irresponsible clique.

### Support

The Right's only substantial support lay in the trade unions. Although Trotsky had abolished these as independent organisations (see page 157), trade unions had been permitted to survive as bodies under state control. Their interests were officially safeguarded by the various branches of the Workers' Central Council. Tomsky chaired the Central Council, while the Moscow branch was led by **Nicolai Uglanov**, who was also the local CPSU secretary. When Stalin realised that these might be a source of opposition he acted quickly and decisively. He sent **Lazar Kaganovich** to undertake a purge of the suspect trade unionists. The Right proved totally incapable of resisting this political blitz. Molotov, Stalin's faithful henchman, was dispatched to Moscow, where he enlisted the support of the pro-Stalin members to achieve a similar purge of the local party officials.

By early 1929, the Right had been undermined beyond recovery:

- Tomsky was no longer the national trade union leader.
- Uglanov had been replaced in the Moscow party organisation.
- Rykov had been superseded as premier by Molotov.
- Bukharin had been voted out as chairman of the Comintern and had lost his place in the Politburo.

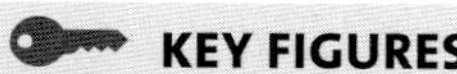
**KEY FIGURES**

**Nicolai Uglanov (1886–1940)**

An admirer and supporter of Bukharin.

**Lazar Kaganovich (1893–1991)**

A ruthless and ambitious young Politburo member from Ukraine.

- Tomsky, Rykov and Bukharin, the main trio of the 'Right Opportunists', as they were termed by the Stalinist press, were allowed to remain in the party, but only after they had publicly admitted the error of their ways.

Stalin's triumph over both Left and Right was complete. He was now in a position to exercise power as the new ***vozhd***. The grey blank was about to become the Red tsar.

**KEY TERM**

***Vozhd*** Russian for supreme leader, equivalent to *Führer* in German.

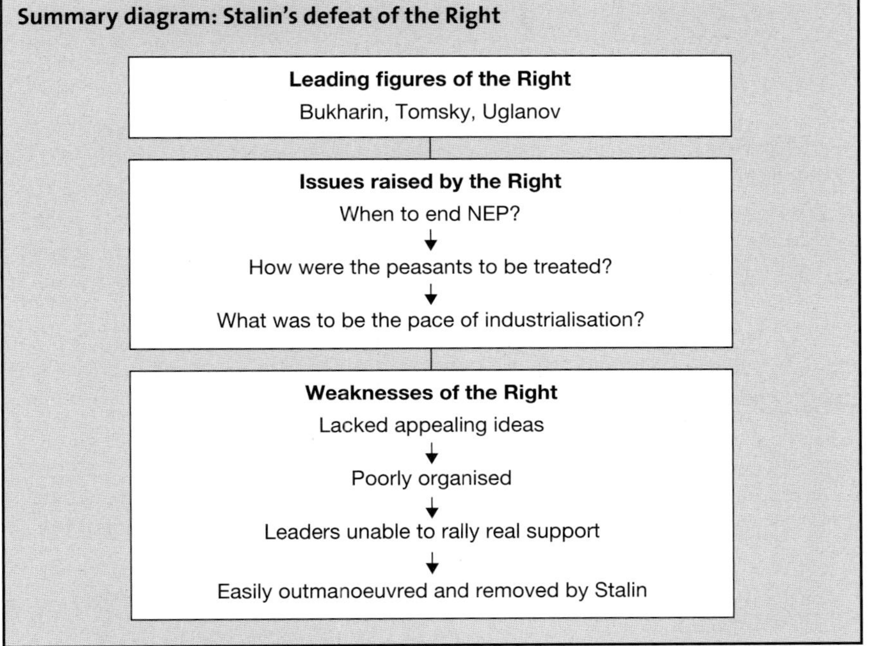

**Summary diagram: Stalin's defeat of the Right**

Leading figures of the Right
Bukharin, Tomsky, Uglanov
Issues raised by the Right
When to end NEP?
How were the peasants to be treated?
What was to be the pace of industrialisation?
Weaknesses of the Right
Lacked appealing ideas
Poorly organised
Leaders unable to rally real support
Easily outmanoeuvred and removed by Stalin



## Chapter summary

Having proved himself a loyal follower of Lenin and a highly active revolutionary terrorist before 1917, Stalin played a part in the October Revolution and went on to serve as a commissar in Lenin's government of Russia. Although criticised in Lenin's last testament, Stalin adroitly used the various positions he had gained within the Bolshevik Party to make himself indispensable as an administrator. As general secretary, his detailed knowledge of all the members left him ideally placed to outmanoeuvre his rivals in the power struggle after Lenin's death.

Stalin isolated Trotsky, his greatest challenger, by convincing the CPSU that if Trotsky's concept of 'Permanent Revolution' was put into practice it would mean the overthrow of the Soviet Union. Stalin's alternative strategy was 'Socialism in One Country', which emphasised the necessity of the besieged Soviet Union making its own survival a priority over the pursuit of international revolution. Stalin also exploited the party dispute over NEP to crush Trotsky and the other Left Bolsheviks. Having rid himself of the Left opposition, Stalin then turned unscrupulously on the Rightists who had supported him against Trotsky and removed them from key positions in party and government, replacing them with his own appointees.

## Refresher questions

Use these questions to remind yourself of the key material covered in this chapter.

**1** How significant was Stalin's revolutionary career before 1924?

**2** How had Stalin been able to rise up the Bolshevik ranks?

**3** What was the significance for Stalin of the 'Lenin enrolment'?

**4** How did Lenin's attack on factionalism assist Stalin?

**5** What gains did Stalin derive from the Lenin legacy?

**6** What were Stalin's advantages in his leadership struggle with Trotsky?

**7** What were Trotsky's weaknesses in his leadership struggle with Stalin?

**8** Why was there a Left–Right division over the question of how the USSR should modernise?

**9** What were the essential features of Trotsky's concept of 'Permanent Revolution'?

**10** What were the essential features of Stalin's concept of 'Socialism in One Country'?

**11** What were the basic weaknesses of the Left in their challenge to Stalin?

**12** Why were the Right unable to mount a successful challenge to Stalin?

## Question practice

### ESSAY QUESTIONS

**1** How important was it, in Stalin's rise to power after 1924, that he held the post of general secretary of the Communist Party?

**2** How far do you agree that Trotsky's own failings were the principal reason for his defeat in the power struggle with Stalin between 1924 and 1929?

**3** Which of the following was the greater obstacle facing Stalin in his rise to power by 1929? i) The Left in the Communist Party. ii) The Right in the Communist Party. Explain your answer with reference to both i) and ii).

**4** 'It was not their ideas but their poor organisation that allowed Stalin to overcome the Left Communists in the late 1920s. How far do you agree?

**5** 'It was Stalin's skilful use of his theory of "Socialism in One Country" that enabled him to dominate the Communist Party between 1924 and 1929.' How far do you agree with this statement?

CHAPTER 7

# Stalin and the Soviet economy 1929–41

Stalin decided that the USSR could not survive unless it rapidly modernised its economy. To this end, he set about completely reshaping Soviet agriculture and industry. This had immense economic, social and political consequences. These are examined as three themes:

★ Stalin's economic aims after 1929

★ Collectivisation: the war against the peasantry

★ Industrialisation: the first three Five-Year Plans

The key debate on *page 221* of this chapter asks the question: Were Stalin's economic policies justified by their results?

## Key dates

| | | | |
|---|---|---|---|
| **1928** | Collectivisation began<br>Start of the first Five-Year Plan | **1935** | Stakhanovite movement |
| **1932–3** | Widespread famine in the USSR | **1938** | Start of the third Five-Year Plan |
| **1933** | Start of the second Five-Year Plan | **1941–5** | The 'Great Patriotic War' |

## 1 Stalin's economic aims after 1929

▶ *What were Stalin's motives in revolutionising the Soviet economy?*

In the late 1920s, Stalin decided to impose on the USSR a crash programme of reform of the Soviet economy. Agriculture and industry were to be revolutionised. This was to prove such a dramatic development that Stalin referred to it as the **'second revolution'**, a way of equating it in importance with that of the 1917 Revolution itself. Historians often used the term the Great Turn to suggest that what Stalin did was as significant as Lenin's introduction of the New Economic Policy (NEP) in 1921 (see page 169). The cue for the great change had been provided in 1926 by a critical resolution of the party congress 'to transform our country from an agrarian into an industrial one, capable by its own efforts of producing the necessary means of modernisation'. Stalin planned to turn that resolution into reality.

**KEY TERM**

**'Second revolution'** The modernisation of the Soviet economy by means of state direction and central control.

## Revolution from above

Stalin's economic policy had one essential aim: the modernisation of the Soviet economy and two essential methods: collectivisation and industrialisation. From 1928 onwards, the attempt to modernise the USSR saw the Soviet state take over the running of the nation's economy. It is also frequently referred to as a 'revolution from above'.

In the Bolshevik interpretation of events, 1917 had been a **revolution from below** (see page 123). The Bolshevik-led proletariat had begun the construction of a state in which the workers ruled. Bukharin and the Right had used this notion to argue that, since the USSR was now a proletarian society, the economy should be left to develop at its own pace, without interference from the government. But Stalin's economic programme ended such thinking. The state would now command and direct the economy from above.

A central planning agency, known as *Gosplan,* had been created earlier under Lenin (see page 133). However, what was different about Stalin's schemes was their scale and thoroughness. Under Stalin, state control was to be total. There was an important political aspect to this. He saw in a hardline policy the best means of confirming his authority over party and government. When he introduced his radical economic changes, Stalin claimed that they marked as significant a stage in Soviet communism as had Lenin's fateful decision to sanction the October Rising in 1917. This comparison was obviously intended to enhance his own status as a revolutionary leader following in the footsteps of Lenin.

## Modernisation

It would be wrong to regard Stalin's policy as wholly a matter of **political expediency**. Judging from his speeches and actions after 1928, he had become convinced that the needs of Soviet Russia could be met only by modernisation. By that, Stalin meant bringing his economically backward nation up to a level of industrial production that would enable it to catch up with and then overtake the advanced economies of Western Europe and the USA. He believed that the survival of the revolution and of Soviet Russia depended on the nation's ability to turn itself into a modern industrial society within the shortest possible time. That was the essence of his slogan 'Socialism in One Country' (see page 195). Asserting that the Soviet Union was 100 years behind the advanced countries, he claimed, 'We must make good this distance in ten years or we shall be crushed.'

### KEY TERMS

**Revolution from below**
The Communist Party consistently claimed that the 1917 Revolution had been a genuine rising of the people rather than a power grab by the Bolsheviks.

**Political expediency**
Pursuing a course of action with the primary aim of gaining a political advantage.

**Summary diagram: Stalin's economic aims after 1929**

**Aims**

- 'Second revolution' to fulfil the first by modernising Soviet economy through state direction and control
- Economic motive:
  - To enable the USSR to catch up with the Western economies
- Political motive:
  - To confirm his authority as leader

↓

**Means**

- Revolution from above
- Collectivisation and industrialisation
- Under Gosplan direction

## Collectivisation: the war against the peasantry

▶ *What part was collectivisation intended to play in Stalin's plan for the modernisation of the USSR?*

Stalin was not a trained economist. He worked to a very simple formula that ran along these lines:

The USSR needed to industrialise.

Industrialisation required large amounts of manpower and capital.

The undeveloped USSR did not have sufficient capital and could not borrow from abroad because of its strained relations with the capitalist world.

Since Russia's natural resources, such as oil and gas, had yet to be effectively exploited, this left land as the only available resource.

Therefore, the peasants must produce surplus food to be sold abroad to raise capital.

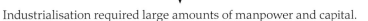

Efficient farming under collectivisation would create a surplus of farm labourers who would thus become available as factory workers.

The necessary first step towards using the land to raise capital was the collectivisation of Russian agriculture. This involved the state's taking the land from the peasants, who would no longer farm for their own individual profit. Instead, they would pool their efforts and receive a wage. Stalin calculated that this change would allow the Soviet Union to use the collective profits from the land to finance a massive industrialisation programme. For him, the needs of the land were always subordinate to those of industry.

**KEY TERMS**

**Collective farms** (*Kolkhozy* in Russian.) Run as co-operatives in which the peasants pooled their resources and shared their labour and wages.

**State farms** (*Sovkhozy* in Russian.) Contained peasants working directly for the state, which paid them a wage.

## Collective and state farms

In introducing collectivisation, Stalin referred to 'the setting up of **collective farms** and **state farms** in order to squeeze out all capitalist elements from the land'. In practice, there was little difference between the two. Both types of farm were to be the means by which private, peasant ownership would be ended and agriculture made to serve the interests of the Soviet state. The plan was to group between 50 and 100 holdings into one unit. It was believed that large farms would be more efficient and would encourage the effective use of agricultural machinery. Indeed, the motorised tractor became the outstanding symbol of this mechanising of Soviet farming. Improved farming methods on the new farms, so ran the argument, would have two vital results. They would:

- decrease the number of rural workers needed
- release the unwanted land workers for the new factories.

## The *kulaks*

Stalin claimed that collectivisation was 'voluntary', the free and eager choice of the peasants. But in truth it was forced on a very reluctant peasantry. In a major propaganda offensive, he copied Lenin in identifying a class of *kulaks*, who were holding back the workers' revolution by monopolising the best land and employing cheap peasant labour to farm it (see page 161). By hoarding their farm produce, they kept food prices high, thus making themselves rich at the expense of the workers and poorer peasants. Unless they were broken as a class, they would prevent the modernisation of the USSR.

The concept of a *kulak* class is now known to have been a Stalinist fabrication. The so-called *kulaks* were really only those peasants who had proved more efficient farmers than their neighbours. In no sense did they constitute the class of exploiting landowners described in Stalinist propaganda. Nonetheless, given the tradition of landlord oppression going back to tsarist times, the notion of grasping *kulaks* proved a very powerful one and provided the grounds for the coercion of the peasantry as a whole – middling and poor peasants, as well as *kulaks*.

### Surplus food, surplus peasants

As a revolutionary, Stalin followed Lenin in having little sympathy for the peasants. Communist theory taught that the days of the peasantry as a revolutionary social force had passed. The future belonged to the urban workers. It was held that October 1917 had been the first stage in the triumph of this proletarian class. Therefore, it was perfectly fitting that the peasantry should, in a time of national crisis, bow to the demands of industrialisation.

It was certainly true that for generations the Russian countryside had been overpopulated, creating a chronic land shortage. Even in the best years of NEP, food production had seldom matched needs. Yet Stalin insisted that the problem was not the lack of food but its poor distribution; food shortages were the result of grain hoarding by the rich peasants. This argument was then used to explain the urgent need for collectivisation as a way of securing adequate food supplies. It also provided the moral grounds for the onslaught on the *kulaks*, who were condemned as enemies of the Soviet nation in its struggle to modernise itself in the face of international, capitalist hostility.

**SOURCE A**

**Members of the Communist youth league unearthing bags of grain hidden by peasants in a cemetery near Odessa, 1930.**

What opportunities did searches such as that shown in Source A give for oppressing the *kulaks*? ?

## De-kulakisation

In some regions the poorer peasants undertook 'de-kulakisation' with enthusiasm, since it provided them with an excuse to settle old scores and give vent to local jealousies. Land and property were seized from the minority of better-off peasants, and they and their families were physically attacked. Such treatment was often the prelude to arrest, and imprisonment or deportation to remote, inhospitable regions by **OGPU** anti-*kulak* squads, authorised by Stalin and modelled on the gangs which had persecuted the peasants during the state-organised terror of the Civil War period (see page 161).

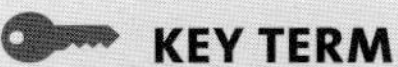

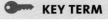

**KEY TERM**

**OGPU** Succeeded the *Cheka* as the state security force. In turn, it became the NKVD, the MVD and the KGB.

**SOURCE B**

**An anti-*kulak* demonstration on a collective farm in 1930. The banner reads 'Liquidate the Kulaks as a Class'.**

? Who was likely to have organised a demonstration like the one shown in Source B?

The renewal of terror also served as a warning to the peasantry of the likely consequences of resisting the state reorganisation of Soviet agriculture. The destruction of the *kulaks* was thus an integral part of the whole collectivisation process. As a Soviet official later admitted: 'most party officers thought that the whole point of de-kulakisation was its value as an administrative measure, speeding up tempos of collectivisation'.

## Resistance to collectivisation

In the period between December 1929 and March 1931, half the peasant farms in the USSR were collectivised. Yet peasants in their millions resisted. What amounted to civil war broke out in the countryside. The following details indicate the scale of the disturbances as recorded in official figures for the period 1929–30:

- 30,000 arson attacks occurred.
- The number of organised rural mass disturbances increased from 172 for the first half of 1929 to 229 for the second half.

## The role of women

A particularly striking feature of the disturbances was the prominent role that women played in them. In Okhochaya, a village in Ukraine, women broke into the barns and seized the bags of grain dumped there by the requisition squads after they had taken them from the peasants. Women, as mothers and organisers of the household, were invariably the first to suffer the harsh consequences of the new agricultural system, and so it was they who were often the first to take action. One peasant explained in illuminatingly simple terms why his spouse was so opposed to collectivisation: 'My wife does not want to socialise our cow.' There were cases of mothers with their children lying down in front of the tractors and trucks sent to break up the private farms and impose collectivisation. One male peasant admitted that the men preferred women to lead the demonstrations since they would be less likely to suffer reprisals from the authorities who certainly, judging by court records, appeared reluctant initially to prosecute female demonstrators.

Peasant resistance, however, no matter how valiant or desperate, stood no chance of stopping collectivisation. The officials and their requisition squads pressed on with their disruptive enforcement policies. Such was the turmoil in the countryside that Stalin called a halt, blaming the troubles on overzealous officials who had become 'dizzy with success'. Many of the peasants were allowed to return to their original holdings. However, the delay was only temporary. Having cleared his name by blaming the difficulties on local officials, Stalin restarted collectivisation in a more determined, if somewhat slower, manner. By the end of the 1930s virtually the whole of the peasantry had been collectivised (see Figure 7.1).

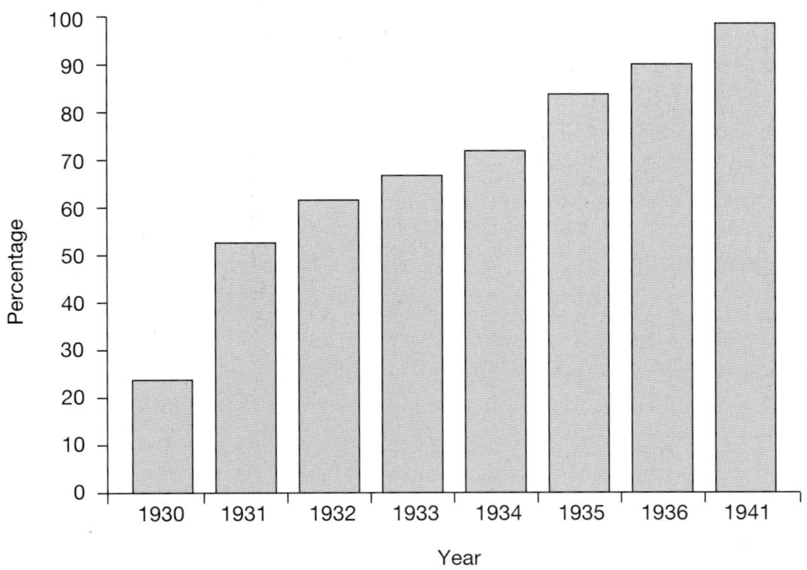


**Figure 7.1** Cumulative percentage of peasant holdings collectivised in the USSR 1930–41.

## Social effects

Behind these remarkable figures lay the story of a massive social upheaval. Bewildered and confused, the peasants either would not or could not co-operate in the deliberate destruction of their traditional way of life. The consequences were increasingly tragic. The majority of peasants ate their seed corn and slaughtered their livestock. There were no crops left to harvest or animals to rear.

The Soviet authorities responded with still fiercer coercion, but this simply made matters worse: imprisonment, deportation and execution could not replenish the barns or restock the herds. Special contingents of party workers were sent from the towns to restore food production levels by working on the land themselves. But their ignorance of farming only added to the disruption. By a bitter irony, even as starvation set in, the little grain that was available was being exported as 'surplus' to obtain the foreign capital that industry demanded. By 1932 the situation on the land was catastrophic.

? In what ways do the data in Figure 7.1 and Tables 7.1 and 7.2 illustrate the impact of collectivisation in the countryside?

**Table 7.1** The fall in food consumption (in kilograms per head)

| Year | Bread | Potatoes | Meat and lard | Butter |
|---|---|---|---|---|
| 1928 | 250.4 | 141.1 | 24.8 | 1.35 |
| 1932 | 214.6 | 125.0 | 11.2 | 0.70 |

**Table 7.2** The fall in livestock (in millions)

| Year | Horses | Cattle | Pigs | Sheep and goats |
|---|---|---|---|---|
| 1928 | 33 | 70 | 26 | 146 |
| 1932 | 15 | 34 | 9 | 42 |

The data in Tables 7.1 and 7.2 refer to the USSR as a whole. In the urban areas there was more food available. Indeed, a major purpose of the grain requisition squads was to maintain adequate supplies to the industrial regions. This meant that the misery in the countryside was proportionally greater, with areas such as Ukraine and Kazakhstan suffering particularly severely. The devastation experienced by the Kazakhs can be gauged from the fact that in this period they lost nearly 90 per cent of their livestock.

### Nationwide famine

Starvation, which in many parts of the Soviet Union persisted throughout the 1930s, was at its worst in the years 1932–3, when a national famine occurred. Collectivisation led to despair among the peasants. In many areas they simply stopped producing, either as an act of desperate resistance or through sheer inability to adapt to the violently enforced land system. Hungry and embittered, they made for the towns in growing numbers. It had, of course, been part of Stalin's collectivisation plan to move the peasants into the industrial regions. However, so great was the migration that a system of internal passports had to be introduced in an effort to control the flow. Some idea of the horrors can be obtained from the following eyewitness account.

**SOURCE C**

**From Victor Serge, *Memoirs of a Revolutionary, 1901–1941*, Oxford University Press, 1963, p. 246.**

*Trainloads of deported peasants left for the icy North, the forests, the steppes, the deserts. These were whole populations, denuded [stripped] of everything; the old folk starved to death in mid-journey, new-born babes were buried on the banks of the roadside, and each wilderness had its little cross of boughs or white wood. Other populations dragging all their mean possessions on wagons, rushed towards the frontiers of Poland, Rumania, and China and crossed them – by no means intact, to be sure – in spite of the machine guns … Agricultural technicians and experts were brave in denouncing the blunders and excesses; they were arrested in thousands and made to appear in huge sabotage trials so that responsibility might be unloaded on somebody.*

What image of peasant suffering and the official Soviet response to it is depicted in Source C? Why was Stalin willing to accept the widespread social disruption described here?

Despite overwhelming evidence of the tragedy that had overtaken the USSR, the official Stalinist line was that there was no famine. In the whole of the contemporary Soviet press there were only two oblique references to it. This conspiracy of silence was of more than political significance. As well as protecting the reputation of Stalin the great planner, it effectively prevented the introduction of measures to remedy the distress. Since the famine did not officially exist, Soviet Russia could not publicly take steps to relieve it. For the same reason, it could not appeal, as had been done during the Russian famine in 1921, for aid from the outside world 1921 (see page 162).

Thus, what Isaac Deutscher, historian and former Trotskyist, called 'the first purely man-made famine in history' went unacknowledged in order to avoid discrediting Stalin. Not for the last time, large numbers of the Soviet people were sacrificed on the altar of Stalin's reputation. There was a strong rumour that Stalin's wife, **Nadezdha Alliluyeva**, had been driven to suicide by the knowledge that it was her husband's brutal policies that had caused the famine. Shortly before her death she had railed at Stalin as an uncaring monster. 'You torment your wife. You torment the whole Russian people.'

**KEY FIGURE**

**Nadezdha Alliluyeva (1902–32)**

Stalin's second wife. His grief at her suicide may help to explain why Stalin became increasingly embittered and unfeeling towards people in general.

The truth of Alliluyeva's charge has now been substantiated by the findings of scholars who have examined the Soviet archives that were opened up after the fall of the USSR in the early 1990s. Lynne Viola in 2007 confirmed the horrific character of Stalin's treatment of the peasantry. She described how, between 1930 and 1932, Stalin drove 2 million peasants into internal exile as slave labourers, a quarter of that number dying of hunger and exposure. Her work, which built on the pioneering studies of Robert Conquest, the first major Western historian to chart Stalin's brutalities, serves as a belated and devastating corrective to the view advanced at the time by pro-Soviet sympathisers in the West that their hero Stalin was creating a paradise on earth.

## Positive aspects of collectivisation

So widespread was the misery produced by collectivisation that it can lead to the overlooking of another important consideration. The hard fact is that Stalin's policies did force a large number of peasants to leave the land. This was a process that Russia needed. Economic historians have often stressed that the land crisis in Russia long pre-dated Stalinism. Since the nineteenth century, land in Russia had proved increasingly incapable of supporting the growing numbers of people who lived unproductively on it. Unless a major shift occurred in the imbalance between urban and rural dwellers, Russia would be in sustained difficulties. The nation needed to change from an agricultural and rural society to an urban and industrial one.

There is a case for arguing, therefore, that Stalin's collectivisation programme, brutally applied though it was, did answer one of the USSR's great needs. Leaving aside questions of human suffering, the enforced migration under Stalin made economic sense. It relieved the pressure on the land and provided the workforce which enabled the industrialisation programme to be started. Perhaps all this could be summed up by saying that Stalin's aims were understandable but his methods unacceptable.

Yet, even allowing for the occasional progressive aspect of collectivisation, such as the building and distributing of mechanised tractors, the overall picture remained bleak. The mass of the peasantry had been uprooted and left bewildered. Despite severe reprisals and coercion, the peasants were unable to produce the surplus food that Stalin demanded. By 1939, Soviet agricultural productivity had barely returned to the level recorded for tsarist Russia in 1913. But the most damning consideration still remains the man-made famine, which in the 1930s killed over 10 million peasants.

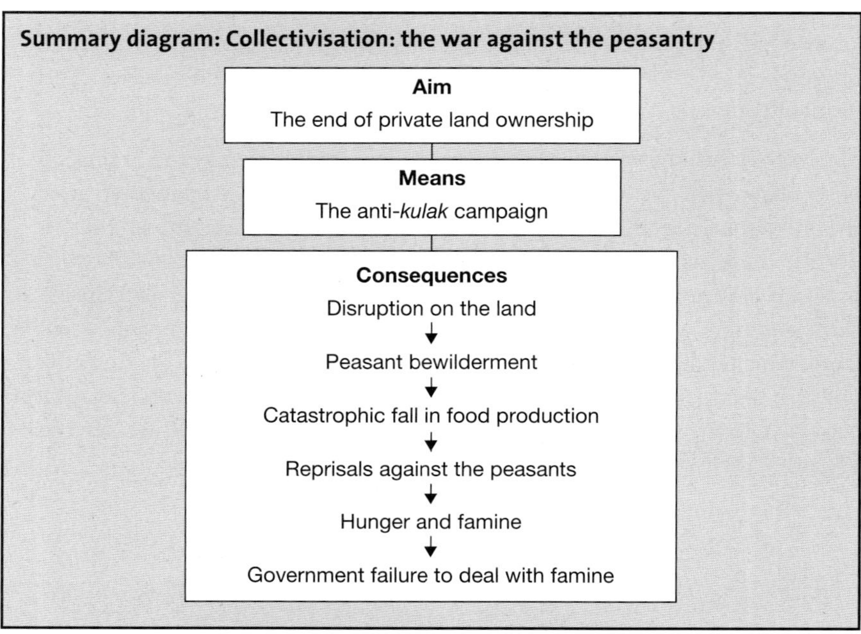

Summary diagram: Collectivisation: the war against the peasantry
Aim
The end of private land ownership
Means
The anti-*kulak* campaign
Consequences
Disruption on the land
Peasant bewilderment
Catastrophic fall in food production
Reprisals against the peasants
Hunger and famine
Government failure to deal with famine

# Industrialisation: the first three Five-Year Plans

► *What were Stalin's aims for Soviet industry in the 1930s and what methods did he use to achieve them?*

Stalin described his industrialisation plans for the USSR as an attempt to establish a war economy. He declared that he was making war on the failings of Russia's past and on the class enemies within the nation. He also claimed that he was preparing the USSR for war against its capitalist foes abroad. This was not simply martial imagery. Stalin regarded iron, steel and oil as the sinews of war. Their successful production would guarantee the strength and readiness of the nation to face its enemies. For Stalin, industry meant heavy industry. He believed that the industrial revolutions which had made Western Europe and North America so strong had been based on iron and steel production. It followed that the USSR must adopt a similar industrial pattern in its drive towards modernisation. The difference would be that, whereas the West had taken the capitalist road, the USSR would follow the path of socialism.

Stalin had grounds for his optimism. It so happened that the Soviet industrialisation drive in the 1930s coincided with the **Great Depression** in the Western world. Stalin claimed that the USSR was introducing into its own economy the technical successes of Western industrialisation but was rejecting the destructive capitalist system that went with them. Socialist planning would enable the USSR to avoid the errors that had begun to undermine the Western economies.

**KEY TERM**

**Great Depression** A period of severe economic stagnation which began in the USA in 1929 and lasted until the mid-1930s, affecting the whole of the industrial world. Marxists regarded it as a portent of the final collapse of capitalism.

Soviet industrialisation under Stalin took the form of a series of Five-Year Plans (FYPs). *Gosplan* was required by Stalin to draw up a list of quotas of production ranging across the whole of Soviet industry. The process began in 1928 and, except for the war years 1941–5, lasted until Stalin's death in 1953. In all, there were five separate plans:

- first FYP: October 1928 to December 1932
- second FYP: January 1933 to December 1937
- third FYP: January 1938 to June 1941
- fourth FYP: January 1946 to December 1950
- fifth FYP: January 1951 to December 1955.

## The first Five-Year Plan: 1928–32

The term 'plan' is misleading. The first FYP laid down what was to be achieved, but did not say how it was to be done. It simply assumed the quotas would be met. What the first FYP represented, therefore, was a set of targets rather than a plan. As had happened with collectivisation, local officials and managers falsified their production figures to give the impression that they had met their targets when, in fact, they had fallen short. For this reason, precise statistics for the first FYP are difficult to determine. A further complication is that three quite distinct versions of the first FYP eventually appeared. Impressed by the apparent progress of the plan in its early stages, Stalin encouraged the formulation of an 'optimal' plan which reassessed targets upwards. These new quotas were hopelessly unrealistic and stood no chance of being reached. Nonetheless, on the basis of the supposed achievements of this 'optimal' plan the figures were amended still higher in 1932. Western analysts suggest the data in Table 7.3 as the closest approximation to the real figures.

**Table 7.3** Industrial output in the USSR under the first Five-Year Plan

| Product (in millions of tonnes) | 1927–8: first plan | 1932–3: 'optimal' | 1932: amended | 1932: actual |
|---|---|---|---|---|
| Coal | 35.0 | 75.0 | 95–105 | 64.0 |
| Oil | 11.7 | 21.7 | 40–55 | 21.4 |
| Iron ore | 6.7 | 20.2 | 24–32 | 12.1 |
| Pig iron | 3.2 | 10.0 | 15–16 | 6.2 |

## Propaganda and collective effort

No matter how much the figures may have been rigged at the time, the first FYP was an extraordinary achievement overall. Coal, iron and the generation of electricity all increased in huge proportions. However, the importance of these figures should not be exaggerated. At the time it was the grand design that mattered, not the detail. The plan was a huge propaganda project aimed at convincing the Soviet people that they were personally engaged in a vast industrial enterprise. By their own efforts, they were changing the character of the society in which they lived and providing it with the means of achieving greatness. Nor was it all a matter of enforcement, fierce though that was. Among the young especially, there was an enthusiasm and a commitment that suggested that many Soviet citizens believed they were genuinely building a new and better world. The sense of the Soviet people as masters of their own fate was expressed in the slogan, 'There is no fortress that we Bolsheviks cannot storm'. John Scott, an American Communist and one of the many pro-Soviet Western industrial advisers who went to the USSR at this time, was impressed by the mixture of idealism and coercion that characterised the early stages of Stalinist industrialisation. He described how the city of Magnitogorsk in the Urals was built from scratch:

? How is the enthusiasm of the workers, as described in Source D, to be explained?

**SOURCE D**

**From J. Scott, *Behind the Urals*, Secker & Warburg, 1942, p. 52.**

*Within several years, half a billion cubic feet of excavation was done, forty-two million cubic feet of reinforced concrete poured, five million cubic feet of fire bricks laid, a quarter of a million tons of structured steel erected. This was done without sufficient labour, without necessary quantities of the most elementary materials. Brigades of young enthusiasts from every corner of the Soviet Union arrived in the summer of 1930 and did the groundwork of railroad and dam construction necessary. Later, groups of local peasants and herdsmen came to Magnitogorsk because of bad conditions in the villages, due to collectivisation. Many of the peasants were completely unfamiliar with industrial tools and processes. A colony of several hundred foreign engineers and specialists, some of whom made as high as one hundred dollars a day, arrived to advise and direct the work.*

*From 1928 until 1932 nearly a quarter of a million people came to Magnitogorsk. About three quarters of these new arrivals came of their own free will seeking work, bread-cards, better conditions. The rest came under compulsion.*

## The plan's neglect of living conditions

A striking feature of the plan was the low priority it gave to improving the material lives of the Soviet people. No effort was made to reward the workers by providing them with affordable consumer goods. Living conditions actually deteriorated in this period. Accommodation in the towns and cities remained substandard.

The Soviet authorities' neglect of basic social needs was not accidental. The plan had never been intended to raise living standards. Its purpose was collective, not individual. It called for sacrifice on the part of the workers in the construction of a socialist state, which would be able to sustain itself economically and militarily against the enmity of the outside world. It was the idea of sacrifice that Stalin used as a justification for demanding that, whatever the social disruption it caused, the relentless industrialisation drive could not be relaxed.

**SOURCE E**

**From Stalin's speech in February 1931, *Works of Josef Stalin*, volume 13, Lawrence & Wishart, 1955, p. 40.**

*It is sometimes asked whether it is not possible to slow down the tempo somewhat, to put a check on the movement. No, comrades, it is not possible! The tempo must not be reduced! To slacken the tempo would mean falling behind. And those who fall behind get beaten. But we do not want to be beaten. No, we refuse to be beaten! One feature of old Russia was the continual beatings she suffered because of her backwardness. She was beaten by the Mongols. She was beaten by the Turks. She was beaten by the Polish and Lithuanian gentry. She was beaten by the British and French capitalists. She was beaten by the Japanese barons. All beat her – because of her backwardness, military backwardness, cultural backwardness, political backwardness, industrial backwardness, agricultural backwardness. They beat her because to do so was profitable and could be done with impunity.*

Why is Stalin so insistent in Source E on emphasising Russia's past humiliations?

## Resistance and sabotage

Stalin's passionate appeal to Russian history subordinated everything to the driving need for national survival, a need which justified the severity that accompanied his enforced transformation of the Soviet economy. He presented the FYP as a defence of the USSR against international hostility. This enabled him to brand resistance to the plan as 'sabotage'. A series of public trials of industrial 'wreckers', including a number of foreign workers, was staged to impress on the party and the masses the futility of protesting against the industrialisation programme. In 1928, in a prelude to the first FYP, Stalin claimed to have discovered an anti-Soviet conspiracy among the mining engineers of Shakhty in the Donbass region of Ukraine. Their subsequent public trial was intended to frighten the workers into line. It also showed that the privileged position of the skilled workers, the '**bourgeois experts**', was to be tolerated no longer.

This attack on the experts was part of a pattern in the first FYP which stressed quantity at the expense of quality. The push towards sheer volume of output was intended to prove the correctness of Stalin's grand economic schemes. Modern historian Sheila Fitzpatrick has described this as being an aspect of Stalin's '**gigantomania**', his love of mighty building projects, such as canals, bridges and docks, which he regarded as proof that the USSR was advancing to greatness. Stalin's emphasis on gross output may also be interpreted as shrewdness on his part. He knew that the untrained peasants who now filled the factories would not turn immediately into skilled workers. It made sense, therefore, in the short term, to ignore the question of quality and to stress quantity.

### KEY TERMS

**Bourgeois experts** A mocking reference to those workers whose skills had enabled them to earn higher wages and thus be less committed to building the new Russia.

**Gigantomania** The worship of size for its own sake.

**Cadres** Party members who were sent into factories and on to construction sites to spy and report back on managers and workers.

## Passing the blame

Stalin was seemingly untroubled by the low quality of production. His notions of industrial 'saboteurs' and 'wreckers' allowed him to place the blame for poor quality and underproduction on managers and workers who were not prepared to play their proper part in rebuilding the nation. He used OGPU agents and party **cadres** to terrorise the workforce. 'Sabotage' became a blanket term used to denounce anyone considered not to be pulling his weight. The simplest errors, such as being late for work or mislaying tools, could lead to such a charge.

At a higher level, those factory managers or foremen who did not meet their production quotas might find themselves on public trial as enemies of the Soviet state. In such an atmosphere of fear and recrimination, doctoring official returns and inflating output figures became normal practice. Everybody at every level engaged in a game of pretence. This was why Soviet statistics for industrial growth were so unreliable and why it was possible for Stalin to claim in mid-course that, since the first FYP had already met its initial targets, it would be shortened to a four-year plan. In Stalin's industrial revolution appearances were everything. This was where the logic of 'gigantomania' had led.

### Stalin: the master planner?

The industrial policies of this time have been described as the 'Stalinist blueprint' or 'Stalin's economic model'. Modern scholars are, however, wary of using such terms. Historian Norman Stone, for example, interprets Stalin's policies not as far-sighted strategy but as 'simply putting one foot in front of the other as he went along'. Despite the growing tendency in all official Soviet documents of the 1930s to include a fulsome reference to Stalin, the master-planner, there was in fact very little planning from the top.

It is true that Stalin's government exhorted, cajoled and bullied the workers into ever-greater efforts towards ever-greater production. But such planning as there was occurred not at national but at local level. It was the regional and site managers who, struggling desperately to make sense of the instructions they were given from on high, formulated the actual schemes for reaching their given production quotas. This was why, when things went wrong, it was easy for Stalin and his Kremlin colleagues to accuse lesser officials of sabotage while themselves avoiding any taint of incompetence.

## The second and third Five-Year Plans

Although the second and third FYPs were modelled on the pattern of the first, the targets set for them were more realistic. Nevertheless, they still revealed the same lack of co-ordination that had characterised the first. Overproduction occurred in some parts of the economy, underproduction in others, which frequently led to whole branches of industry being held up for lack of vital supplies. For example, some projects had too little timber at times, while at other times enough timber but insufficient steel. Spare parts were hard to come by, which often meant broken machines standing unrepaired and idle for long periods.

The hardest struggle was to maintain a proper supply of materials; this often led to fierce competition between regions and sectors of industry, all of them anxious to escape the charge of failing to achieve their targets. As a result, there was hoarding of resources and a lack of co-operation between the various parts of the industrial system. Complaints about poor standards, carefully veiled so as not to appear critical of Stalin and the plan, were frequent. What successes there were occurred again in heavy industry, where the second FYP began to reap the benefit of the creation of large-scale plants under the first plan.

### Scapegoats

The reluctance to tell the full truth hindered genuine industrial growth. Since no one was willing to admit there was an error in the planning, faults went unchecked until serious breakdowns occurred. There then followed the familiar search for scapegoats. It was during the period of the second and third FYPs that Stalin's political purges were at their fiercest (see page 235). In such an all-pervading atmosphere of terror the mere accusation of 'sabotage' was taken as proof of guilt. Productivity suffered as a result. As Russian historian Alec Nove observed: 'Everywhere there were said to be spies, wreckers, diversionists. There was a grave shortage of qualified personnel, so the deportation of many thousands of engineers and technologists to distant concentration camps represented a severe loss.'

## The Stakhanovite movement 1935

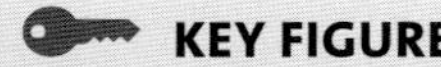

**KEY FIGURE**

**Alexei Stakhanov (1906–77)**

As was admitted by the Soviet authorities in 1988, his achievement was a gross exaggeration. He had not worked on his own but as part of a team, which had been supplied with the best coal-cutting machines available.

The party's control of newspapers, cinema and radio meant that only a favourable view of the plans was ever presented. The official line was that all was well and the workers were happy. Support for this claim was dramatically provided by the Stakhanovite movement. In August 1935, it was officially claimed that **Alexei Stakhanov**, a miner in the Donbass region, had, on his own, cut over 100 tonnes of coal in one five-hour shift, which was more than fourteen times his required quota. His achievement was seized on by the authorities as a glorious example of what was possible in a Soviet Union guided by Josef Stalin.

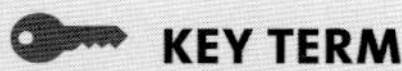

**KEY TERM**

**Storming** An intensive period of work to meet a high set target. Despite the propaganda with which it was introduced, storming proved a very inefficient form of industrial labour and was soon abandoned.

Miners and workers everywhere were urged to match Stakhanov's dedication by similar '**storming**'. But, despite the excitement this aroused, storming proved more loss than gain. While some Stakhanovite groups boasted higher output, this was achieved only by giving them privileged access to tools and supplies and by changing work plans to accommodate them. The resulting disruption led to an overall loss of production in those areas where the Stakhanovite movement was at its most enthusiastic.

## Workers' rights

After 1917, the Russian trade unions had become powerless. In Bolshevik theory, in a truly socialist state such as Russia now was, there was no distinction between the interests of government and those of the workers. Therefore, there was no longer any need for a separate trade union movement. In 1920 Trotsky had taken violent steps to destroy the independence of the unions and bring them directly under Bolshevik control. The result was that after 1920 the unions were simply the means by which the Bolshevik government enforced its requirements on the workers.

Under Stalin's industrialisation programme any vestige of workers' rights disappeared. Strikes were prohibited and the traditional demands for better pay and conditions were regarded as selfish in a time of national crisis. A code of 'labour discipline' was drawn up, demanding maximum effort and output; failure to conform was punishable by a range of penalties from loss of wages to imprisonment in forced labour camps. On paper, wages improved during the second FYP, but in real terms, since there was food rationing and high prices, living standards were lower in 1937 than they had been in 1928.

### Living and working conditions

Throughout the period of the FYPs, Stalin's Soviet government asserted that the nation was under siege. It claimed that unless priority was given to defence needs, the very existence of the USSR was in jeopardy. Set against such a threat, workers' material interests were of little significance. For workers to demand improved conditions at a time when the Soviet Union was fighting for survival was unthinkable; they would be betraying the nation. It was small wonder, then, that food remained scarce and expensive, and severe overcrowding persisted.

Nearly all workers lived in overcrowded apartments. Public housing policy did produce a large number of tenement blocks in towns and cities: usually five-storey structures with no lifts. Quite apart from their architectural ugliness, they were a hazard to health. So great was the overcrowding that it was common for young families to live with their in-laws and equally common for four or five families to share a single lavatory and a single kitchen, which was often no more than an alcove with a gas-ring. There were rotas for the use of these facilities. Queuing to relieve oneself or to cook was part of the daily routine.

There was money available, but the government spent it not on improving social conditions but on armaments. Between 1933 and 1937, defence expenditure rose from four to seventeen per cent of the overall industrial budget. By 1940, under the terms of the third FYP, which renewed the commitment to heavy industrial development, a third of the USSR's government spending was on arms.

## Strengths of the first three Five-Year Plans

In judging the scale of Stalin's achievement, it is helpful to cite such statistics relating to industrial output during the period of the first three FYPs as are reliable. The data in Table 7.4 are drawn from the work of economic historian E. Zaleski, whose findings are based on careful analysis of Soviet and Western sources.

**Table 7.4** Industrial output during the first three Five-Year Plans

| Output | 1927 | 1930 | 1932 | 1935 | 1937 | 1940 |
|---|---|---|---|---|---|---|
| Coal (millions of tonnes) | 35 | 60 | 64 | 100 | 128 | 150 |
| Steel (millions of tonnes) | 3 | 5 | 6 | 13 | 18 | 18 |
| Oil (millions of tonnes) | 12 | 17 | 21 | 24 | 26 | 26 |
| Electricity (millions of kWh) | 18 | 22 | 20 | 45 | 80 | 90 |

The figures indicate a remarkable increase in production overall. In a little over twelve years, coal production had grown five times, steel six, and oil output had more than doubled. Perhaps the most impressive statistic is the one showing that electricity generation quintupled. These four key products provided the basis for the military economy which enabled the USSR not only to survive four years of German occupation but eventually to amass sufficient resources to drive the German army out of Soviet territory. The climax of this was the Soviet invasion and defeat of Germany in 1945.

## Weaknesses of the Five-Year Plans

Stalin's economic reforms succeeded only in the traditional areas of heavy industry. In those sectors where unskilled and forced labour could be easily used, as in large building projects, such as factories, bridges, refineries and canals, the results were impressive. But the Soviet economy itself remained unbalanced. For example, the production of chemicals and textiles declined under the FYPs. Stalin gave little thought to developing an overall economic strategy. Nor were modern industrial methods adopted. Old, wasteful techniques, such as relying on mass labour rather than efficient machines, continued to be used. Vital financial and material resources were squandered.

Stalin's love of what he called 'the Grand Projects of Communism' meant that no real attention was paid to producing quality goods that could then be profitably sold abroad to raise the money the USSR so badly needed. He loved to show off to foreign visitors the great projects that were either completed or under construction. Two enterprises of which he was especially proud were the city of Magnitogorsk (see page 214) and the **White Sea Canal**. Yet, it was all vainglorious. Despite Stalin's boasts and the adulation with which he was regarded by foreign sympathisers, the simple fact remained that his policies had deprived the Soviet Union of any chance of genuinely competing with the modernising economies of Europe and the USA.

**KEY TERM**

**White Sea Canal** In fact three canals linking Leningrad with the White Sea; built predominantly by forced labourers, who died in their thousands, the canal proved practically worthless since it was hardly used after construction.

A serious failing of the FYPs was their neglect of agriculture, which continued to be deprived of funds since it was regarded as wholly secondary to the needs of industry. This neglect proved very damaging. The lack of agricultural growth resulted in constant food shortages which could be met only by buying foreign supplies. This drained the USSR's limited financial resources.

Despite the official adulation of Stalin for his great diplomatic triumph in achieving the Non-aggression Pact with Nazi Germany in August 1939 (see page 249), there was no relaxation within the Soviet Union of the war atmosphere. Indeed, the conditions of the ordinary people continued to deteriorate. An official decree of 1940 empowered Stalin's government to encroach even further on workers' liberties by imposing such measures as:

- direction of labour
- enforced settlement of undeveloped areas
- severer penalties for slacking and absenteeism.

In 1941, when the German invasion effectively destroyed the third FYP, the conditions of the Soviet industrial workers were marginally lower than in 1928. Yet whatever the hardship of the workers, the fact was that in 1941 the USSR was economically strong enough to engage in an ultimately successful military struggle of unprecedented duration and intensity. In Soviet propaganda, this was what mattered, not minor questions of living standards. The USSR's triumph over Nazism would later be claimed as the ultimate proof of the wisdom of Stalin's enforced industrialisation programme.

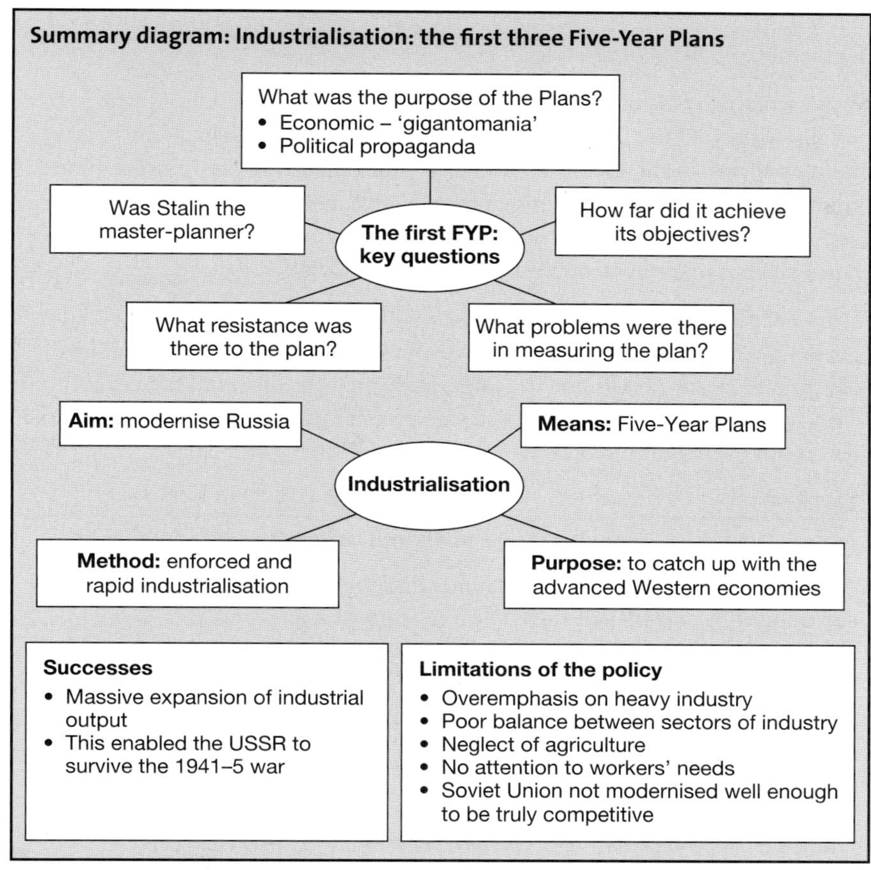

Summary diagram: Industrialisation: the first three Five-Year Plans
What was the purpose of the Plans?
• Economic – 'gigantomania'
• Political propaganda
Was Stalin the master-planner?
The first FYP: key questions
How far did it achieve its objectives?
What resistance was there to the plan?
What problems were there in measuring the plan?
Aim: modernise Russia
Means: Five-Year Plans
Industrialisation
Method: enforced and rapid industrialisation
Purpose: to catch up with the advanced Western economies
Successes
• Massive expansion of industrial output
• This enabled the USSR to survive the 1941–5 war
Limitations of the policy
• Overemphasis on heavy industry
• Poor balance between sectors of industry
• Neglect of agriculture
• No attention to workers' needs
• Soviet Union not modernised well enough to be truly competitive

## 4 Key debate

► *Were Stalin's economic policies justified by their results?*

Many historians have contributed to the analysis of Stalin's economic policies and their impact on the Soviet Union and its people. Some argue that whatever the economic gains resulting from the policies, the methods used to implement them went beyond what was acceptable in human terms. Others suggest that, even putting aside questions of human suffering, the policies did not meet their economic objectives. Another viewpoint is that the problems facing the Soviet Union justified the harsh measures Stalin used. The following introduces the views of some of the main contributors to the debate.

Alec Nove, a Russian scholar who produced his major works in the 1960s and 1970s, argued strongly from a liberal viewpoint that 'Stalin's collectivisation and industrialisation programmes were bad economics' since they caused upheaval on the land and misery to the peasants without producing the industrial growth that the USSR needed. Furthermore, the condition of the industrial workers deteriorated under Stalin's policies.

Nove's approach was matched by British historian Robert Conquest, who initially supported the Soviet experiment, but became disillusioned by Stalin's policies. In the 1960s, he produced a major study of Stalin's economic programme in which he condemned the coercive methods that had been used, remarking: 'Stalinism is one way of attaining industrialisation, just as cannibalism is one way of attaining a high protein diet.'

Sheila Fitzpatrick, a distinguished scholar with left-wing sympathies, broadly agrees with the criticisms made by Nove and Conquest, adding that Stalin's 'gigantomania', his obsession with large-scale projects, distorted the economy at a critical time when what was needed was proper investment and planning. She lays emphasis on Stalin's failure to improve Soviet living standards:

**EXTRACT I**

**From S. Fitzpatrick, *Everyday Stalinism*, Oxford University Press, 1999, p. 100.**

*Despite its promises of future abundance and the massive propaganda that surrounded its current achievements, the Stalinist regime did little to improve the life of its people in the 1930s. Judging by the NKVD's soundings of public opinion, the Stalinist regime was relatively, though not desperately, unpopular in Russian towns. (In Russian villages, especially in the first half of the 1930s, its unpopularity was much greater.) Overall, as the NKVD regularly reported, the ordinary 'little man' in Soviet towns, who thought only of his own and his family's welfare, was 'dissatisfied with Soviet Power', though in a somewhat fatalistic and passive manner. The post NEP situation was compared unfavourably with NEP, and Stalin – despite the officially fostered Stalin cult – was compared unfavourably with Lenin, sometimes because he was more repressive but often because he let people go hungry.*

Significantly, however, Fitzpatrick modifies her criticism by pointing out that Stalin's policies need to be seen in a broad social and political context. Harsh though Stalin was, he was trying to bring stability to a Soviet Russia that had known only turmoil and division since 1917.

This line of reasoning was shared by British historian Peter Gattrell, who, while acknowledging that Stalin was undeniably coercive in his methods, stressed that the outcome of collectivisation and industrialisation was an economy strong enough by 1941 to sustain the USSR through four years of the most demanding of modern wars. Gattrell suggested that Russia could not have been modernised by methods other than those used by Stalin.

David Hoffman, an American analyst, offers a strongly contrary view by arguing that Stalin's use of coercion in seeking economic and social change proved both inhumane and ineffective (see opposite):

**EXTRACT 2**

**From D.L. Hoffman, *Stalinist Values: The Cultural Norms of Soviet Modernity*, Cornell University Press, 2003, p. 111.**

*Social change must be gradual and consensual if it is to succeed. Even if violence achieves superficial change, it does not permanently transform the way people think and act. Moreover in the Soviet case the means and ends were themselves in contradiction. State coercion by its very nature could not create social harmony. The arrest and execution of millions of people only sowed hatred, mistrust and disharmony in Soviet society.*

Robert Service, Stalin's outstanding British biographer, makes the following succinct assessment of the effects of his subject's collectivisation and industrialisation programme by 1940:

**EXTRACT 3**

**From R. Service, *Stalin: A Biography*, Macmillan, 2004, p. 265.**

*Disruption was everywhere in the economy. Ukraine, south Russia, and Kazakhstan were starving. The Gulag [Russia's labour camp system] heaved with prisoners. Nevertheless the economic transformation was no fiction. The USSR under Stalin's rule had been pointed decisively in the direction of becoming an industrial, urban society. This had been his great objective. His gamble was paying off for him, albeit not for millions of victims. Magnitogorsk and the White Sea Canal were constructed at the expense of the lives of Gulag convicts, Ukrainian peasants and even undernourished, overworked factory labourers.*

To what extent do Extracts 1, 2 and 3 concur or differ in their analysis of Stalin's economic policies? ?

The debate is the familiar and unending one about whether the ends justify the means.

## Chapter summary

Judging that economic growth was essential to the very survival of the Soviet Union, Stalin embarked on a massive programme of agricultural and industrial reform. He brushed aside doubters within the Communist Party who were disturbed by the pace of change. Subordinating the land and its peasants to the needs of industry and the workers, he used coercion and terror to enforce his will. Collectivisation created such social and economic disruption that famine followed in its wake. While blaming local officials for their excess of zeal, Stalin declined to relax the pressure. By the mid-1930s the great majority of the peasants had lost their private property and were living in collectives.

The same relentless drive was maintained in the industrialisation programme. In a series of Five-Year Plans, Stalin sought to create a modern economy based on heavy industrial production. There were successes, magnified in Stalinist propaganda, but the pre-set targets were not universally met. Nevertheless, enough was achieved for the level of success to become a matter of historical debate, some analysts claiming that the level of progress justified the harsh methods used to achieve it, others arguing that Stalin's policies were based on a false understanding of modernisation and were, therefore, essentially destructive.

## Refresher questions

Use these questions to remind yourself of the key material covered in this chapter.

1 In what way was collectivisation intended to serve the interests of industrialisation?
2 What were the effects of collectivisation on the peasantry?
3 Why could the famine of the early 1930s not be dealt with effectively?
4 How successful had collectivisation proved to be by 1939?
5 What were Stalin's aims for Soviet industry in the 1930s?
6 What was the purpose of the first Five-Year Plan?
7 How far did the first Five-Year Plan achieve its objectives?
8 Why was there so little resistance to the first Five-Year Plan?
9 How far was the first FYP planned from the top?
10 What were the strengths and weaknesses of the second and third Five-Year Plans?

## Question practice

### ESSAY QUESTIONS

1 Assess the reasons why Stalin decided on a policy of collectivisation of the peasantry in the Soviet Union between 1929 and 1941.
2 How successful was the first Five-Year Plan (1928–32) as an economic programme?
3 To what extent was Soviet industry transformed in the years 1929–41?
4 'The lives of the Russian peasants were hugely disrupted in the years 1929–41.' How far do you agree?
5 Which of the following had the greater consequences for the Soviet people? i) Collectivisation. ii) Industrialisation. Explain your answer with reference to both i) and ii).

CHAPTER 8

# Stalin's dictatorship 1929–41

With victory over his rivals achieved by 1929, Stalin over the next decade followed two interlocking policies: the establishment of total political control and the modernisation of the Soviet economy. This chapter deals with the manner in which the Soviet Union moved towards totalitarianism under Stalin and examines the impact of this on Soviet culture and the lives of the people. The key features covered are:

★ The purges

★ Stalin's totalitarianism

★ Stalin and the cult of personality

★ Stalin's foreign policy

★ Stalin's record by 1941

The key debate on *page 252* of this chapter asks the question: Was Stalin's absolutism a logical progression from the authoritarianism of Lenin?

## Key dates

| | |
|---|---|
| **1929** | Stalin established as *vozhd* |
| **1931–4** | The 'Stalin enrolment' |
| **1933–4** | Stalin's instruments of control created |
| **1932** | Start of the purges |
| **1934–6** | Post-Kirov purges |
| **1936–9** | The 'Great Purge' |
| **1937** | Purge of the armed forces began |
| **1938** | Munich agreement |
| **1938–41** | Spread of purges across USSR |
| **1939–41** | Nazi–Soviet Pact |

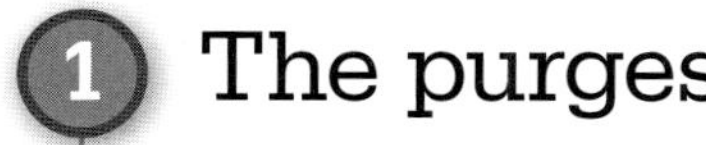

## 1 The purges

▶ *By what means did Stalin consolidate his control over the USSR?*

Having become the *vozhd* of the Soviet Union by 1929, Stalin spent the rest of his life consolidating and extending his authority. The purges were his principal weapon for achieving this. They became the chief mechanism for removing anyone he regarded as a threat to his authority. The Stalinist purges, which began in 1932, were not unprecedented. Public show trials had been held during the early stages of the first Five-Year Plan (FYP) as a way of exposing 'saboteurs' who were accused of damaging the USSR's industrial programme (see page 216).

Prosecutions were not restricted to industrial enemies. In 1932 the trial took place of the M.N. Ryutin, a Right Communist, who had published an attack on Stalin, describing him as 'the evil genius who has brought the revolution to the verge of destruction' and calling for his removal from office. Ryutin and his supporters were publicly tried and expelled from the party. This was the prelude to the first major purge of the Communist Party of the Soviet Union (CPSU) by Stalin. Between 1933 and 1934 nearly a million members, over a third of the total membership, were excluded from the party on the grounds that they were Ryutinites. The purge was organised by **Nicolai Yezhov**, the chief of the Control Commission, the branch of the Central Committee responsible for party discipline.

**KEY FIGURE**

**Nicolai Yezhov (1895–1940)**

Known as the 'poisoned dwarf' because of his diminutive stature and vicious personality, he became head of the NKVD in 1937; he was himself tried and shot three years later.

At the beginning, party purges were not as violent as they later became. The usual procedure was to oblige members to hand in their **party card** for checking, at which point any suspect individuals would not have their cards returned to them. This was tantamount to expulsion since, without cards, members were denied access to all party activities. Under such a system, it became progressively difficult to mount effective opposition.

**KEY TERMS**

**Party card** The official CPSU warrant granting membership to the holder. It was a prized possession in Soviet Russia since it entitled the holder to a wide range of privileges, such as quality accommodation, higher food rations, access to health care and education for the member's children.

**Paranoia** A persecution complex which gives sufferers the conviction that they are surrounded by malicious enemies.

## Stalin's motivation

Despite Stalin's increasing control, attempts were made in the early 1930s to criticise him, as the Ryutin affair illustrates. These efforts were ineffectual, but they led Stalin to believe that organised resistance to him was still possible.

It was such belief that led Stalin to develop the purges into a systematic terrorising not of obvious political opponents but of colleagues and party members. It is difficult to explain precisely why Stalin initiated such a terror. Historians accept that they are dealing with behaviour that sometimes went beyond reason and logic. Stalin was deeply suspicious by nature and suffered from increasing **paranoia** as he grew older. Right up to his death in 1953, he continued to believe he was under threat from actual or potential enemies. In his 2004 biography, Robert Service writes that Stalin had 'a gross personality disorder'. His Georgian origins had given him a fierce sense of honour and revenge; getting even with adversaries was a way of life. He regarded the Bolshevik Revolution of 1917 as the beginning of a process of settling scores with class enemies. 'Violence, dictatorship and terror were methods he and fellow party veterans took to be normal. The physical extermination of enemies was entirely acceptable to them.'

Stalin's daughter, Svetlana, said revealingly about him that once he took a dislike to someone 'he translated that person into the ranks of enemies'. Such thinking meant that everyone was suspect and no one was safe. In Service's words, Stalin saw 'malevolent human agency in every personal or political problem he encountered'. Purges became not so much a series of episodes as a permanent condition of Soviet political life. Terror was all-pervading throughout the remainder of Stalin's life.

## Stalin's instruments of control

In the years 1933–4, as an accompaniment to the purges, Stalin centralised all the major law enforcement agencies:

- the civilian police
- labour camp commandants and guards
- border and security guards.

All these were put under the authority of the NKVD, a body which was directly answerable to Stalin.

## The post-Kirov purges 1934–6

In Leningrad on 1 December 1934, a man named Leonid Nicolaev walked into the Communist Party headquarters and shot dead Sergei Kirov, the secretary of the Leningrad soviet. The apparent motive was revenge; Kirov had been having an affair with the killer's wife. But dramatic though the incident was in itself, its significance went far beyond the tale of a jealous husband shooting his wife's lover. There is a strong probability that the murder of Kirov had been approved, if not planned, by Stalin himself. **Nikita Khrushchev** later stated that Stalin was almost certainly behind the murder. However, a special study concluded in 1993 that while Stalin may well have been guilty, the evidence against him consists of 'unverified facts, rumours and conjectures'.

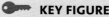

**KEY FIGURE**

**Nikita Khrushchev (1894–1971)**

Leader of the USSR 1956–64; in order to prepare the way for reform he launched 'de-Stalinisation', a fierce attack on Stalin's record.

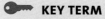

Whatever the truth concerning Stalin's involvement, it was certainly the case that the murder worked directly to his advantage. Kirov had been a highly popular figure in the party. A strikingly handsome Russian, he had made a strong impression at the seventeenth party congress in 1934 and had been elected to the Politburo. He was known to be unhappy with the speed and scale of Stalin's industrialisation drive. He was also opposed to the extreme measures being used as a means of disciplining party members. If organised opposition to Stalin were to form within the party, Kirov was the outstanding individual around whom dissatisfied members might rally. That danger to Stalin had now been removed.

Stalin was quick to exploit the situation further. Within two hours of learning of Kirov's murder he had signed a **'Decree against terrorist acts'**. On the pretext of hunting down the killers, a fresh purge of the party was begun, led by Genrikh Yagoda, head of the NKVD. Three thousand suspected conspirators were rounded up and then imprisoned or executed; tens of thousands of other people were deported from Leningrad. Stalin then filled the vacant positions with his own nominees, as the following list indicates:

**KEY TERM**

**'Decree against terrorist acts'** An order giving the NKVD limitless powers to pursue the enemies of the state and the party.

- In 1935 Kirov's key post as party boss in Leningrad was filled by Andrei Zhdanov, a dedicated Stalinist, who was described by one contemporary Communist as 'a slimy creep without an idea in his head'.

- The equivalent post in Moscow was taken by Nikita Khrushchev, at this stage another ardent Stalin supporter.
- In recognition of his successful courtroom bullying of 'oppositionists' in the earlier purge trials, Andrei Vyshinsky was appointed state prosecutor. A reformed Menshevik, Vyshinsky became notorious for his vengeful and vicious ways.
- Stalin's fellow Georgian, Lavrenti Beria, was entrusted with overseeing state security in the national-minority areas of the USSR. Beria, an obsequious Stalinist and a notorious rapist and child molester, became head of the NKVD, in which position he was feared and hated within the party until his overthrow and execution following Stalin's death.
- Stalin's personal secretary, Alexander Poskrebyshev, was put in charge of the Secretariat. As personal secretary to Stalin after 1929, Poskrebyshev remained totally loyal to his master even though his wife was tortured and shot on Stalin's orders.

As a result of these placements, there was no significant area of Soviet bureaucracy which Stalin did not control.

The outstanding feature of the post-Kirov purge was the status of many of its victims. Prominent among those arrested were Kamenev and Zinoviev. Their arrest sent out a clear message: no party members, whatever their status, were safe. Arbitrary arrest and summary execution became the norm. An impression of this can be gained from noting the fate of the representatives at the party congress of 1934:

- Of the 1996 delegates who attended, 1108 were executed during the next three years.
- In addition, out of the 139 Central Committee members elected at that gathering, all but 41 were executed during the purges.

Historian Leonard Shapiro, in a celebrated study of the CPSU (1960), described these events as 'Stalin's victory over the party'. From this point on, the CPSU was entirely under his control. It ceased, in effect, to have a separate existence. Stalin had become the party.

### The 'Stalin enrolment' 1931–4

Stalin's successful purge was made easier by a recent shift in the make-up of the party, known as the 'Stalin enrolment'. Between 1931 and 1934, the CPSU had recruited a higher proportion of skilled workers and industrial managers than at any time since 1917. Stalin encouraged this as a means of tightening the links between the party and those actually operating the first FYP, but it also had the effect of bringing in a large number of members who joined the party primarily to advance their careers. Acutely aware that they owed their privileged position directly to Stalin's patronage, the new members eagerly supported the elimination of the anti-Stalinist elements in the party. It improved their own chances of promotion. The competition for good jobs in Soviet Russia was invariably fierce. Purges always left positions to be filled. As the chief dispenser of positions, Stalin knew that the self-interest of these new party members would keep them loyal to him.

## The 'Great Purge' 1936–9

It might be expected that, once Stalin's mastery had been established, the purges would stop. But they did not; they increased in intensity. Repeating his constant assertion that the Soviet Union was in a state of siege, Stalin called for still greater vigilance against the enemies within who were in league with the Soviet Union's foreign enemies. Between 1936 and 1939, a progressive terrorising of the Soviet Union occurred, affecting the whole population. Its scale earned it the title of the 'Great Purge' (or the 'Great Terror'), which took its most dramatic form in the public show trials of Stalin's former Bolshevik colleagues. The one-time heroes of the 1917 Revolution were imprisoned or executed as enemies of the state.

The descriptions applied to the accused during the purges bore little relation to political reality. 'Right', 'Left' and Centre' opposition blocs were identified and the groupings invariably had the catch-all term 'Trotskyite' tagged on to them, but such words were convenient prosecution labels rather than definitions of a genuine political opposition. They were intended to isolate those in the CPSU and the Soviet state whom Stalin wished to destroy.

Stalin's 'Great Terror' programme breaks down into three stages:

- the purge of the party
- the purge of the armed services
- the purge of the people.

### The purge of the party

Between 1936 and 1938, Stalin used three major show trials as the means of removing his main political rivals (see box).

**Show trials 1936–8**

- In 1936, Kamenev and Zinoviev and fourteen other leading Bolsheviks were accused of involvement in the Kirov murder and plotting to subvert the Soviet state. After a public trial they were condemned and executed.
- In 1937, seventeen Bolsheviks were denounced collectively as the 'Anti-Soviet Trotskyist Centre', and were charged with spying for Nazi Germany. All but three of them were executed.
- In 1938, Bukharin, Rykov and Tomsky and twenty others, branded 'Trotskyite–Rightists', were publicly tried on a variety of counts, including sabotage, spying and conspiracy to murder Stalin; all were found guilty. Bukharin and Rykov were executed; Tomsky killed himself.

The prelude to the Great Purge of 1936 was a secret letter sent from CPSU headquarters, warning all the local party branches of a terrorist conspiracy by 'the Trotskyite–Kamenevite–Zinovievite–Leftist Counter-Revolutionary Bloc' and instructing Party officials to begin rooting out suspected agents and sympathisers. Once this campaign of denunciation and expulsion had been set in motion in the country at large, Kamenev and Zinoviev were put on public trial in Moscow, charged with involvement in Kirov's murder and with plotting to overthrow the Soviet State. Both men pleaded guilty and read out abject confessions in court.

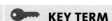

**KEY TERM**

**De-Stalinisation**
The movement, begun by Nikita Khrushchev in 1956, to expose Stalin's crimes and mistakes against the party, which for the first time revealed the scale of the purges.

The obvious question is: 'why did they confess?' After all, these men were tough Bolsheviks. No doubt, as was later revealed during **de-Stalinisation**, physical and mental torture was used. Possibly more important was their sense of demoralisation at having been accused and disgraced by the party to which they had dedicated their lives and which could do no wrong. In a curious sense, their admission of guilt was a last act of loyalty to the party.

Whatever their reasons, the fact that they did confess made it extremely difficult for other victims to plead their own innocence. If the great ones of state and party were prepared to accept their fate, on what grounds could lesser men resist? The psychological impact of the public confessions of such figures as Kamenev and Zinoviev was profound. It helped to create an atmosphere in which innocent victims submitted in open court to false charges, and went to their death begging the party's forgiveness.

It also shows Stalin's astuteness in insisting on a policy of public trials. There is little doubt that he had the power to conduct the purges without using legal proceedings. He could simply have had the victims bumped off. However, by making them deliver humiliating confessions in open court, Stalin was able to reveal the scale of the conspiracy against him and to prove the need for the purging to continue.

### The purging of the Right

This soon became evident after Kamenev and Zinoviev, along with fourteen other Bolsheviks, had been duly executed in keeping with Vyshinsky's notorious demand as prosecutor that they be shot 'like the mad dogs they are'. The details the condemned had revealed in their confessions were used to prepare the next major strike, the attack on 'the Right deviationists'. Bukharin, Rykov and Tomsky were put under investigation, but not yet formally charged. The delay was caused by the reluctance of some of the older Bolsheviks in the Politburo to denounce their comrades. Stalin intervened personally to speed up the process. Yagoda, who was considered to have been too lenient in his recent handling of the 'Trotskyite–Zinovievite bloc', was replaced as head of the NKVD by the less scrupulous Yezhov, whose name, like Vyshinsky's, was to become a byword for terror.

### The 'Anti-Soviet Trotskyist Centre'

Meanwhile, the case for proceeding against Bukharin and the Right was strengthened by the revelations at a further show trial in 1937, at which seventeen Communists, denounced collectively as the 'Anti-Soviet Trotskyist Centre', were charged with spying for Nazi Germany. The accused included **Karl Radek** and **Georgy Pyatakov**, the former favourites of Lenin, and **Grigory Sokolnikov**, Stalin's commissar for finance during the first FYP. Radek's abject confession in which he incriminated his close colleagues, including his friend Bukharin, saved him from the death sentence imposed on all but three of the other defendants. He died two years later, however, in an Arctic labour camp.

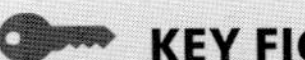

**KEY FIGURES**

**Karl Radek (1885–1939)**

A leading Bolshevik propagandist since 1905, he had been head of the Comintern in the early 1920s.

**Georgy Pyatakov (1890–1937)**

An economist who held a number of important government posts in the 1920s and 1930s.

**Grigory Sokolnikov (1888–1939)**

A finance minister under both Lenin and Stalin.

Yezhov and Vyshinsky now had the evidence they needed. In 1938, in the third of the major show trials, Bukharin and Rykov (Tomsky had taken his own life in the meantime) and eighteen other 'Trotskyite–Rightists' were publicly arraigned on a variety of counts, including sabotage, spying and conspiracy to murder Stalin. The fact that Yagoda was one of the accused was a sign of the speed with which the terror was starting to consume its own kind. **Fitzroy MacLean**, a British diplomat and one of the foreign observers allowed to attend the trial in March 1938, described what he witnessed (Source A).

**SOURCE A**

**From F. McClean, *Eastern Approaches*, Jonathan Cape, 1951, p. 82.**

*To the right of the judges, facing the accused, stood Vyshinski, the Public Prosecutor. In a rapid expressionless voice an officer of the court started to read out the indictment. The trial had begun. The prisoners were charged, collectively and individually, with every conceivable crime: high treason, murder, and sabotage. They had plotted to wreck industry and agriculture, to assassinate Stalin, to dismember the Soviet Union for the benefit of their capitalist allies. They were shown for the most part to have been traitors to the Soviet cause ever since the Revolution. One after another, using the same words, they admitted their guilt: Bukharin, Rykov, Yagoda. Each prisoner incriminated his fellows and was in turn incriminated by them. There was no attempt to evade responsibility.*

*They were men in full possession of their faculties. And yet what they said seemed to bear no relation to reality. The fabric that was being built up was fantastic beyond belief. As the trial progressed it became clearer that the underlying purpose of every testimony was to blacken the leaders of the 'bloc' to represent them not as political prisoners but as common murderers, poisoners and spies.*

Why, in Source A, does the writer stress that the accused were 'in full possession of their faculties'?

At one point in his trial Bukharin embarrassed the court by attempting to defend himself, but he was eventually silenced by Vyshinsky's bullying and was sentenced to be shot along with the rest of the defendants. In his final speech in court, Bukharin showed the extraordinary character of the Bolshevik mentality. Despite the injustice of the proceedings to which he had been subjected, he accepted the infallibility of the party and of Stalin, referring to him as 'the hope of the world.'

The ferocity to which Stalin's prosecutors subjected the accused is evident from Vyshinsky's concluding speech at the trial (Source B).

? In Source B, what is Vyshinsky seeking to establish about the nature of the crimes he is condemning?

**SOURCE B**

**From the summing up on 11 March 1938, by Andre Vyshinsky, chief prosecutor under Stalin, quoted in F.W. Stacey, editor, *Stalin and the Making of Modern Russia*, Edward Arnold, 1970, pp. 33–4.**

*Comrade Judges, as the Court investigation of the present case proceeded, it brought to light ever more the horrors of the chain of unparalleled, monstrous crimes committed by the accused, the entire abominable chain of heinous deeds before which the most base deeds of the most inveterate and despicable criminals fade and grow dim.*

*In what other trial was it possible to uncover the real nature of these crimes with such force to tear the mask of perfidy from the faces of these scoundrels and to show the whole world the bestial countenance of the international brigands who cunningly direct the hands of miscreants against our peaceful Socialist labour that has set up the new, happy, joyously flourishing Socialist society of workers and peasants? Our whole country from young to old is awaiting and demanding one thing: the traitors and spies who are selling our country to the enemy must be shot like dirty dogs. Our people are demanding one thing: crush the accursed reptiles!*

*Over the road cleared of the last scum and filth of the past, we, our people, with our beloved leader and teacher, the great Stalin, at our head, will march as before onwards and onwards, towards Communism.*

## The Stalin constitution 1936

**KEY TERM**

**Popular front** An alliance of socialist and progressive parties.

A particular irony attached to Bukharin's trial and execution. Only two years previously he had been the principal draftsman of the new constitution of the USSR. This 1936 constitution, which Stalin described as 'the most democratic in the world', was intended to impress Western Communists and Soviet sympathisers. This was the period in Soviet foreign policy when, in an effort to offset the Nazi menace to the USSR, Stalin was urging the formation of '**popular fronts**' between the Communist parties and the various left-wing groups in Europe (see page 248). Among the things claimed in the constitution were that:

- Socialism having been established, there were no longer any classes in Soviet society.
- The basic civil rights of freedom of expression, assembly and worship were guaranteed.

**SOURCE C**

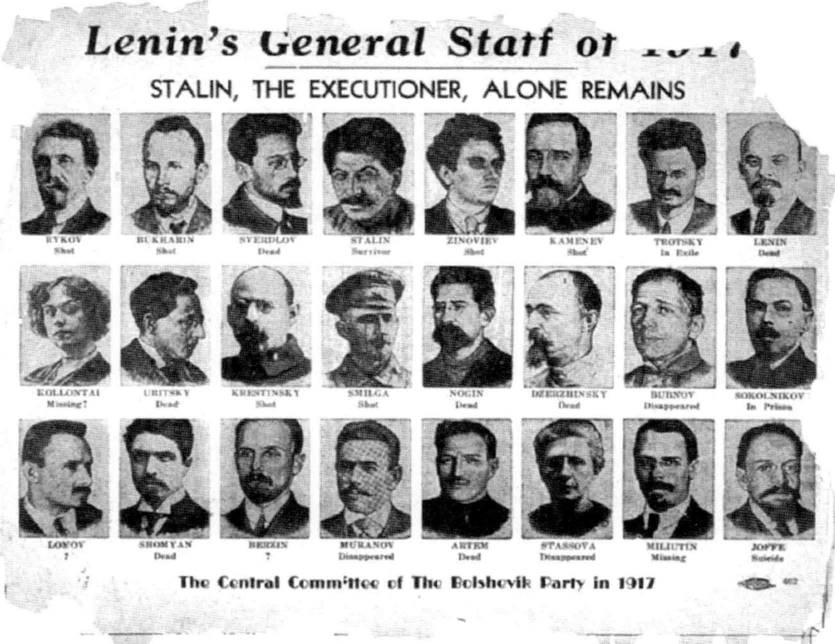


How does the montage in Source C illustrate the extent of the purges against leading members of the CPSU?

**This montage, composed by Trotsky's supporters, illustrates the remarkable fact that of the original 1917 Central Committee of the Bolshevik Party only Stalin had survived by 1938. The majority of the other 23 members had, of course, been destroyed in the purges or were in exile.**

However, the true character of Stalin's constitution lay not in what it said but in what it omitted. Hardly anywhere was the role of the party mentioned; its powers were not defined and, therefore, were not restricted. It would remain the instrument through which Stalin would exercise his total control of the USSR. The contrast between the constitution's democratic claims and the reality of the situation in the Soviet Union could not have been greater.

The show trials that had taken place in Moscow and Leningrad, with their catalogue of accusations, confessions and death sentences, were repeated in all the republics of the USSR. For example, between 1937 and 1939 in Stalin's home state of Georgia:

- two state prime ministers were removed
- four-fifths of the regional party secretaries were dismissed
- thousands of lesser officials lost their posts.

## The purge of the armed forces

A significant development in the purges occurred in 1937 when the Soviet military came under threat. Stalin's control of the Soviet Union would not have been complete if the armed services had continued as an independent force. It was essential that they be kept subservient. Knowing that military loyalties might make a purge of the army difficult to achieve, Stalin took the preliminary step of organising a large number of transfers within the higher ranks in order to lessen the possibility of centres of resistance being formed when the attack came.

With this accomplished, Vyshinsky announced, in May 1937, that 'a gigantic conspiracy' had been uncovered in the Red Army. Marshal Mikhail Tukhachevsky, one of the founders of the Red Army (see page 157), was arrested along with seven other generals, all of whom had been 'heroes of the Civil War'. On the grounds that speed was essential to prevent a military coup, the trial was held immediately, this time in secret. The charge was treason; Tukhachevsky was accused of having spied for Germany and Japan. Documentary evidence, some of it supplied by German intelligence at the request of the NKVD, was produced in proof.

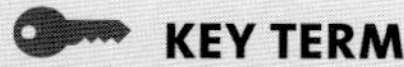

**KEY FIGURE**

**Klimenty Voroshilov (1881–1969)**

One of the founding members of the Bolshevik Party, he became a devoted Stalinist.

**KEY TERM**

**Marshal of the Soviet Union** Equivalent to a field marshal or a five-star general.

The outcome was predetermined and inevitable. In June 1937, after their ritual confession and condemnation, Tukhachevsky and his fellow generals were shot. There appears to have been a particularly personal element in all this. The president of the secret court which delivered the death sentences was Marshal **Voroshilov**, a devoted Stalinist, who had long been jealous of Tukhachevsky's talent and popularity. Tukhachevsky's execution was the signal for an even greater blood-letting. To prevent any chance of a military reaction, a wholesale destruction of the Red Army establishment was undertaken. In the following eighteen months:

- All eleven war commissars were removed from office.
- Three of the five **marshals of the Soviet Union** were dismissed.
- Ninety-one of the 101-man Supreme Military Council were arrested, of whom 80 were executed.
- Fourteen of the sixteen army commanders, and nearly two-thirds of the 280 divisional commanders were removed.
- Thirty-five thousand commissioned officers were either imprisoned or shot.
- The Soviet Navy did not escape; between 1937 and 1939 all the serving admirals of the fleet were shot and thousands of naval officers were sent to labour camps.
- The Soviet Air Force was similarly decimated during that period, only one of its senior commanders surviving the purge.

At the height of the purge extraordinary scenes were witnessed daily in some army camps where whole lorry loads of officers were taken away for execution.

The devastation of the Soviet armed forces, wholly unrelated to any conceivable military purpose, was complete by 1939. It left all three services seriously undermanned and staffed by inexperienced or incompetent replacements. Given the defence needs of the USSR, a theme constantly stressed by Stalin himself, the deliberate crippling of the Soviet military is the aspect of the purges that appears most irrational.

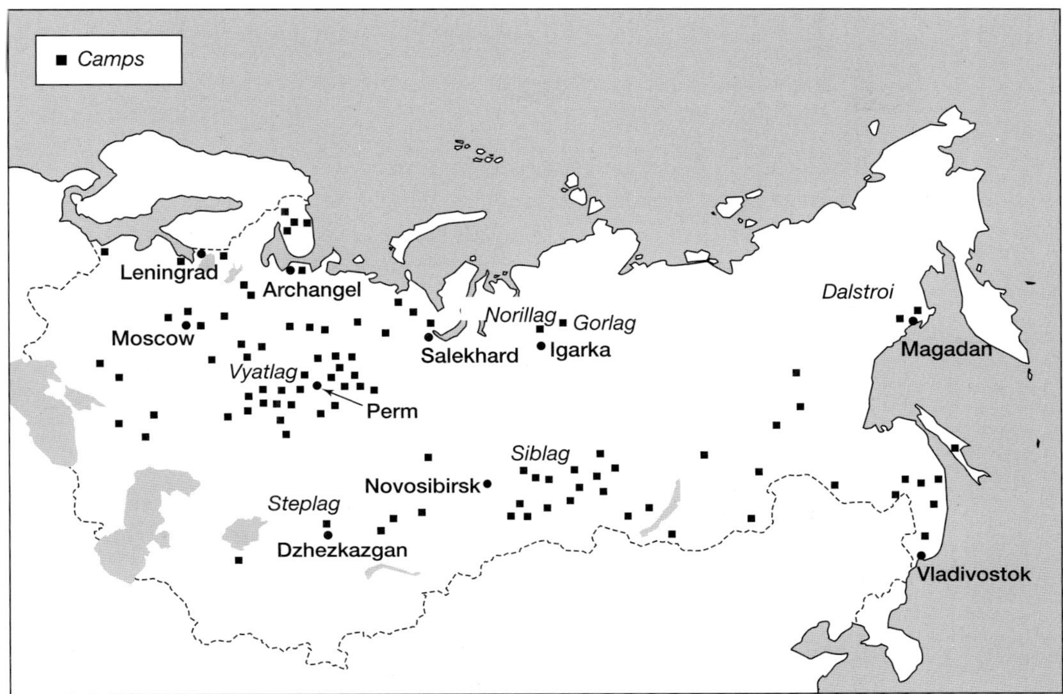


**Figure 8.1** Soviet labour camps 1937–57. What does this map indicate about the extent of Stalin's repression?

## The purge of the people

Stalin's gaining of total dominance over party, government and military did not mean the end of the purges. The apparatus of terror was retained and the search for enemies continued. Purges were used to force the pace of the FYPs, by bringing charges of industrial sabotage against selected managers and workers in the factories. Purges were also a way of forcing the regions and nationalities into total subordination to Stalin. To accommodate the great numbers of prisoners created by the purges, a terrifying development took place in the form of the creation across the USSR of an extensive network of prison and labour camps. These were known collectively as the gulag. By 1941, as a result of the purges, there were an estimated 8 million prisoners in the gulag. The average term for those sent to the gulag was ten years, which, given the conditions in the camps, where starvation and exhausting physical labour, carried out in stifling heat or below-zero temperatures, were routine, was equivalent to a death sentence. As an example of state-organised repression, Stalin's gulag stands alongside Hitler's concentration camps and Mao Zedong's *laogai* (prison camps).

### Mass repression: the 'Yezhovshchina'

No area of Soviet life entirely escaped the purges. The constant fear that this created conditioned the way the Soviet people lived their lives. The greatest impact of the purges was on the middle and lower ranks of Soviet society:

- One person in every eight of the population was arrested during Stalin's purges.
- Almost every family in the USSR suffered the loss of at least one of its members as a victim of the terror.

In the years 1937–8, mass repression was imposed. Known as the 'Yezhovshchina', after its chief organiser, Nicolai Yezhov, this purge was typified by the practice in which NKVD squads entered selected localities and removed hundreds of inhabitants for execution. The number of victims to be arrested was specified in set quotas as if they were industrial production targets. There was no appeal against sentence and the death warrant invariably required that the execution 'be carried out immediately'. The shootings took place in specially designated zones. One notorious example of this was Butovo, a village outside Moscow, which became one of the NKVD's killing fields. Later excavations revealed mass graves there containing over 20,000 bodies, dating back to the late 1930s and indicating that nightly over many months victims had been taken to Butovo and shot in batches of a hundred.

### *The quota system*

It was the numbers not the names that mattered. One incident illustrates the mechanical, dehumanised process. A woman whose neighbour had been arrested called at a police station to ask permission to look after the child the neighbour had had to leave behind.

? In what way does the blueprint in Source D indicate the systematic character of the killings?

**SOURCE D**

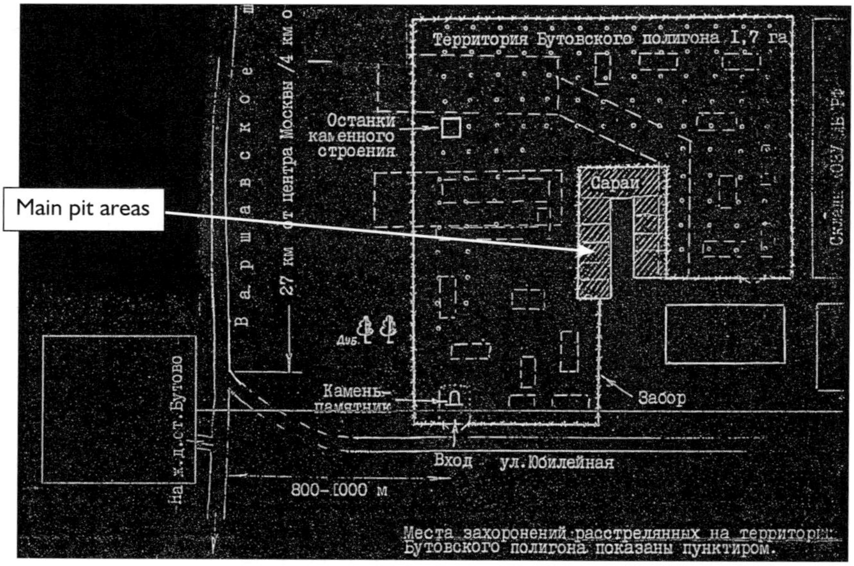

Main pit areas

**Part of an NKVD blueprint of the Butovo killing fields, indicating the pits into which the victims were heaped after being shot.**

**SOURCE E**

**Stalin signing an execution order in 1937; between 1937 and 1938, he authorised over 38,000 execution, a number that was six times greater than that for all those executed for political offences in tsarist Russia between 1815 and 1817.**

Study Source E. What aspects of Stalin's character and personality would have made him capable of signing such an order?

After leaving her waiting for two hours, the police then decided that since they were one short of their daily quota of people to be arrested the caller would make up the number. She was grabbed and thrown into a cell.

## The purges go full circle

In the headlong rush to uncover further conspiracies, interrogators themselves became victims and joined those they had condemned in execution cells and labour camps. Concepts such as innocence and guilt lost all meaning during the purges. The mass of the population were frightened and bewildered. Fear had the effect of destroying moral values and traditional loyalties. The one aim became survival, even at the cost of betrayal. In a 1988 edition devoted to the Stalinist purges, the Moscow *Literary Gazette* referred to 'the special sadism whereby the nearest relatives were forced to incriminate each other – brother to slander brother, husband to blacken wife'.

The chillingly systematic character of the purges was described in the minutes of a plenary session of the Central Committee, held in June 1957 during the de-Stalinisation period. They revealed that between February 1937 and November 1938 the NKVD received formal approval from Stalin to execute 38,697 arrested people and that on one particular day, 12 November 1938, Stalin and Molotov had authorised the execution of 229 prisoners. The batch was made up of:

- 23 members of the Central Committee
- 22 members of the party Control Commission
- 12 regional party secretaries
- 21 people's commissars
- 136 officials from the Secretariat
- 15 leading military personnel.

Insofar as the terrorising of ordinary people had a specific purpose it was to frighten the USSR's national minorities into abandoning any remaining thoughts of challenging Moscow's control and to force them into a full acceptance of Stalin's enforced industrialisation programme.

## Responsibility for the purges

There is little doubt that Stalin himself initiated, and remained the driving force behind, the purges. He exploited the Russian autocratic tradition that he inherited to rid himself of real or imagined enemies. Yet leading scholars, such as Stalin's biographer, Robert Service, now stress that, while Stalin was undoubtedly the architect of the terror, the responsibility for implementing it goes beyond him. The following factors illustrate this:

- Stalinism was not as all-embracing a system of government as has been often assumed. The disorganised state of much of Soviet bureaucracy, particularly at local level, allowed officials to use their own initiative in applying the terror.
- How the purges were actually carried out largely depended on the local party organisation. Many welcomed the purges as an opportunity to settle old scores.
- Revolutionary idealism was mixed with self-interest as party members saw the purges as a way of advancing themselves by filling the jobs vacated by the victims. In this sense, the purges came from below as much as from above, their ferocity being sustained by the lower rank officials in government and party who wanted to replace their superiors, whom they regarded as a conservative elite.
- The purges were popular with those Russians who believed their country could be prevented from slipping back into its historic backwardness only by being powerfully and ruthlessly led. Such people judged that Stalin's unrelenting methods were precisely what the nation needed.
- The disruption of Soviet society, caused by the upheavals of collectivisation and industrialisation, destroyed social cohesion and so encouraged party and government officials to resort to the most extreme measures.
- The notion of civil rights was not strong enough in Russia to offer an alternative to what was being done in the name of the Communist revolution.

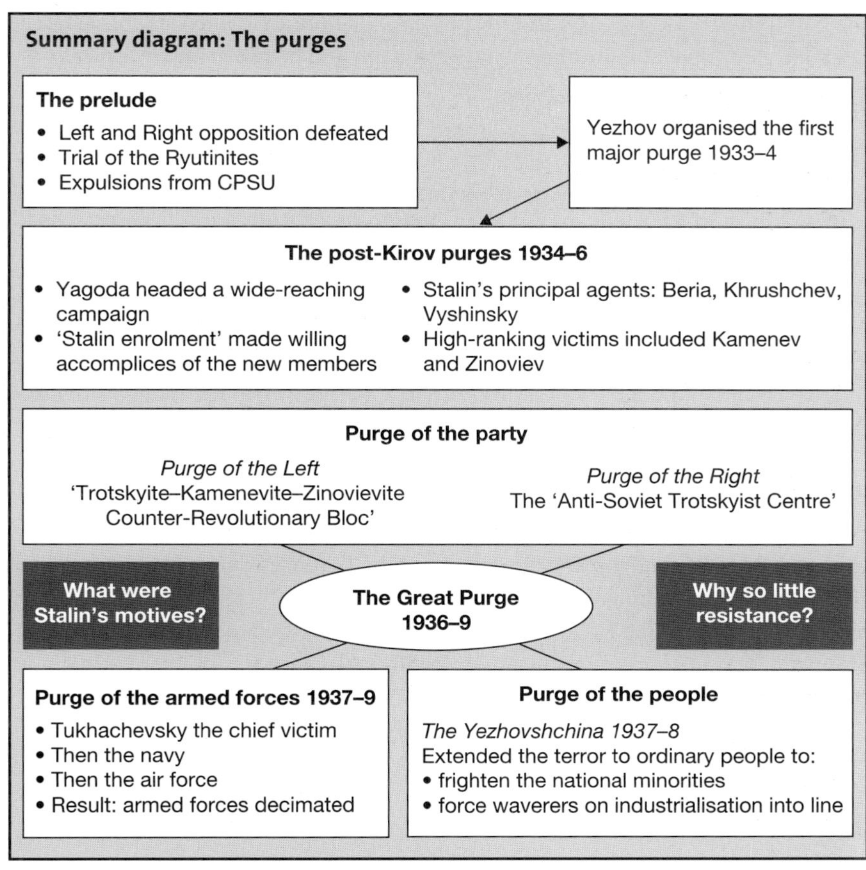

Summary diagram: The purges
The prelude
• Left and Right opposition defeated
• Trial of the Ryutinites
• Expulsions from CPSU
Yezhov organised the first major purge 1933–4
The post-Kirov purges 1934–6
• Yagoda headed a wide-reaching campaign
• 'Stalin enrolment' made willing accomplices of the new members
• Stalin's principal agents: Beria, Khrushchev, Vyshinsky
• High-ranking victims included Kamenev and Zinoviev
Purge of the party
Purge of the Left
'Trotskyite–Kamenevite–Zinovievite Counter-Revolutionary Bloc'
Purge of the Right
The 'Anti-Soviet Trotskyist Centre'
What were Stalin's motives?
The Great Purge 1936–9
Why so little resistance?
Purge of the armed forces 1937–9
• Tukhachevsky the chief victim
• Then the navy
• Then the air force
• Result: armed forces decimated
Purge of the people
The Yezhovshchina 1937–8
Extended the terror to ordinary people to:
• frighten the national minorities
• force waverers on industrialisation into line

# Stalin's totalitarianism

▶ *What were the main characteristics of Stalin's totalitarian state?*

**Totalitarianism** is a governmental system under which individuals become subordinate to the state and lose all personal autonomy. The Soviet Union under Stalin became one of the twentieth-century's outstanding examples of such a system.

## Totalitarianism

By 1941, the basic features of Stalin's totalitarian state had been established. Stalin ran the USSR by a bureaucratic system of government. In doing this, he fulfilled the work begun by Lenin of turning revolutionary Russia into a one-party state. Political and social control was maintained by a terror system whose main instruments were regular purges and show trials directed against

**KEY TERM**

**Totalitarianism** A system in which a regime controls society in all its various features, political, cultural, economic, communal and personal.

the party, the armed services and the people. His political control enabled him to create a **command economy** with agriculture and industry under central direction.

## Absolutism

Stalin's highly individual rule developed into a **cult of personality** which led to his becoming absolute in authority since he was regarded as the embodiment of the Communist Party and the nation. Although all-powerful, Stalin's paranoia led him to create a siege mentality in the USSR. He insisted that even in peacetime the Soviet people had to be on permanent guard from enemies within and hostile nations outside. This was an extension of his concept of 'Socialism in One Country', a policy which subordinated everything to the interests of the Soviet Union as a nation.

## Ideology

Stalin's **absolutism** meant the suppression of any form of genuine democracy, since he operated on the principle, laid down by Lenin, of democratic centralism, which obliged members of the CPSU to accept uncritically and obey all orders and instructions handed down by the party leaders (see page 24). Under Stalin, the Soviet Union recognised only one correct and acceptable ideology, **Marxism–Leninism–Stalinism**. All other belief systems were prohibited. Strict censorship was imposed as a means of enforcing political and cultural conformity in accordance with Stalin's notion of socialist realism.

## Intrinsic violence

Despite his control, Stalin was not all-powerful: no one individual in a nation can be. His authority depended ultimately on the willingness of thousands of underlings to carry out his orders and policies. That he could rely on this is explained for some historians by the character of Soviet communism itself. They draw attention to the violence that was intrinsic to Soviet communism. Stalin once asserted that violence was an 'inevitable law of the revolutionary movement', a restatement of Lenin's declaration that the task of Bolshevism was 'the ruthless destruction of the enemy'. The Stalinist purges are consequently seen by some scholars as a logical historical progression.

## Lack of a tradition of civil rights

In this connection, scholars have also laid weight on how undeveloped the concepts of individual or civil rights were in Russia. Tsardom had been an autocracy in which the first duty of the people had been to obey. The Communists had not changed that. Indeed, Lenin and Stalin had re-emphasised the necessity of obedience to central authority.

### KEY TERMS

**Command economy** A system in which all the main areas of economic activity are under central government control and direction.

**Cult of personality** The projection through constant propaganda of an individual as a heroic figure above ordinary politics and, therefore, entitled to exercise unlimited authority.

**Absolutism** A system, similar to totalitarianism, in which authoritarian control is exercised by government over all aspects of society.

**Marxism–Leninism–Stalinism** The concept of an ideological continuity between the founder of Marxism and its great interpreters, Lenin and Stalin.

## The *nomenklatura*

Among the main beneficiaries of this tradition of obedience were the ***nomenklatura***. The common characteristic of those who led Stalin's purges was their unswerving personal loyalty to him, a loyalty that overcame any doubts they might have had regarding the nature of their work. Stalin had no difficulty in finding eager subordinates to organise the terror campaign. They formed the new class of officials created to replace the old Bolsheviks, decimated in the purges. Dedicated to Stalin, on whom their positions depended, the *nomenklatura* enjoyed rights and privileges denied to the rest of the population. Including their families, they numbered around 600,000 (1.2 per cent of the population) by the late 1930s. Such people, once in post, were unlikely to question Stalin's orders. The more potential rivals they exterminated, the safer their jobs became.

Significantly, the willingness to be totally obedient was not exclusive to minor officials. Of equal note was the eagerness with which Stalin's top ministers carried out his campaigns of terror and persecution. Though they were terrified of him, they did not simply obey him out of fear. People like Beria and Molotov derived the same vindictive satisfaction from their work as their master. Like him, they appeared to have no moral scruples.

**KEY TERM**

***Nomenklatura*** The Soviet establishment, an elite set of privileged officials who ran the party machine.

## Revolution from above

Notwithstanding the attitudes of ordinary Russians, the *nomenklatura* and government ministers, the fact remained that it was Stalin who gave the USSR its essential shape. Whatever the motives of those who carried out Stalin's policies, he was the great motivator. Little of importance took place in the USSR of which he did not approve. That is why some prominent historians describe Stalinism as 'revolution from above', meaning that the changes that occurred under Stalin were directed by him from the top down.

**Summary diagram: Stalin's totalitarianism**

**Key elements**

- Absolutism
- Single imposed Ideology: Marxism–Leninism–Stalinism
- Command economy
- Intrinsic violence
- Lack of a tradition of civil rights
- Obedience

***Nomenklatura***

- The privileged beneficiaries

**But** Stalin controlled the revolution from above

#  Stalin and the cult of personality

▶ *How did Stalin establish a cult of personality?*

Adolf Hitler once wrote that 'the personality cult is the best form of government'. It is not certain whether Stalin ever read this, but it would be a fitting commentary on his leadership of the Soviet Union. One of the strongest charges made by Nikita Khrushchev in his later attack on Stalin was that he had indulged in 'the cult of personality'. He was referring to the way Stalin dominated every aspect of Soviet life, so that he became not simply a leader but the embodiment of the nation itself. Similarly, the Communist Party became indistinguishable from Stalin himself as a person. Communism was no longer a set of theories; it was no longer Leninism. It was whatever Stalin said and did. Soviet communism was Stalinism.

## Stalin as hero

From the early 1930s onwards, Stalin's picture began to appear everywhere. Newspapers, books and films, no matter what their theme, carried a reference to Stalin's greatness. Every achievement of the USSR was credited to Stalin. Such was his all-pervasive presence that Soviet communism became personalised around him. On occasion, in private, Stalin protested that he did not seek the glorification he received but, significantly, he made no effort to prevent it.

Ironically, in view of his later denunciation of Stalin, it was Khrushchev who did as much as anyone to promote the image of Stalin as a glorious hero. At the trial of Zinoviev and Kamenev in August 1936, Khrushchev cursed the defendants as 'Miserable pygmies!' and went on: 'Stalin is hope, Stalin is expectation; he is the beacon that guides all progressive mankind. Stalin is our banner! Stalin is our will! Stalin is our victory!'

Khrushchev was the first to coin the term 'Stalinism' in 1936 when he spoke of the 'Marxism–Leninism–Stalinism that has conquered one sixth of the globe.' At the Eighteenth Congress of the CPSU in March 1939, Khrushchev lauded the Soviet leader as 'our great inspiration, our beloved Stalin', extolling him as 'the greatest genius of humanity, teacher and *vozhd* who leads us towards communism'.

It is one of the many paradoxes of Soviet history that the Communist movement, which in theory drew its authority from the will of the masses, became so dependent on the idea of the great leader. Such was Stalin's standing and authority that he transcended politics. Since he represented not simply the party but the nation itself, he became the personification of all that was best in Russia. This was an extraordinary achievement for a Georgian and it produced a further remarkable development. It became common to assert that many of the great achievements in world history were the work of Russians.

## Propaganda

The claims made for Stalin and his leadership of the Soviet Union developed a surreal quality: that Shakespeare was really a Russian, that Russian navigators had been the first Europeans to discover America and that Russian mathematicians had discovered the secrets of relativity long before Einstein. Eventually Stalin overreached himself. He ordered his scientists to produce a popular soft drink to match the American capitalist Coca-Cola. They tried but finally had to admit that, while Soviet science could achieve marvels, miracles were beyond it.

The cult of personality was not a spontaneous response of the people. It did not come from below; it was imposed from above. The image of Stalin as hero and saviour of the Soviet people was manufactured. It was a product of the Communist Party machine which controlled all the main forms of information: newspapers, cinema and radio. Roy Medvedev, a Soviet historian who lived through Stalinism, later explained that Stalin did not rely on terror alone, but also on the support of the majority of the people, who 'deceived by cunning propaganda, gave Stalin credit for the successes of others and even in fact for "achievements" that were in fact totally fictitious'. A striking example of building on the fictitious was the Stakhanovite movement (see page 218).

## Worship of Stalin

Despite the Soviet attack on the Church, the powerful religious sense of the Russian people remained and it was cleverly exploited by the authorities. Traditional worship, with its veneration of the saints, its **icons**, prayers and incantations, translated easily into the new regime. Stalin became an icon. This was literally true. His picture was carried on giant flags in processions. A French visitor watching at one of the **May Day** celebrations in Moscow's Red Square was staggered by the sight of a flypast of planes all trailing huge portraits of Stalin. 'My God!', he exclaimed. 'Exactly, Monsieur', said his Russian guide.

However, even May Day came to take second place to the celebration of Stalin's birthday each December. Beginning in 1929, on his fiftieth birthday, the occasion was turned each year into the greatest celebration in the Soviet calendar. Day-long parades in Red Square of marching troops, rolling tanks, dancing children, and applauding workers, all presided over by an occasionally smiling Stalin high on a rostrum overlooking Lenin's tomb, became the high moment of the year. It was a new form of tsar worship.

Stalin's wisdom and brilliance were extolled daily in *Pravda* and ***Isvestiya***, the official Soviet newspapers. Hardly an article appeared in any journal that did not include the obligatory reference to his greatness. Children learned from their earliest moments to venerate Stalin as the provider of all good things. At school they were taught continually and in all subjects that Stalin was their guide and protector. It was an interesting aspect of the prescribed school curriculum that history was to be taught not as 'an abstract sociological scheme' but as a

**Icons** Two-dimensional representations of Jesus Christ and the saints, one of the great glories of the Orthodox Church.

**May Day** 'Labour Day', usually 1 May, traditionally regarded as a special occasion for honouring the workers and the achievements of socialism.

***Isvestiya*** Translates as *The Times*.

chronological story full of stirring tales of the great Russian heroes of the past, such as **Ivan the Terrible** and **Peter the Great**, leading up to the triumph of Lenin and the Bolsheviks in 1917.

The climax of this story was Stalin, who, building on the work of Lenin, was securing and extending the Soviet Union. This adulation of Stalin was not confined to history books. There were no textbooks in any subject that did not extol his virtues as the master-builder of the Soviet nation, inspiration to his people and glorious model for struggling peoples everywhere. Eulogies of Stalin poured off the press, each one trying to outbid the other in its veneration of the leader. Every political gathering was a study in the advancement of the Stalin cult. The exaggeration and the sycophantic character of it all are clear in the following extract from a speech given by a delegate to the seventh congress of soviets in 1935.

**KEY FIGURES**

**Ivan the Terrible (reigned 1547–84)**
A powerful tsar who considerably extended Russian territory through conquest.

**Peter the Great (reigned 1682–1725)**
A reforming tsar who attempted to modernise Russia by incorporating Western European ways.

? From your own knowledge, can you think of reasons why the speaker in Source F may not have been as sincere in his praise of Stalin as he appears to be?

**SOURCE F**

**From a speech by A.O. Avdienko, 1 February 1935, quoted in T.H. Rigby, *Stalin*, Prentice-Hall, 1966, p. 111.**

*Thank you, Stalin. Thank you because I am joyful. Thank you because I am well. Centuries will pass, and the generations still to come will regard us as the happiest of mortals, because we lived in the century of centuries, because we were privileged to see Stalin, our inspired leader. Yes and we regard ourselves as the happiest of mortals because we are the contemporaries of a man who never had an equal in world history. The men of all ages will call on thy name, which is strong, beautiful, wise and marvellous. Thy name is engraved on every factory, every machine, every place on the earth and in the hearts of all men. And when the woman I love presents me with a child the first word it will utter shall be: Stalin.*

## Konsomol

A particularly useful instrument for the spread of Stalinist propaganda was **Konsomol** (the Communist Union of Youth), a movement which had begun in Lenin's time but was created as a formal body in 1926 under the direct control of the CPSU. Among its main features were:

- It was open to those aged between 14 and 28 (a Young Pioneer movement existed for those under 14).
- It pledged itself totally to Stalin and the party; in this regard it paralleled the Hitler Youth movement in Nazi Germany.
- Membership was not compulsory but its attraction to young people was that it offered them the chance of eventual full membership of the CPSU, with all the privileges that went with it.
- It grew from 2 million members in 1927 to 10 million in 1940.

The idealism of the young was very effectively exploited by Stalin's regime. Konsomol members were among the most enthusiastic supporters of the FYPs, as they proved by going off in their thousands to help build the new industrial cities such as Magnitogorsk (see page 214). It was Konsomol that provided the flag-wavers and the cheerleaders and which organised the huge gymnastic displays that were the centrepieces of the massive parades on May Day and Stalin's birthday.

## Stalin's popularity

It is difficult to judge how popular Stalin was in real terms. The applause that greeted his every appearance in public or in cinema newsreels was more likely to have been as much a matter of prudence as of real affection. There was no way in which criticism or opposition could be openly expressed. The gulag was full of comrades who had spoken out of turn. The intense **political correctness** that prevailed required that Stalin be publicly referred to as the faultless leader and inspirer of the nation.

A fascinating insight into Stalin's standing with his own people was provided in 1937 by **Leon Feuchtwanger**, who was misled into exaggerating Stalin's economic successes but who remained a shrewd observer of Soviet attitudes. He described 'the worship and boundless cult with which the population surrounds Stalin' and went on to explain the particular character of Stalin's popularity in these terms:

**SOURCE G**

**From L. Feuchtwanger, *Moscow 1937*, Victor Gollancz, 1937, p. 137.**

*The people were grateful to Stalin for their bread and meat, for the order in their lives, for their education and for creating their army which secured this new well-being. The people have to have someone to whom to express their gratitude, and for this purpose they do not select an abstract concept, such as 'communism', but a real man Stalin. Their unbounded reverence is consequently not for Stalin, but for him as a symbol of the patently successful economic reconstruction.*

**KEY TERM**

**Political correctness**
Conformity to a prescribed set of opinions imposed by social pressure and political control.

**KEY FIGURE**

**Leon Feuchtwanger (1884–1958)**
A Jewish novelist and literary critic who was exiled from Nazi Germany in the 1930s.

In Source G, what is meant by the people's reverence for Stalin being 'for him as a symbol'?

**Summary diagram: Stalin and the cult of personality**

**Stalin's cult of personality**
Stalin transcended politics
↓
Everything in Soviet life measured against his standards
↓
Stalin the great arbiter and judge of truth

**Stalinist propaganda**
The means of projecting Stalin's cult of personality
↓
Party machine ensured that Stalinism pervaded every aspect of public life

**How genuinely popular was Stalin?**

# 4 Stalin's foreign policy

*How did Stalin adapt his foreign policy to meet the perceived threats to the Soviet Union?*

## Stalin's attitude to foreign relations

There is an important distinction to be made between the theory and the practice of Soviet foreign policy under Stalin:

- Judged by its propaganda, the USSR was pledged to the active encouragement of worldwide revolution. The Comintern existed for this very purpose (see page 149).
- However, in practice, Stalin did not regard Soviet Russia as being strong enough to sustain a genuinely revolutionary foreign policy. His first task was to ensure the survival of the revolution in Russia itself, with him as its leader.

The Comintern continued to have a role under Stalin but it was limited to protecting the USSR. Far from being the vanguard of international communism, the Comintern became a branch of the Soviet foreign office.

### 'Socialism in One Country'

Stalin conducted his foreign policy in accordance with his basic principle of 'Socialism in One Country'. The defence of the Soviet Union came before all other considerations. He had defeated Trotsky in the power struggle by emphasising that his opponent's call for the Soviet Union to spearhead international revolution put the nation at risk. Having gained power, Stalin kept to that principle.

## The Nazi threat

Stalin's defensiveness made him slow initially to understand the threat posed by Nazi Germany. However, the following developments combined to convince Stalin that Hitler's Germany was a deadly menace:

- violent Nazi attacks on the **KPD**
- the signing of a German–Polish treaty in 1934, which increased the threat to the USSR's western borders
- open talk among German diplomats of their country's intention of expanding into the USSR
- Nazi propaganda against Soviet communism, which was as rabid as its anti-Semitism.

**KEY TERM**

**KPD** The German Communist Party.

For the next six years Soviet foreign policy was primarily concerned with finding allies to nullify the German danger. One of the earliest opportunities for the USSR to lessen its isolation came with its acceptance into the **League of Nations** in 1934. The League provided a platform for the Soviet Union to call for the adoption of the principle of **collective security** in international affairs. One of the fruits of this was an agreement in 1935 between the USSR, France and Czechoslovakia, promising 'mutual assistance' if one of the partners suffered military attack.

In the 1930s collective security was more impressive in principle than in practice. The reason was that Europe's two most powerful states, France and Britain, were not prepared to risk war in order to uphold the principle. Without their participation there was no possibility of collective security becoming a reality.

**KEY TERMS**

**League of Nations** The body set up in 1919 with the aim of resolving international disputes and so maintaining world peace.

**Collective security** Nations acting together to protect individual states from attack.

## Stalin and China

In 1935 in China, the Chinese Communist Party (CCP), led by Mao Zedong, having established its base at Yanan, became locked into what amounted to a civil war with the Nationalists (GMD), led by Chiang Kai-shek. In addition, the CCP was subjected to attacks from Japanese forces that had begun to occupy large parts of China. Yet throughout the years 1935–45, Stalin, declining to act in a spirit of Communist brotherhood, gave little help to Mao and the CCP. Stalin's primary aim was make the Chinese Communists obey Soviet instructions and conform to Soviet notions of Marxist revolution. That was why Mao was engaged in a continuous struggle to prevent his party from being taken over by the pro-Moscow members of the CCP. His success in resisting Soviet pressure reduced Stalin to disparaging Mao and his followers as being Communists only in name; 'they are "white" at heart, even though they wear "red" jackets'.

It was also for reasons of national self-interest that Stalin declined to give the CCP full support in its war with the Japanese. Believing that the Chinese Communists were far weaker than the Nationalists, Stalin gave his main backing throughout the 1930s to Chiang Kai-shek. This was not out of any sense of goodwill towards China. Stalin's hope was that by encouraging GMD resistance to the Japanese occupation of China that began in earnest in 1937, Russia would be less likely itself to be the object of Japanese expansionism. Stalin's concern was that imperialist Japan would exploit the Soviet Union's problems on its European borders to encroach on Russian territory in the Far East.

Broadly, Stalin's policy worked. There were a series of Russo-Japanese incidents in the late 1930s that led to fighting on the Manchurian border, but these were resolved in 1941 with the signing of a non-aggression pact between the Soviet Union and Japan. This held good until August 1945 when, in keeping with a commitment given to the Allies at Yalta in February 1945, the USSR declared war on Japan only days before the Japanese surrender in August of that year.

**KEY TERM**

**Anti-Comintern Pact**
An alliance formed between Germany, Italy and Japan.

## Anti-Comintern Pact 1936

The year 1936 was a very bad one for the USSR's hopes of sheltering under collective security. It saw the creation of an international alliance, the **Anti-Comintern Pact**, aimed directly against the Soviet Union since it carried a clear threat of a two-front attack on the USSR's European and Far-Eastern borders. The danger that this represented had the effect of redoubling Stalin's efforts to obtain reliable allies and guarantees. However, in his attempts to achieve this, Stalin was labouring under a handicap, largely of his own making. The plain fact was that Soviet Russia was not trusted. Enough was known of the Stalinist purges to make neutrals in other countries wary of making alliances with a nation where such treachery or such tyranny was possible.

## Spanish Civil War 1936–9

If Stalin made it difficult for neutrals to sympathise with the defence needs of the Soviet Union, he also put barriers in the way of those on the political left in other countries who should have been his natural supporters. His pursuit of defence agreements with the capitalist powers led to compromises that alienated many Soviet sympathisers. This was especially so with regard to Stalin's attitude towards the Spanish Civil War. The struggle in Spain was a complex affair, but outsiders tended to see it in simple terms as a struggle between the republican left and the fascist right, a reflection of the basic political divide in Europe. Stalin and the Comintern, in keeping with the Soviet policy of encouraging anti-fascist popular fronts (see page 232), sent agents into Spain to organise an alliance of pro-Republican forces.

Stalin's motives and policies were mixed. By focusing on Spain, he hoped to divert foreign attention away from the current Soviet purges. The sending of Soviet military equipment to the Republican side was not simple generosity. In payment, the Spanish Republic had to transfer the greater part of its gold reserves to the USSR. Furthermore, the popular front policy meant in practice that the Soviet Union required all the Republican contingents to put themselves under Soviet direction. The Spanish left came to resent the Soviet Union's attempt to dominate and to doubt whether Stalin really wanted the victory of the Spanish Republic. They were correct; Stalin was anxious not to see a major victory for Marxism in Spain. The explanation of this paradox lies not in Spain, but in Europe at large. Stalin feared that, if communism were installed in south-western Europe, this would so frighten France and Britain that they might well react by forming an anti-Soviet front with Germany and Italy, the very consequence which Soviet foreign policy was struggling to avoid.

## Appeasement: the Munich settlement 1938

Stalin's greatest anxiety yet in foreign affairs came in the autumn of 1938 with the signing by France, Britain, Italy and Germany of the Munich agreement, the climax to the Czechoslovak crisis. Hitler had demanded that the Sudetenland,

**SOURCE H**

**'What, No Chair For Me?' Low's cartoon of September 1938 accurately captured Stalin's response to the Munich settlement, which formally accepted Germany's demand for possession of the Sudeten region of Czechoslovakia. Stalin stands on the far right. The other people represented from left to right are Hitler, Neville Chamberlain of Britain, Daladier of France and Mussolini, fascist leader of Italy.**

In what way does the cartoon in Source H suggest Stalin's sense of isolation from the world stage?

an area which in 1919 had been incorporated into Czechoslovakia, be allowed to become part of Germany. He had threatened invasion if his requirements were not met. Neither Britain nor France was prepared to resist him militarily; instead, they chose appeasement. In the Munich agreement they granted all his major demands.

In the Western world, the Munich settlement has customarily been seen as an act of appeasement, a policy for avoiding war by making concessions to the aggressor. That was not the interpretation put on it by Stalin. For him, Munich was a gathering of the anti-Soviet nations of Europe, intent on giving Germany a free hand to attack a diplomatically isolated USSR. To forestall this, Stalin intensified his efforts to reach agreement with France and Britain. In the year after Munich, the Soviet foreign ministry delivered a series of formal alliance proposals to the French and British governments. These went unanswered. France and Britain could not bring themselves to trust Stalin. Blanked out in this way, Stalin then made a remarkable decision. He entered into an agreement with Nazi Germany.

## The Nazi–Soviet Pact 1939–41

In August 1939, the seemingly impossible happened. The two deadly enemies, Nazi Germany and Communist Russia, came together in a formal agreement, the Nazi–Soviet Pact, in which both countries gave a solemn pledge to maintain peaceful relations with each other for a minimum of ten years. Of equal significance was a 'Secret Additional Protocol', in which it was agreed that the USSR would take over the Baltic States and that Poland would later be divided between Germany and the USSR. At the beginning of September 1939, German forces began to occupy Poland. Within a month, Germany and the Soviet Union had carved up Poland between them.

The Nazi–Soviet Pact seemed to defy history and logic. But there was a rationale to this remarkable change in Soviet foreign policy. Given the real threat that Germany presented and the indifference of France and Britain to his offers of a defensive alliance, Stalin felt he had been left no alternative. He attempted to obviate the danger from Germany by the only move that international circumstances still allowed – an agreement with Germany. By 1941, within two years of the pact, Soviet Russia had regained all the territories it had lost as a result of the First World War. This, added to the ten-year guarantee of peace with Germany, seemed to justify the praise heaped on Stalin inside the Soviet Union for his diplomatic masterstroke. Bitter disillusion was to follow in June 1941 when Hitler tore up the treaty and launched a massive invasion of the Soviet Union.

**Summary diagram: Stalin's foreign policy**

**Soviet policy essentially defensive throughout 1930s**

Stalin concerned to find allies to offset the threat from Nazi Germany

↓

USSR joined League of Nations, 1934

↓

Anti-Comintern Pact in 1936 quickened Stalin's desire to find allies

↓

Stalin saw Munich Agreement of 1938 as a Western plot against USSR

↓

France and Britain unwilling to ally with USSR

↓

Nazi–Soviet Pact, 1939

**Terms of the Nazi–Soviet Pact**

10-year non-aggression agreement
Secret clauses re Baltic States and Poland

**Results**

Hailed as diplomatic triumph for Stalin
Lulled him into false sense of security
Gave Germany free rein in Western Europe
Left Soviet Union exposed to German attack in June 1941

# 5 Stalin's record by 1941

▶ *How did Stalin's reputation stand in 1941?*

On the eve of the launch of **Operation Barbarossa** in June 1941, Stalin's reputation in the Soviet Union could hardly have been higher.

**KEY TERM**

**Operation Barbarossa** The invasion of the Soviet Union, launched without formal warning by Hitler on 22 June 1941.

## Stalin's standing

Stalin was officially lauded as the great leader who had:

- Fulfilled the socialist revolution begun by Lenin.
- Purged the USSR of its internal traitors and enemies.
- Turned the USSR into a great modern economy through collectivisation and industrialisation.
- Made himself an outstanding world statesman.

These, of course, were achievements that Stalin claimed for himself through his propaganda machine. A more sober and more neutral estimate would have to include the negative side of Stalin's exercise of power since the late 1920s. His record judged in this way might include:

- Terror as a state policy.
- Authoritarian one-party rule by the CPSU.
- A single 'correct' ideology of communism as dictated by Stalin.
- A misguided belief in the supremacy of Communist economic planning. Stalin's policy of collectivisation was so disruptive that it permanently damaged Soviet agriculture and left the USSR incapable of feeding itself.
- His policy of enforced industrialisation achieved a remarkable short-term success but prevented the USSR from developing a truly modern economy.

It was the memory of Lenin's dominance of the Bolshevik Party that endured as the most powerful legacy of the 1917 Revolution. After 1917 reverence for the achievements of Lenin became a vital part of Communist tradition. It was Stalin's ability to suggest that he was continuing the work of Lenin that eased his own path to supremacy after 1924. Circumstances had made loyalty to the party and loyalty to Lenin inseparable. Similarly, by the late 1920s Stalin had succeeded in identifying his own authority with that of the rule of the party. This made it extremely difficult for his fellow Communists to oppose him. To criticise Stalin was equivalent to doubting Lenin, the party and the revolution.

The clear proof of how powerful Stalin had become was evident in the 1930s when he launched a series of purges of his real or imagined enemies in the government, the armed services and the party. From then until his death in 1953, he exercised absolute authority over the Soviet Union.

## Key debate

> *Was Stalin's absolutism a logical progression from the authoritarianism of Lenin?*

The reason why this was such a basic and important issue was that it went to the heart of the question as to whether applied Marxism was the perfect social and political system that its adherents claimed it to be. In Communist belief, the justification for the 1917 Revolution led by Lenin was that it had been the first stage in a process that would culminate in the creation of the perfect society. If that process had been corrupted there would have to be an explanation. How could a perfect system become imperfect?

To answer this, committed Communists set out to prove that Stalin had diverted Lenin's revolution away from its true Marxist course. They claimed that the mistakes and terrors of the Stalin years were an aberration caused by Stalin's pursuit of his own personal power. Stalin's methods were not, therefore a continuation of Lenin's policies but a departure from them; Stalinism was not a logical stage in the Communist revolution but a betrayal of it.

Interestingly, Stalin refused to allow the term 'Stalinism' to be used as if it represented something separate from Marxism. He always insisted that his task was to carry Lenin's ideas to fruition. Collectivisation, industrialisation, 'Socialism in One Country' were officially described as 'Marxism–Leninism–Stalinism in action'.

From exile, Trotsky challenged this: he claimed that Stalin had laid his dead bureaucratic hand on Russia, thus destroying the dynamic revolution that Lenin had created. Isaac Deutscher and Roy Medvedev, both of whom suffered personally under Stalin, followed Trotsky in suggesting that Stalin had perverted the basically democratic nature of Leninism into a personal dictatorship.

Alexander Solzhenitsyn, the leading dissident who underwent long years of imprisonment in the gulag, condemned the attempts to explain Stalinism in those terms. In 1974, he wrote that 'Stalin was a very consistent and faithful – if also very untalented – heir to the spirit of Lenin's teaching.' Solzhenitsyn regarded Stalin as a 'blind, mechanical executor of Lenin's will' and stressed that the apparatus of the police state was already in place when Stalin took over: one-party rule, the secret police, the use of terror tactics and show trials. Sozhenitsyn's analysis was backed by Western commentators such as Edward Crankshaw and Robert Conquest, who described Stalin's tyranny as simply a fully developed form of Lenin's essentially repressive creed of revolution.

Dmitri Volkogonov, the Russian biographer of the great trio who made the Russian Revolution, Lenin and Stalin and Trotsky, and who worked under Stalin, went further. He suggested that not only was there a direct line of continuity between Lenin and Stalin but the methods they used to impose communism on Russia meant that the Soviet Union could never become a truly modern state.

**EXTRACT 1**

**From D. Volkogonov, *The Rise and Fall of the Soviet Empire*, HarperCollins, 1998, pp. 84–5.**

*The system designed by Lenin was built by Stalin … The dictatorship of the proletariat became the dictatorship of a single party, which had in turn become the dictatorship of a single leader … Stalin personified the regime and symbolised a way of thinking and acting …*

*Stalinism, as the materialisation of Lenin's ideas, arose not only from the peculiarities of Russian history. Russia has always been a country of faith, the USSR no less, if only of the faith of anti-Christianity. Stalin was the embodiment of the system's drive for ideological faith …*

*The one-dimensional approach laid down by Lenin doomed Stalinism historically. Created as the theory and practice of 'Lenin's precepts', Stalinism from its inception was hidebound by ossified dogmatism. By welding the Party organisation to that of the state, Stalinism gradually reshaped the legions of 'revolutionaries' into an army of bureaucrats. By adopting revolutionary methods to speed up the natural course of events, Stalinism ultimately brought the country to real backwardness.*

Such interpretations were given powerful support by the opening up of the Soviet state archives in the 1990s, following the fall of communism and the break-up of the USSR. Such analysts as Robert Tucker, Richard Pipes and Walter Laqueur produced compelling evidence to establish the claim that Stalin, far from corrupting Lenin's policies, had fulfilled them. Pipes was insistent that all the main features of the tyranny that Stalin exerted over the Soviet state had been inherited directly from Lenin.

**EXTRACT 2**

**From R. Pipes, *Russia Under the Bolshevik Regime 1919–1924*, Harvill, 1994, p. 508.**

*Stalin was a true Leninist in that he faithfully followed his patron's political philosophy and practices. Every ingredient of what has come to be known as Stalinism save one – murdering fellow Communists – he had learned from Lenin, and that includes the two actions for which he is most severely condemned: collectivization and mass terror. Stalin's megalomania, his vindictiveness, his morbid paranoia, and other odious personal qualities should not obscure the fact that his ideology and modus operandi were Lenin's. A man of meager education, he had no other source of ideas.*

*By throttling democratic impulses in the party in order to protect his dictatorship, and by imposing on the Party a top-heavy command structure, Lenin ensured that the man who controlled the central party apparatus controlled the Party and through it, the state. And that man was Stalin.*

Strongly argued though the case for seeing a continuity between Leninism and Stalinism is, it is not the final word. For example, Stephen Cohen, an American revisionist historian, holds that the continuity thesis takes too little account of the complexities attaching to the notion of Stalinism, which needs much more analysis.

**EXTRACT 3**

**From S.F. Cohen, 'Bolshevism and Stalinism', in R.C. Tucker, editor, *Stalinism: Essays in Historical Interpretation*, Transaction Publishers, 1997, p. 24.**

*In treating Stalinism as 'full-blown' Bolshevism, and the Soviet 1930s as a function and extension of 1917, the main scholarly disservice of the continuity thesis has been to discourage close examination of Stalinism as a specific system with its own history. I am persuaded that essential, even definitive, aspects of Stalinism, including critical turning points in its history and the 'excesses,' cannot be understood apart from Stalin as a political personality …*

*It is important to shed the ahistorical habit of thinking of the Stalinist system as an unchanging phenomenon. The historical development of Stalinism must be traced and analyzed through its several stages …*

*We are confronted here with the difficulty inherent in applying Western concepts, whether of the Marxist or modernization variety, to a Soviet political and social reality shaped by Russian historical and cultural tradition.*

? How convincing as analyses of Stalinism are the arguments put forward in Extracts 1, 2 and 3?

Clearly, some historians think the evidence overwhelmingly points to the conclusion that Stalin fulfilled what Lenin had begun, while others regard this as essentially a Western interpretation which oversimplifies the issue. It is unlikely that there will ever be universal agreement over the precise nature of the Lenin–Stalin historical link.

## Defining Stalinism

As the key debate indicated, there is much dispute over what Stalinism actually was, but the following list suggests some of the principal features of the system which operated during the quarter of a century in which Stalin had mastery over the USSR, and which need to be considered when working towards a definition:

- Stalin ran the USSR by a bureaucratic system of government.
- Stalin completed the work begun by Lenin of turning revolutionary Russia into a one-party state in which all parties, other than the CPSU, were outlawed.
- Political and social control was maintained by a terror system whose main instruments were regular purges and show trials directed against the party, the armed services and the people.

- A climate of fear was deliberately created so that no one could relax or challenge Stalin's policies.
- Stalin created a command economy, with agriculture and industry centrally directed and no allowance made for local knowledge or initiative.
- Stalin's highly individual rule developed into a 'cult of personality' which led to his being regarded as the embodiment of the Communist Party and the nation
- Stalin encouraged the development of an elite *nomenklatura;* officials who were loyal to Stalin because it was on his favour that their privileges depended. This stifled all criticism and made every official complicit in Stalin's crimes.
- Stalin created a siege mentality in the USSR. Even in peacetime, Stalin insisted that the Soviet people had to be on permanent guard from enemies within and hostile nations outside.
- Stalin was as intense a nationalist as ever the tsars had been. Notwithstanding its claim to be leading an international revolution, the Soviet Union under Stalin abandoned the active pursuit of revolution, making its priority instead the strengthening of the USSR as a nation.
- The Comintern, officially pledged to foment international revolution, spent its time defending the interests of USSR.
- As the only Communist state in existence, the USSR was internationally isolated in a largely capitalist, hostile world.
- Stalin imposed his concept of 'Socialism in One Country', a policy which subordinated everything to the interests of the Soviet Union as a nation. This involved the rejection of the Trotskyist alternative of 'Permanent Revolution', which would have engaged the USSR in leading the movement for international revolution.
- Stalin's rule meant the suppression of any form of genuine democracy, since he operated on the principle, laid down by Lenin, of democratic centralism, which obliged members of the CPSU to accept uncritically and obey all orders and instructions handed down by the party leaders.
- Under Stalin it was claimed that the Soviet Union was a single-class nation. Recognition was given only to the proletariat, in whose name and by whose authority Stalin held power. It was the role of the proletariat to destroy the remnants of all other classes.
- The USSR recognised only one correct and acceptable ideology, Marxism–Leninism–Stalinism. All other political, philosophical or religious belief systems were rejected.

One can predict that no matter how studies of Stalin may develop, the points in the above list will remain central to any analysis.

## Chapter summary

The means Stalin chose to consolidate his political control of the Soviet Union were the purges. With the NKVD as the chief instrument of enforcement, Stalin organised the repression in three stages: the purges of the party, of the armed services and of the people. So extensive was this fiercely coercive system that the Soviet Union became a terror state. Despite the danger of this undermining any chance of genuine social cohesion, an increasingly paranoid Stalin pressed on unrelentingly, backed by a *nomenklatura* that saw in the purges the opportunity to become the new Soviet establishment.

Intense propaganda developed the cult of personality around Stalin, which portrayed him as a uniquely gifted leader successfully solving all the problems facing the Soviet Union and its people. In keeping with his concept of 'Socialism in One Country', Stalin adopted an essentially defensive attitude towards the other countries, seeking alliances rather than confrontation. The character of Stalinism remains a matter of debate, particularly on the question of whether there was a direct causal link between Leninism and Stalinism.

## Refresher questions

Use these questions to remind yourself of the key material covered in this chapter.

1. Why was Stalin able to extend the purges on such a huge scale?
2. What consequences followed the murder of Kirov in 1934?
3. In what sense did the post-Kirov purges mark 'Stalin's victory over the party'?
4. What were the main features of the Great Purge?
5. Was there any logic behind the purge of the armed services?
6. In what sense was Stalin's rule totalitarian?
7. What were the main characteristics of Stalin's cult of personality?
8. How was state propaganda used to promote Stalin's image?
9. Why was Stalin reluctant to give full support to Mao and the CCP in China?
10. Why was the Soviet Union willing to sign a non-aggression pact with Nazi Germany in 1939?
11. Was there an unbroken link between Leninism and Stalinism?
12. What was Stalin's record as national and party leader?

## Question practice

### ESSAY QUESTIONS

1. 'Stalin's aim in launching the Great Purge, 1936–9, was to make his power absolute in the Soviet Union.' How far do you agree with this statement?
2. Assess the reasons why there was so little opposition to the Stalinist purges of the 1930s.
3. How successfully had Stalin's cult of personality been developed by 1941?
4. 'It was Stalin's ability to suggest that he was continuing the work of Lenin that enabled him to establish his dominance of the Soviet Union between 1929 and 1941.' How far do you agree with this statement?

# OCR A level History

## Essay guidance

The assessment of this OCR Unit Y219 and Y249: Russia 1894–1941 depends on whether you are studying it for AS or A level:

- for the AS exam, you will answer one essay question from a choice of two, and one interpretation question, for which there is no choice
- for the A level exam, you will answer one essay question from a choice of two and one shorter essay question, also from a choice of two.

The guidance below is for answering both AS and A level essay questions. Guidance for the shorter essay question is at the end of this section. Guidance on answering interpretation questions is on page 255.

For both OCR AS and A level History, the types of essay questions set and the skills required to achieve a high grade for Unit Group 2 are the same. The skills are made very clear by both mark schemes, which emphasise that the answer must:

- focus on the demands of the question
- be supported by accurate and relevant factual knowledge
- be analytical and logical
- reach a supported judgement about the issue in the question.

There are a number of skills that you will need to develop to reach the higher levels in the marking bands:

- understand the wording of the question
- plan an answer to the question set
- write a focused opening paragraph
- avoid irrelevance and description
- write analytically
- write a conclusion which reaches a supported judgement based on the argument in the main body of the essay.

These skills will be developed in the section below, but are further developed in the 'Period Study' chapters of the *OCR A level History* series (British Period Studies and Enquiries).

### Understanding the wording of the question

To stay focused on the question set, it is important to read the question carefully and focus on the key words and phrases. Unless you directly address the demands of the question, you will not score highly. Remember, in questions where there is a named factor you must write a good analytical paragraph about the given factor, even if you argue that it was not the most important.

### Planning an answer

Many plans simply list dates and events – this should be avoided as it encourages a descriptive or narrative, rather than analytical, answer. The plan should be an outline of your argument; this means you need to think carefully about the issues you intend to discuss and their relative importance before you start writing your answer. It should therefore be a list of the factors or issues you are going to discuss and a comment on their relative importance.

| Types of AS and A level questions you might find in the exams | The factors and issues you would need to consider to answer them |
|---|---|
| 1 Assess the reasons why the Reds won the Russian Civil War. | Weigh up the relative importance of a range of factors as to why the Reds won the Russian Civil War. |
| 2 To what extent was White weakness the most important cause of the victory of the Reds in the Russian Civil War? | Weigh up the relative importance of a range of factors, including comparing the importance of White weakness with other factors. |
| 3 'The leadership of Trotsky was the most important reason for the victory of the Reds in the Russian Civil War.' How far do you agree? | Weigh up the relative importance of a range of factors, including comparing the importance of Trotsky's leadership with other issues to reach a balanced judgement. |
| 4 How successful was Trotsky as the Reds' war leader? | This question requires you to make a judgement about Trotsky's war leadership. As well as thinking about factors you need to think about issues such as:<br>• Trotsky's relationship with Lenin<br>• His success as a converted Menshevik<br>• His suppression of the trade unions<br>• His role as a political figure and in the organisation of the war<br>• His administrative abilities<br>• Red brutality. |

For question 1 in the table, your plan might look something like this:

### Logistical control

- Reds controlled central areas and railways.
- Reds retained Moscow and Leningrad.
- Reds maintained regular supplies.
- Whites, in contrast, were widely scattered and so unable to maintain supply lines effectively.
- Whites denied control of the railways were always at a logistical disadvantage.

### Leadership

- Lenin's strong political leadership and Trotsky's strong military leadership combined to give the Reds a major advantage.
- The Whites never developed a strong central committed leadership.

### Division

- As a consequence of strong leadership, the Reds able to present a united front.
- The White forces were divided between various leaders who seldom co-operated effectively.

### Morale

- Reds, inspired by a committed sense of purpose, maintained high morale.
- Whites, without agreed strategic and political aims, suffered low morale.

## The opening paragraph

Many students spend time 'setting the scene'; the opening paragraph becomes little more than an introduction to the topic – this should be avoided. Instead, make it clear what your argument is going to be. Offer your view about the issue in the question – what was the most important reason for the victory of the Reds? – and then introduce the other issues you intend to discuss. In the plan it is suggested that the Reds' control of the central areas and railways was the most important factor. This should be made clear in the opening paragraph, with a brief comment as to why – central control allowed the Reds to maintain vital supplies and move troops swiftly, advantages denied to the Whites. This will give the examiner a clear overview of your essay, rather than it being a mystery tour where the argument becomes clear only at the end. You should also refer to any important issues that the question raises. For example:

*The most important reason why the Reds won the Civil War was the availability of regular supplies*[1]. *Although there were many other factors, including leadership, military strength and White disunity, it was the availability of regular supplies that enabled the Reds to assert control*[2]. *The Reds' logistical advantages proved critical during a two-year struggle that ranged over a wide area*[3].

1 The student is aware that there were a number of important reasons.
2 The answer offers a clear view as to what it considers to be the most important reason – a thesis is offered.
3 There is a brief justification to support the thesis.

## Avoid irrelevance and description

A well-prepared plan will stop you from simply writing all you know about why the Reds won and force you to weigh up the role of a range of factors. Similarly, it should also help prevent you from simply writing about the military events of the Civil War. You will not lose marks if you do that, but neither will you gain any credit, and you will waste valuable time.

## Write analytically

This is perhaps the hardest, but most important skill you need to develop. An analytical approach can be helped by ensuring that the opening sentence of each paragraph introduces an idea, which directly answers the question and is not just a piece of factual information. In a very strong answer it should be possible to simply read the opening sentences of all the paragraphs and know what argument is being put forward.

If we look at question 2 on the importance of White weakness (see page 255), the following are possible sentences with which to start paragraphs:

- White weakness became an important factor once it became clear that the Reds were fighting a desperate war of survival that they could not afford to lose.
- Red strength, particularly in regard to their maintenance of supplies, ensured that in a long two-year war they were more likely to be successful.
- The political leadership of Lenin was important because he was able to keep the Red armies and their civilian supporters wholly committed to the struggle.
- Trotsky provided the military leadership that raised Red morale and contrasted sharply with White half-heartedness.

You would then go on to discuss both sides of the argument raised by the opening sentence, using relevant knowledge about the issue to support each side of the argument. The final sentences of the paragraph would reach a judgement on the role played by the factor you are discussing in the victory of the Reds. This approach would ensure that the final sentence of each paragraph links back to the actual question you are answering. If you can do this for each paragraph you will have a series of mini-essays, which discuss a factor and reach a conclusion or judgement about the importance of that factor or issue. For example:

*Military leadership was an important factor in securing the Reds' victory, but this would not have been conclusive had the Red armies not been able to move rapidly, sure in the knowledge that they would be readily and adequately supplied*[1]. *It was the Whites' inability to match the Reds in speed of movement and maintenance of vital resources that weakened morale and led to growing disputes among the White generals, whose separate armies rarely acted as a united force and failed to link with the foreign interventionist forces. Aware of the Reds' growing logistical superiority, the morale of the Whites sank, leaving them weakened militarily and psychologically.*[2]

1 The sentence puts forward a clear view that military leadership needed other supporting factors to make it a conclusive reason.
2 The claim is developed by referring to some of the evidence that supports the argument.

### The conclusion

The conclusion provides the opportunity to bring together all the interim judgements to reach an overall judgement about the question. Using the interim judgements will ensure that your conclusion is based on the argument in the main body of the essay and does not offer a different view. For the essay answering question 1 (see page 259), you can decide what was the most important factor in the victory of the Reds, but for questions 2 and 3 you will need to comment on the importance of the named factor – White weakness or Trotsky's leadership – as well as explain why you think a different factor is more important, if that has been your line of argument. Or, if you think the named factor is the most important, you will need to explain why that was more important than the other factors or issues you have discussed.

Consider the following conclusion to question 2: To what extent was White weakness the most important cause of the victory of the Reds in the Russian Civil War?

*Although the Whites certainly had numerous limitations such as low morale, the incompatible aims of their four major leaders and the failure to use foreign support effectively, the weakness of the Whites was not the most important factor in their defeat***[1]***. After all, weaknesses have to be exploited. Unless the Reds had had the means to do this they could not have been successful. But, under Lenin's political direction and Trotsky's military leadership, the Reds used their control of the railways and their geographical and logistical advantages, initially to defend their position, and then to take the offensive against the separated White forces***[2]***. It is these considerations that lead to the conclusion that, although White weakness was clearly an important factor, it was Red strength that was the most important cause of the Reds' victory in the Russian Civil War.*

1. This is a strong conclusion because it considers the importance of the named factor – White weakness – but weighs that up against a range of other factors to reach an overall judgement.
2. It is also able to show links between the other factors to reach a balanced judgement, which brings in a range of issues, showing the interplay between them.

## How to write a good essay for the A level short-answer questions

The short-answer question will require you to weigh up the importance of two factors or issues in relation to an event or a development. For example:

> Which of the following was the greater threat to the tsarist government by 1917?
>
> (i) Social unrest in Petrograd.
>
> (ii) Opposition in the *duma*.
>
> Explain your answer with reference to both (i) and (ii).

As with the long essays, the skills required are made very clear by the mark scheme, which emphasises that the answer must:

- analyse the two issues
- evaluate the two issues
- support your analysis and evaluation with detailed and accurate knowledge
- reach a supported judgement as to which factor was more important in relation to the issue in the question.

The skills required are very similar to those for the longer essays. However, there is no need for a long introduction, nor are you required to compare the two factors or issues in the main body of the essay, although either approach can still score full marks. For example, an opening could be:

*Social unrest in Petrograd was certainly a threat to the tsarist government since it showed the Russian people's growing dissatisfaction with the way the war had reduced their living conditions***[1]***. However, the duma opposition was protest from within the top level of political society* *and consequently the more disturbing. By the end of 1916, Russia's poor performance in the war had brought hardship to ordinary Russians and disillusion to those within the highly influential political class. It was the latter who made the first open move against the government, thereby giving greater significance to popular protests***[2]**. *Street protests were containable. Duma opposition threatened government itself***[3]**.

1. The answer explains why street protests were taking place.
2. The implications of this development are considered.
3. The wider implications are hinted at, and this could be developed and contrasted with the opposition within the *duma*.

The answer could go on to argue how the resistance within the *duma* was a deeply disturbing development for the government since it revealed that the upper class, by tradition the natural supporters of tsardom, had turned against it.

Most importantly, the conclusion must reach a supported judgement as to the relative importance of the factors in relation to the issue in the question. For example:

*Both the developments were a serious worry to the tsarist government. However, the Petrograd street protests were not specifically against the government, whereas the duma opposition was a direct attack on it and, therefore, the greater threat***[1]**. *The people who demonstrated on the streets had been angered by the grim conditions that the war had brought. Food and fuel shortages and long casualty lists had made them embittered. But their anger lacked focus; it did not directly challenge the tsar's government. In contrast, the duma protests were expressly anti-government. Milyukov, the Kadet leader, fiercely accused the government of stupidity and treason and declared that the duma would fight until the government removed itself. The threat could not have been greater***[2]**.

1. The response explains the relative importance of the two factors and offers a clear view.
2. The response supports the view offered in the opening sentence and therefore reaches a supported judgement.

# Interpretations guidance

## How to write a good essay

The guidance below is for answering the AS interpretation question for OCR Unit Y249: Russia 1894–1941. Guidance on answering essay questions is on page 259.

The OCR specification outlines the two key topics from which the interpretation question will be drawn. For this book these are:

- The rule of Tsar Nicholas II.
- The Civil War and Lenin.

Chapters 1, 2 and 5 of this book cover the AS key topics for interpretation questions.

The specification also lists the main debates to consider.

It is also worth remembering that this is an AS unit and not an A level historiography paper. The aim of this element of the Unit is to develop an awareness that the past can be interpreted in different ways.

The question will require you to assess the strengths and limitations of a historian's interpretation of an issue related to one of the specified key topics.

You should be able to place the interpretation within the context of the wider historical debate on the key topic.

There are a number of skills you need to develop if you are to reach the higher levels in the mark bands:

- To be able to understand the wording of the question.
- To be able to explain the interpretation and how it fits into the debate about the issue or topic.
- To be able to consider both the strengths and weaknesses of the interpretation using your own knowledge of the topic.

Here is an example of a question you will face in the exam:

> Read the interpretation and then answer the question that follows:
>
> 'Nicholas II faced no popular pressure to abdicate; the pressure stemmed exclusively from the ranks of politicians and generals who thought the Crown's removal essential to victory.'
>
> (From Richard Pipes, *Three Whys of the Russian Revolution*, 1998.)
>
> Evaluate the strengths and limitations of this interpretation, making reference to other interpretations that you have studied.

## Approaching the question

There are several steps to take to answer this question:

### 1 Explain the interpretation and put it into the context of the debate on the topic

In the first paragraph you should explain the interpretation and the view it is putting forward. This paragraph places the interpretation in the context of the historical debate and explains any key words or phrases relating to the given interpretation. A suggested opening might be as follows:

*The interpretation puts forward the view that it was not the rising of the people which forced the tsar to abdicate. The author suggests that the exclusive factor was the demand of the army leaders and the politicians who pressured Nicholas II into giving up the throne***[1]***. In referring to the role of the army and the politicians, Pipes is introducing the idea that the February Revolution was not a rising 'from below' but a coup 'at the top'. Tsardom was not overthrown; it collapsed from within***[2]***. Popular demonstrations did take place but the vital moves were made by the upper class. The interpretation argues that the events of February were not a people's revolution but a change of power at the top***[3]***.*

1 The opening two sentences are clearly focused on the given interpretation. They clearly explain that the February Revolution was 'exclusively' a result of the pressure applied by the army and the politicians.
2 The second sentence explains that the 'pressure' on Nicholas II to abdicate came from the top of society, and this is developed in the following sentence.
3 The last sentence begins to develop the idea, advanced by Pipes, that the common perception of the tsar's being overthrown by the rising of the people is a historical misjudgement.

In order to place Pipes' view in the context of the debate about the importance of various factors, you could go on to suggest that there are other important factors that have to be considered, including the economic situation, living conditions in Petrograd, and the progress of the war against Germany and Austria.

## 2 Consider the strengths of the interpretation

In the second paragraph consider the strengths of the interpretation by bringing in your own knowledge that supports the given view. A suggested response might start as follows when considering the strengths of the view:

*Pipes makes a strong case. It was on the advice of the army leaders and those in government, who had been formerly loyal to the tsar, that Nicholas chose to abdicate***[1]***. The first open challenge to the tsar had come when the duma refused his order to disband. It was the leading generals in the army command who had physically prevented Nicholas returning to Petrograd from the front by diverting his train and telling him that his cause was hopeless***[2]***. These actions combined to convince the tsar that those who should have been his natural supporters were no longer willing to support or defend him. It did not need the popular risings to turn this into a revolution. The revolution had already taken place***[3]***.*

1 The answer clearly focuses on the strength of the given interpretation.
2 The response provides some support for the view in the interpretation from the candidate's own knowledge. This is not particularly detailed or precise, but could be developed in the remainder of the paragraph.
3 The final sentence links together the two factors.

In the remainder of the paragraph you could show how these two factors were linked and how the full impact of the popular risings came after the tsar had met resistance from within the army and the government.

## 3 Consider the limitations of the interpretation

In the third paragraph consider the limitations of the given interpretation by bringing in knowledge that can challenge the given interpretation and explains what is missing from the interpretation.

A suggested response might start as follows when considering the limitations of the view:

*However, there are a number of qualifications that could be applied to Pipes' interpretation***[1]***. Most importantly, it does not take into account the prevailing economic conditions in Petrograd. By saying that the pressure on the tsar stemmed 'exclusively' from stavka and the politicians, the author does not allow for the threat posed to the government by increasingly violent street demonstrations. The pressure that the high command and politicians applied to the tsar to abdicate was a response to the fear they had of an uncontrollable movement by a hungry populace, embittered by three years of war***[2]***. The interpretation also ignores the growing, organised militancy of the factory workers in Petrograd***[3]***.*

1 The opening makes it very clear that this paragraph will deal with the limitations of the interpretation.
2 It explains clearly the first weakness and provides evidence to support the claim. The evidence is not detailed and could be developed, but the answer focuses on explaining the weakness, rather than providing lots of detail.
3 Although more detail could have been provided about the influence of economic factors, the answer goes on to explain a second limitation, lack of reference to the growth of a militant worker movement, and this could be developed in the remainder of the paragraph.

Answers might go on to argue that a key area of research among historians is the role of worker movements in 1917. It is arguable that the organisation, for example of the Putilov factory workers in Petrograd, represented a swelling wave of working-class agitation that has to be taken account of in any analysis of the February Revolution.
The paragraph might, therefore, suggest that the interpretation provides a partial answer which needs further development. There is no requirement for you to reach a judgement as to which view is more convincing or valid.

## Assessing the interpretation

In assessing the interpretation you should consider the following:

- Identify and explain the issue being discussed in the interpretation: the factors that led to *stavka* and the *duma* pressing Nicholas to abdicate.
- Explain the view being put forward in the interpretation: the interpretation argues that it was 'exclusively' pressure from the generals and politicians that led to the abdication.
- Explain how the interpretation fits into the wider debate about the issue: the relative importance of the conflicting notions of a coup 'at the top' and 'revolution from below', economic factors, conditions in Petrograd, the impact of an increasingly desperate war situation and the growth of worker militancy.

In other interpretations you might need to:

- Consider whether there is any particular emphasis within the interpretation that needs explaining or commenting on, for example, if the interpretation says something is 'the only reason' or 'the single most important reason'.
- Comment on any concepts that the interpretation raises, such as 'exclusively', 'revolution from below', 'collapse from within'.
- Consider the focus of the interpretation, for example, if an interpretation focuses on an urban viewpoint, what was the rural viewpoint? Is the viewpoint given in the interpretation the same for all areas of society?

Summary: this is what is important for answering interpretation questions:

- Explaining the interpretation.
- Placing it in the context of the wider historical debate about the issue it considers.
- Explaining the strengths *and* weaknesses of the view in the extract.

# Glossary of terms

**Absolutism** A system, similar to totalitarianism, in which authoritarian control is exercised by government over all aspects of society.

**Accommodationism** The idea that the Bolsheviks should co-operate with the Provisional Government and work with the other revolutionary and reforming parties.

**Administrative fiat** Strict command from above.

***Agents provocateurs*** Government agents who infiltrated opposition movements to stir up trouble so that the ringleaders could be exposed.

**Agrarian economy** A system in which food is produced on the land by arable and dairy farming and then traded.

**All-Russian Congress of Soviets** A gathering of representatives from all the soviets formed in Russia since February.

**Amazons** A special corps of female soldiers recruited by Kerensky to show the patriotism of Russia's women in the anti-German struggle.

**Anarchy** Absence of government or authority, leading to disorder.

**Anti-Comintern Pact** An alliance formed between Germany, Italy and Japan.

**Anti-Semitism** Hatred of the Jewish race; for centuries Russia had been notorious for its vicious treatment of the Jews.

**ARA** The American Relief Association, formed to provide food and medical supplies for post-war Europe.

**Autocratic** The absolute rule of one person – in Russia this meant the tsar.

**Autonomy** National self-government.

**Balkans** The area of south-eastern Europe (fringed by Austria-Hungary to the north, the Black Sea to the east, Turkey to the south and the Aegean Sea to the west), which had largely been under Turkish control.

**Baltic States** Estonia, Latvia and Lithuania.

**Bi-cameral** A parliament made up of two chambers, an upper and a lower.

**Bolsheviks** From *bolshinstvo*, Russian for majority.

**Bosphorus** The narrow waterway linking the Black Sea with the Dardanelles.

**Bourgeois experts** A mocking reference to those workers whose skills had enabled them to earn higher wages and thus be less committed to building the new Russia.

**Bourgeoisie** The owners of capital, the boss class, who exploited the workers but who would be overthrown by them in the revolution to come.

**Buffer state** An area that lies between two states, providing protection for each against the other.

**Bureaucratisation** The growth in power of the Secretariat, which was able to make decisions and operate policies without reference to ordinary party members.

**Cadres** Party members who were sent into factories and on to construction sites to spy and report back on managers and workers.

**Capital** The essential financial resource which provides the means for investment and expansion.

**Capitalist methods of finance** The system in which the owners of private capital (money) increase their wealth by making loans on which interest has to be paid later by the borrower.

**Capitalists** Russia's financiers and industrialists.

**Catechism** The manual used for instructing the people in the essential points of the faith.

**Central Powers** Germany, Austria-Hungary and Turkey.

***Cheka*** 'The All-Russian Extraordinary Commission for Fighting Counter-Revolution, Sabotage and Speculation', a long title for what was essentially a secret police force, modelled on the tsarist *Okhrana*.

**Class struggle** A continuing conflict at every stage of history between those who possess economic and political power and those who do not – in simple terms 'the haves' and 'the have-nots'.

**Collective farms** (*Kolkhozy* in Russian.) Run as co-operatives in which the peasants pooled their resources and shared their labour and wages.

**Collective security** Nations acting together to protect individual states from attack.

**Collectivisation** The taking over by the Soviet state of the land and property previously owned by the peasants, accompanied by the requirement that the peasants now live and work communally.

**Comintern** The Communist International, a body set up in Moscow in March 1919 to organise worldwide revolution.

**Command economy** A system in which all the main areas of economic activity are under central government control and direction.

**Commissar for foreign affairs** Equivalent to the secretary of state in the USA or the foreign secretary in Britain.

**Commissar for nationalities** Minister responsible for liaising with the non-Russian national minorities.

**Commissars** Russian for ministers: Lenin chose the word because he said 'it reeked of blood'.

**Commissions** The holding of officer rank.

**Committee system** A process in which the *duma* deputies formed various subgroups to consider particular issues.

***Confidant*** A person in whom another places a special trust and to whom one confides intimate secrets.

**Conscription** The forcing of large numbers of peasants into the army or navy.

**Constitutional monarchy** A system of government in which the king or emperor rules but governs only through elected representatives whose decisions he cannot countermand.

**Co-operatives** Groups of workers or farmers working together on their own enterprise.

**Cossacks** The remnants of the elite cavalry regiment of the tsars.

**Council of People's Commissars** A cabinet of ministers, responsible for creating government policies.

**CPSU** The Communist Party of the Soviet Union, the new name for the Bolshevik Party from 1918 onwards.

**Cult of personality** The projection through constant propaganda of an individual as a heroic figure above ordinary politics and, therefore entitled to exercise unlimited authority.

**'Dark masses'** Used contemptuously in the imperial court and government circles to describe the peasants, who made up four-fifths of the population.

***De facto*** 'By the very fact' – a term used to denote the real situation, as compared to what it should or might be in theory or in law.

**'Decree against terrorist acts'** An order giving the NKVD limitless powers to pursue the enemies of the state and the party.

**De-Stalinisation** The movement, begun by Nikita Khrushchev in 1956, to expose Stalin's crimes and mistakes against the party, which for the first time revealed the scale of the purges.

**Dialectic** The violent struggle which takes place in nature and in human society between opposites.

***Diktat*** A settlement imposed on a weaker nation by a stronger one.

**Double-agent** A government agent who pretends to be spying for the opposition against the authorities but who reports plans and secrets back to the authorities.

**Dual Authority** Lenin first coined this term to describe the balance of power between the Provisional Government and the Petrograd soviet.

***Duma*** The Russian parliament, which existed from 1906 to 1917.

**Economism** Putting the improvement of the workers' conditions before the need for revolution.

**Emancipation Decree of 1861** This reform had abolished serfdom – a Russian form of slavery in which the landowner had total control over the peasants who lived or worked on his land.

***Émigré*** One who flees from his own country; in the Russian case, *émigrés* were those who left after October 1917 from fear or a desire to plan a counter-strike against the Bolsheviks.

**Entente** An agreement to remain on friendly terms.

**Entrepreneurialism** The dynamic, expansionist attitude associated with Western commercial and industrial activity in this period.

**Factionalism** The forming within the party of groups with a particular complaint or grievance.

***Fait accompli*** An established situation that cannot be changed.

**Finance-capital** The resource used by stronger countries to exploit weaker ones. By investing heavily in another country, a stronger power made that country dependent on it.

**General strike** An organised stoppage by all or a majority of the workers.

**Ghettoes** Particular areas where Jews were concentrated and to which they were restricted.

**Gigantomania** The worship of size for its own sake.

**God's anointed** At their coronation tsars were anointed with holy oil to symbolise that they governed by divine will.

**Gold standard** The system in which a nation's basic unit of currency, in Russia's case the rouble, had a fixed gold content, thus giving it strength when exchanged against other currencies.

***Gosplan*** The government body responsible for national economic planning.

**Great Depression** A period of severe economic stagnation which began in the USA in 1929 and lasted until the mid-1930s, affecting the whole of the industrial world. Marxists regarded it as a portent of the final collapse of capitalism.

**'Great spurt'** The spread of industry and the increase in production that occurred in the 1890s.

**Haemophilia** A genetic condition in which the blood does not clot, leaving the sufferer with painful bruising and internal bleeding, which can be life threatening.

**Icons** Two-dimensional representations of Jesus Christ and the saints, one of the great glories of the Orthodox Church.

**Indemnities** Payment of war costs demanded by the victors from the defeated.

**Industrialisation** The introduction of a vast scheme for the building of factories, which would produce heavy goods such as iron and steel.

**Inflation rate** A measure of the decline in the value of money over a period of time, more money being needed to buy the same quantity of goods.

**Intelligentsia** A cross-section of the educated and more enlightened members of Russian society who wanted to see their nation adopt progressive changes along Western lines.

**Interior minister** Equivalent to Britain's home secretary.

**International revolutionaries** Those Marxists who were willing to sacrifice mere national interests in the cause of the worldwide rising of the workers.

***Isvestiya*** Translates as *The Times*.

**KPD** The German Communist Party.

***Kulaks*** The Bolshevik term for the class of allegedly rich, exploiting peasants.

**Labourists** The SRs as a party officially boycotted the elections to the first *duma*, but stood as Labourists.

**League of Nations** The body set up in 1919 with the aim of resolving international disputes and so maintaining world peace.

**'Left Communists'** Those Bolsheviks who were convinced that their first task was to consolidate the October Revolution by driving the German imperialist armies from Russia.

**Left SRs** Social revolutionaries who sided with the Bolsheviks in their recognition of the legitimacy of the peasant land seizures and in their demand that Russia withdraw from the war.

**Legislative *duma*** A parliament with law-making powers.

**Leningrad** Petrograd had been renamed in Lenin's honour.

**Liberal ideas** Notions that called for limitations on the power of rulers and greater freedom for the people.

**Little Father** A traditional term denoting the tsar's paternal care of his people.

**Mandate** The authority to govern granted by a majority of the people through elections.

**Marshal of the Soviet Union** Equivalent to a field marshal or a five-star general.

**Martial law** The placing of the population under direct military authority.

**Marxism–Leninism** The notion that Marx's scientific analysis of class war had been developed by Lenin into a practical, workable programme.

**Marxism–Leninism–Stalinism** The concept of an ideological continuity between the founder of Marxism and its great interpreters, Lenin and Stalin.

**May Day** 'Labour Day', usually 1 May, traditionally regarded as a special occasion for honouring the workers and the achievements of socialism.

**Mensheviks** From *menshinstvo*, Russian for minority.

**Militia** Local citizens called together and granted arms to deal with a crisis requiring force.

***Mir*** The traditional village community.

**Monarchists** Reactionaries who wanted a restoration of tsardom.

**National insurance** A system of providing workers with state benefits, such as unemployment pay and medical treatment, in return for the workers' contributing regularly to a central fund.

**Nepmen** Those who stood to gain from the free trading permitted under NEP: the rich peasants, the retailers, the traders and the small-scale manufacturers.

**Nepotism** A system in which positions are gained through family connections rather than on merit.

***Nomenklatura*** The Soviet establishment, an elite set of privileged officials who ran the party machine.

**Non-determinist approach** Rejection of the idea that history follows a fixed, inevitable course.

***Obschina*** Peasant communes set up within the localities.

**'October deserters'** Those Bolsheviks who in October 1917, believing that the party was not yet strong enough, had advised against a Bolshevik rising.

**OGPU** Succeeded the *Cheka* as the state security force. In turn, it became the NKVD, the MVD and the KGB.

***Okhrana*** The tsarist secret police, whose special task was to hunt down subversives who challenged the tsarist regime.

**Operation Barbarossa** The invasion of the Soviet Union, launched without formal warning by Hitler on 22 June 1941.

**Orgburo** Organisation Bureau, which turned policies into practice.

**Paranoia** A persecution complex which gives sufferers the conviction that they are surrounded by malicious enemies.

**Parliamentary-bourgeois republic** Lenin's contemptuous term for the Provisional Government, which he dismissed as an unrepresentative mockery that had simply replaced the rule of the tsar with the rule of the reactionary *duma*.

**Party card** The official CPSU warrant granting membership to the holder. It was a prized possession in Soviet Russia since it entitled the holder to a wide range of privileges, such as quality accommodation, higher food rations, access to health care and education for the member's children.

**'Party democracy'** The right of all party members to express their opinion on policy.

**Passive disobedience** Opposing government not by violent challenge but by refusing to obey particular laws.

**Patronage** The right to appoint individuals to official posts in the party and government.

**The 'people'** The part of the population that the SRs believed truly represented the character and will of the Russian nation.

**People's militia** A new set of volunteer law-enforcement officers drawn from ordinary civilians.

**Petrograd** For patriotic reasons, soon after the war began, the German name for the capital, St Petersburg, was changed to the Russian form, Petrograd.

**Pogroms** Fierce persecutions which often involved the wounding or killing of Jews and the destruction of their property.

**Politburo** The Political Bureau, responsible for major policy decisions.

**Political activists** Those who believed that necessary change could be achieved only through direct action.

**Political commissars** Party officials who accompanied the officers and reported on their political correctness.

**Political correctness** Conformity to a prescribed set of opinions imposed by social pressure and political control.

**Political expediency** Pursuing a course of action with the primary aim of gaining a political advantage.

**Popular front** An alliance of socialist and progressive parties.

**Populists** *Narodniks*, from the Russian word for 'the people'.

**Private enterprise** Economic activity organised by individuals or companies, not the government.

**Progressists** A party of businessmen who favoured moderate reform.

**Progressive** Promoting necessary change.

**Progressives** Those who believed in parliamentary government for Russia.

**Prohibition** The state's banning of the production and sale of alcohol.

**Proletariat** The exploited industrial workers who would triumph in the last great class struggle.

**Quantitative easing (QE)** The printing of extra currency notes to meet the demand for ready money; a risky process since the money is not tied to an actual increase in genuine wealth.

**Radicalisation** A movement towards more sweeping or revolutionary ideas.

**Radicalism** The desire to change society fundamentally, literally at its roots.

**Reactionary** Resistant to any form of progressive change.

**Red Guards** A force, some 10,000 in number, largely made up at this time of elderly men recruited from the workers in the factories.

**Reformers** Strong critics of the tsarist system who believed it could be changed for the better by pressure from without and reform from within.

**Reparations** Payment of war costs by the loser to the victor.

**Representative government** A form of rule in which ordinary people choose their government and have the power to replace it if it does not serve their interests.

**Requisitioning** State-authorised takeover of property or resources.

**Revolution from below** The Communist Party consistently claimed that the 1917 Revolution had been a genuine rising of the people rather than a power grab by the Bolsheviks.

**Revolutionaries** Those who believed that Russia could not progress unless the tsarist system was destroyed.

**Revolutionary socialism** The belief that change could be achieved only through the violent overthrow of the tsarist system.

**Rightists** Not a single party; they represented a range of conservative views from right of centre to extreme reaction.

**Romanov dynasty** The royal house that ruled Russia between 1613 and 1917.

**Rural crisis** The problem of land shortage and overpopulation in the countryside produced by the huge increase in the number of people living in Russia by the late nineteenth century.

**Russian constituent assembly** A full gathering of the elected representatives of the Russian people.

***Samogon*** Illicitly distilled vodka, the equivalent of 'moonshine' or 'hooch', Western forms of unlicensed alcohol.

**Schlieffen Plan** A strategy entailing a lightning knockout blow against France, which would then enable German forces to turn fully on Russia.

**'Second revolution'** The modernisation of the Soviet economy by means of state direction and central control.

**Secretariat** A form of civil service that administered policies.

**Serbian nationalists** Activists struggling for Serbia's independence from Austria-Hungary.

**'Slavophiles'** Those who regarded Western values as corrupting and urged that the nation should preserve itself as 'holy Russia', glorying in its Slav culture and traditions.

**Smolny** The Bolshevik headquarters in Petrograd, housed in what had been a young ladies' finishing school.

**Social Democrats** The All-Russian Social Democratic Workers' Party.

**Soviet** Russian word for a council made up of elected representatives.

***Sovnarkom*** Russian for government or cabinet.

**Spartacists** Named after Spartacus, the leader of a slave rebellion in ancient Rome.

***Starets*** Russian for holy man, the name given to Rasputin by the impressionable peasants who believed he had superhuman powers.

**State capitalism** The direction and control of the economy by the government, using its central power and authority.

**State farms** (*Sovkhozy* in Russian.) Contained peasants working directly for the state, which paid them a wage.

**State grain procurements** Enforced collections of fixed quotas of grain from the peasants.

***Stavka*** The high command of the Russian army.

**Storming** An intensive period of work to meet a high set target. Despite the propaganda with which it was introduced, storming proved a very inefficient form of industrial labour and was soon abandoned.

**System of dating** Until February 1918 Russia used the Julian calendar, which was thirteen days behind the Gregorian calendar, the one used in most Western countries by this time. That is why different books may give different dates for the same event. This book uses the older dating for the events of 1917.

**Tariffs** Duties imposed on foreign goods to keep their prices high and, therefore, discourage importers from bringing them into the country.

**Tax in kind** The peasant surrendering a certain amount of his produce, equivalent to a fixed sum of money.

**'Telescoped revolution'** The notion that the final two stages of revolution, bourgeois and proletarian, could be compressed into one.

**'Testament'** A set of reflections and comments that Lenin made on his fellow Communist leaders.

**'To deliver the votes'** To use control of the party machine to gain majority support in key divisions.

**Total war** A struggle in which the whole nation, people, resources and institutions, is involved.

**Totalitarianism** A system in which a regime controls society in all its various features, political, cultural, economic, communal and personal.

**Triple Entente** Not a formal alliance, but a declared willingness by three powers to co-operate.

**Triumvirate** A ruling or influential bloc of three people.

**Union of Municipal Councils** A set of patriotic urban local councils.

**Union of *Zemstvos*** A set of patriotic rural local councils.

**United Opposition** The group led by Kamenev and Zinoviev, sometimes known as the New Opposition, who called for an end to NEP and the adoption of a rapid industrialisation programme.

**Universal suffrage** An electoral system in which all adults have the right to vote.

***Vesenkha*** The Supreme Council of the National Economy, later known as *Gosplan*.

***Vozhd*** Russian for supreme leader, equivalent to *Führer* in German.

**War-credits** Money loaned on easy repayment terms to Russia to finance its war effort.

**'Westerners'** Those who believed that to remain a great nation Russia would have to adopt the best features of the advanced countries of Western Europe.

**White Sea Canal** In fact three canals linking Leningrad with the White Sea; built predominantly by forced labourers, who died in their thousands, the canal proved practically worthless since it was hardly used after construction.

***Zemgor*** The joint body that devoted itself to helping Russia's war wounded.

***Zemstva*** These local councils were elected bodies, but the voting regulations left them very much in the hands of the landowners.

# Further reading

## Books relevant to the whole period

**David Christian, *Imperial and Soviet Russia* (Macmillan, 1997)**
A very helpful combination of documents, commentary and analysis across the whole period

**Michael Court, *The Soviet Colossus History and Aftermath* (M.E. Sharpe, 1996)**
A clear informed narrative from the fall of tsardom to the fall of Khrushchev and beyond

**Sheila Fitzpatrick, *The Russian Revolution 1917–1932* (Oxford University Press, 1994)**
A short, stimulating survey by a celebrated expert in the field

**Geoffrey Hosking, *Russia and the Russians* (Allen Lane, 2001)**
A very readable coverage of the whole period by a leading authority

**Martin Malia, *The Soviet Tragedy: A History of Socialism in Russia, 1917–1991* (Free Press, 1994)**
A survey of why the 74-year Soviet experiment failed

**Martin McCauley, *The Rise and Fall of the Soviet Union: 1917–1991* (Routledge, 2013)**
Especially good on political and cultural developments

**Martin McCauley, *Who's Who in Russian History since 1900* (Routledge, 1997)**
An exceptionally helpful reference book of mini-biographies

**Alec Nove, *An Economic History of the USSR* (Penguin, 1992)**
Established as the most reliable short account of economic developments across the period

**Richard Sakwa, *The Rise and Fall of the Soviet Union 1917–1991* (Routledge, 1999)**
An excellent selection of key documents, linked with a very well-informed commentary

**Robert Service, *The Penguin History of Modern Russia: From Tsarism to the Twenty-first Century* (Penguin, 2009)**
Informed coverage of the whole period by an outstanding Western historian

**Ian D. Thatcher, editor, *Regime and Society in Twentieth-Century Russia* (Macmillan, 1999)**
A set of important essays by international scholars, analysing key themes such as late tsarist Russia, Lenin and Trotsky

**Dmitri Volkogonov, *The Rise and Fall of the Soviet Empire: Political Leaders from Lenin to Gorbachev* (HarperCollins, 1998)**
Intrinsically valuable as an analysis and made more so by the fact that the Russian author lived and worked under Stalin

## Website

**www.marxists.org/history/ussr/events/revolution/index.htm**
Soviet History Archive: a rich set of sources, starting with 1917 and covering politics, economics, culture and foreign affairs

## Chapter 1

**Anna Geifman, editor, *Russia Under the Last Tsar: Opposition and Subversion 1894–1917* (Blackwell, 1999)**
A Russian writer's insights into the anti-tsarist movements before 1917

**Sidney Harcave, *Count Sergei Witte and the Twilight of Imperial Russia: A Biography* (M.E. Sharpe, 2004)**
A study of Witte's ultimately doomed attempts to modernise tsarist Russia

**Richard Pipes, *Russia Under the Old Regime* (Penguin, 1995)**
Fascinatingly describes how the Russian state came to be regarded as the personal property of the tsar

**Thomas Calnan Sorenson, *The Thought and Policies of Konstantin P. Pobedonostsev* (University of Washington Press, 1978)**
An illuminating study of the most influential conservative in late imperial Russia

**Ian D. Thatcher, editor, *Late Imperial Russia: Problems and Perspectives* (Manchester University Press, 2005)**
A collection of stimulating essays on the major issues by a group of leading scholars

## Chapter 2

**Abraham Ascher, *P.A. Stolypin: The Search for Stability in Late Imperial Russia* (Stanford University Press, 2001)**
Offers stimulating insights into the efforts made by late tsardom's outstanding minister

**R.W. Davies, *From Tsarism to the New Economic Policy* (Cornell UP, 1991)**
Analysis by a writer who remains the leading authority on economic developments

**Dominic Lieven, *Nicholas II: Emperor of All the Russias* (Pimlico, 1993)**
An outstanding biography, especially impressive on tsardom's lost opportunities pre-1914

## Chapter 3

**Joseph Fuhrmann, *Rasputin: The Untold Story* (John Wiley, 2013)**
An absorbing study of the man who helped to bring down tsardom

**Dominic Lieven, *Towards the Flame: Empire, War and the End of Tsarist Russia* (Allen Lane, 2015)**
A stimulating analysis of collapsing tsardom by an outstanding authority

**Norman Stone, *The Eastern Front 1914–17* (Penguin, 1998)**
A lively account by a thought-provoking historian

**James D. White, *Lenin: The Practice and Theory of Revolution* (Palgrave, 2001)**
Particularly strong on Lenin pre-1917

## Chapter 4

**Edward Acton, *Rethinking the Russian Revolution* (Edward Arnold, 1990)**
An interesting survey of many of the major interpretations of 1917

**E.H. Carr, *The Russian Revolution from Lenin to Stalin 1917–1929* (Palgrave, 2004)**
An accessible, shortened version of a monumental study by a pioneering historian in Russian studies

**Richard Pipes, *The Russian Revolution 1899–1919* (Collins Harvill, 1990)**
Strongly critical of Lenin and the Bolsheviks, but a very detailed and readable account by a Polish-American historian

**Richard Pipes, *Three Whys of the Russian Revolution* (Pimlico, 1998)**
A short but very useful summary of the major points in the previous book

**S.A. Smith, *The Russian Revolution: A Very Short Introduction* (Oxford University Press, 2002)**
Belies its self-deprecating title by being a brilliant analysis of the 1917 Revolutions

**Rex A. Wade, *The Russian Revolution 1917* (Cambridge University Press, 2000)**
A reliable narrative account

## Chapter 5

**Silvana Malle, *The Economic Organization of War Communism 1917–21* (Cambridge University Press, 1985)**
Traces in detail Lenin's economic programme from War Communism to NEP

**Evan Mawdsley, *The Russian Civil War* (Birlinn, 2008)**
Very detailed account of the struggle that confirmed the Bolsheviks in power

**Richard Pipes, *Russia under the Bolshevik Regime, 1919–24* (Collins Harvill, 1994)**
A detailed study of the Bolshevik consolidation of power

**Robert Service, *Lenin: A Biography* (Macmillan, 2004)**
First part of the writer's classic trilogy of the three great revolutionary figures of the period

## Chapter 6

**Isaac Deutscher, *Trotsky* (Oxford University Press, 1954–70)**
A classic three-volume study of Stalin's great rival, written by a Trotsky admirer

**Stephen Kotkin, *Stalin: Paradoxes of Power* (Allen Lane, 2014)**
The first in an intended three volume biography of Stalin, this book provides a detailed and gripping analysis of Stalin's rise to power

**Robert Service, *Trotsky: A Biography* (Macmillan, 2004) and *Stalin: A Biography* (Macmillan, 2009)**
Especially authoritative treatment of the rise of Stalin and his conflict with Trotsky

**Dmitri Volkogonov, *Stalin: Triumph and Tragedy* (Weidenfeld & Nicolson, 1991)**
Written from a Russian perspective with Stalin as the central figure

## Chapter 7

**Robert Conquest, *Harvest of Sorrow* (Macmillan, 1988)**
A pioneering study of Stalin's shattering collectivisation programme

**R.W. Davies, editor, *The Economic Transformation of the Soviet Union* (Cambridge University Press, 1994)**
The most authoritative analysis of Stalin's economic reforms

**Peter Gattrell, *Under Command: The Soviet Economy 1924–53* (Routledge, 1992)**
Acknowledged as an outstanding study of Stalin's economic policies

**Alec Nove, *Stalinism and After* (Unwin Hyman, 1975)**
A masterly survey of the impact of Stalinism

**Simon Sebag Montefiore, *Stalin: The Court of the Red Tsar* (Alfred A. Knopf, 2004)**
An absorbing study of Stalin's style of government

## Chapter 8

**Anne Applebaum, *Gulag: A History of the Soviet Camps* (Penguin, 2003)**
A detailed account of the human consequences of Stalin's repressive measures

**Robert Conquest, *The Great Terror: A Reassessment* (Pimlico, 2008)**
A republication of the first book in the West to reveal the scale and character of Stalin's purges

**Sheila Fitzpatrick, *Everyday Stalinism. Ordinary Life in Extraordinary Times: Soviet Russia in the 1930s* (Oxford University Press, 1999)**
A leading Western scholar's absorbing study of the impact of Stalin's policies on ordinary Russians

**Sheila Fitzpatrick, editor, *Stalinism: New Directions* (Routledge, 2000)**
A collection of scholarly revisionist essays analysing the character of Stalinism

**J.A. Getty and R.T. Manning, *Stalinist Terror: New Perspectives* (Cambridge University Press, 1993)**
Brings together informed thinking on the motives behind, and the results of, Stalin's terror programme

**David L. Hoffman, *Stalinist Values: The Cultural Norms of Soviet Modernity* (Cornell University Press, 2003)**
Brings together many of the major ideas on Stalinism as a cultural phenomenon

**Oleg V. Khevniuk, *Stalin: New Biography of a Dictator* (Yale University Press, 2015)**
Fascinating insights from a modern Russian perspective into Stalin's character and personality

**Robert C. Tucker, *Stalinism – Essays in Historical Interpretation* (Transaction Publishers, 1999)**
Reflections and analysis by one of the major experts on the character of Stalinism

**Lynne Viola, *The Unknown Gulag: The Lost World of Stalin's Special Settlements* (Oxford University Press, 2007)**
A study that reveals the involvement in the terror of those below Stalin

# Index


1905 Revolution 31–8

Agriculture 6, 132, 161–2, *see also* Collectivisation; Land; NEP; Stolypin, Peter
Alexander II 4
Alexander III 12
Alexandra, Tsarina 82–3
Alliluyeva, Nadezdha 211
Anti-Comintern Pact 248
Anti-Semitism 12–13, 190
'Anti-Soviet Trotskyist Centre' 231
Antonov, Alexander 164
*April Theses* 102–3
August Manifesto 36

Balkans 55, 57, 58–9, 68, 69
Bismarck, Otto von 57
Bloody Sunday 32
Bolsheviks
- and Lenin 24
- effect of Civil War 146–7
- impact of First World War 71
- in power 130–3
- on land question 109–10
- reasons for success 119–22, 143–6
- Revolution 115–17
- role in February Revolution 89
- tactics 24–5, 137–8
- taking power 118
- *see also* Lenin, Vladimir Ilyich

Brest-Litovsk, Treaty of 136–9, 148
Britain
- Russian relations with 58
- *see also* Triple Entente

Bukharin, Nikolai 163, 171–2, 197, 199, 200–1, 204, 229, 230–2
Butovo killing fields 236

*Cheka* 154–6, 160, 161, 163, 164, 167, 168, 177, 207
China, and Stalin 247
Chkheidze, Nikolai 107
Civil rights, under Stalin 240
Collectivisation 199–200, 205–12
Conscription 7, 49, 158–9, 160
Constituent Assembly dissolution 134–5
Constitutional Democrats, *see* Kadets
Cult of personality 240, 242–5

De-kulakisation 207–8
Denikin, Anton 143, 144
Dual Authority 97
*Dumas* 47, 48–51
Dzerzhinsky, Felix 154, 155, 156

Factionalism 171, 187
Famine 141, 162–3, 210–11
February Revolution 85–9, 90–1, 92–4
Feuchtwanger, Leon 245
First World War 60–2, 68–70, 104–6, 149
Five-Year Plans 213–19
Franco-Russian Convention 57, *see also* Triple Entente

Gapon, Georgy, Father 32, 33
General strike 36, 37, 54, 86
Germany
- First World War and mobilisation plans 70
- Russian relations with 56–7
- *see also* Nazi Germany

Goremykin, Ivan 49
Gorky, Maxim 135
'Great Purge' 229–37
Guchkov, Alexander 26, 54, 105

Herzen, Alexander 8–9
Hitler, Adolf 242, *see also* Nazi Germany

Industrialisation
- effect of War Communism 160–1
- great spurt 14–18, 46, 62, 64
- in nineteenth century 5
- Marx's analysis 21
- results of NEP 172, 193, 194, 197
- Stalin's plans 198–9, 204, 205–6, 207, 212, 222–3, 225–6, 227, 238, 251, 252
- *see also* Five-Year Plans; Witte, Sergei

Inflation 46, 72, 90, 131, 160
International Women's Day 86, 87
Ivan the Terrible 244

Japan, war with Russia 28–30
'July Days' 106–9

Kadets 27
Kaganovich, Lazar 200
Kamenev, Lev 100–1, 102, 107, 114, 115, 118, 156, 185, 189, 191, 192, 196, 197, 228, 229, 230, 242
Kerensky, Alexander 81, 88, 97, 105–6, 107–8, 110–11, 113–15, 116, 117, 119, 121, 122, 126
Kirov, Sergei 197, 227–8, 229, 230
Kolchak, Alexander 143, 144
Kollontai, Alexandra 165, 168
Kornilov, General 106, 108, 110–11, 112–13, 115, 121
Khrushchev, Nikita 227, 242
Konsomol 244–5
Kornilov affair 110–12
Kronstadt Rising 166–8
*Kulaks* 206–7 *see also* De-kulakisation

Labour camps 155, 235
Land 43–6, 109–10, 132
'Left Communists' 138–9
Lena Goldfields incident 53
Lenin, Vladimir Ilyich 21, 103
- and Bolsheviks (before 1917) 24
- approach to foreign affairs 152–3
- as international revolutionary 176
- authoritarian rule 178–81
- decrees 131–3
- enrolment 187
- exploitation of Russia's authoritarian tradition 174
- funeral 189–90
- impact on Social Democrats 22
- legacy 174–8
- on Russian proletariat 175
- outlawing of all socialist parties except Bolsheviks 171
- overthrow of Provisional Government 114
- return after tsar's abdication 101–4
- strategy to overthrow Kerensky's government 113
- strengths 176
- telescoped revolution 175
- testament 185, 191
- weaknesses 176–8
- *see also* Marxism–Leninism; NEP

Liberals 25–6
Lvov, Prince 97, 105, 106

Magnitogorsk 214–15, 220, 245
Marx, Karl 20–1, 22
Marxism 24, 103, 109, 120–1, 124, 125, 127, 130, 137, 171, 174, 175, 176, 179, 193, 248, 252
Marxism–Leninism 103, 153–4, 174, 175, 176, 179
Marxism–Leninism–Stalinism 240, 242, 252, 255
Milyukov, Paul 25, 27, 33, 49. 80, 84, 97, 105, 121
Modernisation 109, *see also* Industrialisation
Molotov, Vyacheslav 197, 200, 238, 241
Munich settlement 248–9

*Narodniks*, *see* Populists
Nationalisation 160
Nazi Germany 246
Nazi–Soviet Pact 249–50
NEP, *see* New Economic Policy
New Economic Policy 168, 169–73
Nicholas II 81
- abdication 88–9
- and *dumas* 47, 49
- as a war leader 77–8
- execution of tsar and family 155
- February Revolution 86, 87
- foreign policy 28–30
- growth of opposition 80–2
- opposition groups 18–27
- policies 11–13
- position at outbreak of First World War 60–2, 63–4
- resistance to change 64
- *see also* August Manifesto; October Manifesto; Stolypin, Peter; Witte, Sergei

*Nomenklatura* 241

October Manifesto 36–7
October Revolution 112–18, 119–22, 123–7
Octobrists 26
*Okhrana* 4, 11, 33, 51, 53, 74, 85, 154

Peasants 5–7, 19–20, 33, 34, 37, 52, 72, 146, 159, 161, 175, 194, *see also* Collectivisation; Famine; Land; NEP; Tambov Rising
People's Will 4, 19, 20
'Permanent Revolution' 192, 195
Peter the Great (Peter I) 4, 9, 244
Petrograd
- political shift 112–13
- role in February Revolution 89
- soviet 88, 97

Plehve, Vyacheslav 28, 33
Plekhanov, George 21, 22–3
Pobedonostsev, Konstantin 11–12, 78, 81
Poland 56, 152, 250
Populists 19
*Potemkin* mutiny 35–5
Preobrazhensky, Yevgeny 163
Prohibition 74
Propaganda 206, 214, 220, 243, 244, 246
Provisional Committee 86, 88–9
Provisional Government 89 97, 98–9, 104–6, 115–16, 119–20
Purges 225–7, 229–38
Pyatakov, Georgy 231

Radek, Karl 231
Railways 15–16
Rasputin, Gregory Efimovich 82–4
Red Army 152, 156–9
Red Terror 153–6
Reformers 25
Religion, *see* Russian Orthodox Church
Rodzianko, Mikhail 26, 51, 60, 76, 77, 86, 88
Russia
- army 7
- authoritarian tradition 174
- civil service 8–9
- economy 5–6, 14–17, 42–7, 71–2, 175, *see also* Collectivisation; Five-Year Plans; New Economic Policy
- entry into First World War 68
- foreign policy 55–9, 62–3
- impact of First World War 71–9
- political backwardness 4
- problems of modernisation 9–11
- relations with Austria-Hungary 58–9
- social structure 5
- state oppression 4
- urban unrest 52–4
- *see also* USSR

Russian Civil War
- atrocities 145
- challenge from Social Revolutionaries 141
- effect on Bolsheviks 146–7
- foreign intervention 148–52
- Greens 140
- reasons for Bolshevik victory 143–6
- role of Lenin 139–40
- role of Trotsky 145
- White resistance 143

Russian Empire 1–3, 55
Russian Orthodox Church 4–5, 83, 162, 178, 243
Russian Revolution (1905), *see* 1905 Revolution
Russian Revolution (1917)
- causes 71
- importance of First World War 90, 104–5
- *see also* February Revolution; 'July Days'; October Revolution

Russification 12, 13
Rykov, Aleksei 189, 197, 199, 200, 201, 229, 230, 231
Ryutin, M.N. 226

Sazonov, Sergei 68, 69
Serbia, *see* Balkans
Show trials 229
Shlyapnikov, Alexander 88, 165
Shulgin, Vasily 81
Social Democrats (SDs) 20–1, 22–4
Social Revolutionary Party (SRs) 19–20
'Socialism in One Country' 246
Society
- Five-Year Plans and living conditions 215, 219
- impact of First World War 72–5, 78–9, 126
- *see also* Collectivisation; Industrialisation; Purges; Russia; Russian Civil War

Sokolnikov, Grigory 137, 231
Soviet Order Number 1: 98
Soviets
- formation 36

Spanish Civil War 248
Stakhanov, Alexei 218
Stakhanovite movement 218
Stalin
- and China 247
- as hero 242
- as dominant figure of Right 188
- attitude to foreign relations 246
- background 183–4
- centralisation of law enforcement agencies 227
- constitution 232
- defeat of Right 198–201
- defeat of Trotsky and Left 196–8
- early revolutionary career 184
- economic policies 203–4, 205, 221–3, *see also* Collectivisation; Five-Year Plans
- 'enrolment' 228–9
- exploitation of NEP question 193
- in Civil War 185
- in October Revolution 184–5
- personality 226–7
- popularity 245
- position on Lenin's death 186
- propaganda 243–5
- reputation in Soviet Union (1941) 251
- totalitarianism 239–40
- worship 243–4
- *see also* Industrialisation; Purges

Stalinism 242, 252–5
State capitalism 14–15
Stolypin, Peter 14, 44
- and *dumas* 50, 61
- and Witte 46–7
- assassination 52
- economic policies 42–7
- policy of repression 49, 50

Strikes 52–3, 64, 90, 92, 93, 165–6, 167, 218, *see also* General strike
Struve, Peter 25, 38 121
Sukhanov, Nicolai 99, 121, 184

Tambov Rising 164
Tolstoy, Leo 31
Tomsky, Mikhail 189, 197, 199, 200–1, 229, 230, 231
Totalitarianism 239–40
Trade unions 20, 23, 24, 27, 36, 46, 53, 99, 150, 157, 166, 177, 200, 218
Triple Entente 58
Trotsky, Leon 192
- and NEP 193–4
- as war commissar 156–9
- character 190–1
- defeat by Stalin 196
- exile 197–8
- ideological divide with Stalin 195–6
- party members' attitudes towards 191
- reasons for failure of 1905 Revolution 38
- role in Bolshevik Revolution 115
- *see also* Bureaucratisation

Tsarism 3–4, *see also individual tsars*
Tseretelli, Iraklii 121

Uglanov, Nicolai 200
USSR 159, 178, 186, 194, 195–6

Voroshilov, Klimenty 234
Vyborg group 49

War Communism 160–4
Western Allies, intervention in Russia 148–52
Witte, Sergei 14
- and Japan 28, 35
- and Stolypin 44, 46–7
- frustration with tsar's policies 36, 78
- influence 46
- modernisation policies 14–17
- problems 17–18
- return in 1905: 36

Women
- Amazons 118, 119
- and Rasputin 82
- role in resistance to collectivisation 208
- voting 47
- *see also* International Women's Day

'Workers' Opposition' movement 165
Wrangel, Baron Pyotr 143, 144

Yezhov, Nicolai 226, 230, 231
'Yezhovshchina' 235–6
Youth movement, *see* Konsomol
Yudenich, Nicolai 144

Zinoviev, Grigor 114, 115, 185, 189, 191, 192, 196, 197, 228, 229, 230, 242

**Acknowledgements:** Allen Lane, *Russia and the Russians* by Geoffrey Hosking, 2001. Berg Publishers, *The Russian Revolution* by Dietrich Geyer, 1987. Blackwell, *Russia and the Last Tsar: Opposition and Subversion 1894–1917* by Anna Geifman, editor, 1999. Collins Harvill, *The Russian Revolution* by R. Pipes, 1990. Cornell University Press, *Stalinist Values: The Cultural Norms of Soviet Modernity* by D.L. Hoffman, 2003. Edward Arnold, *Stalin and the Making of Modern Russia* by F.W. Stacey, editor, 1970. Granada, *Russia in Revolution 1890–1918* by Lionel Kochan, 1966. HarperCollins, *The Rise and Fall of the Soviet Empire* by D. Volkogonov, 1998. Harvill, *Russia Under the Bolshevik Regime 1919–1924* by R. Pipes, 1994. Hollis & Carter, *Stalin, An Appraisal of the Man and His Influence* by Leon Trotsky, 1966. Izdatel'stro Z-oe, *O Samagone [Oh, Vodka!]* by D.N. Voronov, 1929. Jonathan Cape, *Eastern Approaches* by F. McClean, 1951. Lawrence & Wishart, *Stalin's Works* by Josef Stalin, 1955; *Works of Josef Stalin* by Josef Stalin, 1955; *Reminiscences of Lenin* by K.K. Krupskaya, 1959; *Collected Works of Lenin* by V.I. Lenin, 1959. Macmillan, *Imperial and Soviet Russia* by David Christian, 1997; *The Russian Revolution & the Soviet State 1917–21 Documents* by M. McCauley, 1984; *The Russian Revolution and the Soviet State* by M. McCauley, editor, 1975; *Lenin: A Biography* by Robert Service, 2000; *Stalin: A Biography* by R. Service, 2004. Marxists Internet Archive. Michael Joseph, *Age of Extremes* by Eric Hobsbawm, 1994. Oxford University Press, *Endurance and Endeavour: Russian History 1812–1980* by J.N. Westwood, 1985; *Everyday Stalinism* by S. Fitzpatrick, 1999; *The Russian Revolution* by S.A. Smith, 2002; *Memoirs of a Revolutionary, 1901–1941* by Victor Serge, 1963. Paladin, *Russia in Revolution* by Lionel Kochan, 1974. Penguin, *An Economic History of the USSR* by Alex Nove, 1973; *Lenin and the Russian Revolution* by Christopher Hill, 1971; *Lenin* by David Shub, 1976; *The Bolshevik Revolution* by E.H. Carr, 1973; *Nicholas II: The Last of the Tsars* by Marc Ferro, 1990. Pimlico, *Nicholas II* by Dominic Lieven, 1993; *Three Whys of the Russian Revolution* by R. Pipes, 1998. Pluto Press, *The History of the Russian Revolution* by Leon Trotsky, 1977, 1985. Prentice-Hall, *Russia 1917: The February Revolution* by G. Katkov, 1967; *Stalin* by T.H. Rigby, 1966. Random House, *The Structure of Russian History* by M. Cherniavsky, editor, 1970. Secker & Warburg, *Behind the Urals* by J. Scott, 1942. Sutton Publishing, *The Russian Revolution* by Harold Shukman, 1998. Transaction Publishers, *Stalinism: Essays in Historical Interpretation* by R.C. Tucker, editor, 1997. University of Chicago Press, *Readings in Russian Civilization* by T. Riha, editor, 1964. University of Exeter Press, *The Soviet Union: A Documentary History* by E. Acton, editor, 2005. Van Nostrand, *The Social Crucible* by S. Hendel, 1959. Victor Gollancz, *Moscow 1937* by L. Feuchtwanger, 1937. Yale University Press, *A Source Book for Russian History* by G. Vernadsky, editor, 1972. *The Routledge Atlas of Russian History*, Sir Martin Gilbert, copyright © 2007 Routledge, reproduced by permission of Taylor & Francis Books UK, www.martingilbert.com